RUSSIA

FINLAND
St. Petersburg
Moscow
ESTONIA
LATVIA

KAZAKHSTAN

MONGOLIA

UKRAINE

UZBEKISTAN
TURKMENISTAN
KYRGYZSTAN
TAJIKISTAN

Beijing
(Peking)
Tianjin

Shenyang
NORTH
KOREA
SOUTH
KOREA

JAPAN

Tokyo
Osaka
Seoul

CHINA
Asia

Wuhan
Chongqing

Shanghai

PACIFIC

Tropic of Cancer

BULGARIA
GREECE TURKEY
GEORGIA
AZER.

ITALY
ALB.

CYPRUS SYRIA
LEB.
ISRAEL
JORDAN

IRAQ
IRAN

AFGHAN.

Tehran

Baghdad

KUWAIT

PAKISTAN

Lahore

Delhi

BANGLA.
Dacca

BURMA
(Myanmar)

Hong Kong

TAIWAN

Cairo

TUNISIA
MALTA

LIBYA

EGYPT

BAHRAIN QATAR
SAUDI U.A.E.
ARABIA
OMAN

Karachi

Ahmadabad

Mumbai
(Bombay)

INDIA

Hyderabad

Kolkata
(Calcutta)

LAOS
THAI-
LAND

Manila

OCEAN

NORTHERN
MARIANAS

20

Guam
(U.S.A.)

PHILIPPINES

frica

NIGER

CHAD

SUDAN

YEMEN

DJIBOUTI

ETHIOPIA

Bangalore

Chennai
(Madras)

Bangkok

CAMBODIA
VIETNAM

Ho Chi Minh City

PALAU

FEDERATED STATES
OF MICRONESIA

NGERIA

AMEROON

GABON

CENTRAL
AFRICAN
REP.

SOMALI
REP.

MALDIVES

SRI
LANKA

MALAYSIA

BRUNEI
SINGAPORE

Equator

CONGO
(Dem. Rep.
of the)

Kinshasa

CABINDA
(Angola)

RWANDA
BURUNDI

KENYA

TANZANIA

SEYCHELLES

INDIAN

Borneo

INDONESIA

Jakarta

EAST
TIMOR

New
Guinea

PAPUA
NEW
GUINEA

ANGOLA

ZAMBIA

MALAWI

COMOROS

OCEAN

Cocos Islands
(Australia)

Christmas
Island
(Australia)

Oceania

New
Caledonia
(Fr.)

NAMIBIA

ZIMBABWE

BOTSWANA

MADAGASCAR

MAURITIUS

SWAZILAND

Réunion
(Fr.)

AUSTRALIA

Tropic of Capricorn

SOUTH
AFRICA

LESOTHO

Sydney

NEW
ZEALAND

Prince Edward
Islands
(South Africa)

Crozet Is.
(Fr.)

Kerguelen Is.
(Fr.)

SOUTHERN OCEAN

om Greenwich

ica

Antarctic Circle

COPYRIGHT PHILIP'S

OXFORD

POCKET
WORLD
ATLAS

SIXTH EDITION

CONTENTS

WORLD STATISTICS

4–7	Countries
8–9	Cities
10–11	Time zones
12–13	Flight paths
14–15	Distance table
16–19	World climate

CITY PLANS

20	City plans – legend
21	Amsterdam
22	Athens
23	Bangkok
24	Barcelona
25	Berlin
26	Brussels
27	Cape Town
28	Chicago
29	Dublin
30	Hong Kong
31	London
32	Madrid
33	Mexico City
34	Moscow
35	Mumbai
36	New York
37	Paris
38	Prague
39	Rio de Janeiro
40	Rome
41	San Francisco
42	Singapore
43	Sydney
44	Tokyo
45	Toronto
46	Vienna

GAZETTEER OF NATIONS

47	Gazetteer of Nations – contents
48–72	Country-by-country profiles

NOTE:
For reasons of safety or politics, there may be times when it is not advisable, or desirable, to visit one or more of the countries described in the Gazetteer of Nations section. If in doubt, please check with the US Department of State (www.state.gov/travel).

Copyright © 2008 Philip's
Reprinted 2018

Philip's, a division of Octopus Publishing Group Limited
50 Victoria Embankment, London EC4Y 0DZ
www.octopusbooks.co.uk
An Hachette Livre UK Company
www.hachettelivre.co.uk

Cartography by Philip's

CITY PLANS
Page 29, Dublin: The town plan of Dublin is based on Ordnance Survey Ireland by permission of the Government Permit Number 8408. © Ordnance Survey Ireland and Government of Ireland.

 Ordnance Survey®

Page 31, London: This product includes mapping data licensed from Ordnance Survey® with the permission of the Controller of Her Majesty's Stationery Office. © Crown copyright 2008. All rights reserved. Licence number 100011710.

Vector data: Courtesy of Gräfe and Unser Verlag GmbH, München, Germany (city-center maps of Bangkok, Cape Town, Mexico City, Singapore, Sydney, and Tokyo).

Published in North America by Oxford University Press, Inc., 198 Madison Avenue, New York, NY 10016

www.oup.com/us/atlas

OXFORD
UNIVERSITY PRESS
Oxford is a registered trademark of Oxford University Press

Library of Congress Cataloging-in-Publication Data available

ISBN 978-0-19-537453-7

Printing (last digit): 9 8 7 6 5 4

Printed in Malaysia

WORLD MAPS

I	World Maps – general reference
2–3	The Land Hemisphere 1:133.3M
4–5	The Water Hemisphere 1:133.3M

EUROPE

6–7	Europe 1:26.7M
8–9	Scandinavia and the Baltic Lands 1:13.3M
10–11	British Isles 1:6.7M
12–13	France 1:6.7M
14–15	Germany and Benelux 1:6.7M
16–17	Central Europe 1:6.7M
18–19	Spain and Portugal 1:6.7M
20–21	Italy and the Adriatic 1:6.7M
22–23	Greece and the Balkans 1:6.7M
24–25	Eastern Europe 1:13.3M

ASIA

26–27	Asia 1:67M
28–29	Western Russia and Central Asia 1:26.7M
30–31	Eastern Siberia 1:26.7M
32–33	Japan 1:8.5M
34–35	China 1:26.7M
36–37	Philippines and Eastern Indonesia 1:16.7M
38–39	Southeast Asia 1:16.7M
40–41	Eastern India, Bangladesh and Burma 1:13.3M
42–43	Western India, Pakistan and Sri Lanka 1:13.3M
44–45	Persian Gulf, Iran and Afghanistan 1:13.3M
46–47	The Middle East and Turkey 1:13.3M
48–49	Arabia and the Horn of Africa 1:20M

AFRICA

50–51	Africa 1:56M
52–53	Northwest Africa 1:20M
54–55	Northeast Africa 1:20M
56–57	Central Africa 1:20M
58–59	Southern Africa 1:20M

AUSTRALASIA

60–61	Australia 1:26.7M
62–63	Southeast Australia 1:10.7M
64–65	New Zealand 1:8M
	Central and Southwest Pacific

NORTH AMERICA

66–67	North America 1:46.7M
68–69	Western Canada and Alaska 1:20M
70–71	Eastern Canada 1:20M
72–73	Northwest USA 1:8M
74–75	North-central USA 1:8M
76–77	Northeast USA 1:8M
78–79	Southwest USA 1:8M
80–81	Southern USA 1:8M
82–83	Southeast USA 1:8M
84–85	Mexico 1:20M
86–87	Caribbean and Central America 1:20M

SOUTH AMERICA

88–89	South America 1:46.7M
90–91	South America – Northwest 1:21.3M
92–93	South America – Northeast 1:21.3M
94–95	South America – South 1:21.3M

POLAR REGIONS

96	Antarctica 1:46.7M

INDEX

97–160	Index to World Maps

Country/Territory	Area (1,000 sq km)	Area (1,000 sq mi)	Population (1,000s)	Density (persons per sq km)	Capital City	Annual Income US$
Afghanistan	652	252	31,890	49	Kabul	800
Albania	28.7	11.1	3,601	125	Tirana	5,500
Algeria	2,382	920	33,333	14	Algiers	8,100
American Samoa (US)	0.20	0.08	58	290	Pago Pago	5,800
Andorra	0.47	0.18	72	153	Andorra La Vella	38,800
Angola	1,247	481	12,264	10	Luanda	6,500
Anguilla (UK)	0.10	0.04	14	134	The Valley	8,800
Antigua & Barbuda	0.44	0.17	69	157	St John's	10,900
Argentina	2,780	1,074	40,302	15	Buenos Aires	13,000
Armenia	29.8	11.5	2,972	100	Yerevan	5,700
Aruba (Netherlands)	0.19	0.07	100	518	Oranjestad	21,800
Australia	7,741	2,989	20,434	3	Canberra	37,500
Austria	83.9	32.4	8,200	98	Vienna	39,000
Azerbaijan	86.6	33.4	8,120	94	Baku	9,000
Azores (Portugal)	2.2	0.86	236	107	Ponta Delgada	15,000
Bahamas	13.9	5.4	306	22	Nassau	22,700
Bahrain	0.69	0.27	709	1,066	Manama	34,700
Bangladesh	144	55.6	150,448	1,045	Dhaka	1,400
Barbados	0.43	0.17	281	652	Bridgetown	19,700
Belarus	208	80.2	9,725	47	Minsk	10,200
Belgium	30.5	11.8	10,392	340	Brussels	36,500
Belize	23.0	8.9	294	13	Belmopan	7,800
Benin	113	43.5	8,078	72	Porto-Novo	1,500
Bermuda (UK)	0.05	0.02	66	1,196	Hamilton	69,900
Bhutan	47.0	18.1	2,328	50	Thimphu	1,400
Bolivia	1,099	424	9,119	8	La Paz/Sucre	4,400
Bosnia-Herzegovina	51.2	19.8	4,552	89	Sarajevo	6,600
Botswana	582	225	1,816	3	Gaborone	14,700
Brazil	8,514	3,287	190,011	22	Brasília	9,700
Brunei	5.8	2.2	372	65	Bandar Seri Begawan	25,600
Bulgaria	111	42.8	7,323	66	Sofia	11,800
Burkina Faso	274	106	14,326	52	Ouagadougou	1,200
Burma (= Myanmar)	677	261	47,374	70	Rangoon/Naypyidaw	1,900
Burundi	27.8	10.7	8,391	301	Bujumbura	800
Cambodia	181	69.9	13,996	77	Phnom Penh	1,800
Cameroon	475	184	18,060	38	Yaoundé	2,300
Canada	9,971	3,850	33,390	3	Ottawa	38,200
Canary Is. (Spain)	7.2	2.8	1,682	234	Las Palmas/Santa Cruz	19,900
Cape Verde Is.	4.0	1.6	424	105	Praia	7,000
Cayman Is. (UK)	0.26	0.10	47	178	George Town	43,800
Central African Republic	623	241	4,369	7	Bangui	700
Chad	1,284	496	9,886	8	Ndjamena	1,600
Chile	757	292	16,285	22	Santiago	14,400
China	9,597	3,705	1,321,852	138	Beijing	5,300
Colombia	1,139	440	44,380	39	Bogotá	7,200
Comoros	2.2	0.86	711	328	Moroni	600
Congo	342	132	3,801	11	Brazzaville	3,700
Congo (Dem. Rep. of the)	2,345	905	65,752	28	Kinshasa	300
Cook Is. (NZ)	0.24	0.09	22	91	Avarua	9,100
Costa Rica	51.1	19.7	4,134	79	San José	13,500
Croatia	56.5	21.8	4,493	80	Zagreb	15,500
Cuba	111	42.8	11,394	103	Havana	4,500
Cyprus	9.3	3.6	788	85	Nicosia	24,600
Czech Republic	78.9	30.5	10,229	130	Prague	24,400
Denmark	43.1	16.6	5,468	127	Copenhagen	37,400

Listed above are the principal countries and territories of the world. If a territory is not completely independent, then the country it is associated with is named. The area figures give the total area of land, inland water, and ice. The population figures are 2007 estimates. The annual income is the Gross Domestic Product per capita in US dollars. [Gross Domestic Product per capita has been measured

Country/Territory	Area (1,000 sq km)	Area (1,000 sq mi)	Population (1,000s)	Density (persons per sq km)	Capital City	Annual Income US$
Djibouti	23.2	9.0	496	22	Djibouti	1,000
Dominica	0.75	0.29	72	96	Roseau	3,800
Dominican Republic	48.5	18.7	9,366	192	Santo Domingo	9,200
East Timor	14.9	5.7	1,085	72	Dili	800
Ecuador	284	109	13,756	49	Quito	7,100
Egypt	1,001	387	80,335	80	Cairo	5,400
El Salvador	21.0	8.1	6,948	330	San Salvador	5,200
Equatorial Guinea	28.1	10.8	551	20	Malabo	4,100
Eritrea	118	45.4	4,907	40	Asmara	1,000
Estonia	45.1	17.4	1,316	29	Tallinn	21,800
Ethiopia	1,104	426	76,512	68	Addis Ababa	700
Faroe Is. (Denmark)	1.4	0.54	48	34	Tórshavn	31,000
Fiji	18.3	7.1	919	50	Suva	4,100
Finland	338	131	5,238	16	Helsinki	35,500
France	552	213	60,876	111	Paris	33,800
French Guiana (France)	90.0	34.7	196	1	Cayenne	8,300
French Polynesia (France)	4.0	1.5	279	67	Papeete	17,500
Gabon	268	103	1,455	5	Libreville	13,800
Gambia, The	11.3	4.4	1,688	149	Banjul	800
Gaza Strip	0.36	0.14	1,482	4,118	–	1,100
Georgia	69.7	26.9	4,646	67	Tbilisi	4,200
Germany	357	138	82,401	231	Berlin	34,400
Ghana	239	92.1	22,931	96	Accra	1,400
Gibraltar (UK)	0.006	0.002	28	4,303	Gibraltar Town	38,200
Greece	132	50.9	10,706	81	Athens	30,500
Greenland (Denmark)	2,176	840	56	0.03	Nuuk (Godthåb)	20,000
Grenada	0.34	0.13	90	262	St George's	3,900
Guadeloupe (France)	1.7	0.66	449	264	Basse-Terre	7,900
Guam (US)	0.55	0.21	173	316	Agana	15,000
Guatemala	109	42.0	12,728	117	Guatemala City	5,400
Guinea	246	94.9	9,948	40	Conakry	1,000
Guinea-Bissau	36.1	13.9	1,473	41	Bissau	600
Guyana	215	83.0	769	4	Georgetown	5,300
Haiti	27.8	10.7	8,706	314	Port-au-Prince	1,900
Honduras	112	43.3	7,484	67	Tegucigalpa	3,300
Hong Kong (China)	1.1	0.42	6,980	6,392	–	42,000
Hungary	93.0	35.9	9,956	107	Budapest	19,500
Iceland	103	39.8	302	3	Reykjavik	39,400
India	3,287	1,269	1,129,866	344	New Delhi	2,700
Indonesia	1,905	735	234,694	122	Jakarta	3,400
Iran	1,648	636	65,398	40	Tehran	12,300
Iraq	438	169	27,500	63	Baghdad	3,600
Ireland	70.3	27.1	4,109	58	Dublin	45,600
Israel	20.6	8.0	6,427	309	Jerusalem	28,800
Italy	301	116	58,148	193	Rome	31,000
Ivory Coast (= Côte d'Ivoire)	322	125	18,013	56	Yamoussoukro	1,800
Jamaica	11.0	4.2	2,780	253	Kingston	4,800
Japan	378	146	127,433	337	Tokyo	33,800
Jordan	89.3	34.5	6,053	66	Amman	4,700
Kazakhstan	2,725	1,052	15,285	6	Astana	11,100
Kenya	580	224	36,914	63	Nairobi	1,600
Kiribati	0.73	0.28	108	133	Tarawa	1,800
Korea, North	121	46.5	23,302	193	Pyŏngyang	1,900
Korea, South	99.3	38.3	49,045	498	Seoul	24,600
Kosovo	10.9	4.2	2,127	195	Priština	1,800

using the purchasing power parity method. This enables comparisons to be made between countries through their purchasing power (in US dollars), showing real price levels of goods and services rather than using currency exchange rates.] The figures are the latest available, usually 2007 estimates. *OPT = Occupied Palestinian Territory; N/A = Not available.

Country/Territory	Area (1,000 sq km)	Area (1,000 sq mi)	Population (1,000s)	Density (persons per sq km)	Capital City	Annual Income US $
Kuwait	17.8	6.9	2,506	141	Kuwait City	55,300
Kyrgyzstan	200	77.2	5,284	27	Bishkek	2,000
Laos	237	91.4	6,522	28	Vientiane	1,900
Latvia	64.6	24.9	2,260	35	Riga	17,700
Lebanon	10.4	4.0	3,926	377	Beirut	10,400
Lesotho	30.4	11.7	2,125	70	Maseru	1,500
Liberia	111	43.0	3,196	29	Monrovia	500
Libya	1,760	679	6,037	3	Tripoli	13,100
Liechtenstein	0.16	0.06	34	214	Vaduz	25,000
Lithuania	65.2	25.2	3,575	55	Vilnius	16,700
Luxembourg	2.6	1.0	480	186	Luxembourg	80,800
Macau (China)	0.02	0.007	457	18,280	–	24,300
Macedonia (FYROM)	25.7	9.9	2,056	81	Skopje	8,400
Madagascar	587	227	19,449	33	Antananarivo	1,000
Madeira (Portugal)	0.78	0.30	241	309	Funchal	22,700
Malawi	118	45.7	13,603	115	Lilongwe	800
Malaysia	330	127	24,821	75	Kuala Lumpur/Putrajaya	14,400
Maldives	0.30	0.12	369	1,230	Malé	3,900
Mali	1,240	479	11,995	10	Bamako	1,200
Malta	0.32	0.12	402	1,272	Valletta	23,200
Marshall Is.	0.18	0.07	62	342	Majuro	2,900
Martinique (France)	1.1	0.43	433	394	Fort-de-France	14,400
Mauritania	1,026	396	3,270	3	Nouakchott	1,800
Mauritius	2.0	0.79	1,251	613	Port Louis	11,900
Mexico	1,958	756	108,701	55	Mexico City	12,500
Micronesia, Fed. States of	0.70	0.27	108	154	Palikir	2,300
Moldova	33.9	13.1	4,320	128	Chişinău	2,200
Monaco	0.001	0.0004	33	33,000	Monaco	30,000
Mongolia	1,567	605	2,952	2	Ulan Bator	2,900
Montenegro	14.0	5.4	685	49	Podgorica	3,800
Montserrat (UK)	0.10	0.04	10	94	Plymouth	3,400
Morocco	447	172	33,757	76	Rabat	3,800
Mozambique	802	309	20,906	26	Maputo	900
Namibia	824	318	2,055	2	Windhoek	5,200
Nauru	0.02	0.008	14	644	Yaren District	5,000
Nepal	147	56.8	28,902	205	Katmandu	1,100
Netherlands	41.5	16.0	16,571	399	Amsterdam/The Hague	38,600
Netherlands Antilles (Neths)	0.80	0.31	224	233	Willemstad	16,000
New Caledonia (France)	18.6	7.2	222	12	Nouméa	15,000
New Zealand	271	104	4,116	15	Wellington	27,300
Nicaragua	130	50.2	5,675	44	Managua	3,200
Niger	1,267	489	12,895	10	Niamey	700
Nigeria	924	357	135,031	146	Abuja	2,200
Northern Mariana Is. (US)	0.46	0.18	85	177	Saipan	12,500
Norway	324	125	4,628	14	Oslo	55,600
Oman	310	119	3,205	15	Muscat	19,100
Pakistan	796	307	164,742	205	Islamabad	2,600
Palau	0.46	0.18	21	46	Melekeok	7,600
Panama	75.5	29.2	3,242	41	Panamá	9,000
Papua New Guinea	463	179	5,796	13	Port Moresby	2,900
Paraguay	407	157	6,669	16	Asunción	4,000
Peru	1,285	496	28,675	22	Lima	7,600
Philippines	300	116	91,077	304	Manila	3,300
Poland	323	125	38,518	123	Warsaw	16,200
Portugal	88.8	34.3	10,643	115	Lisbon	21,800
Puerto Rico (US)	8.9	3.4	3,944	433	San Juan	19,600
Qatar	11.0	4.2	907	79	Doha	29,400
Réunion (France)	2.5	0.97	777	311	St-Denis	6,200

Country/Territory	Area (1,000 sq km)	Area (1,000 sq mi)	Population (1,000s)	Density (persons per sq km)	Capital City	Annual Income US$
Romania	238	92.0	22,276	94	Bucharest	11,100
Russia	17,075	6,593	141,378	8	Moscow	14,600
Rwanda	26.3	10.2	9,908	376	Kigali	1,000
St Kitts & Nevis	0.26	0.10	39	151	Basseterre	8,200
St Lucia	0.54	0.21	171	277	Castries	4,800
St Vincent & Grenadines	0.39	0.15	118	304	Kingstown	3,600
Samoa	2.8	1.1	214	73	Apia	2,100
San Marino	0.06	0.02	30	485	San Marino	34,100
São Tomé & Príncipe	0.96	0.37	200	199	São Tomé	1,200
Saudi Arabia	2,150	830	27,601	14	Riyadh	20,700
Senegal	197	76.0	12,522	64	Dakar	1,700
Serbia	77.5	29.9	8,024	104	Belgrade	7,700
Seychelles	0.46	0.18	82	180	Victoria	18,400
Sierra Leone	71.7	27.7	6,155	86	Freetown	800
Singapore	0.68	0.26	4,553	6,570	Singapore City	48,900
Slovak Republic	49.0	18.9	5,448	112	Bratislava	19,800
Slovenia	20.3	7.8	2,009	99	Ljubljana	27,300
Solomon Is.	28.9	11.2	567	20	Honiara	600
Somalia	638	246	9,119	14	Mogadishu	600
South Africa	1,221	471	43,998	36	Cape Town/Pretoria	10,600
Spain	498	192	40,448	80	Madrid	33,700
Sri Lanka	65.6	25.3	20,926	319	Colombo	4,100
Sudan	2,506	967	39,379	16	Khartoum	2,500
Suriname	163	63.0	471	3	Paramaribo	7,800
Swaziland	17.4	6.7	1,133	65	Mbabane	4,800
Sweden	450	174	9,031	20	Stockholm	36,900
Switzerland	41.3	15.9	7,555	183	Bern	39,800
Syria	185	71.5	19,315	104	Damascus	4,500
Taiwan	36.0	13.9	22,859	635	Taipei	29,800
Tajikistan	143	55.3	7,077	49	Dushanbe	1,600
Tanzania	945	365	39,384	42	Dodoma	1,100
Thailand	513	198	65,068	127	Bangkok	8,000
Togo	56.8	21.9	5,702	100	Lomé	900
Tonga	0.65	0.25	117	156	Nuku'alofa	2,200
Trinidad & Tobago	5.1	2.0	1,057	206	Port of Spain	21,700
Tunisia	164	63.2	10,276	63	Tunis	7,500
Turkey	775	299	71,159	91	Ankara	7,500
Turkmenistan	488	188	5,097	10	Ashkhabad	9,200
Turks & Caicos Is. (UK)	0.43	0.17	22	51	Cockburn Town	11,500
Tuvalu	0.03	0.01	12	461	Fongafale	1,600
Uganda	241	93.1	30,263	128	Kampala	1,100
Ukraine	604	233	46,300	77	Kiev	6,900
United Arab Emirates	83.6	32.3	4,444	53	Abu Dhabi	55,200
United Kingdom	242	93.4	60,776	248	London	35,300
United States of America	9,629	3,718	301,140	31	Washington, DC	46,000
Uruguay	175	67.6	3,461	20	Montevideo	10,700
Uzbekistan	447	173	27,780	62	Tashkent	2,200
Vanuatu	12.2	4.7	212	17	Port-Vila	2,900
Venezuela	912	352	26,024	29	Caracas	12,800
Vietnam	332	128	85,262	259	Hanoi	2,600
Virgin Is. (UK)	0.15	0.06	24	154	Road Town	38,500
Virgin Is. (US)	0.35	0.13	108	308	Charlotte Amalie	14,500
Wallis & Futuna Is. (France)	0.20	0.08	16	60	Mata-Utu	3,800
West Bank (OPT)*	5.9	2.3	2,536	433	–	1,100
Western Sahara	266	103	383	1	El Aaiún	N/A
Yemen	528	204	22,231	42	Sana'	2,400
Zambia	753	291	11,477	15	Lusaka	1,400
Zimbabwe	391	151	12,311	32	Harare	500

	Population (1,000s)		Population (1,000s)		Population (1,000s)		Population (1,000s)
Afghanistan		**China**		Changde	1,429	**El Salvador**	
Kabul	3,288	Shanghai	14,503	Huainan	1,420	San Salvador	1,517
Algeria		Beijing	10,717	Liuzhou	1,409	**Ethiopia**	
Algiers	3,260	Guangzhou	8,425	Suining, Sichuan	1,401	Addis Ababa	2,899
Angola		Shenzhen	7,233	Quanzhou	1,377	**Finland**	
Luanda	2,839	Wuhan	7,093	Xintai	1,334	Helsinki	1,091
Argentina		Hong Kong	7,041	Mianyang	1,322	**France**	
Buenos Aires	13,349	Tianjin	7,040	Heze	1,318	Paris	9,820
Córdoba	1,592	Chongqing	6,363	Yiyang	1,318	Lyons	1,403
Rosario	1,312	Shenyang	4,720	Yueyang	1,286	Marseilles	1,382
Mendoza	1,072	Dongguan	4,320	Suqian	1,258	Lille	1,029
Armenia		Chengdu	4,065	Changzhou	1,249	**Georgia**	
Yerevan	1,103	Xi'an	3,926	Huaian	1,243	Tbilisi	1,406
Australia		Harbin	3,695	Chifeng	1,238	**Germany**	
Sydney	4,388	Nanjing	3,621	Jingmen	1,228	Berlin	3,387
Melbourne	3,663	Guiyang	3,447	Yuzhou	1,226	Hamburg	1,705
Brisbane	1,769	Dalian	3,073	Zaoyang	1,210	Munich	1,195
Perth	1,484	Changchun	3,046	Huzhou	1,203	**Ghana**	
Adelaide	1,137	Zibo	2,982	Tianshui	1,199	Accra	1,981
Austria		Kunming	2,837	Yongzhou	1,182	Kumasi	1,517
Vienna	2,260	Hangzhou	2,831	Mudanjiang	1,171	**Greece**	
Azerbaijan		Qingdao	2,817	Liupanshui	1,149	Athens	3,238
Baku	1,856	Taiyuan	2,794	Leshan	1,143	**Guatemala**	
Bangladesh		Jinan	2,743	Jining, Shandong	1,143	Guatemala City	3,242
Dhaka	12,560	Zhengzhou	2,590	Xiaoshan	1,130	**Guinea**	
Chittagong	4,171	Fuzhou	2,453	Yixing	1,129	Conakry	1,465
Khulna	1,497	Changsha	2,451	Zigong	1,087	**Haiti**	
Rajshahi	1,035	Lanzhou	2,411	Xianyang	1,072	Port-au-Prince	2,129
Belarus		Xiamen	2,371	Fuyu	1,068	**Honduras**	
Minsk	1,778	Shijiazhuang	2,275	Yulin	1,060	Tegucigalpa	1,061
Belgium		Jinxi	2,268	Baoding	1,042	**Hungary**	
Brussels	1,012	Jilin	2,255	Xinyi, Jiangsu	1,022	Budapest	1,693
Bolivia		Wenzhou	2,212	Zhuzhou	1,016	**India**	
La Paz	1,533	Nanchang	2,188	Jixi	1,012	Mumbai	18,336
Santa Cruz	1,352	Zaozhuang	2,096	Linqing	1,009	Delhi	15,334
Brazil		Nanchong	2,046	Jiamusi	1,006	Kolkata	14,299
São Paulo	18,333	Nanning	2,040	Xiangfan	1,006	Chennai	6,915
Rio de Janeiro	11,469	Linyi	2,035	Zhangjiakou	1,001	Bangalore	6,532
Belo Horizonte	5,304	Ürümqi	2,025	**Colombia**		Hyderabad	6,145
Pôrto Alegre	3,795	Yantai	1,991	Bogotá	7,594	Ahmedabad	5,171
Recife	3,527	Wanxian	1,963	Medellín	3,236	Pune	4,485
Brasília	3,341	Xuzhou	1,960	Cali	2,583	Surat	3,671
Salvador	3,331	Baotou	1,920	Barranquilla	1,918	Kanpur	3,040
Fortaleza	3,261	Hefei	1,916	Bucaramanga	1,069	Jaipur	2,796
Curitiba	2,871	Suzhou	1,849	Cartagena	1,002	Lucknow	2,589
Campinas	2,640	Nanyang	1,830	**Congo**		Nagpur	2,359
Belém	2,097	Tangshan	1,825	Brazzaville	1,173	Patna	2,066
Goiânia	1,878	Ningbo	1,810	**Congo**		Indore	1,941
Manaus	1,673	Datong	1,763	**(Dem. Rep.)**		Vadodara	1,686
Santos	1,634	Yancheng	1,678	Kinshasa	6,049	Bhopal	1,656
Vitória	1,602	Tianmen	1,676	Kolwezi	1,207	Coimbatore	1,628
Maceió	1,137	Shangqui	1,650	Lubumbashi	1,179	Ludhiana	1,583
Natal	1,049	Lu'an	1,647	**Costa Rica**		Agra	1,526
Bulgaria		Wuxi	1,646	San José	1,217	Visakhapatnam	1,468
Sofia	1,093	Luoyang	1,644	**Croatia**		Cochin	1,461
Burma (= Myanmar)		Hohhot	1,644	Zagreb	1,067	Nashik	1,408
Rangoon	4,107	Anshan	1,611	**Cuba**		Meerut	1,340
Cambodia		Qiqihar	1,607	Havana	2,192	Faridabad	1,330
Phnom Penh	1,364	Tai'an	1,598	**Czech Republic**		Varanasi	1,300
Cameroon		Daqing	1,594	Prague	1,171	Ghaziabad	1,277
Douala	1,980	Xinghua	1,587	**Denmark**		Asansol	1,272
Yaoundé	1,727	Pingxiang	1,562	Copenhagen	1,091	Jamshedpur	1,246
Canada		Handan	1,535	**Dominican**		Madurai	1,245
Toronto	5,312	Xiantao	1,528	**Republic**		Jabalpur	1,234
Montréal	3,640	Zhanjiang	1,514	Santo Domingo	2,563	Rajkot	1,205
Vancouver	2,188	Weifang	1,498	**Ecuador**		Dhanbad	1,195
Ottawa	1,156	Shantou	1,495	Guayaquil	2,387	Amritsar	1,162
Calgary	1,058	Fushun	1,456	Quito	1,514	Allahabad	1,153
Edmonton	1,015	Xianyang	1,450	**Egypt**		Vijayawada	1,093
Chile		Luzhou	1,447	Cairo	11,146	Srinagar	1,093
Santiago	5,683	Neijiang	1,441	Alexandria	3,760	Aurangabad	1,065

Population (1,000s)		Population (1,000s)		Population (1,000s)		Population (1,000s)	
Bhilainagar-Durg	1,051	Benghazi	1,114	Novosibirsk	1,425	Odessa	1,027
Solapur	1,012	**Madagascar**		Nizhniy Novgorod	1,288	**United Arab Emirates**	
Indonesia		Antananarivo	1,808	Yekaterinburg	1,281	Dubai	1,330
Jakarta	13,215	**Malaysia**		Samara	1,140	**United Kingdom**	
Bandung	4,126	Kuala Lumpur	1,405	Omsk	1,132	London	8,505
Surabaya	2,992	**Mali**		Kazan	1,108	Birmingham	2,280
Medan	2,287	Bamako	1,379	Rostov	1,081	Manchester	2,228
Palembang	1,733	**Mexico**		Chelyabinsk	1,067	Liverpool	1,519
Ujung Pandang	1,284	Mexico City	19,013	Ufa	1,035	Glasgow	1,159
Iran		Guadalajara	3,905	Volgograd	1,016	**United States of America**	
Tehran	7,352	Monterrey	3,517	Perm	1,014	New York	18,718
Mashhad	2,147	Toluca	1,987	**Saudi Arabia**		Los Angeles	12,298
Esfahan	1,547	Puebla	1,880	Riyadh	5,514	Chicago	8,814
Tabriz	1,396	Tijuana	1,570	Jedda	3,807	Miami	5,434
Karaj	1,235	Ciudad Juárez	1,469	Mecca	1,529	Philadelphia	5,392
Shiraz	1,230	León	1,438	Medina	1,044	Dallas–Fort Worth	4,655
Qom	1,045	Torreón	1,057	**Senegal**		Boston	4,361
Iraq		**Morocco**		Dakar	2,313	Houston	4,320
Baghdad	5,910	Casablanca	3,743	**Serbia**		Atlanta	4,304
Mosul	1,236	Rabat	1,859	Belgrade	1,116	Washington	4,238
Basra	1,187	Fès	1,032	**Sierra Leone**		Detroit	4,034
Ireland		**Mozambique**		Freetown	1,007	Phoenix–Mesa	3,416
Dublin	1,037	Maputo	1,316	**Singapore**		San Francisco	3,385
Israel		**Nepal**		Singapore City	4,372	Seattle	2,989
Tel Aviv-Yafo	3,025	Katmandu	1,176	**Somalia**		San Diego	2,852
Italy		**Netherlands**		Mogadishu	1,320	Minneapolis–St Paul	2,556
Rome	3,348	Amsterdam	1,157	**South Africa**		Tampa–St Petersburg	2,252
Milan	2,953	Rotterdam	1,112	Johannesburg	3,254	Denver	2,239
Naples	2,245	**New Zealand**		Cape Town	3,083	Baltimore	2,205
Turin	1,660	Auckland	1,152	Durban	2,631	St Louis	2,159
Ivory Coast		**Nicaragua**		Pretoria	1,271	Cleveland	1,855
(= Côte d'Ivoire)		Managua	1,165	Vereeniging	1,027	Portland	1,810
Abidjan	3,516	**Nigeria**		Port Elizabeth	1,006	Pittsburgh	1,806
Japan		Lagos	11,135	**Spain**		Las Vegas	1,720
Tokyo	12,064	Kano	2,884	Madrid	5,608	San Bernardino	1,690
Yokohama	6,427	Ibadan	2,375	Barcelona	4,795	San Jose	1,631
Osaka	2,599	Kaduna	1,329	**Sudan**		Cincinnati	1,599
Nagoya	2,172	Benin City	1,022	Khartoum	4,518	Sacramento	1,555
Sapporo	1,922	**Pakistan**		**Sweden**		Norfolk–Virginia Beach	1,460
Kobe	1,493	Karachi	11,819	Stockholm	1,729	Kansas City	1,437
Kyoto	1,468	Lahore	6,373	**Syria**		San Antonio	1,436
Fukuoka	1,341	Faisalabad	2,533	Aleppo	2,505	Indianapolis	1,387
Kawasaki	1,250	Rawalpindi	1,794	Damascus	2,317	Milwaukee	1,316
Hiroshima	1,126	Gujranwala	1,466	**Taiwan**		Orlando	1,306
Kitakyushu	1,011	Multan	1,459	Taipei	2,606	Providence	1,248
Sendai	1,008	Hyderabad	1,392	Kaohsiung	1,515	Columbus	1,236
Jordan		Peshawar	1,255	T'aichung	1,033	Austin	1,107
Amman	1,292	**Panama**		**Tanzania**		Memphis	1,053
Kazakhstan		Panamá	1,216	Dar es Salaam	2,683	New Orleans	1,010
Almaty	1,156	**Paraguay**		**Thailand**		**Uruguay**	
Kenya		Asunción	1,858	Bangkok	6,604	Montevideo	1,353
Nairobi	2,818	**Peru**		**Togo**		**Uzbekistan**	
Korea, North		Lima	8,180	Lomé	1,337	Tashkent	2,181
Pyŏngyang	3,351	**Philippines**		**Tunisia**		**Venezuela**	
N'ampo	1,102	Manila	10,677	Tunis	2,063	Caracas	3,276
Korea, South		Davao	1,326	**Turkey**		Valencia	2,330
Seoul	9,888	**Poland**		Istanbul	9,712	Maracaibo	2,182
Busan	3,830	Warsaw	1,680	Ankara	3,573	Maracay	1,138
Incheon	2,884	**Portugal**		Izmir	2,487	**Vietnam**	
Daegu	2,675	Lisbon	2,761	Bursa	1,414	Ho Chi Minh City	5,065
Daejeon	1,522	Porto	1,309	Adana	1,245	Hanoi	4,164
Gwangju	1,379	**Puerto Rico**		**Uganda**		Haiphong	1,873
Seongnam	1,353	San Juan	2,604	Kampala	1,345	**Yemen**	
Ulsan	1,340	**Romania**		**Ukraine**		Sana'	1,801
Lebanon		Bucharest	1,934	Kiev	2,621	**Zambia**	
Beirut	2,070	**Russia**		Kharkov	1,521	Lusaka	1,450
Libya		Moscow	10,672	Dnepropetrovsk	1,122	**Zimbabwe**	
Tripoli	2,098	Saint Petersburg	5,315	Donetsk	1,065	Harare	1,527

Listed above are the principal cities with more than 1,00,000 inhabitants. The figures are taken from the most recent census or estimate available (usually 2007), and as far as possible are for the metropolitan area or urban agglomeration.

The world is divided into 24 time zones, each centered on meridians at 15° intervals, which is the longitudinal distance the Sun travels every hour. The Prime Meridian running through Greenwich in London, England, passes through the middle of the first time zone. Zones to the east of Greenwich are ahead of Universal Time (UT) by one hour for every 15° of longitude, while zones to the west are behind UT by one hour.

When it is 12 noon at the Greenwich meridian, 180° east it is midnight of the same day, while at 180° west the day is only just beginning. To overcome this, the International Date Line was established in 1883 – an imaginary line which approximately follows the 180th meridian. Therefore, if one traveled eastward from Japan (140° East) toward Samoa (170° West), one would pass from Sunday night straight into Sunday morning.

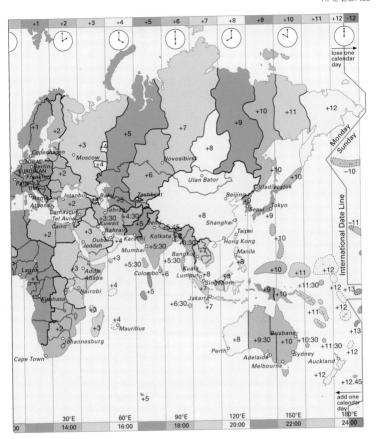

+1	+2	+3	+4	+5	+6	+7	+8	+9	+10	+11	+12 -12

lose one calendar day

Monday / Sunday

International Date Line

add one calendar day

30°E	60°E	90°E	120°E	150°E	180°E
14:00	16:00	18:00	20:00	22:00	24:00

TIME DIFFERENCES FROM EASTERN STANDARD TIME

BEIJING	+13	LONDON	+5
CAIRO	+7	LOS ANGELES	−3
CHICAGO	−1	MOSCOW	+8
DALLAS	−1	MEXICO CITY	−1
DELHI	+10.5	SANTIAGO	+1
DENVER	−2	SYDNEY	+15
HONOLULU	−5	TOKYO	+14
KUWAIT	+8	VANCOUVER	−3

KEY TO TIME ZONES MAP

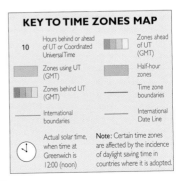

10 — Hours behind or ahead of UT or Coordinated Universal Time

Zones using UT (GMT)

Zones behind UT (GMT)

International boundaries

Actual solar time, when time at Greenwich is 12:00 (noon)

Zones ahead of UT (GMT)

Half-hour zones

Time zone boundaries

International Date Line

Note: Certain time zones are affected by the incidence of daylight saving time in countries where it is adopted.

WORLD'S BUSIEST AIRPORTS

TOTAL NUMBER OF PASSENGERS IN MILLIONS (2006)

ATLANTA HARTSFIELD INTL. (ATL)	**84.8**
CHICAGO O'HARE INTL. (ORD)	**77.0**
LONDON HEATHROW (LHR)	**67.5**
TOKYO HANEDA (HND)	**65.8**
LOS ANGELES INTL. (LAX)	**61.0**
DALLAS/FORT WORTH INTL. (DFW)	**60.2**
PARIS CHARLES DE GAULLE (CDG)	**56.8**
FRANKFURT INTL. (FRA)	**52.8**
BEIJING CAPITAL INTL. (PEK)	**48.7**

The flight paths shown on the maps above usually follow the shortest, most direct route from A to B, known as the *great-circle route*. A great circle is any circle that divides the globe into equal halves. Aircraft do not always fly along great-circle routes, however. Lack of search and rescue and emergency landing provisions, together with limits on fuel consumption and minimum flying altitudes, mean that commercial aircraft do not usually fly across Antarctica.

FLIGHT TIMES FROM NEW YORK

FRANKFURT	8hrs 35mins
JOHANNESBURG	17hrs 45mins
MEXICO CITY	5hrs 45mins
PARIS	8hrs 15mins
ROME	9hrs 35mins
SANTIAGO	12hrs 55mins
SINGAPORE	23hrs 10mins
TOKYO	14hrs 35mins
VANCOUVER	7hrs 25mins

FLIGHT TIMES FROM LONDON

ATHENS	4hrs 05mins
AUCKLAND	24hrs 20mins
BANGKOK	14hrs 30mins
BUENOS AIRES	14hrs 20mins
HONG KONG	14hrs 10mins
LOS ANGELES	12hrs 00mins
MOSCOW	3hrs 50mins
MUMBAI (BOMBAY)	11hrs 15mins
NEW YORK	6hrs 50mins

DISTANCE TABLE

Kms (upper-right values) / Miles (lower-left values)

	Beijing	Buenos Aires	Cairo	Caracas	Chicago	Hong Kong	Honolulu	Johannesburg	Kolkata	Lagos	London	Los Angeles
Beijing	Beijing	11972	4688	8947	6588	1220	5070	7276	2031	7119	5057	6251
Buenos Aires	19268	Buenos Aires	7341	3167	5599	11481	7558	5025	10268	4919	6917	6122
Cairo	7544	11814	Cairo	6340	6127	5064	8838	3894	3541	2432	2180	7580
Caracas	14399	5096	10203	Caracas	2502	10166	6009	6847	9609	4810	4664	3612
Chicago	10603	9011	3206	4027	Chicago	7783	4247	8689	7978	5973	3949	1742
Hong Kong	1963	18478	8150	16360	12526	Hong Kong	5543	6669	1653	7360	5980	7232
Honolulu	8160	12164	14223	9670	6836	8921	Honolulu	11934	7048	10133	7228	2558
Johannesburg	11710	8088	6267	11019	13984	10732	19206	Johannesburg	5256	2799	5637	10362
Kolkata	3269	16524	5699	15464	12839	2659	11343	8459	Kolkata	5727	4946	8152
Lagos	11457	7916	3915	7741	9612	11845	16308	4505	9216	Lagos	3118	7713
London	8138	11131	3508	7507	6356	9623	11632	9071	7961	5017	London	5442
Los Angeles	10060	9852	12200	5812	2804	11639	4117	16676	13120	12414	8758	Los Angeles
Mexico City	12460	7389	12372	3586	2726	14122	6085	14585	15280	11071	8936	2493
Moscow	5794	13477	2902	9938	8000	7144	11323	9161	5534	6254	2498	9769
Mumbai	4757	14925	4355	14522	12953	4317	12914	6974	1664	7612	7190	14000
Nairobi	9216	10402	3536	11544	12883	8776	17282	2927	6179	3807	6819	15544
New York	10988	8526	9020	3430	1145	12950	7980	12841	12747	8477	5572	3936
Paris	8217	11051	3210	7625	6650	9630	11968	8732	7858	4714	342	9085
Rio de Janeiro	17338	1953	9896	4546	8547	17704	13342	7113	15073	6035	9299	10155
Rome	8126	11151	2133	8363	7739	9284	12916	7743	7219	4039	1431	10188
Singapore	4478	15879	8267	18359	15078	2599	10816	8660	2897	11145	10852	14123
Sydney	8949	11800	14418	15343	14875	7374	8168	11040	9138	15519	16992	12073
Tokyo	2099	18362	9571	14164	10137	2874	6202	13547	5141	13480	9562	8811
Wellington	10782	9981	16524	13122	13451	9427	7513	11761	11354	16050	18814	10814

The table above shows air distances in miles and kilometers between 30 major cities.

Mexico City	Moscow	Mumbai	Nairobi	New York	Paris	Rio de Janeiro	Rome	Singapore	Sydney	Tokyo	Wellington	
7742	3600	2956	5727	6828	5106	10773	5049	2783	5561	1304	6700	**Beijing**
4591	8374	9275	6463	5298	6867	1214	6929	9867	7332	11410	6202	**Buenos Aires**
7687	1803	2706	2197	5605	1994	6149	1325	5137	8959	5947	10268	**Cairo**
2228	6175	9024	7173	2131	4738	2825	5196	11407	9534	8801	8154	**Caracas**
1694	4971	8048	8005	711	4132	5311	4809	9369	9243	6299	8358	**Chicago**
8775	4439	2683	5453	8047	5984	11001	5769	1615	4582	1786	5857	**Hong Kong**
3781	7036	8024	10739	4958	7437	8290	8026	6721	5075	3854	4669	**Honolulu**
9063	5692	4334	1818	7979	5426	4420	4811	5381	6860	8418	7308	**Johannesburg**
9494	3438	1034	3839	7921	4883	9366	4486	1800	5678	3195	7055	**Kolkata**
6879	3886	4730	2366	5268	2929	3750	2510	6925	9643	8376	9973	**Lagos**
5552	1552	4467	4237	3463	212	5778	889	6743	10558	5942	11691	**London**
1549	6070	8700	9659	2446	5645	6310	6331	8776	7502	5475	6719	**Los Angeles**
	6664	9728	9207	2090	5717	4780	6365	10321	8058	7024	6897	**Mexico City**
10724		3126	3942	4666	1545	7184	1477	5237	9008	4651	10283	**Moscow**
15656	5031		2816	7793	4356	8332	3837	2432	6313	4189	7686	**Mumbai**
14818	6344	4532		7358	4029	5548	3350	4635	7552	6996	8490	**Nairobi**
3264	7510	12541	11842		3626	4832	4280	9531	9935	6741	8951	**New York**
9200	2486	7010	6485	5836		5708	687	6671	10539	6038	11798	**Paris**
7693	11562	13409	8928	7777	9187		5725	9763	8389	11551	7367	**Rio de Janeiro**
10243	2376	6175	5391	6888	1105	9214		6229	10143	6127	11523	**Rome**
16610	8428	3914	7460	15339	10737	15712	10025		3915	3306	5298	**Singapore**
12969	14497	10160	12153	15989	16962	13501	16324	6300		4861	1383	**Sydney**
11304	7485	6742	11260	10849	9718	18589	9861	5321	7823		5762	**Tokyo**
11100	16549	12370	13664	14405	18987	11855	18545	8526	2226	9273		**Wellington**

Miles

Known as "great-circle" distances, these measure the shortest routes between the cities.

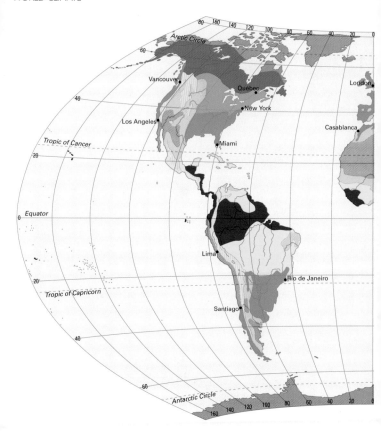

Climate is weather in the long term: the seasonal pattern of temperature and precipitation averaged over a period of time. Temperature roughly follows latitude, and is warmest near the equator and coldest near the poles. The interplay of various factors, however, namely the differential heating of land and sea, the influence of landmasses and mountain ranges on winds and ocean currents, and the effect of vegetation, all combine to add complexity. Thus New York and Naples share almost the same latitude, but their resulting climates are quite different. Most scientists are now in agreement that the world's climate is changing, due partly to atmospheric pollution. By the year 2050, average world temperatures are predicted to rise by approximately 3°F to make the climate hotter than it has been at any time during the last 120,000 years. Climate graphs for 24 cities are given on pages 18 and 19.

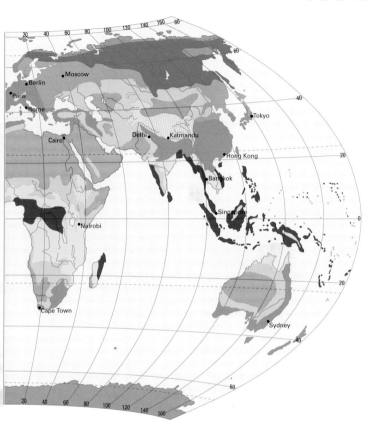

SEASONAL WEATHER EXTREMES

- **Caribbean**
  Hurricanes – August to October
- **Northern Latitudes**
  Blizzards – November to March
- **Southern Asia**
  Cyclones and typhoons – June to November
- **Southern Asia**
  Monsoon rains – July to October

CLIMATIC REGIONS

- Tropical climate (hot and wet)
- Desert climate (hot and very dry)
- Savanna climate (hot with dry season)
- Steppe climate (Warm and dry)
- Mild climate (Warm and wet)
- Continental climate (cold with wet winter)
- Subarctic climate (very cold winter)
- Polar climate (very cold and dry)
- Mountainous climate (altitude affects climate)
- Lima • Climate graphs on pages 18 and 19

Note: Climate comprises a description of the condition of the atmosphere over a considerable area for a long time (at least 30 years).

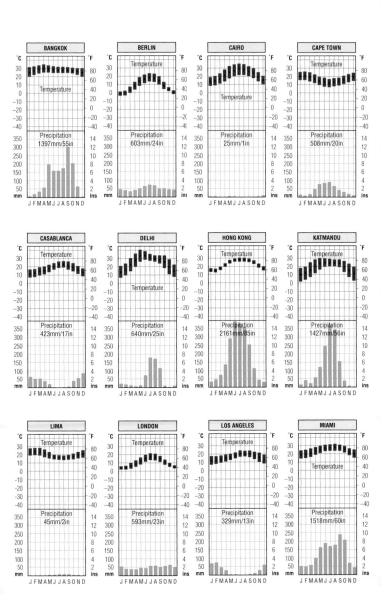

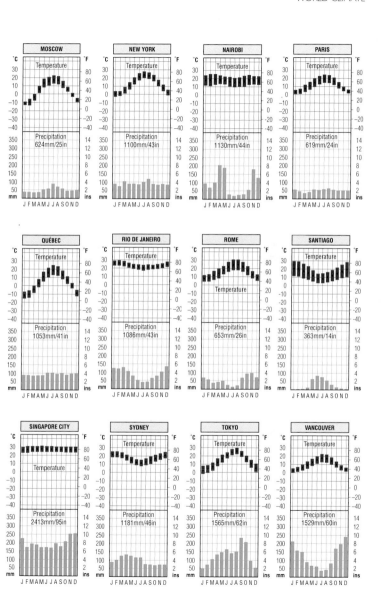

CITY PLANS

21 Amsterdam   **34** Moscow

22 Athens   **35** Mumbai

23 Bangkok   **36** New York

24 Barcelona   **37** Paris

25 Berlin   **38** Prague

26 Brussels   **39** Rio de Janeiro

27 Cape Town   **40** Rome

28 Chicago   **41** San Francisco

29 Dublin   **42** Singapore

30 Hong Kong   **43** Sydney

31 London   **44** Tokyo

32 Madrid   **45** Toronto

33 Mexico City   **46** Vienna

LEGEND TO CITY PLANS

Motorway		†	Abbey/cathedral
Through route		†	Church of interest
Secondary road		⊞	Hospital
Other road		⸸	Mosque
Limited access / pedestrian road		♠	Shrine
Railroad		✿	Synagogue
Tramway/monorail		🏯	Temple
Elevated rail lines		🄸	Tourist information center
Rail/bus station		☐	Public building
Underground/Metro station		Museum	Place of interest

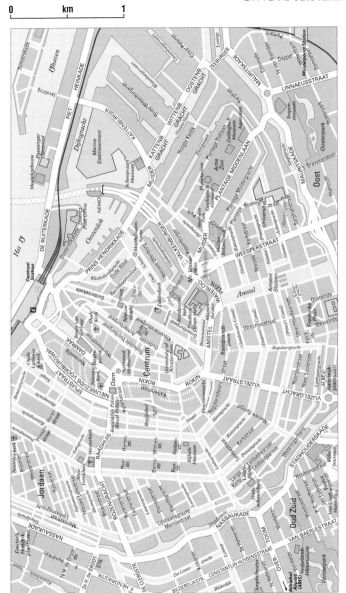

0   km   1

COPYRIGHT PHILIPS

21

0   km   1

Atiki
Ilission
Aristou
Agorakritou
Michail
Parrasiou
Alkamenous
Eynardou
Alkiviadou
Peoniou
Vodaa
Ioulianou
Domokou
Samou
KODRICTONOS
Derigny
Septemvriou
Aristotelous
Aristovriou
ACHARNON
Philis
PATISSION
Ferron
EVELPIDON
Mavrommateon
Pl. Victorias
Pedion Areos
Valtinon
Soutsou
Papargopoulou
Lomvardou
Paraschou
Lastareos
Komninon

Larisis
Samou
LIOSSION
Larisis
Theodorou
Peloponnisos
Neof. Metaxa Ipirou
Aghios Pavlos
Kritis
Akominatou
Psaron
Hiou
Mezonos
Deligiani
Keramaon
Favierou
Victor Ougo
Karolou
Metaxovrgio
Mami
Kapodistriou
CHALKOKONDILI
National Santovriandou
Theatre
AG. KONSTANTINOU

LEOFOROS
Plapouta
Ioustinianou
Voulgaroktonou
Lofos Strefi
Kallidromiou
Dervenakion
Benaki
Pigis
TRIKOUPI
Mavromichali
Isavron
IPPOKRATOUS
Aghios Nikolaos

28 OKTOVRIOU
PATISSION
Metsovou
Irakliou
Bouboulinas
Trikoupi
Ipirou
Tritis
Averof
Iositsa
Spiridonos
National Archeological Museum
Stournara
Solomou
Canigos
Themistokleous
Emmanouil
Solonos
Zoodhou
Akadimias
Valtetsiou
H.AR.
Mavromichali
Askilpiou Didotou
Didotou
Aghios Dionysios
Sina
Solonos
Akadimias
Dimotirou
Pindarou

Pl. Omonia
Omonia
(Omonia Sq.)
ELEFTHERIOU VENIZELOU
Opera House
Ethniki Vivliothiki
Panepistimio
Aghios Dionysios
Akadimia

Panepistimio
Panepistimio
STADIOU
Pl. Klafthmonos
Sokratous
Sofokleous
Kendriki Agora
Evripdou
Megalou Alexandrou
Kolokotroni
Agiou Markou
Pericleous
ERMOU

PIREOS
Deligirgi
Zinonos
Kolofon
Mitera
Leonidou
Kyrnthous
Agisilaou
Keramikou
Therniopylon
Salaminos
Plataion
Asomaton
Sachtouri
Aristofanous Miouli
Kriezi
Keramikos
ERMOU

ATHINAS
EOLOU
AREOS
Mitropoleos
Monastiraki
VASILISSIS
SOFIAS
AMALIAS
FILELLINON
NIKIS

ERMOU
Eptachalkou
Thisio
Poulopoulou
Irakleidon
Nileos
Akamantos
Thisio
Agora
Plaka
Polignotou Lysiou
Adrianou
Nikodimou
Tripodon Kidathineon
Apollonos
Mitropoleos
(Cathedral of Athens)
Syntagma Square (Constitution Square)
Syntagma
Vouli (Parliament Building)
Ethnikos Kipos
Zappeion

APOSTOLOU PAVLOU
Aghia Marina
Lofos Nimfon
Pnika
Dimofontos
Acropolis
Arios Pagos
Odeon of Herodes Atticus
Parthenon
Theorias
Museum
Lisicratous
Theatre of Dionysos
LEOFOROS OLGAS
Temple of Olympian Zeus
ARDITOU

DIONYSIOU
Rovertou
AREOPAGITOU
Acropolis
Parthenonos
Erechthiou
Galli
Mitseon
Makrigianni
SINGROU
KALLIRROIS
Anapafseos
Vachi

Troon
Kalisthenous
Arakinthou
Lofos Filopapou
Garivaldi
Misaralloti
Propyleou

● **Greek Dance Theatre**

Athens Airport (AMS)

0 km 2

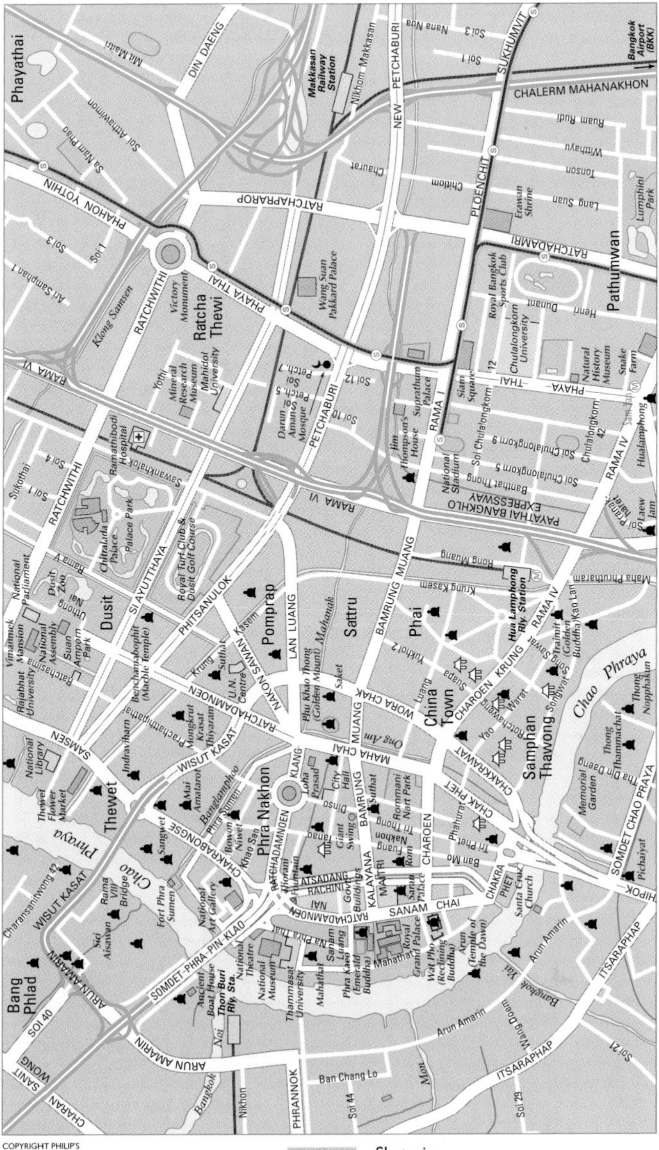

Skytrain

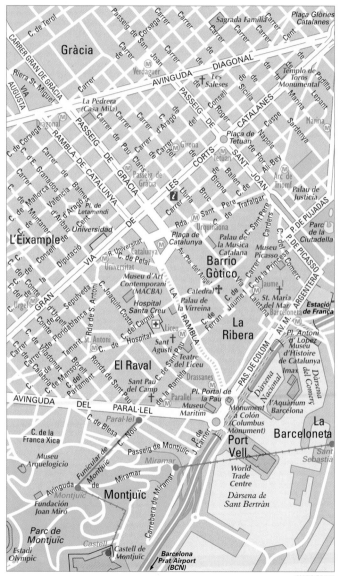

0   km   1

Gràcia

CARRER GRAN DE GRÀCIA
VIA AUGUSTA
C. de Terol
Riera St. Miguel
Passeig de Corsega
Carrer
Carrer
de
Carrer
de
Carrer
Sagrada Família
Carrer
Cent
Plaça Glòries Catalanes

Verdaguer
AVINGUDA
DIAGONAL
de
Sicilia
Marina
Lepant
Templo de Padilla Toros Monumental

RAMBLA DE CATALUNYA
PASSEIG DE GRÀCIA
La Pedrera (Casa Mila)
Diagonal
C. de Corsega
Carrer de Pau Claris
C. d'Arago
PASSEIG DE
CORTS
Les Saleses
de
Consell
C. de Roger
Casp
Napols
Sardenya
Marina
Arc de Triomf
Palau de Justicia

L'Eixample
C. d'E Granados
Carrer de Balmes
Valencia
d'Aribau
Carrer d'Arago
Pl. de Letamendi
Carrer
C. Aragó
Girona
de
CATALANES
Plaça de Tetuan
Bailen
de
Ali Bey
SANT JOAN
Tetuan
de
de
Girona
Trafalgar
de C. Sant Pere
Carders
P. DE PUJADAS
Parc de la Ciutadella
Palau de Justicia

C. de Mallorca
C. de Muntaner
Carrer
Cent
Universidad
LES
Carrer
Rda.
Sant
Pere
de
Museu Picasso
P. DE PICASSO

C. C.
C. del Comte d'Urgell
C. de Villaret
Diputació
VIA
GRAN
R. Universitat
C. de Pelai
Universitat
Catalunya
Plaça de Catalunya
Urquinaona
Palau de la Musica Catalana
de la Princesa
Comerc
ARGENTERA

C. Urgel
d'Urgell
Sepulveda
C. de S. Antoni
C. Joaquim Costa
Museu d'Art Contemporani (MACBA)
Hospital Santa Creu
Av Pta de Angel
LA RAMBLA
Caldral
Palau de la Virreina
C. de Jaume
Jaume I
Via
St. Maria del Mar
Estació de França

El Raval
C. del
Rda de Sant Pau
Carrer de Villadomat
C. de Calàbria
C. del Parlament
St. Antoni
Tamarit
Borrell
C. del Hospital
Liceu
Sant Agusti
Sant Pau del Camp
Teatre del Liceu
Drassanes
Carrer de la Rambla
C. de Ferran
Barri Gòtic
La Ribera
AV IM
PAS DE COLOM
Pl. Antoni d' Lopez
Museu d'Histoire de Catalunya
Imax
Dàrsena del Comerc

AVINGUDA DEL PARAL·LEL
C. de Blesa
C. de la Franca Xica
Museu Arqueologicio
Paral·lel
C. de Nou
Passeig de Montjuïc
Pl. Portal de la Pau
Museu Maritim
Monument a Colón (Columbus Monument)
Dàrsena Nacional
l'Aquàrium Barcelona
Port Vell
La Barceloneta
Sant Sebastià

Fundación Joan Miró
Avinguda
Montjuïc
Funicular de Montjuïc
Miramar
de
Miramar
Carretera de Miramar
Montjuïc
World Trade Centre
Dàrsena de Sant Bertràn

Parc de Montjuïc
Estadi Olympic
Castell
Castell de Montjuïc
Barcelona Prat Airport (BCN)

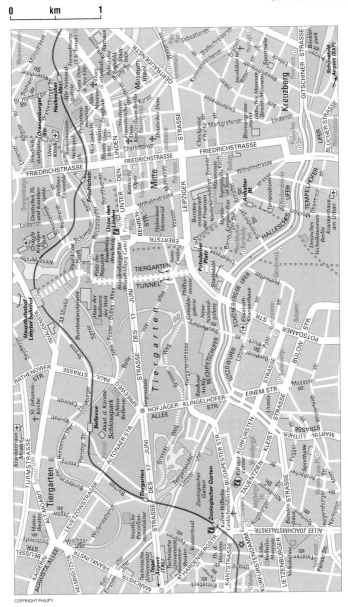

0   km   1

COPYRIGHT PHILIP'S

25

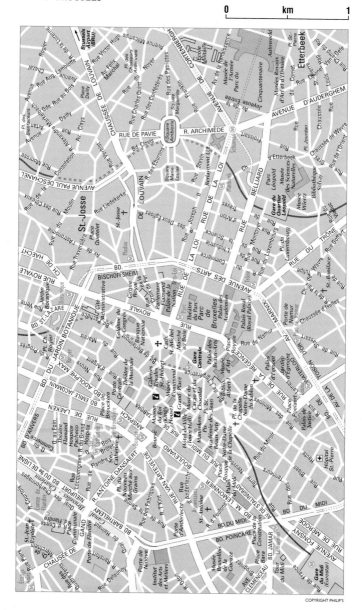

0   km   1

COPYRIGHT PHILIP'S

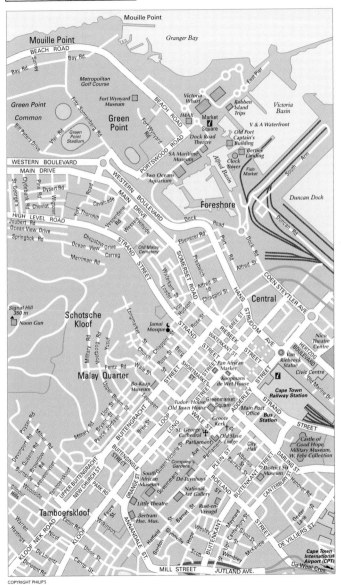

0   km   1

Mouille Point

Mouille Point
BEACH ROAD

Granger Bay

Bay Rd.

Bay Rd.
Surrey

Metropolitan
Golf Course

East Pier

Fort Wynard
Museum

Victoria
Wharf

Robben
Island
Trips

Victoria
Basin

Green Point Common

Fritz Sonnenburg Rd

Green
Point
Stadium

Green Point

IMAX

Market
Square

V & A Waterfront

Vlei Rd.

Bitt Peters Drive

Fort Wynard

Dock Road
Theatre

Old Port
Captain's
Building

Berties
Landing

WESTERN BOULEVARD

BEACH ROAD

PORTSWOOD ROAD

SA Maritime
Museum

Clock
Tower

Fish
Market

MAIN DRIVE

St. George's

Pinehurst Rd

Dysart Rd

Two Oceans
Aquarium

Alfred Basin

South Arm

Cheviot

York Road

Cavalcade

Cloete

WESTERN BOULEVARD

MAIN DRIVE

Foreshore

Duncan Dock

HIGH LEVEL ROAD

Wigmore

Joubert Rd

Thornhill

Vesperdene

Wessels

Chepstow Drive

Dock

Road

Port

Duncan Rd.

Ocean View Drive

Springbok Rd

Ocean View

Carreg

Merriman Rd

STRAND STREET

Old Malay
Cemetery

Ebenezer Rd

Alfred St.

Rd.

Prestwich

SOMERSET ROAD

Alfred St.

COEN STEYTLER AVE

Waterkant

Loader

Vos
Museum

Rose St.

Chiappini St.

HANS STRIDOM AVE

Central

Signal Hill
350 m

Noon Gun

Schotsche Kloof

Longmarket

Jamai
Mosque

STRAND

Chiappini

Rose St.

Bree

RIEBEEK STREET

STRIDOM STREET

WATERKANT ST

Nico
Theatre
Centre

HERTZOG BOULEVARD

Van
Riebeeck
Statue

Civic Centre

Military Rd.

Vogelbog Rd.

Yusuf

Church

Rose St.

STRAND STREET

SHORTMARKET ST

Pan African
Market

STRAND

Old Marine Dr.

Malay Quarter

Pentz Rd

Wale St.

Koopmans
de Wet House

Cape Town
Railway Station

Upper Bloem St.

Bo-Kaap
Museum

Leeuwen

Greenmarket
Square

ADDERLEY

Main Post
Office

Lion St.

Braam St.

Tudor House
Old Town House

WALE ST.

Groote
Kerk

Bus
Station

Military Rd.

Peace Jordan

BUTENGRACHT

Bree St.

LOOP

LONG

St. George's
Cathedral

Old Slave
Lodge

STRAND

Power Rd

Milner Rd

Parliament

City
Hall

DARLING ST.

Queens rd

Brownlow

BUITENSINGLE STREET

Upper Queen Victoria St

Company's
Gardens

Government

Parliament

Albertus

Barrack

Castle of
Good Hope,
Military Museum,
W. Fehr Collection

Burnside

UPPER BUITENGRACHT

PARK RD

South African
Museum

De Tuynhuys

PLEIN ST

District Six

BUITENKANT

Woodside

NEW CHURCH ST

ORANGE ST

National
Art Gallery

ROELAND

CANTERBURY Rd.

Harvey Rd.

Gilmour
Hill

Tamboerskloof

Faure St.

Little Theatre

Rust-en-
Vreugd

Oyster
Lane

KLOOF NEK ROAD

Nicol

Wilkinson

Bertram
Hse. Mus.

Barnet

ANNANDALE ST

Wesley

Maynard

Glvin St.

Gevin St.

Mckenzie

DE VILLIERS ST.

Warren

Hastings

Eaton Rd

De Lorentz

Union St.

Hatfield

Glynnville

Scott

Canterbury

BUITENKANT STREET

Wembley

Cape Town
International
Airport (CPT)

Gilmour

KLOOF

Camp St.

Gardon

Da Waal Cres.

Derwent Rd

MILL STREET

JUTLAND AVE.

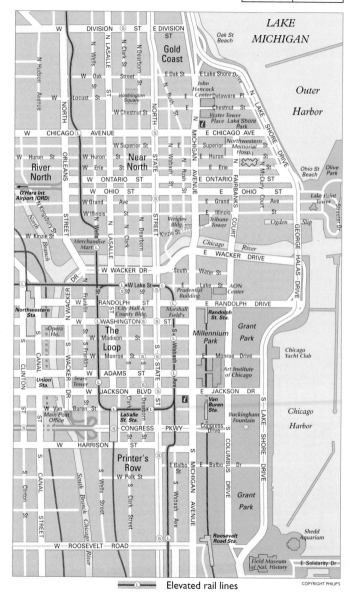

0   km   0.5

LAKE
MICHIGAN

Oak St
Beach

Gold
Coast

E Lake Shore Drive

John
Hancock
Center

Outer
Harbor

Delaware Pl

Chestnut St

Water Tower
Place Lake Shore
Park

E CHICAGO AVE

Near
North

Northwestern
Memorial
Hosp.

River
North

Ohio St
Beach

Olive
Park

O'Hara Int.
Airport (ORD)

Lake Point
Tower

Wrigley
Bldg.

Tribune
Tower

Ogden

Slip

Merchandise
Mart

Chicago

River

E WACKER DRIVE

South

Water St

Northwestern
Sta.

Prudential
Building

AON
Center

E RANDOLPH DRIVE

City Hall &
County Bldg.

Marshall
Field's

Randolph
St. Sta.

Grant
Park

Opera
Ho.

The
Loop

Millennium
Park

Chicago
Yacht
Club

Monroe Drive

Art Institute
of Chicago

Union
Sta.

Sears
Tower

Chicago
Harbor

Van
Buren
Sta.

LaSalle
St. Sta.

Main Post
Office

Buckingham
Fountain

Congress
Drive

Printer's
Row

Grant
Park

Shedd
Aquarium

Roosevelt
Road Sta.

Field Museum
of Nat. History

E Solidarity Dr

COPYRIGHT PHILIP'S

Elevated rail lines

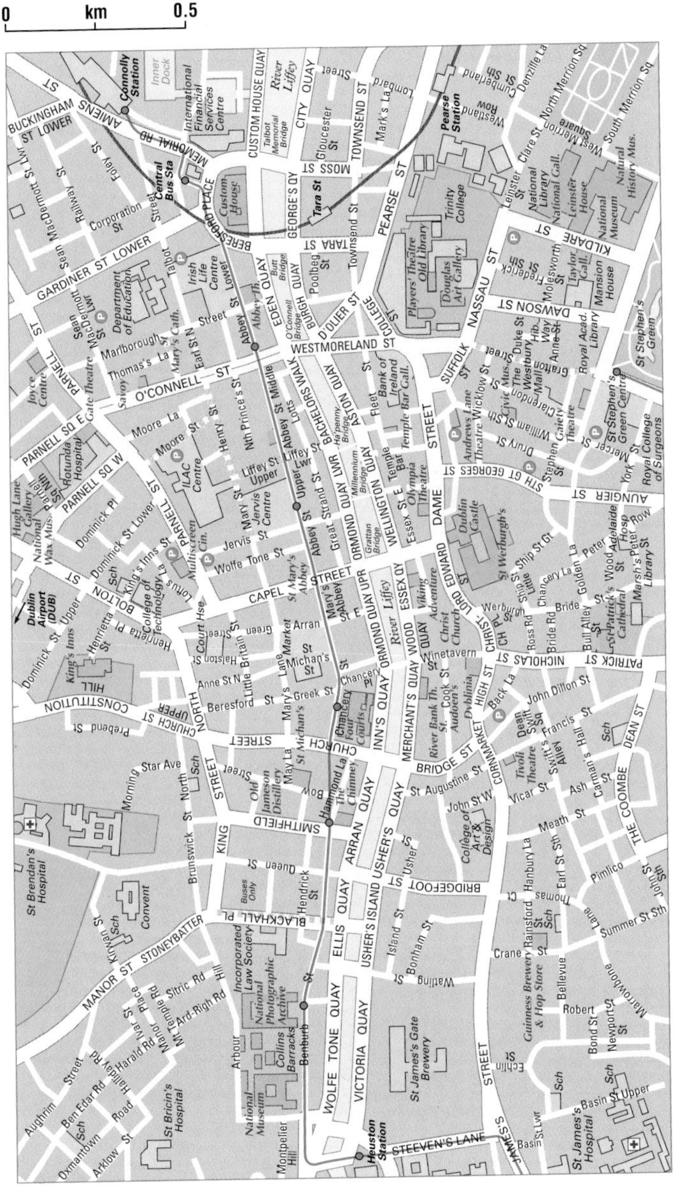

0   km   0.5

Light Rail (LUAS)

COPYRIGHT PHILIP'S

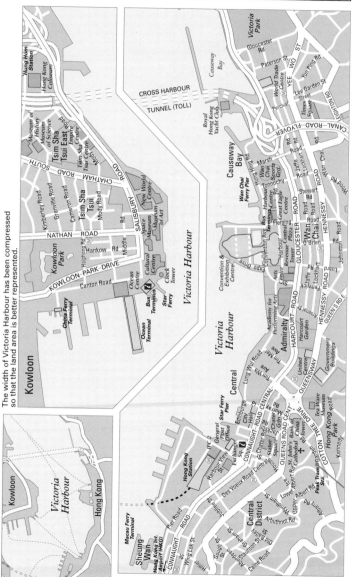

The width of Victoria Harbour has been compressed so that the land area is better represented.

COPYRIGHT PHILIP'S

30

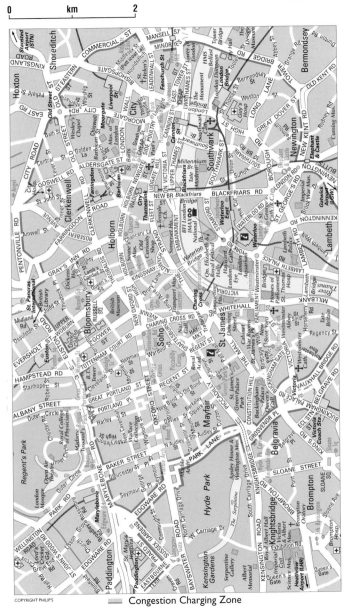

Congestion Charging Zone

COPYRIGHT PHILIP'S

0   km   1

Barajas
Airport
(MAD)

AVENIDA DE
MENÉNDEZ PELAYO

Paseo del Duque de Fernán Núñez

Palacio de
Velázquez

Palacio de
Cristal

Paseo del Ecuador

Estanque

Parque   del   Retiro

La Chopera

Plaza Mariano
de Cavia

Basílica de
Atocha

Plaza de la
Independencia

Casa de
América

Observatorio
Astronómico

CALLE DE ALFONSO XII

Puerta de
Alcalá

CALLE DE GOYA

Biblioteca
Nacional
(National
Library)

Museo
Arqueológico
Nacional

Museo
del
Ejército

Jardín
Botánico

Estación
de Atocha

PASEO REINA CRISTINA

Plaza de
Colón

Palacio de
Communicaciones

Museo Naval

Museo
del Prado

Plaza del
Emperador
Carlos V

RONDA DE ATOCHA

PASEO DE RECOLETOS

Cuartel
General
del Ejército

Museo del
Castillo

C. de Espalter

Plaza
Cánovas
del Castillo

Centro de
Arte
Reina Sofía

Justicia

Plaza de
la Cibeles

Plaza de
España

Banco de
España

Museo
Thyssen-
Bornemisza

Real Acad.
de la Historia

Convento de
Santa Isabel

ALCALÁ

Min. de
Educación

Jardín Botánico

Carrera de San Jerónimo

CALLE DE

Chueca

Min. de
Hacienda

Teatro Español
(National Theatre)

Cortes

Calle de las Huertas

CALLE DE LAVAPIÉS

Real Academia
de Bellas Artes

Oratorio del
Caballero de
Gracia

Embajadores

Universidad

GRAN VÍA

Sol

Puerta
del Sol

Comisaría
de policía

Descalzas
Reales

Palacio de
Santa Cruz

Catedral de
San Isidro

El Rastro

CALLE DE SAN BERN.

Convento de
la Encarnación

Plaza
Mayor

Ribera de Curtidores

CALLE DE TOLEDO

RONDA DE TOLEDO

C. DE LA PRINCESA

Torre de
Madrid

Museo
Cerralbo

Teatro
Real

Palacio del
Senado

Palacio

CALLE MAYOR

Centro

Parque
del Rastro

GRAN VÍA

Argüelles

Estación
Príncipe Pío

Jardines
Sabatini

Palacio
Real
(Royal
Palace)

BAILÉN

San
Andrés

Plaza de
San
Francisco

GRAN VÍA DE
SAN FRANCISCO

Glorieta Puerta
de Toledo

PASEO DEL PINTOR
ROSALES

Templo de
Debod

Parque de
la Montaña

CUESTA DE

Catedral de
Nuestra Señora
de la Almudena

CALLE DE FERRAZ

Campo
del
Moro

San
Francisco
el Grande

CALLE DE SEGOVIA

RONDA DE SEGOVIA

Paseo   Imperial

Imperial

Glorieta de
S. Vicente

Puente
del Rey

Paseo Virgen del Puerto

Calle de Juan Duque

PASEO DE LA FLORIDA

Río   Manzanares

AV. DE PORTUGAL

Paseo Virgen del Puerto

DA DE LA VIRGEN DEL PUERTO

DA DEL MANZANARES

Paseo de la Ermita del Santo

Paseo de los Melancólicos

COPYRIGHT PHILIP'S

0 km 1

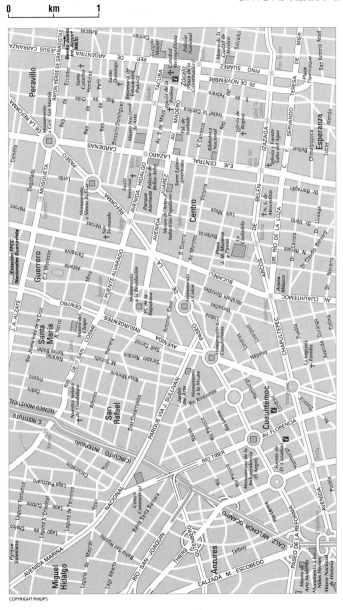

Peravillo

Benito Juárez Int. Airport (MEX)

Arcas

Carmen

Azteca

JESÚS CARRANZA

Ecatitla

ARGENTINA

DE

Salvador

Museo de la Ciudad de México

Templo Mayor

Santo Domingo

REP.

Catedral Metropolitana

Palacio Nacional

RAYÓN HÉROE DE GRANADITAS

DE LA REFORMA

Santa Catarina

Honduras

de

Chile

Perú

Rep. de

Belisario Domínguez

Rep.

Rep.

de

Santo Domingo

Secretaría de Educación Pública

Iglesia de la Profesa

TACUBA

20 DE NOVIEMBRE

Zócalo (Plaza de la Constitución)

PINO SUÁREZ

Monumento a Gral. San Martín

Camelia

Museo Nacional de Arte

Av. 5 de Mayo

Isabel la Católica

AV. MADERO

Pal. de Iturbide

5 de Febrero

Plaza Tlaxcoaque

San Antonio Abad

PASEO

MOSQUETA

Dagolilla

Lerdo

Guerrero

PASEO

REFORMA

Saúco

Santa Veracruz

AVENIDA HIDALGO

V. Carranza

Biblioteca Nacional

Iglesia de Regina

ISAZAGA

F. SERVANDO

TERESA

Chimalpopoca

DE

Esperanza

Lucas

Alamán

Monumento a Simón Bolívar

San Fernando

CÁRDENAS

AVENIDA JUÁREZ

Parque Alameda Central

Iglesia y Fuente Salto del Agua

Bolívar

LÁZARO

Museo de Artes e Industrias Populares

Torre Latinoamericana

Palacio de Bellas Artes

EJE CENTRAL

Victoria

Luis Moya

BELÉN

ARCOS

DR. RÍO DE LA LOZA

Dr. Barragán

Heroes

Estación FFCC Nacionales Buenavista

Zaragoza

Mina

AVENIDA

D. Guerra

Av. Morelos

La Ciudadela

Plaza J. M. Morelos y Pavón

Balderas

BUCARELI

Abraham González

Dr. Vértiz

Dr. Lavista

Dr. Liceaga

N. Heroes

Tres de Mercedes

J. A. ALZATE

CENTRO

Reforma

Aldama

C.J. Menezas

Guerrero

DE PUENTE ALVARADO

Monumento a la Revolución

Pl. de la República

Arena México

DR. CLAUDIO BERNARD

AV. CUAUHTÉMOC

Navarro

Versalles

Lisboa

Liverpool

CHAPULTEPEC

Puebla

Durango

Colima

MIER

San Juana Inés de la Cruz

Santa María

Museo del Chopo

Naranjo

Sadi Carnot

Antonio Caso

Serapio Rendón

DE SAN COSME

Jesús Terán

Ponciano Arriaga

Monumento a Cuauhtémoc

PASEO

Monumento a Colón

Lisboa

Liverpool

Nápoles

La Sagrada Familia

INSURGENTES

Cedro

Fresno

Nuestra Señora de Guadalupe

Alfonso

M. Schultz

Rosa Moreno

Díaz Covarrubias

PARQUE VÍA J. SULLIVAN

Río Amazonas

Monumento a la Madre

Jardín del Arte

Río Sena

INSTITUTO

TECNICO INDUSTRIAL

San Rafael

(CIRCUITO INTERIOR)

RÍO TIBER

RÍO Pánuco

Río Lerma

Cuauhtémoc

AV. FLORENCIA

Sevilla

NACIONAL

Bahía Santa Bárbara

Centro Commercial

Monumento de la Independencia (El Ángel)

Fuente de D. Cazador

PASEO DE LA REFORMA

Oaxaca

Mérida

Lago de Pátzcuaro

Lago Texcoco

Lago de Términos

Laguna de Mayrán

Ixtaccíhuatl

Tirac

RÍO SAN JOAQUÍN

GUTENBERG

Leibniz

AVENIDA

AVENIDA

Parque Salesiano

Laguna Tamiahua

Cuitzeo

Laguna S. Cristóbal

Chalco

Lago Chalco

AVENIDA MARINA

Bahía San Hipólito

THIERS

CALZ. MELCHOR OCAMPO

CALZADA M. ESCOBEDO

Miguel Hidalgo

Anzures

Museo de Arte Moderno

Monumento a los Niños Héroes

Museo Nacional de Historia

COPYRIGHT PHILIPS

33

0   km   1

SAD.-SAMOTECHNAYA

SAD.-SUHAREVSKAYA

SAD.-TRIUMFALNAYA UL.

Svetnoy Boulevard

Suharevskaya

Old Moscow Circus

Sergievskiy Per.

U. SRETENKA

SVETNOY

BOULEVARD

CHEKHOVA U.

PETROVSKIY

Trubnaya Pl.

'BOULEVARD RING'

BOULEVARD

ROZHDESTVENSKIY

Moscow Sheremetyevo Airport (SVO)

Russian Cinema

BOULEVARD

Convent of the Nativity of the Virgin

Pushkinskaya Tverskaya

Ulitsa Rozhdestvenka

STRASTNOY BLD.

Chekovskaya

PETROVKA

NEGLININAYA

Varsonofyevskiy Per.

Museum of the Revolution

Pushkin Ploshchad

PUSHKINSKAYA

ULITSA LUBYANKA

Stoleshnikov

Petrovskiy Passage

ULITSA

Kuznetskiy Most

Gorky Theatre

Pereulok

ULITSA

Bolshoy Theatre

ULITSA

Detskiy Theatre

Lubyanka

Ulitsa Stanislavskovo

Chekhov Theatre

Central Post Office

Teatralnaya

Theatre Square

TEATRALNIY PROJ.

Ploshchad Lubyanskaya

Ulitsa Nezhdanovo

Ulitsa Ogaryova

Belinskogo Ul.

Ermolovoy Theatre

Okhotniy Ryad

Slavanskiy Bazar

Polytech. Museum

NOVAYA PL.

Ul. Nikolskaya

Bolshoy Per. Devyatsinskiy

Revolution Square

PL. Revolyutsiy

GERSENA

ULITSA

Manezhnaya Ploshchad

Lenin Museum

Gum Shopping Arcade

Ulitsa Ilinka

Moscow Conservatoire

Semazhko Ul.

University

Historical Museum

Red Square

Lenin Mausoleum

Central Exhibition Hall

Garden

Arsenal

Council of Ministers

VOZDVIZHENKA U.

ULITSA RYAD

Museum of Russian Architecture

Aleksandrovsky Sad

Presidium of the Supreme Soviet

St. Basil's Cathedral

OKHOTNIY

MANEZHNAYA

Alexander

Ivan Square

Lenin State Library

Palace of Congress

Kremlin

Central Concert Hall

U. ZNAMENKA

Terem Palace

Cathedral Square

Archangel Cathedral

Marx-Engels Ulitsa

Boroviskaya Ploshchad

Armoury Palace

Kremlin Palace

Pushkin Fine Arts Museum

Moskva (Moscow)

KREMLEVSKAYA NABEREZHNAYA

VOLKHONKA ULITSA

Cathedral of Christ the Saviour

SOFIYSKAYA NABEREZHNAYA

BOLSHOY KAMENNY MOST

BOLOTNAYA NAB.

Vodootvodny Kanal

KADASHEVSKAYA NAB.

0   km   2

Haji Ali Mosque
Causeway
Mahalaxmi Race Course
Mumbai Chhatrapati Shivaji Airport (BOM)
N. M. JOSHI MARG
Rambhau Bhogle Mg
BARRISTER NATH PAI MARG
Jijamata Udyan (Victoria Gardens)
LALA LAJPATRAI MARG
Keshavrao Khadye Marg
Sane Guruji Marg
Bapurao Jagtap Mg
Maulana Azad Mg
Byculla
Sant Savta Mg
Mascarenhas Rd
Mahalaxmi
Willingdon Sports Club
DESHMUKH RD.
TARDEO RD.
Mumbai Central Station
DR. A. Nair Rd.
Mirra Galib Mg
SIR JAMSHEDJI JIJIBHOY MARG
R. C. Cathedral
Mazagaon
Balwantsingh
Champsi Mg
Dodi Mg
State Road Transport Terminus
Jehangir Boman Behram Marg
PATTHE BAPURAO MARG
Dr. Bhadkamkar Marg
R.S. Nimbkar Rd
Shaukatali
Maulana Azad Rd
Tardeo
GOPALRAO
Barodawala Mg
Jalojee Dadaji Rd
S. K.
Maulana
Wadi Bandar Rd
ROAD
Ramchandra Bhatt Mg.
Raudat Tahera Mosque
Umerkhadi
Mani Bhavan (Gandhi Museum)
N. Desai
SARDAR VALLABHBHAI PATEL RD
Patel Rd
Rd
S. V. PATEL RD
Mandvi
D'MELLO
Babulnath Temple
SITARAM PATKAR
Bhuleshwar
C. Patel Tank Rd
Jaykar Mg
I. M. Merchant Rd
Dr. N.A. Purandare Mg.
Netaji Subhash Rd
Jagannath Dr. Babasaheb
MAHARSHI
KARVE
MARINE DRIVE
Chowpatty Beach
Taraporewala Aquarium
Mumbadevi Temple
ALI RD
MOHAMED
Meherali Rd
Nandlal Jani Rd
P.
N. Natha St
Tilak Rd
N. Natha Rd
Kalbadevi
Kalbadevi Rd
Shankarshier Rd
Girgaum
Jama Masjid Mosque
Crawford Market (Mahatma Phule)
PALTON
Pydhuni
St. George's Hospital
Lokmanya
NAVROJI RD
DR. DADABHAI
Ahless & Cama Hospital
Azad Maidan
Chhatrapati Shivaji (Victoria) Terminus
Back Bay
Wankhede Stadium
V. Thackersey Mg
Mahatma Gandhi
H. Somani
DR. D. Mg
G.P.O.
W. Hirachand Mg
S. B. SINGH RD
S.Vallabhdas Mg
The Mint
Custom Basin
Churchgate Station
ROAD
NAVROJI RD
Fort
Rajabai Twr.
University
Jehangir Art Gallery
Town Hall
West Basin
Mumbai Harbour
Brabourne Stadium
Marine Drive
J. Tata Rd
Maharshi B. Patil Mg
Madame
Oval Maidan
Cama Rd
Nariman Point
National Centre for Performing Arts
J. Bajaj Mg
Gen. J. Bhonsale Mg
N Parekh Mg
N Parekh
Chhatrapati Shivaji Museum
National Gallery of Modern Art
Colaba
Gateway of India
S. B. SINGH RD

35

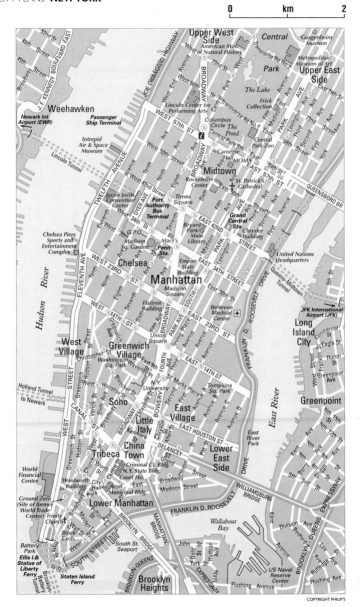

0   km   2

Upper West Side
American Mus. of Natural History
West of Natural History
Central Park
Guggenheim Museum
Transverse Rd No.2
Metropolitan Museum of Art
The Lake
Upper East Side
East 79th St
Frick Collection
J.F. KENNEDY BOULEVARD EAST
52nd St
48th St
45th Street
Broadway
Weehawken
Newark Int. Airport (EWR)
Passenger Ship Terminal
Lincoln Tunnel
Intrepid Air & Space Museum
West End Avenue
WEST 57th ST
Lincoln Center for Performing Arts
Columbus Circle
Central Park So.
The Pond
Central Park Zoo
72nd Street
66th Street
PARK AVE
Madison
Lexington
Third
Second
First
York
72nd Street
Street
TWELFTH AVENUE
West 50th Street
West 42nd Street
Ninth
Tenth
Eighth
Carnegie Hall
MOMA
Midtown
Rockefeller Center
St. Patrick's Cathedral
EAST 57th ST
Queensboro Br
Jacob Javits Convention Center
Port Authority Bus Terminal
Tenth
Times Square
BROADWAY
Grand Central Sta.
Chrysler Building
EAST 42ND STREET
Bryant Park
Main Library
PARK AVENUE
DYER AVE
ELEVENTH AVENUE
G.P.O.
Madison Sq. Garden
Penn Sta.
Empire State Building
EAST 34TH STREET
United Nations Headquarters
Chelsea Piers Sports and Entertainment Complex
Hudson River
WEST 23RD ST
Chelsea
Manhattan
Madison Square
East 30th St
Bellevue Medical Center
Queens-Midtown Tunnel
Ninth
Eighth
Seventh
WEST 14TH ST
Flatiron Building
EAST 23RD STREET
FRANKLIN D. ROOSEVELT DRIVE
West Village
Greenwich Village
Union Square
PARK AVE
EAST 14TH ST
JFK International Airport (JFK)
Long Island City
Greenwich St
Washington Sq. Park
Christopher St
Waverly Pl
N.Y. University
St Marks Place
FOURTH AVE
Tompkins Sq. Park
East Eagle St
Huron St
Bleecker St
Houston St
BOWERY
East Village
Avenue D
Greenpoint
East River
Holland Tunnel to Newark
Soho
Little Italy
China Town
Tribeca
CANAL STREET
Kenmare
DELANCEY
EAST HOUSTON ST
Lower East Side
East River Park
WEST STREET
World Financial Center
Criminal Ct. Bldg.
N.Y. State Bldg.
Court Ho.
Broadway
WILLIAMSBURG BRIDGE
Woolworth Building
City Hall Park
East Municipal Bldg.
Madison Street
BROOKLYN-QUEENS EXPRESSWAY
Ground Zero (Site of former World Trade Center)
Trinity Church
Fulton
Pearl
FRANKLIN D. ROOSEVELT
DRIVE
Kent Ave
Division Ave
Lower Manhattan
Stock Exch.
South Seaport
BROOKLYN BRIDGE
MANHATTAN BRIDGE
John St
York St
Wallabout Bay
US Naval Reserve Center
Battery Park
Ellis I.& Statue of Liberty Ferry
SOUTH STREET
Staten Island Ferry
Brooklyn-Battery Tunnel
Brooklyn Heights
BROOKLYN QUEENS
Flushing Avenue

COPYRIGHT PHILIP'S

0   km   1

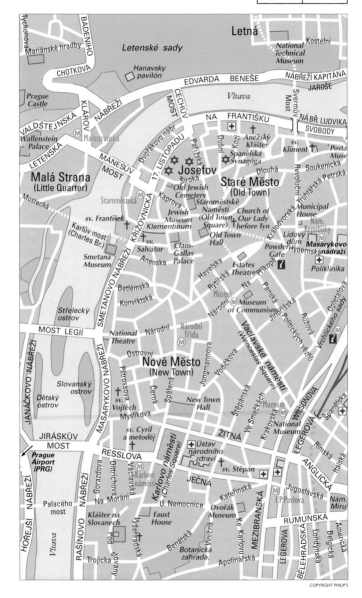

0   km   0.5

Letná

Tychonova
Mariánské hradby
BADENIHO
CHOTKOVA
Prague
Castle
KLÁROV
NÁBŘEŽÍ
VALDŠTEJNSKÁ
Wallenstein
Palace
LETENSKÁ
Malostranská
Malá Strana
(Little Quarter)
Mostecká
MÁNESŮV
MOST
Dvořákovo nábř
17. LISTOPADU
sv. Františka
KŘIŽOVNICKÁ
Karlův most
(Charles Br.)
sv.
Salvátor
Smetana
Museum
SMETANOVO NÁBŘEŽÍ
Betlémská
Konviktská
Střelecký
ostrov
MOST LEGIÍ
National
Theatre
Ostrovní
Nové Město
(New Town)
MASARYKOVO NÁBŘEŽÍ
Slovanský
ostrov
Dětský
ostrov
Petrossova
sv.
Vojtěch
Myslíkova
Černá
JIRÁSKŮV
MOST
Prague
Airport
(PRG)
HOŘEJŠÍ NÁBŘEŽÍ
Palackého
most
Vltava
RAŠÍNOVO NÁBŘEŽÍ
RESSLOVA
Na Moráni
Václavská
Dittrichova
Gorazdova
Kláštěr na
Slovanech
Pod
Trojická
Slovany
Vyšehradská
Faust
House
Benátská
Botanická
zahrada
Apolinářská
Vítězná

Letenské sady
Hanavský
pavilón
EDVARDA BENEŠE
Vltava
CECHŮV MOST
NA FRANTIŠKU
Dušní
Josefov
Široká
Old Jewish
Cemetery
Jewish
Museum
Klementinum
Anenska
Clam-
Gallas
Palace
Havelská
Rytířská
Na
Můstku
Muzeum
Národní
Třída
Jungmannova
Spálená
New Town
Hall
ŽITNÁ
Ústav
národního
zdraví
JEČNÁ
Karlovo náměstí
(Charles Square)
U. Nemocnice
Dvořák
Museum
Ke Karlovu
Kateřinská

National
Technical
Museum
Kostelní
NÁBŘEŽÍ KAPITÁNA JAROŠE
Švermův Most
NÁ BŘ. LUDVIKA
SVOBODY
Anežský
Klášter
Revoluční
Kozí
sv.
Kliment
Pošta
Muse
Soukenická
Staré Město
(Old Town)
Pařížská
Španělská
Synagóga
Dlouhá
Truhlářská
Petrská
Staroměstská
Kaprova
Staroměstské
Náměstí
(Old Town
Square)
Church of
Our Lady
before Týn
Old Town
Hall
Estates
Theatre
Králodvorská
Municipal
House
Nám.
Republiky
Lidový
dům
Hybernská
Masarykovo
nádraží
Powder
Gate
Příkopě
Poliklinika
Na
Panská
Jindřišská
Museum
of Communism
Václavské náměstí
(Wenceslas Square)
Politických vězňů
Růžová
Vrchlického sady
Opletalova
Vodičkova
Štěpánská
Ve Smečkách
Krakovská
WILSONOVA
Muzeum
National
Museum
LEGEROVA
ANGLICKÁ
Spálená
Rímská
Jugoslávská
I.P.Pavlova
Nám.
Miru
RUMUNSKÁ
MEZIBRANSKÁ
sv. Štěpán
BĚLEHRADSKÁ
LEGEROVA
Belgická
Londýnská
Americká

COPYRIGHT PHILIP'S

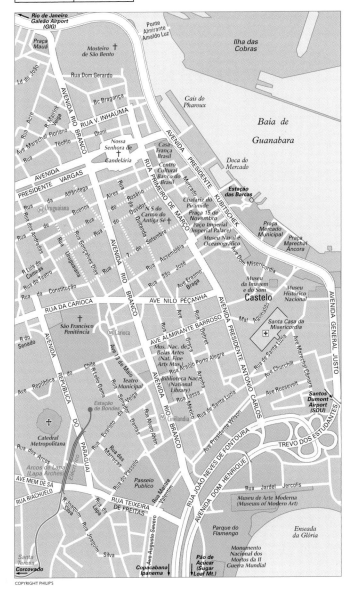

COPYRIGHT PHILIP'S

0   km   1

VIALE REGINA
VIALE NOMENTANA
VIALE DEL CASTRO
Min. dei Transporti
Viale di Alessandria
Viale Castrense
Palestro
Via de' Mille
Via Marsala
VIA SOMMEISINTA
Piazza della Croce Rossa
V. Nazaro Romano
Piazza del Popolo
Mus. Naz. Romano
Piazza dei Cinquecento
Stazione Centrale Roma Termini
Via Giovanni
Piazza Vitt.
Emanuele II
VIA MERULANA
VIA LABICANA

VIA SALARIA
Via Tevere
VIA PLAVE
XX SETTEMBRE
S.M. Maggiore
S. Maria d'Angeli
Piazza della Repubblica
Via Cavour
Via Principe Amedeo
Via Principe Amedeo
VIA GIOVANNI LANZA
Museo d'Arte Orientale
Parco di Traiano
Domus Aurea (Golden House)

CORSO D'ITALIA
Via Sicilia
Via Toscana
Piemonte
Min. Agricoltura e Foreste
Min. Industria
Piazza Barberini
Via del Tritone
Teatro dell'Opera
VIA NAZIONALE
Min. d. Difesa Esercito
Ministero dell'Interni
Via Panisperna
Via Cavour
VIA GIOVANNI LANZA
Colle Oppio
Colosseo (Colosseum)

Museo e Gall. Borghese
Via Pinciana
Vle. d. Museo Borghese
VIALE DEL MURO TORTO
Vittorio Veneto
Pal. Barberini
VIA DEL QUIRINALE
VIA DEI FORI IMPERIALI
Colonna Traiana (Trajan's Column)
S. Maria in Aracoeli
Piazza d. Campidoglio
Foro Romano (Roman Forum)
Arco di Costantino
Monte Palatino

Villa Borghese
Galoppatoio
V. di S. Paolo d. Brasile
VIA DEL MURO TORTO
Giardino del Pincio
Trinità dei Monti
Piazza di Spagna (Spanish Steps)
Via Sistina
Palazzo del Quirinale
Giardino del Quirinale
Fontana di Trevi (Trevi Fountain)
SS. Apostoli
Capitolio
Conservatori
Via di S. Teodoro

VIALE WASHINGTON
Viale del Giardino Zoo
S. Maria del Popolo
Piazza del Popolo
Posta Centrale
Piazza San Silvestro
Via Del Corso
Via del Babuino
Ospedale S. Giacomo
Mausoleo di Augusto
Piazza Colonna
Palazzo Chigi
Palazzo Doria Pamphili
Via del Corso
PLEBISCITO
Palazzo Venezia
Mon. a Vittorio Emanuele II
V. D. TEATRO DI MARCELLO
Teatro di Marcello

V. Flaminia
S. Maria del Popolo
Ripetta
Via del Corso
Camera dei Deputati
Pantheon
Piazza d. Minerva
Via d. Scrofa
Piazza Navona
LUNG. DEI CENCI
Leonardo da Vinci Airport (FCO)

V. Flaminia
LUNGOTEVERE
LUNG. IN AUGUSTA
ARNALDO DA BRESCIA
LUNGOTEVERE MELLINI
Tevere (Tiber)
LUNG MARZIO
Via Fed. Cesi
S. Agostino
C. d. Rinascimento
Palazzo della Cancelleria
Campo d. Fiori
Palazzo Farnese
LUNG. DEI VALLATI
LUNG. FARNESINA
L. R. SANZIO

L. MICHELANGELO
Piazza della Libertà
Via Cicerone
Piazza Cavour
Palazzo di Giustizia
Castel Sant'Angelo
Via dei Coronari
CORSO VITTORIO EMANUELE II
Giulia
Palazzo d. Sangallo
L. D. FARNESINA
L. D. TEBALDI
V. d. Lungara
V. d. Scala
Museo Torlonia
Palazzo Corsini

P. Garibaldi
L. MICHELANGELO
Lepanto
Via Pompeo Magno
Via Cola di Rienzo
Via Virgilio
Via Crescenzio
L. TOR DI NONA
L. VATICANO
L. CASTELLO
SASSIA
L. GIANICOLENSE
Palazzo Corsini
Gianicolo
Mon. a G. Garibaldi
Via Garibaldi

Museo d. Poste e Tel.
S. Pellico
Via MILIZIE
Via Brofferio
Via Fabio Massimo
Via Germanico
Via Ottaviano
VIA DELLA CONCILIAZIONE
Borgo Vittorio
VIA DELLA
Ospedale S. Spirito
Via Nuova delle Fornaci

VIALE GIULIO CESARE
Via Gra. Lente
Via della Giuliana
Via Candia
VIA ANGELICO
VIA LEONE IV
Musei Vaticani
Cappella Sistina (Sistine Chapel)
Piazza San Pietro (St Peter's Square)
S. Pietro in Vaticano (St. Peter's)
Via delle Fornaci
Via delle Fornaci
Villa Abamelek

CIRCONV. TRIONFALE
Via TRIONFALE
VIA ANDREA DORIA
Via Tunisi
Via G. Savonarola
Via Pisani
CITTÀ DEL VATICANO (VATICAN CITY)
Via Vaticano
Stazione Vaticana
VIA PORTA CAVALLEGGERI
VIA AURELIO
VIA GREGORIO VII
Via della Cava Aurelia
Stazione S. Pietro
V. Innocenzo III

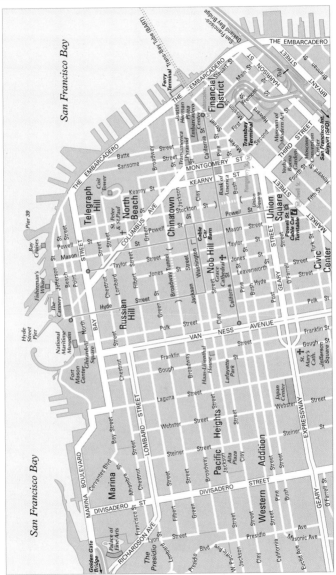

Cable Car route

0   km   1

CAIRNHILL ROAD
CLEMENCEAU AVE
Cairnhill Rise
Cairnhill Road
BUKIT TIMAH RD
Kandang Kerbau Hospital
Zhujiao Centre
Veerama Kaliamman Temple
Cuff Rd
Upper Wld
Sim Lim Tower
Sim Lim Square
Istana (President's Residence)
Emerald Hill Rd
Edinburgh Road
Sophia Road
Mackenzie Road
Clive
Dunlop
Abdul Gaffoor Mosque
ROCHOR CANAL RD
Central Park
BIDEFORD RD
Thong Sia Building
Orchard Road
Cuppage Centre
Faber House
Centre point
Orchard Plaza
Orchard Point
Mount Emily Park
Wilkie Road
Sophia Road
Handy Road
SELEGIE ROAD
SHORT STREET
Sim Lim Square
Bus Station
Blanco Court
PENANG ROAD
ORCHARD ROAD
N2 Somerset
EBER ROAD
KILLINEY
OXLEY ROAD
Lloyd Rd
Chesed-El synagogue
Sacred Heart Church
FORT CANNING ROAD
Handy Road
N1 Dhoby Ghaut
Bencoolen Mosque
BENCOOLEN
WHITLEY
St. Joseph's Church
Singapore Art Museum
BRAS BASAH
MIDDLE ROAD
Colonial District
RIVER VALLEY ROAD
Sri Thandayuthapani Temple
TANK ROAD
Hong San See Temple
Shan Rd
Yong San See Rd
Kim Yam Rd
CLEMENCEAU
Clarke Quay
Nanson
Boat Quay
MERCHANT ROAD
Singapore River
HAVELOCK ROAD
Melaka Mosque
CENTRAL EXPRESSWAY
Chin Swee Road
UPPER CROSS ROAD
Pearl's Hill City Park
Pearl's Hill Reservoir
People's Park Complex
PICKERING ST
NORTH CANAL RD
NEW BRIDGE ROAD
Pagoda St
Smith St
Oriental Theatre
W2 Outram Park
Chinatown
Jamae Mosque
Sri Mariamman Temple
Sago St
Wak Hai Cheng Bio Temple
Tuk Lak Ch'i Temple
Ann Siang Rd
Boon Tat St
Thian Hock Keng Temple
Al-Abrar Mosque
MAXWELL ROAD
TELOK AYER
Lau Pa Sat Festival Market
ROBINSON ROAD
Singapore General Hospital
NEW BRIDGE ROAD
NEIL ROAD
Everton Park
CRAIG RD
SOUTH BRIDGE ROAD
CANTONMENT ROAD
WALLICH ST
W1 Tanjong Pagar
Dixon Rd
SHENTON WAY
ANSON ROAD
MARINA STATION RD
H1 Marina Bay
Spottiswoode Park
Spottiswoode Park Road
Singapore Railway Station
AYER RAJAH EXPRESSWAY
EAST COAST PARKWAY
Hock Teck See Temple
Changi Int. Airport (SIN)
Finger Pier

Sri Temasek
Singapore Hist. Mus.
Fort Canning Park
Battle Box
Fort Canning Reservoir
Van Kleef Aquarium
Asian Civ. Mus.
STAMFORD ROAD
BRIDGE ROAD
Cath. of the Good Shepherd
VICTORIA STREET
Seah St
Raffles Hotel
BEACH ROAD
Raffles City
C2 City Hall
St. Andrew's Cathedral
War Memorial Park
HILL STREET
NORTH BRIDGE ROAD
Singapore Philatelic Mus.
Funan Centre
City Hall
Supreme Court
Parliament Hse.
Victoria Concert Hall & Theatre
Singapore Cricket Club
Padang
CONNAUGHT DR
ESPLANADE DRIVE
Esplanade-Theatres on the Bay
Raffles Landing Site
Empress Place Museum
Merlion Park
Marina Bay
FULLERTON RD
Clifford Pier
Bus Station
OUB Centre
C1 Raffles Place
RAFFLES QUAY
Boat Quay
Telok Ayer Basin

COPYRIGHT PHILIP'S

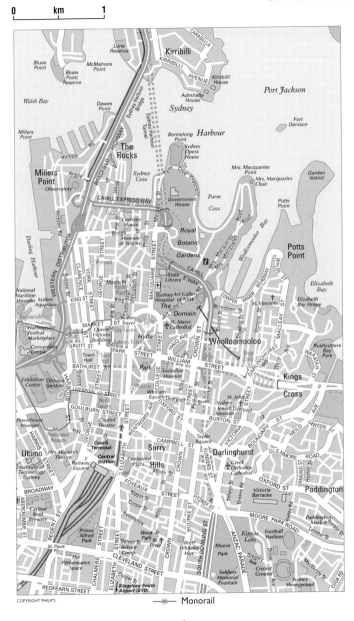

0 km 1

Blues Point

McMahons Point

Luna Reserve

KIRRIBILLI

Kirribilli

CABARELLA ST

KIRRIBILLI AVENUE

Kirribilli House

Blues Point Reserve

Walsh Bay

Dawes Point

Sydney Harbour Bridge

Admiralty House

Port Jackson

Sydney

Millers Point

Hickson Rd

BRADFIELD HIGHWAY

Sydney Harbour Tunnel

The Rocks

George St

Bennelong Point

Sydney Harbour

Fort Denison

Millers Point

Argyle St

Observatory

Sydney Cove

Farm Cove

Sydney Opera House

Mrs. Macquaries Point

Mrs. Macquaries Chair

Garden Island

CAHILL EXPRESSWAY

Circular Quay

Government House

Farm Cove

Potts Point

Darling Harbour

Hickson Rd

WESTERN DISTRIBUTOR

Pitt St

Customs House

Bridge St

Museum of Sydney

Royal Botanic Gardens

Mrs. Macquaries Road

Woolloomooloo Bay

Potts Point

National Maritime Museum

Sydney Aquarium

CLARENCE ST

YORK STREET

GEORGE STREET

KING ST

Wynyard

Martin Place

Martin Pl

King St

MACQUARIE STREET

State Library

Hospital of NSW

CAHILL E-WAY

COWPER WHARF ROADWAY

Nicholson St

St. Vincents

Elizabeth Bay

Elizabeth Bay House

Harbourside

Darling Park

MARKET ST

Sydney Tower

City Centre

Sydney Centre

St James

The Domain

Art Gallery of NSW

Bourke St

Victoria St

Macleay St

Harbourside Festival Marketplace

Convention Centre

PYRMONT BRIDGE

Sussex St

Queen Victoria Building

Galeries Victoria

Hyde Park

St. Marys Cathedral

HAIG AVE

CROWN ST

Woolloomooloo

Kings Cross

DARLINGHURST RD

Rushcutters Bay Park

WARATAH ST

Exhibition Centre

Chinese Garden

DRUITT ST

Town Hall

Town Hall

PARK ST

STREET

BATHURST STREET

Australian Museum

WILLIAM STREET

Kings Cross

MACLEAY ST

LIVERPOOL STREET

HARBOUR ST

GEORGE STREET

COLLEGE ST

William

St. John

Darlinghurst

GLENMORE ROAD

Powerhouse Museum

GOULBURN STREET

Capitol Theatre

Riley St

Square

Liverpool St

Jewish Museum

Liverpool St

BURTON ST

BOUNDARY ST

NEILD AVE

LANSON ST

Her Majesty's Theatre

HARRIS ST

Powerhouse Museum

Hay St

Coach Terminal

Surry

Campbell St

Taylor Square

FLINDERS ST

Darlinghurst

Greek Orthodox Cathedral

OXFORD ST

Paddington

Ultimo

ABERCROMBIE ST

Institute of Technology Sydney

WENTWORTH AVE

ELIZABETH STREET

Central Station

Central Plaza

Hills

CROWN ST

Albion St

Victoria Barracks

MOORE PARK ROAD

Paddington Market

Leinster St

Carlton Keat Brewery

BROADWAY

REGENT ST

GEORGE STREET

Railway Square

FOVEAUX STREET

FITZROY ST

BOURKE STREET

SOUTH DOWLING STREET

GLENMORE ROAD

ORMOND ST

COOK RD

Prince Alfred Park

Belvoir St

Ward Park St

Kippax St

Cooper St

Devonshire St

Riley St

St Peter

Brett Whiteley Mus.

Moore Park

Kippax Lake

Football Stadium

Gordon St

St Pauls

CHALMERS ST

BELVOIR ST Comp.

Crown St

ANZAC PARADE

Gregory Ave

Soldiers Memorial Fountain

Cricket Ground

Mackenzie St

Sydney Showground

The Performance Space

REDFERN STREET

CLEVELAND STREET

ELIZABETH STREET

Cooper St

Kingsford-Smith Airport (SYD)

— Ⓜ — Monorail

0   km   2

Akihabara Station

CHUO-DORI

Naiko Int. Airport (NRT)

SHOWA-DORI

Transport Museum

Nikolaido Church

Kanda

KANDA-HEISEI

HONGO-DORI

Chūō

CHUO-DORI

EITAI-DORI

Bridgestone Mus. of Art

SOTOBORI-DORI

Tsukiji

HARUMI-DORI

St. Luke's Int. Hospital

Tsukiji Honganji Temple

Sumida-Gawa

Jimbōchō

Jimbocho

Science & Technology Museum

Kitano-maru Park

Budōkan

Kudankita

National Mus. of Modern Art

Tokyo Station

Marunouchi

UCHIBORI-DORI

Tokyo International Forum

Ginza

Kabuki-za Theatre

CHUO-DORI

Sony Centre

Shimbashi

Central Wholesale Market

HIBIYA

YASUKUNI-DORI

SOTOBORI-DORI

East Garden

Fukiage Imperial Garden

Imperial Palace

Chiyoda

UCHIBORI-DORI

Outer Garden

Hibiya Park

Nissei Theatre

HIBIYA-DORI

Shiba

DAIICHI-KEIHIN-DORI

Hama Rikyu Garden

Haneda Int. Airport (HND)

Science & Technology Museum

National Theatre

Kasumigaseki

ATAGO-DORI

Shiba Park

Tokyo Tower

Zōjōji Temple

Minato

Sanbanchō

SHINJUKU-DORI

St. Ignatius

Yotsuya Station

SOTOBORI-DORI

National Diet Building

Government Buildings

SOTOBORI-DORI

Toranomon

Reinanzaka Church

Ichigaya

GAIEN-HIGASHI-DORI

YASUKUNI-DORI

Suntory Art Museum

Jingū Inner Garden

Akasaka Palace Garden

AOYAMA-DORI

Akasaka

Nogi-jinja Shrine

Roppongi

GAIEN

Azabu

GAIEN-NISHI-DORI

Yotsuya

Shinanomachi Station

GAIEN-HIGASHI-DORI

National Stadium

Jingū Outer Garden

Jingū Baseball Stadium

Aoyama Cemetery

Aoyama

GAIEN-NISHI-DORI

GAIEN-NISHI-DORI

Nezu Art Museum

KOTTO-DORI

SHINJUKU-DORI

Sendagaya Station

YASUKUNI-DORI

Shinjuku National Garden

Shinjuku

Hanazono-jinja

SHINJUKU-DORI

Shinjuku Station

Minami-shinjuku Station

MEIJI-DORI

KOSHU-KAIDO

Yoyogi Station

EXPRESSWAY NO.4

SHINJUKUSEN

Yoyogi Park

Sangūbashi Station

Meiji Shrine Inner Garden

Meiji Shrine Treasurehouse

Meiji Shrine

MEIJI-DORI

Yayū Memorial Hall

Harajuku Station

INOKASHIRA-DORI

Omotesandō

OMOTESANDO

Oriental Bazaar

Shibuya

Shibuya Station

SHIBUYA-SEN

AOYAMA-DORI

MEIJI-DORI

DOGEN-ZAKA

EXPRESSWAY NO.3

Kanze Nō Plg Theatre

Sumitomo Building

Tokyo City Hall

⊖ Toei Subway   Ⓜ Tokyo Metro

COPYRIGHT PHILIP'S

0   km   1

Royal Ontario Museum
Gardiner Museum of Ceramic Art
Charles St West
Isabella Street
Wellesley La
Wellesley Pl
Inkerman Street
Gloucester Street
Irwin Ave
Dundonald Street
Cawthra Square Park
Bleecker Street
Sherbourne Street
Varsity Stadium
St Joseph St
PHIPPS St
BAY STREET
St. West
Wellesley Street East
JARVIS STREET
Maitland Street
Homewood Avenue
Maitland Pl
Wellesley
HOSKIN AVE
Queen's Park
Wellesley
Ontario Government Buildings
Breadalbane Street
Orthopedic & Arthritic Hospital
Alexander Street
CBC Museum
Tower Rd
QUEEN'S PARK CRESCENT WEST
QUEEN'S PARK CRESCENT EAST
Hart House Circle
Grosvenor St
Wood Street
STREET
Sigmund Samuel Building
Provincial Legislature
Queen's Park
Women's College Hospital
Grenville Street
Police HQ
CARLTON
Conservatory
Allan Gdns
Galbraith Road
University of Toronto
Granby Street
McGill Street
JARVIS STREET
Glenholme Pl
Pembroke St
COLLEGE STREET
Queen's Park
College
Barbara Ann Scott Park
YONGE
Gerrard Street East
Mutual Street
George
COLLEGE STREET
Toronto General Hospital
Elizabeth St
Laplante Ave
Gerrard Street West
Ryerson University
Church Street
Gould Street
Dalhousie St
Bond
Beverley Street
Henry Street
Orde Street
Princess Margaret Hospital
Mt Sinai Hospital
Hospital for Sick Children
BAY
O'Keefe Lane
Elm St
Edward St
McCaul Street
Toronto Rehab Institute
Elm St
Coach Terminal
Victoria Street
DUNDAS STREET EAST
St Michael's Cathedral
Armoury
Baldwin Street
St Patrick's Church
UNIVERSITY
Edward St
St Patrick
DUNDAS STREET WEST
Foster Pl
STREET
Trinity Sq
Toronto Eaton Centre
Massey Hall
Shuter Street
Metro United Church
Mutual St
D Arcy Street
DUNDAS STREET WEST
The Art Gallery of Ontario
Simcoe Street
St Patrick
County Courthouse
City Hall
St. Michael's Hospital
Bond St
QUEEN STREET EAST
China Town
Grange Ave
Grange Park
McCaul Street
Osgoode Hall
Nathan Philips Square
Old City Hall
Queen
RICHMOND ST EAST
Downtown
Lombard Street
Phoebe St
Stephanie Street
John St
Renfrew Place
Campbell Ho
WEST
Osgoode
WEST
Richmond Adelaide Centre
ADELAIDE STREET EAST
P.O.
St. James Park
Bulwer Street
QUEEN
RICHMOND
STREET
Bank of Canada
National Bank Bldg
WEST
YONGE
St James Cathedral
STREET
Nelson Street
STREET
Toronto Stock Exchange
BAY
Scotia Plaza
King
KING STREET EAST
ADELAIDE
Widmer St
UNIVERSITY
WEST
Colborne Street
Royal Alexandra Theatre
Pearl St
St Andrew
WEST
Gallery of Inuit Art
Toronto Dominion Centre
Commerce Court
Hockey Hall of Fame
Hummingbird Centre
Peter St
KING
STREET
Roy Thomson Hall
Wellington
Canada Trust Tower
The Esplanade
Mercer Street
Wellington Street West
AVENUE
WEST
Union
Canada Custom Building
Metro Hall
Simcoe Park
WEST
P.O.
Clarence Square Park
CBC Broadcast Centre & Mus
FRONT
STREET
Union Station
Bus Terminal
SPADINA
Metro Toronto Conv. Cen. (Nth)
Convention Centre (Sth)
Air Canada Centre
GARDINER
LAKE SHORE BOULEVARD EAST
Isabella Valancy Crawford Park
Boulevard
Freeland St
AVENUE
Rogers Centre (Sky Dome)
C.N. Tower
Bremner
Police Station
Queen's Quay East
Old Bremner Boulevard
Roundhouse
Roundhouse Park
HARBOUR ST
Harbour Square Park
City Core Golf & Driving Range
LAKE SHORE BOULEVARD WEST
West
EXPRESSWAY
Toronto Island Ferry Terminal
Lester B. Pearson Int. Airport (YYZ)
GARDINER EXPRESSWAY
Queen's Quay
Harbourfront Park
Queen's Quay Terminal
Lake Ontario

45

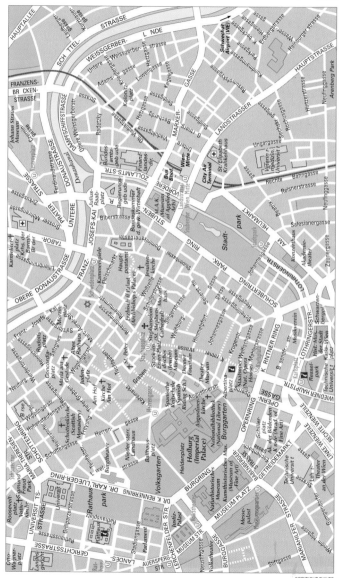

0   km   1

COPYRIGHT PHILIP'S

GAZETTEER OF NATIONS

48 Afghanistan
Albania
Algeria
American
   Samoa
Andorra
Angola

49 Anguilla
Antigua &
   Barbuda
Argentina
Armenia
Aruba
Australia

50 Austria
Azerbaijan
Azores
Bahamas
Bahrain
Bangladesh

51 Barbados
Belarus
Belgium
Belize
Benin
Bermuda

52 Bolivia
Bosnia-
   Herzegovina
Botswana
Brazil
Bulgaria
Burma

53 Cambodia
Canada
Canary Is.
Cape Verde
Cayman Is.
Chad

54 Chile
China
Colombia
Comoros
Costa Rica
Croatia

55 Cuba
Cyprus
Czech Rep.
Denmark
Dominica
Dominican Rep.

56 Ecuador
Egypt
El Salvador
Estonia
Ethiopia
Fiji Is.

57 Finland
France
French Polynesia
Gambia, The
Georgia
Germany

58 Gibraltar
Greece
Grenada
Guadeloupe
Hong Kong
Hungary

59 Iceland
India
Indonesia
Iran
Ireland
Israel

60 Italy
Jamaica

Japan
Jordan
Kenya
Korea, South

61 Kuwait
Latvia
Lebanon
Libya
Liechtenstein
Lithuania

62 Luxembourg
Madagascar
Malawi
Malaysia
Maldives
Malta

63 Martinique
Mauritius
Mexico
Mongolia
Montenegro
Morocco

64 Namibia
Nepal
Netherlands
Neth. Antilles
New Zealand
Nigeria

65 Norway
Oman
Pakistan
Paraguay
Peru
Philippines

66 Poland
Portugal
Puerto Rico
Qatar

Réunion
Romania

67 Russia
St Kitts & Nevis
St Lucia
St Vincent
Samoa
Saudi Arabia

68 Serbia
Seychelles
Singapore
Slovak Rep.
Slovenia
South Africa

69 Spain
Sri Lanka
Sweden
Switzerland
Syria
Taiwan

70 Tanzania
Thailand
Trinidad & T.
Tunisia
Turkey
Uganda

71 Ukraine
UAE
UK
USA
Uruguay
Venezuela

72 Vietnam
Virgin Is., British
Virgin Is., US
Yemen
Zambia
Zimbabwe

AFGHANISTAN

GOVERNMENT Transitional
LANGUAGES Pashtu, Dari/Persian, Uzbek
CURRENCY Afghani = 100 puls
MEDICAL Visitors should protect against yellow fever, polio, typhoid and malaria
TRAVEL Most governments currently advise against all travel to Afghanistan. The security situation remains serious, with danger away from main roads from mines and unexploded ordnance
WEATHER Jun to Aug very hot; Dec to Mar very cold; Jun to Sep scanty rainfall; mild at other times
BANKING 0800–1200 and 1300–1630 Sat to Wed; 0830–1330 Thu. However, at the time of writing, many banks are closed
EMERGENCY Unavailable
TIME ZONE GMT +4.30
INTERNATIONAL DIALING CODE Unavailable

ALGERIA

GOVERNMENT Socialist republic
LANGUAGES Arabic and Berber (both official), French
CURRENCY Algerian dinar = 100 centimes
MEDICAL There is a risk of yellow fever, malaria, hepatitis A, typhoid, and polio
TRAVEL Most governments currently advise against all tourist and non-essential travel to Algeria. Travel by public transport should be avoided and only secure accommodation used
WEATHER Jun to Sep in the north is usually hot with high humidity along the coast; Oct to Feb wet and mild
BANKING 0900–1630 Sun to Thu
EMERGENCY Unavailable
TIME ZONE GMT +1
INTERNATIONAL DIALING CODE 213

ANDORRA

GOVERNMENT Parliamentary co-princedom
LANGUAGES Catalan, Spanish, French
CURRENCY Euro = 100 cents
MEDICAL There are no specific health risks
TRAVEL In Andorra, visitors will find some of the most stunning scenery and the best skiing in the Pyrenees. Shopping around, prices may often be up to 30% below those in France and Spain
WEATHER Jun to Sep warm and pleasant; Dec to Apr sunny but cold with abundant snow; rain falls throughout the year; snow often remains on the peaks of mountains until July
BANKING 0900–1300 and 1500–1700 Mon to Fri; 0900–1200 Sat
EMERGENCY Police 110; Fire/Ambulance 118
TIME ZONE GMT +1
INTERNATIONAL DIALING CODE 376

ALBANIA

GOVERNMENT Multiparty republic
LANGUAGES Albanian (official)
CURRENCY Lek = 100 qindars
MEDICAL Water is untreated and not safe to drink. Medical facilities in the country are poor
TRAVEL Crime is high throughout parts of the country and visitors should remain vigilant at all times. It is advisable to dress down and avoid carrying expensive items. Street demonstrations against the government are common
WEATHER Jun to Sep warm and dry; Oct to May cool and wet
BANKING 0700–1500 Mon to Fri
EMERGENCY Police 24445; Fire 23333; Ambulance 22235
TIME ZONE GMT +1
INTERNATIONAL DIALING CODE 355

AMERICAN SAMOA

GOVERNMENT US overseas territory
LANGUAGES Samoan, English
CURRENCY US dollar = 100 cents
MEDICAL Water is untreated and is unsafe to drink. Vaccination against polio and typhoid is recommended
TRAVEL Most visits to American Samoa are trouble-free and crime is low. Tourists should respect local culture and take usual precautions, especially in the towns
WEATHER Hot, tropical climate with heavy rainfall from Dec to Apr. The most comfortable time to visit is May to Sep
BANKING 0900–1500 Mon to Fri
EMERGENCY All services 911
TIME ZONE GMT –11
INTERNATIONAL DIALING CODE 1 684

ANGOLA

GOVERNMENT Multiparty republic
LANGUAGES Portuguese (official), many others
CURRENCY Kwanza = 100 lwei
MEDICAL There is a risk of yellow fever, hepatitis A, polio, typhoid, and malaria
TRAVEL Most governments currently advise against tourist and non-essential travel to Angola due to the aftermath of civil war. Visitors should remain vigilant, particularly after dark. Crime levels are high and land mines are widely distributed and unmarked
WEATHER Warm to hot all year; Nov to Apr wet; cooler and wetter climate in the south
BANKING 0845–1600 Mon to Fri
EMERGENCY Unavailable
TIME ZONE GMT +1
INTERNATIONAL DIALING CODE 244

ANGUILLA

GOVERNMENT UK overseas territory
LANGUAGES English (official)
CURRENCY East Caribbean dollar = 100 cents
MEDICAL There are no specific health risks, but medical facilities are limited on the island
TRAVEL Most visits are trouble-free, but beachwear should be confined to resort areas. Travelers should take normal precautions, such as locking doors and securing valuables
WEATHER Tropical climate. Hurricane risk from Jun to Nov; Oct to Dec is the rainy season. Optimum diving conditions in summer months
BANKING 0800–1500 Mon to Thu; 0800–1700 Fri
EMERGENCY All services 911
TIME ZONE GMT –4
INTERNATIONAL DIALING CODE 1 264

ANTIGUA & BARBUDA

GOVERNMENT Constitutional monarchy
LANGUAGES English (official), English patois
CURRENCY East Caribbean dollar = 100 cents
MEDICAL Visitors should take normal precautions against mosquito bites. Vaccinations recommended against polio and typhoid
TRAVEL Generally trouble-free, but visitors should avoid isolated areas, including beaches, after dark
WEATHER Tropical with little variation between the seasons; rainfall is minimal. The islands are at risk from hurricanes from Jun to Nov
BANKING 0800–1400 Mon to Thu; 0800–1700 Fri
EMERGENCY All services 999/911
TIME ZONE GMT –4
INTERNATIONAL DIALING CODE 1 268

ARGENTINA

GOVERNMENT Federal republic
LANGUAGES Spanish (official)
CURRENCY Argentine peso = 10,000 australs
MEDICAL Cholera is a risk in the subtropical northern region
TRAVEL Occasional outbreaks of social unrest. It is inadvisable to walk in isolated, poorly-lit areas. Visitors should avoid carrying too much cash or wearing jewelry. Avoid military areas, which usually allow no stopping
WEATHER Jun to Aug cool in Buenos Aires area; Dec to Feb hot and humid; rain falls all year round
BANKING 1000–1500 Mon to Fri
EMERGENCY Police 101/107
TIME ZONE GMT –3
INTERNATIONAL DIALING CODE 54

ARMENIA

GOVERNMENT Multiparty republic
LANGUAGES Armenian (official)
CURRENCY Dram = 100 couma
MEDICAL Visitors should protect against hepatitis and bacterial infection
TRAVEL The border areas with Azerbaijan should be avoided at all times. Crime remains relatively low in Armenia, but occasional thefts from cars and pickpocketing may occur. The local standard of driving is poor, but most visits are generally trouble-free
WEATHER Apr to Oct hot and sunny; Jul to Sep little rainfall; Dec to Feb cold with heavy snow
BANKING 0930–1730 Mon to Fri
EMERGENCY Unavailable
TIME ZONE GMT +4
INTERNATIONAL DIALING CODE 374

ARUBA

GOVERNMENT Parliamentary democracy
LANGUAGES Dutch, English, Spanish, Papiamento
CURRENCY Aruba florin = 100 cents
MEDICAL Water is purified and should be safe; normal precautions should be taken with food
TRAVEL Beachwear should be confined to the beach. Travelers should take normal precautions, such as avoiding isolated areas after dark
WEATHER Tropical marine climate, warm and dry with average temperatures of 82°F [28°C]. Nov and Dec experience short showers
BANKING 0800–1200 and 1300–1600 Mon to Fri
EMERGENCY Police 11 000; Ambulance 74 300; Fire 115
TIME ZONE GMT –4
INTERNATIONAL DIALING CODE 297

AUSTRALIA

GOVERNMENT Federal constitutional monarchy
LANGUAGES English (official)
CURRENCY Australian dollar = 100 cents
MEDICAL No vaccinations required. There are few health hazards, but visitors should protect against sunburn, spider, and snake bites
TRAVEL Visitors should exercise caution in major urban areas, particularly after dark
WEATHER Tropical to temperate; Nov to Mar warm or hot in all areas; Jun to Aug mild in south-eastern region; Sep to May warm to hot; rain falls all year round and is heaviest Mar to Jul
BANKING 0930–1600 Mon to Thu; 0930–1700 Fri, but hours vary throughout the country
EMERGENCY Emergency Services 000
TIME ZONE East GMT +10; Cen. +9.30; West +8
INTERNATIONAL DIALING CODE 61

AUSTRIA

GOVERNMENT Federal republic
LANGUAGES German (official)
CURRENCY Euro = 100 cents
MEDICAL There are no specific health risks in Austria
TRAVEL Visitors to the Alps should contact the Austrian Tourist Agency for advice on safety. Austria benefits all year round by providing summer sightseeing and winter sports
WEATHER Jun to Aug warm and pleasant; Oct to Apr cold; Mar to Aug higher rainfall
BANKING 0800–1230 and 1330–1500 Mon, Tue, Wed and Fri; Thu 0800–1230 and 1330–1730
EMERGENCY Emergency Services 112; Police 133; Ambulance 144
TIME ZONE GMT +1
INTERNATIONAL DIALING CODE 43

AZERBAIJAN

GOVERNMENT Federal multiparty republic
LANGUAGES Azerbaijani (official), Russian
CURRENCY Azerbaijani manat = 100 gopik
MEDICAL Visitors should protect against malaria, yellow fever, diptheria, tick-borne encephalitis, hepatitis, rabies, and typhoid fever
TRAVEL Travel to the western region of Nagorno-Karabakh and surrounding occupied area should be avoided. Passport photocopies should be carried at all times. Do not enter or leave the country via the land borders with Russia
WEATHER May to Sep sunny, warm, and dry; Oct to Apr mild with some rain
BANKING 0930–1730 Mon to Fri
EMERGENCY Unavailable
TIME ZONE GMT +4
INTERNATIONAL DIALING CODE 994

AZORES

GOVERNMENT Portuguese autonomous region
LANGUAGES Portuguese
CURRENCY Euro = 100 cents
MEDICAL There are no specific health risks in the Azores
TRAVEL Most visits to the Azores are trouble-free. The nine large islands and numerous small ones are situated in the middle of the Atlantic Ocean and offer the traveler a wealth of stunning scenery
WEATHER Mild throughout the year; Jun to Sep sunny and warm; Jan to Apr changeable; Oct to Mar wet
BANKING Visitors should check at their hotel
EMERGENCY Unavailable
TIME ZONE GMT –1
INTERNATIONAL DIALING CODE Unavailable

BAHAMAS

GOVERNMENT Constitutional parliamentary democracy
LANGUAGES English (official), Creole
CURRENCY Bahamian dollar = 100 cents
MEDICAL Visitors should protect against dehydration, sunburn, tetanus, and jellyfish
TRAVEL Most visits are trouble-free, but crime exists in the cities of Nassau and Freeport. Keep valuables hidden and avoid walking alone
WEATHER Mild throughout the year; May to Oct warm and wet; Dec to Mar cooler and drier; Jun to Nov hurricanes occur
BANKING 0930–1500 Mon to Thu; 0930–1700 Fri, but hours on each island vary
EMERGENCY All Services 911
TIME ZONE GMT –5
INTERNATIONAL DIALING CODE 1 242

BAHRAIN

GOVERNMENT Monarchy (emirate) with a cabinet appointed by the Emir
LANGUAGES Arabic (official), English, Farsi, Urdu
CURRENCY Bahrain dinar = 1,000 fils
MEDICAL There are no specific health risks
TRAVEL Generally calm, but any increase in regional tension may affect travel advice. Visitors should avoid village areas, particularly after dark. Keep cash and valuables out of sight at all times
WEATHER Jun to Sep very hot; Nov to Mar milder and pleasant
BANKING 0800–1200 and 1600–1800 Sat to Wed; 0800–1100 Thu
EMERGENCY All Services 999
TIME ZONE GMT +3
INTERNATIONAL DIALING CODE 973

BANGLADESH

GOVERNMENT Multiparty republic
LANGUAGES Bengali (official), English
CURRENCY Taka = 100 paisas
MEDICAL Visitors should protect against cholera, dysentery, hepatitis, malaria, and meningitis
TRAVEL Avoid political gatherings. Driving conditions are very poor. Visitors should keep valuables hidden and avoid travel after dark
WEATHER Jun to Sep monsoon with heavy rain and very high humidity; Nov to Feb sunny and cool; Mar to Jun hot with thunderstorms
BANKING 0830–1430 Sun to Wed; 0830–1300 Thu. Closed Fri and Sat
EMERGENCY Police Dhaka 866 551–3; Fire and Ambulance Service Dhaka 9 555 555
TIME ZONE GMT +6
INTERNATIONAL DIALING CODE 880

BARBADOS

GOVERNMENT Parliamentary democracy
LANGUAGES English (local Bajan dialect also spoken)
CURRENCY Barbados dollar = 100 cents
MEDICAL The sun is intense and visitors should wear strong sunscreen at all times. Other health risks include dengue fever
TRAVEL Travel is generally risk-free, but visitors should avoid deserted beaches at night
WEATHER Warm all year round; Jun to Dec wet season; Feb to May cooler and drier
BANKING 0800–1500 Mon to Thu; 0800–1300 and 1500–1700 Fri
EMERGENCY Police 112; Ambulance 115; All Services 119
TIME ZONE GMT −4
INTERNATIONAL DIALING CODE 1 246

BELGIUM

GOVERNMENT Federal constitutional monarchy
LANGUAGES Dutch, French, German (all official)
CURRENCY Euro = 100 cents
MEDICAL There are no specific health risks, but medical care is expensive
TRAVEL Most visits are trouble-free, but visitors should take sensible precautions to avoid the increasing threat of mugging, bag-snatching, and pickpocketing, particularly in Brussels
WEATHER May to Sep mild; Nov to Mar cold; rain falls all year round, often as snow in winter
BANKING 0900–1200 and 1400–1600 Mon to Fri. Some banks open 0900–1200 Sat
EMERGENCY Police 101; Emergency Services 112 Fire/Ambulance 100 (112 from a mobile phone)
TIME ZONE GMT +1
INTERNATIONAL DIALING CODE 32

BENIN

GOVERNMENT Multiparty republic
LANGUAGES French (official), Fon, Adja, Yoruba
CURRENCY CFA franc = 100 centimes
MEDICAL Visitors should protect against cholera and malaria. Yellow fever vaccination certificates are required for entry. Water is unsafe to drink
TRAVEL Travel is generally safe, but driving out of towns at night should be avoided due to poor street lighting. Occasional incidents of mugging and armed robberies occur in Cotonou
WEATHER Warm to hot all year round; Mar to Jul and Sep to Oct are rainy seasons in the south
BANKING 0800–1100 and 1500–1600 Mon to Fri
EMERGENCY Consult foreign embassy
TIME ZONE GMT +1
INTERNATIONAL DIALING CODE 229

BELARUS

GOVERNMENT Multiparty republic
LANGUAGES Belarusian and Russian (both official)
CURRENCY Belarusian rouble = 100 kopecks
MEDICAL Visitors should avoid eating dairy produce, mushrooms, and fruits of the forests which can carry high levels of radiation. Other health risks include hepatitis A and B, and typhoid
TRAVEL Pickpocketing and theft from vehicles or hotel rooms is common. Visitors should avoid demonstrations and rallies, and remain vigilant at all times
WEATHER May to Aug mild; Oct to Apr cold; Jan to Mar snow cover; rain falls all year round
BANKING 0900–1730 Mon to Fri
EMERGENCY Police 02; Ambulance 03
TIME ZONE GMT +2
INTERNATIONAL DIALING CODE 375

BELIZE

GOVERNMENT Constitutional monarchy
LANGUAGES English (official), Spanish, Creole
CURRENCY Belizean dollar = 100 cents
MEDICAL Precautions should be taken against polio, typhoid, and cholera. Malaria is present throughout the year, excluding urban areas
TRAVEL Nov to May is the best time to visit, but this is the busy tourist season when prices rise and hotels fill up. Belize has one of the longest barrier reefs in the world
WEATHER Hot and humid climate. Monsoon and hurricane season runs from Jun to Sep
BANKING 0800–1300 Mon to Thu; 0800–1200 and 1500–1800 Fri
EMERGENCY All services 911
TIME ZONE GMT −6
INTERNATIONAL DIALING CODE 501

BERMUDA

GOVERNMENT Self-governing British dependency
LANGUAGES English (some Portuguese is also spoken)
CURRENCY Bermuda dollar = 100 cents
MEDICAL There are no specific health risks
TRAVEL Most visits to Bermuda are trouble-free. Accommodation can be up to 40% cheaper between Nov and Mar, but events and entertainment are less plentiful at this time
WEATHER Jun to Sep very warm; Nov to Apr mild; rainfall is abundant and evenly distributed all year round
BANKING 0930–1500 Mon to Thu; 0930–1500 and 1630–1730 Fri
EMERGENCY All Services 911
TIME ZONE GMT −4
INTERNATIONAL DIALING CODE 1 441

BOLIVIA

GOVERNMENT Multiparty republic
LANGUAGES Spanish, Aymara, Quechua (official)
CURRENCY Boliviano = 100 centavos
MEDICAL Altitude sickness is common. Visitors should drink plenty of water and protect against cholera, hepatitis, malaria, polio, and tetanus
TRAVEL Pickpocketing is common and visitors are advised to remain vigilant at all times. The country is going through a period of unrest
WEATHER Average max. daily temperature of 62–66°F [17–19°C] all year round; low annual rainfall, most falling Dec to Mar
BANKING 0930–1500 Mon to Thu; 0930–1500 and 1630–1730 Fri
EMERGENCY All Services 911
TIME ZONE GMT −4
INTERNATIONAL DIALING CODE 591

BOSNIA-HERZEGOVINA

GOVERNMENT Federal republic
LANGUAGES Bosnian, Serbian, Croatian
CURRENCY Convertible marka = 100 convertible pfenniga
MEDICAL Medical facilities are limited. There is a risk of hepatitis and typhoid fever
TRAVEL Crime level is generally low, but isolated incidents of violence can flare up. Unexploded land mines and other ordnance still remain in certain areas
WEATHER Jun to Sep warm; Dec to Feb cold; spring and fall mild; rain falls all year round
BANKING 0730–1530 Mon to Fri
EMERGENCY Consult foreign office in country of residence before departure
TIME ZONE GMT +1
INTERNATIONAL DIALING CODE 387

BOTSWANA

GOVERNMENT Multiparty republic
LANGUAGES English (official), Setswana
CURRENCY Pula = 100 thebe
MEDICAL There are no specific health risks, but visitors should protect against malaria
TRAVEL Most visits are trouble-free, but there is an increasing incidence of crime. Prolonged rainfall may cause flooding and block roads from Dec to Apr
WEATHER In the east, May to Sep mild with little rainfall; Nov to Mar warm, rainy season but nights can be cold
BANKING 0900–1430 Mon, Tue, Thu and Fri; 0815–1200 Wed; 0815–1045 Sat
EMERGENCY Police 351161
TIME ZONE GMT +2
INTERNATIONAL DIALING CODE 267

BRAZIL

GOVERNMENT Federal republic
LANGUAGES Portuguese (official)
CURRENCY Real = 100 centavos
MEDICAL Visitors should take precautions against AIDS, malaria, meningitis, and yellow fever
TRAVEL High crime rate in major cities of Rio de Janeiro and São Paulo. Dress down and avoid wearing jewelry
WEATHER Jun to Sep pleasant in southeast; Dec to Mar hot and humid with high rainfall
BANKING 1000–1630 Mon to Fri
EMERGENCY All Services 0
TIME ZONE Eastern GMT −3; North East and East Pará −3; Western −4; Amapa and West Para −4; Acre State −5; Fernando de Noronha Archipelago −2
INTERNATIONAL DIALING CODE 55

BULGARIA

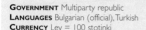

GOVERNMENT Multiparty republic
LANGUAGES Bulgarian (official), Turkish
CURRENCY Lev = 100 stotinki
MEDICAL There are no specific health risks
TRAVEL Most visits to Bulgaria are trouble-free, but there is a risk of robbery. Pickpockets operate in downtown Sofia and in the Black Sea resorts. Car theft is commonplace
WEATHER May to Sep warm with some rainfall; Nov to Mar cold with snow; rain falls frequently during spring and fall
BANKING 0800–1130 and 1400–1800 Mon to Fri; 0830–1130 Sat
EMERGENCY Police 166; Fire 160; Ambulance 150
TIME ZONE GMT +2
INTERNATIONAL DIALING CODE 359

BURMA (= MYANMAR)

GOVERNMENT Military regime
LANGUAGES Burmese (official); minority ethnic groups have their own languages
CURRENCY Kyat = 100 pyas
MEDICAL Visitors should protect against cholera, dysentery, hepatitis, malaria, rabies, and typhoid
TRAVEL Politically unsettled. Visitors should avoid large crowds and should not visit Aung San Suu Kyi without prior arrangement. Terrorist attacks have been reported in some areas
WEATHER Monsoon climate; Feb to May hot with very little rain; May to Oct wet; Nov to Feb cooler and drier
BANKING 1000–1400 Mon to Fri
EMERGENCY Unavailable
TIME ZONE GMT +6.30
INTERNATIONAL DIALING CODE 95

CAMBODIA

GOVERNMENT Constitutional monarchy
LANGUAGES Khmer (official), French, English
CURRENCY Riel = 100 sen
MEDICAL Visitors should protect against cholera, hepatitis, malaria, typhoid, and rabies
TRAVEL Visitors should seek advice before traveling. The greatest risks are from traffic accidents and armed robbery after dark. Land mines exist in certain rural areas
WEATHER Tropical monsoon climate; May to Oct monsoon; Dec to Jan lower humidity and little rainfall; Feb to Apr hot; temperatures are constant throughout the country
BANKING 0800–1500 Mon to Fri
EMERGENCY Unavailable
TIME ZONE GMT +7
INTERNATIONAL DIALING CODE 855

CANADA

GOVERNMENT Federal multiparty constitutional monarchy
LANGUAGES English and French (both official)
CURRENCY Canadian dollar = 100 cents
MEDICAL Medical treatment is expensive and it is essential that visitors have travel insurance. Blackfly and mosquitoes can cause problems in areas near water
TRAVEL Most visits to Canada are trouble-free
WEATHER Varies considerably; Jul to Aug tend to be warm all round the country; Nov to Mar very cold everywhere except west coast
BANKING 1000–1500 Mon to Fri
EMERGENCY Emergency Services 911 or 0
TIME ZONE Six zones exist from GMT –3.30 in Newfoundland to –8 on the Pacific coast
INTERNATIONAL DIALING CODE 1

CANARY ISLANDS

GOVERNMENT Spanish autonomous region
LANGUAGES Spanish
CURRENCY Euro = 100 cents
MEDICAL The Canary Islands are part of Spain and there are no specific health risks
TRAVEL The islands are volcanic and the landscape is varied. Many resorts suffer the effects of mass tourism, but beyond these areas there are stunning, peaceful regions to be enjoyed
WEATHER Subtropical climate; generally hot and sunny all year round, but Dec to Feb slightly cooler than rest of year
BANKING Visitors should enquire at hotel
EMERGENCY Unavailable
TIME ZONE GMT
INTERNATIONAL DIALING CODE 34

CAPE VERDE

GOVERNMENT Multiparty republic
LANGUAGES Portuguese, Creole
CURRENCY Cape Verde escudo = 100 centavos
MEDICAL Water is untreated and unsafe to drink. Avoid dairy products as they are unpasteurized. Polio and typhoid vaccinations are recommended; there is a risk of cholera and malaria
TRAVEL Most visits to Cape Verde are trouble-free. Visitors should avoid carrying valuables in public and remain vigilant at all times
WEATHER Warm and temperate climate with a dry summer. The islands suffer periodically from drought
BANKING 0800–1400 Mon to Fri
EMERGENCY All services 87
TIME ZONE GMT –1
INTERNATIONAL DIALING CODE 238

CAYMAN ISLANDS

GOVERNMENT British crown colony
LANGUAGES English (local dialects also spoken)
CURRENCY Cayman Islands dollar = 100 cents
MEDICAL There is a risk of sunburn and poisonous plants are present
TRAVEL Most visits to the Cayman Islands are trouble-free. Car hire is a good way to move around the islands
WEATHER Warm tropical climate all year round; May to Oct wet season with usually brief showers
BANKING 0900–1600 Mon to Thu; 0900–1630 Fri
EMERGENCY Police 911; Ambulance 555; All Services 911
TIME ZONE GMT –5
INTERNATIONAL DIALING CODE 1 345

CHAD

GOVERNMENT Multiparty republic
LANGUAGES French and Arabic (both official)
CURRENCY CFA franc = 100 centimes
MEDICAL Visitors should be vaccinated against yellow fever, tetanus, cholera, and hepatitis A
TRAVEL Visitors to Chad should remain vigilant at all times especially in the southwest region along the border with Cameroon. Areas to avoid include the Aozou Strip and the Tibesti area on the border with Libya, where minefields exist
WEATHER Hot tropical climate; Mar to May very hot; May to Oct wet in south; Jun to Sep wet in central areas; little rain in northern regions
BANKING 0900–1400 Mon to Fri
EMERGENCY Unavailable
TIME ZONE GMT +1
INTERNATIONAL DIALING CODE 235

CHILE

Government Multiparty republic
Languages Spanish (official)
Currency Chilean peso = 100 centavos
Medical Visitors should protect themselves against cholera
Travel Most visits are trouble-free, but visitors are advised to keep in groups and avoid walking alone, particularly after dark. Pickpockets and muggers are active in cities. Passport photocopies should be carried at all times
Weather Variable climate; Sep to Nov and Feb to Apr pleasant temperatures; Dec to Mar hotter; skiing is popular from Jun to Aug
Banking 0900–1400 Mon to Fri
Emergency Police 133; Fire 132
Time zone GMT –4; Easter Island –6
International dialing code 56

CHINA

Government Single-party Communist republic
Languages Mandarin Chinese (official)
Currency Renminbi yuan = 10 jiao = 100 fen
Medical Rabies is widespread. A virulent strain of viral pneumonia has emerged in the southeast and malaria is common in southern areas
Travel Violent crimes are rare. Crime occurs in cities, and extra care should be taken around street markets and popular bar areas at night
Weather Climate varies; Apr to Sep humid and hot; Jan to Mar very cold; rainfall high in central areas; Jul to Sep typhoon season in the south
Banking 0930–1200 and 1400–1700 Mon to Fri; 0900–1700 Sat
Emergency Police 110; Fire 119
Time zone GMT +8
International dialing code 86

COLOMBIA

Government Multiparty republic
Languages Spanish (official)
Currency Colombian peso = 100 centavos
Medical Visitors should protect against altitude sickness, cholera, hepatitis A, B and D, and malaria
Travel Guerrilla and criminal attacks close to Bogota are increasing. Violence and kidnapping are serious problems in Colombia. The border area with Panama and the Uraba region of Antioquia are particularly dangerous
Weather Hot and humid; May to Nov rainy season; cooler in upland areas
Banking 0900–1500 Mon to Fri
Emergency All Services 112 (01 in smaller towns and rural areas)
Time zone GMT –5
International dialing code 57

COMOROS

Government Multiparty republic
Languages Arabic and French (both official)
Currency CFA franc = 100 centimes
Medical Strict food hygiene precautions are essential. Cholera and malaria are prevalent and medical facilities are basic and limited
Travel Generally crime-free, but be aware of pickpockets. Visitors should not walk around town centres unaccompanied at night
Weather Tropical climate with average temperatures of 77°F [25°C]. Cyclone risk between Jan and Apr
Banking 0730–1300 Mon to Thu; 0730–1100 Fri
Emergency Unavailable
Time zone GMT +3
International dialing code 269

COSTA RICA

Government Multiparty republic
Languages Spanish (official), English
Currency Costa Rican colón = 100 céntimos
Medical Cases of dengue fever have been confirmed. Visitors should protect themselves against malaria, cholera, and hepatitis
Travel Daylight muggings can occur. Do not wear jewelry or carry large amounts of cash. Riptides are very common on all beaches
Weather Coastal areas warmer than inland low-lying regions; Dec to Apr warm and dry; May to Nov rainy season; landslides can occur
Banking 0900–1500 Mon to Fri
Emergency Police 104; Fire 103; Ambulance 225/1436 and 228/2187
Time zone GMT –7
International dialing code 506

CROATIA

Government Multiparty republic
Languages Croatian
Currency Kuna = 100 lipas
Medical No specific health risks, although the health system is severely stretched at present
Travel Exercise caution in the areas bordering Bosnia-Herzegovina, Serbia, and Montenegro. There continue to be incidents of violence and many unexploded land mines remain undetected. It is inadvisable to use the Debelli Brijeg crossing-points into Montenegro
Weather Continental climate in the north and Mediterranean on the Adriatic Coast
Banking 0700–1500 Mon to Fri
Emergency Police 92; Fire 93; Ambulance 94
Time zone GMT +1
International dialing code 385

CUBA

GOVERNMENT Socialist republic
LANGUAGES Spanish (official)
CURRENCY Cuban peso = 100 centavos
MEDICAL Tap water is unsafe to drink, with a risk of contracting hepatitis A
TRAVEL Street theft occurs, especially in Old Havana and major tourist sites. Do not carry large amounts of cash or jewelry. Do not travel with anyone other than your recognized tour operator. Avoid military zones
WEATHER May to Oct hot rainy season; Aug to Nov hurricane season; Dec to Apr cooler
BANKING 0830–1200 and 1330–1500 Mon to Fri; 0830–1030 Sat
EMERGENCY All Services 26811
TIME ZONE GMT –4
INTERNATIONAL DIALING CODE 53

CYPRUS

GOVERNMENT Multiparty republic
LANGUAGES Greek and Turkish (both official)
CURRENCY Euro = 100 cents
MEDICAL There are no specific health risks, but visitors should be protected against hepatitis
TRAVEL Travel is generally trouble-free, but attempts to pass overland from the northern Turkish sector into the southern Greek region are not recommended
WEATHER Apr to May and Sep to Oct cool and pleasant; Jun to Aug hot and dry; Nov to Mar rainfall is heavier, but temperatures remain warm
BANKING 0815–1230 in tourist areas; 1530–1730 in winter; 1630–1830 in summer
EMERGENCY All Services 199
TIME ZONE GMT +2
INTERNATIONAL DIALING CODE 357

CZECH REPUBLIC

GOVERNMENT Multiparty republic
LANGUAGES Czech (official)
CURRENCY Czech koruna = 100 haler
MEDICAL Visitors to forested areas should seek advice about immunization against tick-borne encephalitis and lyme disease
TRAVEL Most visits are trouble-free, but petty theft is a growing problem, particularly in Prague. Pickpocketing is very common at tourist attractions
WEATHER May to Sep mild; Apr and Oct much cooler
BANKING 0800–1800 Mon to Fri
EMERGENCY Police 158; Fire 150; Ambulance 155
TIME ZONE GMT +1
INTERNATIONAL DIALING CODE 42

DENMARK

GOVERNMENT Parliamentary monarchy
LANGUAGES Danish (official), English
CURRENCY Danish krone = 100 øre
MEDICAL There are no specific health risks in Denmark
TRAVEL Visits to Denmark are generally trouble-free. Visitors will enjoy relatively low prices compared to other European countries
WEATHER Jun to Aug warm summer season; Oct to Mar cold and wet with chance of frost; spring and fall are usually mild and pleasant
BANKING 0930–1700 Mon, Tue, Wed and Fri; 0930–1800 Thu. Some foreign exchange bureaux remain open until midnight
EMERGENCY Emergency Services 112
TIME ZONE GMT +1
INTERNATIONAL DIALING CODE 45

DOMINICA

GOVERNMENT Parliamentary democracy
LANGUAGES English (official), Creole, French
CURRENCY East Caribbean dollar = 100 cents
MEDICAL Dengue fever is prevalent and visitors should guard against mosquito bites
TRAVEL Most visits are trouble-free. Visitors are advised to take sensible precautions and be vigilant at all times
WEATHER Tropical climate with heavy rainfall, particularly in Jun to Oct, which is also the hottest period. Tropical storms and hurricanes can occur between Jun and Nov
BANKING 0800–1500 Mon to Thu; 0800–1700 Fri
EMERGENCY All services 999
TIME ZONE GMT –4
INTERNATIONAL DIALING CODE 1 767

DOMINICAN REPUBLIC

GOVERNMENT Multiparty republic
LANGUAGES Spanish (official)
CURRENCY Dominican peso = 100 centavos
MEDICAL Tourists should protect against polio and typhoid. There are occasional outbreaks of malaria and dengue fever; anti-mosquito skin repellants are recommended
TRAVEL Border areas should be avoided while the political unrest in neighbouring Haiti continues. Avoid any excursions that are not recommended by tour operators
WEATHER Hot tropical climate; Jun to Nov rainy season with the risk of hurricanes
BANKING 0800–1600 Mon to Fri
EMERGENCY Emergency Services 711
TIME ZONE GMT –4
INTERNATIONAL DIALING CODE 1 809

ECUADOR

GOVERNMENT Multiparty republic
LANGUAGES Spanish (official), Quechua
CURRENCY US dollar = 100 cents
MEDICAL There is a risk of dengue fever, hepatitis, malaria, typhoid, diptheria, and rabies
TRAVEL Street crimes such as muggings and pickpocketing are common in the cities. Visitors should avoid travel to the provinces bordering Colombia due to incidents of kidnapping
WEATHER Jan to Apr warm and rainy on mainland and Galapagos; Jun to Aug cold; Jun to Aug dry in Highlands; Aug to Feb dry in Oriente
BANKING 0900–1330 and 1430–1830 Mon to Fri
EMERGENCY Police 101; Ambulance 131
TIME ZONE GMT –5; Galapagos Islands –6
INTERNATIONAL DIALING CODE 593

EGYPT

GOVERNMENT Republic
LANGUAGES Arabic (official), French, English
CURRENCY Egyptian pound = 100 piastres
MEDICAL There are no specific health risks in Egypt
TRAVEL Due to continuing tensions, visitors should keep in touch with developments in the Middle East and remain vigilant at all times. Particular care should be taken when traveling in Luxor and beyond in the Nile Valley
WEATHER Jun to Aug very hot and dry; Sep to May dry and cooler; spring and fall months are pleasant; dusty Saharan winds during Apr
BANKING 0830–1400 Sun to Thu
EMERGENCY Unavailable
TIME ZONE GMT +2
INTERNATIONAL DIALING CODE 20

EL SALVADOR

GOVERNMENT Republic
LANGUAGES Spanish (official)
CURRENCY US dollar = 100 cents
MEDICAL Tourists should protect against cholera, hepatitis, malaria, rabies, and typhoid
TRAVEL El Salvador is more politically stable than ever, but has high levels of violent crime. Visitors traveling alone should be vigilant at all times
WEATHER Hot subtropical climate; Nov to Apr dry season; May to Oct rainy season with cooler evenings
BANKING 0900–1300 and 1345–1600 Mon to Fri
EMERGENCY All Services 123/121
TIME ZONE GMT –6
INTERNATIONAL DIALING CODE 503

ESTONIA

GOVERNMENT Multiparty republic
LANGUAGES Estonian (official), Russian
CURRENCY Estonian kroon = 100 senti
MEDICAL There are no specific health risks
TRAVEL Most visits are trouble-free. Despite independence in 1991, much tradition exists in Estonia. Skiing, skating, and ice fishing are popular during the winter months
WEATHER Large temperature variations; Apr to May warm and pleasant; Jun to Sep hot.; Dec to Mar very cold with heavy snowfall; rain falls all year round
BANKING 0930–1630 Mon to Fri
EMERGENCY Police 02; Fire 01; Ambulance 03 (dial an extra 0 first if in Tallinn)
TIME ZONE GMT +2
INTERNATIONAL DIALING CODE 372

ETHIOPIA

GOVERNMENT Federation of nine provinces
LANGUAGES Amharic (official), many others
CURRENCY Birr = 100 cents
MEDICAL Water-borne diseases and malaria are prevalent. Medical facilities outside the capital are extremely poor
TRAVEL Most governments advise against travel to the Gambella region and the Eritrean border. There is currently a high risk of terrorism throughout the country
WEATHER Lowlands are hot and humid, it is warm in the hills and cool in the upland areas
BANKING 0800–1200 and 1300–1700 Mon to Thu; 0830–1100 and 1300–1700 Fri
EMERGENCY Not available
TIME ZONE GMT +3
INTERNATIONAL DIALING CODE 251

FIJI ISLANDS

GOVERNMENT Transitional
LANGUAGES English (official), various Fijian dialects
CURRENCY Fijian dollar = 100 cents
MEDICAL Visitors should protect against dengue fever and should avoid mosquito bites
TRAVEL There has been an increase in petty crime due to the unsettled economic and political situations
WEATHER Tropical climate; Dec to Apr humid, rainy season with a risk of tropical cyclones; May to Oct cooler, dry season
BANKING 0930–1500 Mon to Thu; 0930–1600 Fri
EMERGENCY All Services 000
TIME ZONE GMT +12
INTERNATIONAL DIALING CODE 679

FINLAND

GOVERNMENT Multiparty republic
LANGUAGES Finnish and Swedish (both official)
CURRENCY Euro = 100 cents
MEDICAL There are no specific health risks, but if mushroom-picking/eating, seek advice on safety
TRAVEL Visits to Finland are generally trouble-free
WEATHER Temperate climate; May to Sep warm with midnight sun; Oct to Mar very cold; Nov to May snow cover in the north; skiing starts in Feb, the coldest month, and continues until Jun in Lapland
BANKING 0915–1615 Mon to Fri
EMERGENCY Police 002; Fire/Ambulance 000; Emergency Services 112; Doctor 008
TIME ZONE GMT +2
INTERNATIONAL DIALING CODE 358

FRANCE

GOVERNMENT Multiparty republic
LANGUAGES French (official)
CURRENCY Euro = 100 cents
MEDICAL There are no specific health risks
TRAVEL Most visits to France are trouble-free. There have been sporadic bomb attacks on the island of Corsica and care should be exercised
WEATHER Temperate climate in the north; rain falls all year round; Mediterranean climate in the south; mild in the west; May to Sep hot and sunny; Oct to Nov pleasant temperatures
BANKING 0900–1200 and 1400–1600 Mon to Fri. Some banks close on Mondays
EMERGENCY Police 17; Fire 18; Ambulance 15; Emergency Services 112
TIME ZONE GMT +1
INTERNATIONAL DIALING CODE 33

FRENCH POLYNESIA

GOVERNMENT French overseas territory
LANGUAGES French and Polynesian (both official)
CURRENCY French Pacific franc = 100 cents
MEDICAL Water is untreated and dairy foods are unpasteurized. Vaccinations against polio and typhoid are recommended
TRAVEL Most visits are trouble-free, but visitors should remain vigilant at al times. French Polynesia is made up of 130 islands, Tahiti being the most popular
WEATHER Tropical but moderate climate with occasional cyclonic storms in Jan. Cool and dry Mar to Nov
BANKING 0745–1530 Mon to Fri
EMERGENCY Dial operator
TIME ZONE GMT –9 to GMT –10
INTERNATIONAL DIALING CODE 689

GAMBIA, THE

GOVERNMENT Military regime
LANGUAGES English (official), Mandinka, Wolof
CURRENCY Dalasi = 100 butut
MEDICAL Water-borne diseases and malaria are common. Other health risks include yellow fever, hepatitis, rabies, and typhoid .
TRAVEL Exercise caution when walking at night. Do not travel with valuables and dress modestly
WEATHER Nov to Mar dry and cool with winds from the Sahara; Jun to Oct rainy season; inland the cool season is shorter and temperatures are hot from Mar to Jun
BANKING 0800–1330 Mon to Thu; 0800–1100 Fri
EMERGENCY Consult foreign embassy
TIME ZONE GMT
INTERNATIONAL DIALING CODE 220

GEORGIA

GOVERNMENT Multiparty republic
LANGUAGES Georgian (official), Russian
CURRENCY Lari = 100 tetri
MEDICAL Diptheria and rabies cases have been reported. Tap water is unsafe to drink. Anthrax has been reported in the east. Medical care is poor and visitors should carry their own syringes
TRAVEL The regions of Abkhazia and South Ossetia should be avoided. Do not attempt access across the land borders with Russia
WEATHER Jul to Sep hot; Dec to Mar mild, especially in the southwest; low temperatures in alpine areas; rainfall heavy in southwest
BANKING 0930–1730 Mon to Fri
EMERGENCY Police 02; Fire 01; Ambulance 03
TIME ZONE GMT +4
INTERNATIONAL DIALING CODE 995

GERMANY
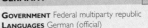

GOVERNMENT Federal multiparty republic
LANGUAGES German (official)
CURRENCY Euro = 100 cents
MEDICAL There are no specific health risks, but medical care is expensive
TRAVEL Visits to Germany are generally trouble-free. Travelers are able to enjoy a wealth of arts and culture, plus stunning natural scenery
WEATHER Very variable, temperate climate throughout the country; May to Oct warm; Nov to Apr cold; rain falls all year round
BANKING 0830–1300 and 1400/30–1600 Mon to Fri
EMERGENCY Police 110; Fire 112; Emergency Services 112
TIME ZONE GMT +1
INTERNATIONAL DIALING CODE 49

GIBRALTAR

GOVERNMENT UK overseas territory
LANGUAGES English and Spanish
CURRENCY Gibraltar pound = 100 pence
MEDICAL There are no specific health risks in Gibraltar
TRAVEL Most visits to Gibraltar are trouble-free. The country was recognized as a British possession in 1713, and despite Spanish claims, its population has consistently voted to retain its contacts with Britain
WEATHER Warm all year round; Jun to Sep hot and can be humid; Nov to Mar mild
BANKING 0900–1530 and 1630–1800 Mon to Fri
EMERGENCY All Services 999
TIME ZONE GMT +1
INTERNATIONAL DIALING CODE 350

GREECE

GOVERNMENT Multiparty republic
LANGUAGES Greek (official)
CURRENCY Euro = 100 cents
MEDICAL There is a risk of sunburn
TRAVEL Visitors should exercise normal precautions regarding safety and security. Tourists are strongly advised not to hire motorcycles, scooters, or mopeds
WEATHER Mediterranean climate; Aug to Nov pleasant temperatures; Nov to Mar heavy rainfall; Apr to Jun hot
BANKING 0800–1400 Mon to Fri
EMERGENCY Police 100; Fire 199; Ambulance 166; Emergency Services 112
TIME ZONE GMT +2
INTERNATIONAL DIALING CODE 30 + 1 for Athens; 31 Thessaloniki; 81 Heraklion; 661 Corfu

GRENADA

GOVERNMENT Constitutional monarchy
LANGUAGES English (official)
CURRENCY East Caribbean dollar = 100 cents
MEDICAL Tourists should protect against polio and typhoid. Anti-mosquito repellants are recommended
TRAVEL Trips are mostly trouble-free; however, tourists should remain vigilant at all times
WEATHER Tropical climate, rainy season is Jun to Sep when tropical storms and hurricanes occur. Jan to May is drier and less humid
BANKING 0800–1400 Mon to Thu; 0800–1300 and 1400–1700 Fri
EMERGENCY Police 112; Ambulance 434; Emergency services 911
TIME ZONE GMT –4
INTERNATIONAL DIALING CODE 1 473

GUADELOUPE

GOVERNMENT French overseas territory
LANGUAGES French (official), Creole
CURRENCY Euro = 100 cents
MEDICAL Polio and typhoid vaccinations are recommended. Water is untreated and unsafe to drink
TRAVEL Visits to Guadeloupe are generally trouble-free, and the French culture and influence is clearly evident. Soufriere de Guadeloupe is an active volcano
WEATHER Warm, humid weather all year round. Rainy season from Jun to Oct, when there is a risk of hurricanes
BANKING 0800–1600 Mon to Fri
EMERGENCY Police 17; Fire and Ambulance 18
TIME ZONE GMT –4
INTERNATIONAL DIALING CODE 590

HONG KONG

GOVERNMENT Special administrative region of China
LANGUAGES Chinese and English; Cantonese is most widely spoken
CURRENCY Hong Kong dollar = 100 cents
MEDICAL Visitors should protect against polio and typhoid. Slight risk of malaria in rural areas
TRAVEL Most visits are trouble-free
WEATHER Nov to Dec warm with pleasant breeze; Jan to Feb much cooler; Mar to Apr warmer; May to Sep very humid and uncomfortable, with a risk of cyclones in Sep
BANKING 0900–1630 Mon to Fri; 0900–1330 Sat
EMERGENCY All Services 999
TIME ZONE GMT +8
INTERNATIONAL DIALING CODE 852

HUNGARY
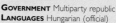

GOVERNMENT Multiparty republic
LANGUAGES Hungarian (official)
CURRENCY Forint = 100 fillér
MEDICAL There are no specific health risks in Hungary
TRAVEL Street theft is common in tourist areas, particularly in Budapest. It is illegal to drive having consumed alcohol. Passports to be carried at all times. Do not take photographs of anything connected with the military
WEATHER Jun to Aug very warm and sunny; spring and fall mild and pleasant; Jan to Mar very cold
BANKING 0900–1400 Mon to Fri
EMERGENCY Police 107; Fire/Ambulance 104
TIME ZONE GMT +1
INTERNATIONAL DIALING CODE 36

ICELAND

GOVERNMENT Multiparty republic
LANGUAGES Icelandic (official)
CURRENCY Icelandic króna = 100 aurar
MEDICAL There is a risk of hypothermia if trekking during the winter months
TRAVEL Visitors planning to travel off-road do so at their own risk and must contact the local authorities (Vegagerdin) prior to departure. Interior roads are closed in winter
WEATHER Weather is highly changeable all year round; May to Aug is mild with nearly 24 hours of daylight in Reykjavik; Sep to Apr is cold
BANKING 0915–1600 Mon to Fri
EMERGENCY Unavailable
TIME ZONE GMT
INTERNATIONAL DIALING CODE 354

INDIA

GOVERNMENT Multiparty federal republic
LANGUAGES Hindi, English, Telugu, Bengali, Marathi, Tamil, Urdu, Gujarati, Malayalam, Kannada, Oriya, Punjabi, Assamese, Kashmiri, Sindhi and Sanskrit (all official)
CURRENCY Indian rupee = 100 paisa
MEDICAL There is a risk of malaria, AIDS, and intestinal problems. Precautions should be taken
TRAVEL Visitors are advised to avoid the Pakistan border areas, as well as Jammu and Kashmir
WEATHER Hot tropical climate that varies from region to region; Apr to Sep very hot with monsoon rains
BANKING 1000–1400 Mon to Fri
EMERGENCY Unavailable
TIME ZONE GMT +5.30
INTERNATIONAL DIALING CODE 91

INDONESIA

GOVERNMENT Multiparty republic
LANGUAGES Bahasa Indonesian (official)
CURRENCY Indonesian rupiah = 100 sen
MEDICAL There is a risk of polio, typhoid, hepatitis B, yellow fever, and TB. Unpasteurized dairy produce should be avoided
TRAVEL Non-essential travel to Indonesia is not recommended due to the risk of terrorism against Western interests
WEATHER Tropical, varying climate; May to Oct dry weather from eastern monsoon; Nov to Apr rains from western monsoon. In northern Sumatra this pattern is reversed
BANKING 0800–1500 Mon to Fri
EMERGENCY Police 110; Ambulance 118
TIME ZONE West GMT +7; Central +8; East +9
INTERNATIONAL DIALING CODE 62

IRAN

GOVERNMENT Islamic republic
LANGUAGES Persian, Turkic, Kurdish
CURRENCY Iranian rial = 100 dinars
MEDICAL There is a risk of polio, typhoid, malaria and cholera
TRAVEL Visitors should monitor media reports before traveling. Any increase in regional tension will affect travel advice. Visitors should exercise caution and avoid carrying large sums of money since robbery and bag-snatching are common
WEATHER Dec to Mar very cold; Apr to Jun and Sep to Nov warm; Jun to Sep extremely hot
BANKING 0900–1600 Sat to Wed; 0900–1200 Thu. Closed on Fri
EMERGENCY Unavailable
TIME ZONE GMT +3.30
INTERNATIONAL DIALING CODE 98

IRELAND

GOVERNMENT Multiparty republic
LANGUAGES Irish (Gaelic) and English (both official)
CURRENCY Euro = 100 cents
MEDICAL There are no specific health risks
TRAVEL The Irish usually have close community bonds. Visitors should find people very friendly. Strong economic growth continues
WEATHER Rain falls all year round; Jul to Sep warm; Nov to Mar wet and cold; spring and fall mild
BANKING 1000–1600 Mon to Fri. Banks may open later in Dublin
EMERGENCY Emergency Services 112; All Services 999
TIME ZONE GMT
INTERNATIONAL DIALING CODE 353

ISRAEL

GOVERNMENT Multiparty republic
LANGUAGES Hebrew and Arabic (both official)
CURRENCY New Israeli shekel = 100 agorat
MEDICAL There are no specific health risks
TRAVEL Most governments currently strongly advise against travel to the West Bank, Gaza, and Jerusalem, or near their border areas with Israel. Visitors should keep car doors locked when traveling and avoid carrying large sums of cash
WEATHER Jul to Sep hot and windy; Dec to Mar cool in the north; spring and fall are warm and pleasant
BANKING 0830–1230 and 1600–1730 Mon, Tue and Thu; 0830–1230 Wed; 0830–1200 Fri
EMERGENCY Police/Fire 100; Ambulance 101
TIME ZONE GMT +2
INTERNATIONAL DIALING CODE 972

ITALY

GOVERNMENT Multiparty republic
LANGUAGES Italian (official), German, French, Slovene
CURRENCY Euro = 100 cents
MEDICAL There are no specific health risks
TRAVEL Crime is rare, but visitors in tourist areas and city centres should remain vigilant after dark
WEATHER Apr to May and Oct to Nov warm and pleasant; Jun to Sep hot; Dec to Mar colder temperatures with heavy snow in mountain areas; warmer in the south
BANKING Generally 0830–1330 and 1530–1930 Mon to Fri
EMERGENCY Police 112; Fire 115; Ambulance 113; Emergency Services 112
TIME ZONE GMT +1
INTERNATIONAL DIALING CODE 39

JAPAN

GOVERNMENT Constitutional monarchy
LANGUAGES Japanese (official)
CURRENCY Yen = 100 sen
MEDICAL Health and hygiene standards are high and visitors are not required to have vaccinations
TRAVEL Most visits remain trouble-free. There is a high risk of earthquakes and typhoons which often hit the country
WEATHER Sep to Nov typhoons and rain; Jun to Sep warm/very hot with rain in Jun; Mar to May pleasant; Dec to Feb cold winds and snow in western areas, but dry and clear on Pacific coast
BANKING 0900–1500 Mon to Fri
EMERGENCY Tokyo English Life Line 3403 7106; Japan Helpline 0120 461 997
TIME ZONE GMT +9
INTERNATIONAL DIALING CODE 81

KENYA

GOVERNMENT Multiparty republic
LANGUAGES Kiswahili and English (both official)
CURRENCY Kenyan shilling = 100 cents
MEDICAL Malaria is endemic and AIDS is widespread. Water is unsafe to drink
TRAVEL Be alert at all times, particularly in Nairobi and Mombasa. Avoid traveling after dark and in isolated areas
WEATHER Complex and changeable; Jan to Feb hot and dry; Mar to May hot and wet; Jun to Oct warm and dry; Nov to Dec warm and wet; Cooler with rain at any time at higher altitudes
BANKING 0900–1500 Mon to Fri; 0900–1100 on first and last Sat of each month
EMERGENCY All Services 336886/501280
TIME ZONE GMT +3
INTERNATIONAL DIALING CODE 254

JAMAICA

GOVERNMENT Constitutional monarchy
LANGUAGES English (official), patois English
CURRENCY Jamaican dollar = 100 cents
MEDICAL There are no specific health risks
TRAVEL Most visits are trouble-free, but violent crime does exist, mainly in Kingston. Visitors should avoid walking alone in isolated areas, and be particularly alert after dark and using public transport
WEATHER Tropical climate; temperatures remain high all year round; May to Oct rainy season, but showers can occur at any time
BANKING 0900–1400 Mon to Thu; 0900–1500 Fri
EMERGENCY Police 119; Fire/Ambulance 110
TIME ZONE GMT –5
INTERNATIONAL DIALING CODE 1 876

JORDAN

GOVERNMENT Constitutional monarchy
LANGUAGES Arabic (official)
CURRENCY Jordan dinar = 1,000 fils
MEDICAL There are no specific health risks, but visitors should consider vaccination against hepatitis, polio, tetanus, typhoid, and diptheria
TRAVEL Before traveling, visitors should monitor media reports for any increase in regional tension. Crime is low, but visitors should dress modestly and respect local customs
WEATHER Jun to Sep hot and dry with cool evenings; Nov to Mar cooler with rainfall
BANKING 0830–1230 and 1530–1730 Sat to Thu; 0830–1000 during Ramadan
EMERGENCY Police 192; Fire/Ambulance 193
TIME ZONE GMT +2
INTERNATIONAL DIALING CODE 962

KOREA, SOUTH

GOVERNMENT Multiparty republic
LANGUAGES Korean (official)
CURRENCY South Korean won = 100 chon
MEDICAL There are no specific health risks, but medical and dental treatment can be expensive
TRAVEL Travel to South Korea is generally trouble-free, but some form of identification should be carried at all times
WEATHER Jul to Aug hot with heavy rainfall and a chance of typhoons; Sep to Nov and Apr to May mild and dry; Dec to Mar cold but dry, with good skiing
BANKING 0930–1630 Mon to Fri; 0930–1330 Sat
EMERGENCY Unavailable
TIME ZONE GMT +9
INTERNATIONAL DIALING CODE 82

KUWAIT

GOVERNMENT Constitutional monarchy
LANGUAGES Arabic (official), English
CURRENCY Kuwaiti dinar = 1,000 fils
MEDICAL Vaccinations against polio, typhoid, and cholera are recommended
TRAVEL Visitors should monitor media reports before traveling. Any increase in regional tension will affect travel advice. There is a danger from unexploded bombs and land mines on beaches and in rural areas. All Islamic laws should be respected. Photography permits are required
WEATHER Apr to Oct hot, humid with little rain; Nov to Mar cool and dry
BANKING 0800–1200 Sun to Thu
EMERGENCY Unavailable
TIME ZONE GMT +3
INTERNATIONAL DIALING CODE 965

LEBANON

GOVERNMENT Multiparty republic
LANGUAGES Arabic (official), French, English
CURRENCY Lebanese pound = 100 piastres
MEDICAL Protection against polio and typhoid is recommended
TRAVEL Visitors should remain alert to international developments in the Middle East. Most governments currently advise against travel to areas within the Israeli Occupied Zone
WEATHER Jun to Sep hot and dry, but humid along the coast; Dec to May high rainfall with snow in mountains; spring and fall pleasant
BANKING 0830–1200 Mon to Sat
EMERGENCY Police 386 440 425; Fire 310 105; Ambulance 386 675
TIME ZONE GMT +2
INTERNATIONAL DIALING CODE 961

LIECHTENSTEIN

GOVERNMENT Hereditary constitutional monarchy
LANGUAGES German (official)
CURRENCY Swiss franc = 100 centimes
MEDICAL There is a risk of altitude sickness, sunburn, and hypothermia in the Alps
TRAVEL Most visits to Liechtenstein are trouble-free. The country is culturally and economically extremely similar to Switzerland. Winter sports are very popular in the Alps from Nov to Apr
WEATHER Temperate climate; Nov to Apr cool or cold; Jun to Sep warm with high rainfall
BANKING 0800–1630 Mon to Fri
EMERGENCY Police 117; Ambulance 144
TIME ZONE GMT +1
INTERNATIONAL DIALING CODE 41 75

LATVIA

GOVERNMENT Multiparty republic
LANGUAGES Latvian (official), Lithuanian, Russian
CURRENCY Latvian lat = 10 santimi
MEDICAL Visitors should protect themselves against tick-borne encephalitis, particularly if visiting forested areas
TRAVEL Most visits are trouble-free, but tourists should exercise caution since muggings and pickpocketing have increased recently. Use guarded car parks and keep valuables hidden
WEATHER Temperate climate; Apr to Sep warm and clear; Nov to Mar extremely cold; spring and fall mild
BANKING 1000–1800 Mon to Fri
EMERGENCY Police 02; Fire 01; Ambulance 03
TIME ZONE GMT +2
INTERNATIONAL DIALING CODE 371

LIBYA

GOVERNMENT Single-party socialist state
LANGUAGES Arabic (official), Berber
CURRENCY Libyan dinar = 1,000 dirhams
MEDICAL There is a slight risk of malaria, cholera, and hepatitis
TRAVEL Most visits to Libya are trouble-free, but any increase in regional tension will affect travel advice
WEATHER Warm all year round; Nov to Mar occasional rainfall; Apr to Sep can be very hot; May to Jun severe sandstorms from the south
BANKING 0800–1200 Sat to Wed (during winter); 0800–1200 Sat to Thu; 1600–1700 Sat and Wed (during summer)
EMERGENCY Unavailable
TIME ZONE GMT +1
INTERNATIONAL DIALING CODE 218

LITHUANIA

GOVERNMENT Multiparty republic
LANGUAGES Lithuanian (official), Russian, Polish
CURRENCY Litas = 100 centai
MEDICAL Travelers to forested areas should seek advice about protection against rabies and tick-borne encephalitis
TRAVEL There is a risk of pickpocketing, mugging, and bag-snatching, particularly on public transport. Be alert at all times and avoid quiet areas after dark
WEATHER Temperate climate; May to Sep warm; Oct to Nov mild; Nov to Mar can be very cold with snowfall common
BANKING 0900–1700 Mon to Fri
EMERGENCY Police 02; Fire 01; Ambulance 03
TIME ZONE GMT +2
INTERNATIONAL DIALING CODE 370

LUXEMBOURG

GOVERNMENT Constitutional monarchy (Grand Duchy)
LANGUAGES Luxembourgish (official), French, German
CURRENCY Euro = 100 cents
MEDICAL There are no specific health risks
TRAVEL Most travel to Luxembourg is trouble-free. The country is prosperous with a very high quality of life. Visitors may find it expensive compared to other European countries
WEATHER May to Sep warm with rainfall; Oct to Apr cold with snow
BANKING Varies greatly but generally 0900–1200 and 1330–1630 Mon to Fri
EMERGENCY Police 113; Fire/Ambulance 112
TIME ZONE GMT +1
INTERNATIONAL DIALING CODE 352

MADAGASCAR

GOVERNMENT Republic
LANGUAGES Malagasy and French (both official)
CURRENCY Malagasy franc = 100 centimes
MEDICAL There is a risk of polio, typhoid, bilharzia, cholera, rabies, and hepatitis. Precautions should be taken. Water is unsafe to drink and unpasteurized dairy products should be avoided
TRAVEL Locals are very welcoming and have a relaxed attitude toward time. Local culture should be respected
WEATHER Generally hot and subtropical with varying temperatures. Inland is more temperate, and the south is dry and arid
BANKING 0800–1300 Mon to Fri
EMERGENCY Unavailable
TIME ZONE GMT +3
INTERNATIONAL DIALING CODE 261

MALAWI

GOVERNMENT Multiparty republic
LANGUAGES Chichewa and English (both official)
CURRENCY Malawian kwacha = 100 tambala
MEDICAL AIDS and malaria are very common. Outbreaks of cholera do occur, particularly during the rainy season
TRAVEL Be alert at all times, particularly after dark. Avoid travel out of town at night since the condition of roads is poor. Cases of muggings and bag-snatching are increasing. Do not resist demands since attacks can be very violent
WEATHER Apr to Oct hot and dry; May to Jul cool and cold at night; Nov to Apr rainy season
BANKING 0800–1300 Mon to Fri
EMERGENCY Unavailable
TIME ZONE GMT +2
INTERNATIONAL DIALING CODE 265

MALAYSIA

GOVERNMENT Federal constitutional monarchy
LANGUAGES Malay (official), Chinese, English
CURRENCY Ringgit (Malaysian dollar) = 100 cents
MEDICAL No vaccinations required, but visitors should be up-to-date with typhoid, tetanus, and hepatitis B. Also check malarial status of region
TRAVEL The penalty for all drug offences is harsh. There has been a recent increase in street crime in Kuala Lumpur
WEATHER Nov to Feb heavy rains in eastern areas; Apr to May and Oct thunderstorms in western areas; showers can occur all year round
BANKING 1000–1500 Mon to Fri
EMERGENCY All Services 999
TIME ZONE GMT +8
INTERNATIONAL DIALING CODE 60

MALDIVES

GOVERNMENT Republic
LANGUAGES Maldivian Dhivehi, English
CURRENCY Rufiyaa = 100 laari
MEDICAL There is a high risk of sunburn all year round
TRAVEL Travel to the Maldives is generally trouble-free, but visitors should be aware that there are very harsh penalties for drug offences. Visitors should respect the Islamic religion and act accordingly
WEATHER Hot, tropical climate; May to Oct warm, but humid and wet from the southwest monsoon; Nov to Apr hot and dry
EMERGENCY Police 119; Fire 118; Ambulance 102
TIME ZONE GMT +5
INTERNATIONAL DIALING CODE 960

MALTA

GOVERNMENT Multiparty republic
LANGUAGES Maltese and English (both official)
CURRENCY Euro = 100 cents
MEDICAL There are no specific health risks
TRAVEL Most visits are trouble-free and crime is rare. However, bag-snatching and pickpocketing can occur. Caution should be exercised when traveling by car since many roads are poorly maintained. Visitors should dress modestly when visiting churches
WEATHER Jul to Sep hot with cool breezes; Feb to Jun mild; occasional sudden bursts of rain
BANKING 0800–1200 Mon to Thu; 0800–1200 and 1430–1600 Fri; 0800–1130 Sat
EMERGENCY Police 191; Ambulance 196
TIME ZONE GMT +1
INTERNATIONAL DIALING CODE 356

MARTINIQUE

GOVERNMENT Overseas department of France
LANGUAGES French, French Creole patois, English
CURRENCY Euro = 100 cents
MEDICAL There is a risk of sunburn and intestinal parasites. Bilharzia (schistosomiasis) may be present in fresh water
TRAVEL Travel to Martinique is generally trouble-free
WEATHER Warm all year round; Sep can be very humid; Feb to May cooler and dry; Oct to Dec higher rainfall; upland areas are cooler than lowlands
BANKING 0800–1600 Mon to Fri
EMERGENCY Police 17; Fire/Ambulance 18
TIME ZONE GMT −4
INTERNATIONAL DIALING CODE 596

MAURITIUS

GOVERNMENT Multiparty democracy
LANGUAGES French (official), Creole, English
CURRENCY Mauritian rupee = 100 cents
MEDICAL Malaria exists in the northern rural areas and there is a risk of bilharzia
TRAVEL Visitors should always respect local customs and traditions. Most visits are trouble-free, crime levels are low, but sensible precautions should be taken
WEATHER The weather is warm with a year-round sea breeze. Jan to May are the best months to visit. Tropical storms are likely to occur from Dec to Mar
BANKING 0930–1430 Mon to Fri; 0930–1130 Sat
EMERGENCY Unavailable
TIME ZONE GMT +4
INTERNATIONAL DIALING CODE 230

MEXICO

GOVERNMENT Federal republic
LANGUAGES Spanish (official)
CURRENCY Mexican peso = 100 centavos
MEDICAL Visitors should protect themselves against polio, tetanus, typhoid, and hepatitis A
TRAVEL Most visits are trouble-free, but visitors should remain aware of incidents of armed robbery in urban areas, particularly Mexico City, and should dress down accordingly
WEATHER May to Oct humid, rainy season; Oct to May warm and dry; lowland areas are warmer and upland areas are cooler all year round
BANKING 0900–1330 Mon to Fri
EMERGENCY All Services 08
TIME ZONE Spans three time zones from GMT −6 to −8
INTERNATIONAL DIALING CODE 52

MONGOLIA

GOVERNMENT Multiparty republic
LANGUAGES Khalkha Mongolian (official), Turkic, Russian
CURRENCY Tugrik = 100 möngös
MEDICAL Visitors should protect against brucellosis, cholera, and meningitis
TRAVEL Petty street crime is increasing. Visitors should avoid traveling alone after dark. In rural areas always carry a GPS and satellite phone
WEATHER May to Oct dry and mild; Nov to Apr bitterly cold. Note that between Oct and May sudden snowstorms can block roads and bring transport systems to a standstill
BANKING 1000–1500 Mon to Fri
EMERGENCY Unavailable
TIME ZONE GMT +9
INTERNATIONAL DIALING CODE 976

MONTENEGRO

GOVERNMENT Republic
LANGUAGES Serbian
CURRENCY Euro = 100 cents
MEDICAL There are no specific health risks, but the health system suffers from widespread shortages of medicines and other essentials
TRAVEL Most visits to Montenegro are trouble free but sensible precautions should be taken. Visitors should be vigilant for pickpocketing in public places and on public transport.
WEATHER Montenegro has a continental climate; Nov to Mar very cold; Jun to Sep warm with colder conditions in the mountain regions
BANKING 0700–1500 Mon to Fri; 0800–1400 Sat
EMERGENCY Police 92; Fire 93; Ambulance 94
TIME ZONE GMT +1
INTERNATIONAL DIALING CODE 382

MOROCCO

GOVERNMENT Constitutional monarchy
LANGUAGES Arabic (official), Berber, French
CURRENCY Moroccan dirham = 100 centimes
MEDICAL There are no specific health risks, but malaria is present in northern coastal areas
TRAVEL Visits are usually trouble-free, but visitors should only use authorized guides. Theft is increasing in major cities and valuables should be hidden at all times
WEATHER Winter cool and wet in north; Oct to Apr warm to hot in lowlands; Dec to Mar very cold in upland areas
BANKING 0830–1130 and 1430–1700 Mon to Fri (winter); 0800–1530 Mon to Fri (summer)
EMERGENCY Police 19; Fire/Ambulance 15
TIME ZONE GMT
INTERNATIONAL DIALING CODE 212

NAMIBIA

GOVERNMENT Multiparty republic
LANGUAGES English (official), Afrikaans, German
CURRENCY Namibian dollar = 100 cents
MEDICAL Malaria and bilharzia are endemic in the north and east respectively
TRAVEL Most visits are trouble-free. The Angola border should be avoided because of land mines left undetected after the civil war. Visitors should seek advice before traveling to townships
WEATHER Oct to Apr rain inland; May to Oct hot and dry; the coast is cool and relatively free of rain all year round
BANKING 0900–1530 Mon to Fri
EMERGENCY Police 1011; Fire 2032270; Ambulance 2032276
TIME ZONE GMT +2
INTERNATIONAL DIALING CODE 264

NETHERLANDS
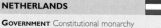

GOVERNMENT Constitutional monarchy
LANGUAGES Dutch (official), Frisian
CURRENCY Euro = 100 cents
MEDICAL There are no specific health risks in the Netherlands
TRAVEL Most visits to the Netherlands are trouble-free. Attitudes here are very liberal. Locals are extremely welcoming and speak very good English
WEATHER Jun to Sep usually warm but changeable; Nov to Mar can be bitterly cold with some snow; rain falls all year round; Apr is best for daffodils and May is best for tulips
BANKING 0900–1600 Mon to Fri
EMERGENCY Emergency Services 112
TIME ZONE GMT +1
INTERNATIONAL DIALING CODE 31

NEW ZEALAND

GOVERNMENT Constitutional monarchy
LANGUAGES English and Maori (both official)
CURRENCY New Zealand dollar = 100 cents
MEDICAL There are no specific health risks
TRAVEL Most visits are trouble-free, but visitors should take precautions against street crime in urban areas after dark. Travel within the country is relatively cheap and efficient, and accommodation is varied and affordable
WEATHER Subtropical climate in North Island; no extremes of heat or cold, but Nov to Apr warmer; temperate in South Island with cool temperatures; rainfall occurs all year round
BANKING 0900–1630 Mon to Fri
EMERGENCY All Services 111
TIME ZONE GMT +12
INTERNATIONAL DIALING CODE 64

NEPAL

GOVERNMENT Multiparty republic
LANGUAGES Nepali (official), local languages
CURRENCY Nepalese rupee = 100 paisa
MEDICAL There is a risk of altitude sickness, hepatitis A, malaria (in lowland areas), and typhoid
TRAVEL Trekkers are advised to use professional guides and should obtain up-to-date advice regarding the safety of their chosen route
WEATHER Oct to Nov clear and dry, and not too cold at higher altitudes; Dec to Jan cool; Feb to Apr warm; Jun to Sep monsoon season
BANKING 1000–1450 Sun to Thu; 1000–1230 Fri
EMERGENCY Unavailable
TIME ZONE GMT +5.45
INTERNATIONAL DIALING CODE 977

NETHERLANDS ANTILLES

GOVERNMENT Parliamentary democracy
LANGUAGES Dutch (official), French, English, Spanish, many others
CURRENCY Netherlands Antillean gilder = 100 cents
MEDICAL Polio and typhoid vaccinations are recommended. Water is considered drinkable and normal precautions should be taken with food
TRAVEL Most visits to the Netherlands Antilles are trouble-free
WEATHER Hot and tropical climate with cool sea breezes
BANKING 0830–1530 Mon to Fri
EMERGENCY Police 599/5/22222; Ambulance 599/5/22111
TIME ZONE GMT –4
INTERNATIONAL DIALING CODE 599

NIGERIA

GOVERNMENT Federal multiparty republic
LANGUAGES English (official), Hausa, Yoruba, Ibo
CURRENCY Naira = 100 kobo
MEDICAL Visitors must have a yellow fever vaccination and protect against cerebral malaria
TRAVEL Incidences of kidnapping are increasing. Violent street crime, armed robberies, and car theft are common throughout the country. Visitors should avoid using public transport and traveling after dark outside tourist areas
WEATHER Mar to Nov hot, humid and wet; Apr to Sep wet; Dec to Mar dusty winds, but cooler
BANKING 0800–1500 Mon; 0800–1330 Tue to Fri
EMERGENCY Unavailable
TIME ZONE GMT +1
INTERNATIONAL DIALING CODE 234

NORWAY

GOVERNMENT Constitutional monarchy
LANGUAGES Norwegian (official)
CURRENCY Norwegian krone = 100 ore
MEDICAL There are no specific health risks in Norway
TRAVEL Most visits to Norway remain trouble-free. The country offers beautiful mountain scenery and year-round skiing
WEATHER May to Sep sunny and warm with long daylight hours; Dec to Mar very cold and dark; midnight sun occurs from 13 May to 29 Jul, and from 28 May to 14 Jul in the Lofoten Islands
BANKING 0900–1700 Mon to Thu; 0900–1530 Fri
EMERGENCY Police (Oslo) 002; Ambulance 003
TIME ZONE GMT +1
INTERNATIONAL DIALING CODE 47

OMAN

GOVERNMENT Monarchy with consultative council
LANGUAGES Arabic (official), Baluchi, English
CURRENCY Omani rial = 100 baizas
MEDICAL Visitors should protect against malaria
TRAVEL Most visits to Oman are trouble-free, but visitors should remain informed of developments in the Middle East. There are harsh penalties, including the death penalty, for drug offences. Driving conditions are hazardous
WEATHER Jun to Sep very hot; Oct to Mar pleasant; the rest of the year is cooler
BANKING 0800–1200 Sat to Wed; 0800–1130 Thu
EMERGENCY All Services 999
TIME ZONE GMT +4
INTERNATIONAL DIALING CODE 698

PAKISTAN

GOVERNMENT Military regime
LANGUAGES Urdu (official), many others
CURRENCY Pakistan rupee = 100 paisa
MEDICAL Visitors should protect against dengue fever, hepatitis A, and malaria. There is also a risk of encephalitis in rural regions
TRAVEL Due to the threat from terrorism, most Western governments advise against all travel to Pakistan, except for their nationals of Pakistan origin
WEATHER Nov to Apr warm; Apr to Jul hot; Jul to Sep monsoon with high rainfall in upland areas
BANKING 0900–1300 and 1500–2000 Sun to Thu; closed on Fri. Some banks open on Sat
EMERGENCY Unavailable
TIME ZONE GMT +5
INTERNATIONAL DIALING CODE 92

PARAGUAY

GOVERNMENT Multiparty republic
LANGUAGES Spanish and Guaraní (both official)
CURRENCY Guaraní = 100 céntimos
MEDICAL There is a risk of cholera, hepatitis, hookworm, typhoid, malaria, and tuberculosis
TRAVEL Most visits to Paraguay are trouble-free, but there is economic recession and some political instability. Attractions include several national parks, including the Chaco – South America's great wilderness
WEATHER Subtropical climate; Dec to Mar is the hottest and wettest season, but rain falls all year round
BANKING 0845–1215 Mon to Fri
EMERGENCY All Services 00
TIME ZONE GMT +5
INTERNATIONAL DIALING CODE 595

PERU

GOVERNMENT Transitional republic
LANGUAGES Spanish and Quechua (both official), Aymara
CURRENCY New sol = 100 centavos
MEDICAL Visitors should protect against altitude sickness, cholera, typhoid, hepatitis, and malaria
TRAVEL Tourist areas are generally safe, but visitors should exercise caution, particularly in Lima and Cuzco, where crime has become a serious problem for foreign visitors
WEATHER Oct to Apr hot and dry in coastal areas, but much rainfall in highlands; May to Sep is dry and the best time to visit the highlands
BANKING 0930–1600 Mon to Fri
EMERGENCY All Services 011/5114
TIME ZONE GMT –5
INTERNATIONAL DIALING CODE 51

PHILIPPINES

GOVERNMENT Multiparty republic
LANGUAGES Filipino (Tagalog) and English (both official), Spanish, many others
CURRENCY Philippine peso = 100 centavos
MEDICAL Visitors should protect against cholera, malaria, rabies and hepatitis
TRAVEL Visitors should check developments before traveling. Bomb explosions and kidnapping by organized gangs or terrorists have occurred in Manila and Mindanao
WEATHER Tropical climate with sea breeze; Jun to Sep wet; Oct to Feb cool and dry; Mar to May hot and dry; Jun to Sep typhoons occur
BANKING 0900–1600 Mon to Fri
EMERGENCY Unavailable
TIME ZONE GMT +8
INTERNATIONAL DIALING CODE 63

POLAND

GOVERNMENT Multiparty republic
LANGUAGES Polish (official)
CURRENCY Zloty = 100 groszy
MEDICAL Medical care is generally poor,
particularly in rural regions
TRAVEL Most visits to Poland are trouble-free,
but there is a serious risk of robbery when using
public transport. Locals are very hospitable and
welcoming
WEATHER Temperate climate; May to Sep
warm; Nov to Mar cold and dark; spring and fall
are warm and pleasant; rain falls all
year round
BANKING 0800–1800 Mon to Fri
EMERGENCY Police 997; Ambulance 999
TIME ZONE GMT +1
INTERNATIONAL DIALING CODE 48

PORTUGAL

GOVERNMENT Multiparty republic
LANGUAGES Portuguese (official)
CURRENCY Euro = 100 cents
MEDICAL Sunburn is a risk during summer
TRAVEL Most visits are trouble-free. Children
under 18 years traveling to Portugal should be
accompanied by parents/guardians, or someone
in the country should be authorized to have
responsibility for them
WEATHER Apr to Oct hot and sunny; Nov to
Mar wetter, particularly in the north; summers
are hotter and winters are longer in the north
BANKING 0830–1500 Mon to Fri
EMERGENCY Emergency Services 112;
All Services 115
TIME ZONE GMT
INTERNATIONAL DIALING CODE 351

PUERTO RICO

GOVERNMENT Commonwealth of the
United States
LANGUAGES Spanish and English (both official)
CURRENCY US dollar = 100 cents
MEDICAL There is a risk of sunburn and a slight
risk of hepatitis and bilharzia
TRAVEL Most visits to Puerto Rico are
trouble-free
WEATHER Tropical climate with little variation
in temperature all year round; May to Nov
hurricane season; cooler in upland regions
BANKING 0900–1430 Mon to Thu; 0900–1430
and 1530–1700 Fri
EMERGENCY Police 787 343 2020; Fire 787 343
2330; All Services 911
TIME ZONE GMT –4
INTERNATIONAL DIALING CODE 1 787

QATAR

GOVERNMENT Constitutional absolute monarchy
LANGUAGES Arabic (official), English,
CURRENCY Qatari riyal = 100 dirhams
MEDICAL There are no specific health risks
TRAVEL Visitors should keep informed of
international developments before traveling.
It is prohibited to bring drugs, alcohol, religious
material, or pork products into the country;
videos may be censored. Visitors should dress
modestly and respect local customs
WEATHER Jun to Sep very hot and dry; Apr
to May and Dec to Feb frequent sandstorms;
Nov and Feb to Mar warm with little wind
BANKING 0730–1130 Sat to Thu
EMERGENCY All Services 999
TIME ZONE GMT +3
INTERNATIONAL DIALING CODE 974

RÉUNION

GOVERNMENT Overseas department of France
LANGUAGES French (official), Creole
CURRENCY Euro = 100 cents
MEDICAL Precautions should be taken against
typhoid and rabies. Water is unsafe to drink and
dairy products should be avoided as they are
unpasteurized
TRAVEL Most trips to Réunion are trouble-free.
Its society and culture are similar to Western
Europe. Usual precautions should be taken
WEATHER Hot and tropical with cooler
temperatures in the hills. Cool and dry from
May to Nov; hot and wet from Dec to Apr
BANKING 0800–1600 Mon to Fri
EMERGENCY Police 17; Fire 18; Ambulance 15
TIME ZONE GMT +4
INTERNATIONAL DIALING CODE 262

ROMANIA

GOVERNMENT Multiparty republic
LANGUAGES Romanian (official), Hungarian
CURRENCY Leu = 100 bani
MEDICAL Visitors should protect against rabies,
typhoid, and encephalitis
TRAVEL Petty theft is common in urban areas.
It is illegal to exchange money on the street.
Corruption is widespread. Roads are poorly
maintained
WEATHER May to Oct warm, but coastal areas
are cooled by sea breezes; Nov to Apr harsh
winter with snow, but milder along the coast
BANKING 0900–1200 Mon to Fri; 1300–1500
Mon to Fri (currency exchange only)
EMERGENCY Police 955; Fire 981; Ambulance 961
TIME ZONE GMT +2
INTERNATIONAL DIALING CODE 40

RUSSIA

GOVERNMENT Federal multiparty republic
LANGUAGES Russian (official), many others
CURRENCY Russian ruble = 100 kopeks
MEDICAL Visitors should protect against diptheria, hepatitis A, typhoid, and encephalitis
TRAVEL Travel to the Chechen Republic and northern Caucasus is inadvisable. Visitors should keep all valuables out of sight
WEATHER Variable climate in north and central regions; Jul to Aug warm and wet; May to Jun and Sep to Oct dry; Nov to Apr very cold with snow
BANKING 0930–1730 Mon to Fri
EMERGENCY Police 02; Fire 01; Ambulance 03
TIME ZONE GMT +3 in Moscow and St Petersburg. Other areas vary
INTERNATIONAL DIALING CODE 7

ST KITTS & NEVIS

GOVERNMENT Constitutional monarchy
LANGUAGES English
CURRENCY East Caribbean dollar = 100 cents
MEDICAL Visitors should protect against mosquito bites as dengue fever is present. Water is untreated and is unsafe to drink
TRAVEL Most visits are trouble-free. The islands are now commercialized and tourists are welcomed. Usual precautions should be taken
WEATHER Hot and tropical with cooling sea breezes. There is little seasonal temperature variation. Hurricane season is Aug to Oct
BANKING 0800–1500 Mon to Thu; 0800-1500/1700 Fri; 0830-1100 Sat
EMERGENCY All Services 911
TIME ZONE GMT –4
INTERNATIONAL DIALING CODE 1 869

ST LUCIA

GOVERNMENT Parliamentary democracy
LANGUAGES English (official), French patois
CURRENCY East Caribbean dollar = 100 cents
MEDICAL Dengue fever is present; precautions should be taken against mosquito bites. Polio and typhoid vaccinations are recommended
TRAVEL Most trips to St Lucia are trouble-free, but sensible precautions should be taken. Beachwear should not be worn in towns
WEATHER Tropical climate moderated by trade winds. Temperatures are uniform at about 79°F [26°C]. St Lucia lies in the hurricane belt
BANKING 0800–1500 Mon to Thu; 0800–1700 Fri; 0800–1200 Sat
EMERGENCY All Services 999
TIME ZONE GMT –4
INTERNATIONAL DIALING CODE 1 758

ST VINCENT & THE GRENADINES

GOVERNMENT Parliamentary democracy
LANGUAGES English
CURRENCY East Caribbean dollar = 100 cents
MEDICAL Protection from polio, typhoid, and mosquito bites are recommended
TRAVEL Sensible precautions should be taken. There is a relaxed society and most visits are trouble-free. Excellent West Indian cuisine can be found on St Vincent
WEATHER Tropical climate with cooling trade winds. Hottest months are Jun and Jul. Tropical storms may occur from Jun to Nov
BANKING 0800–1500 Mon to Thu; 0800–1700 Fri
EMERGENCY All Services 999
TIME ZONE GMT –4
INTERNATIONAL DIALING CODE 1 809

SAMOA

GOVERNMENT Mix of parliamentary democracy and constitutional monarchy
LANGUAGES Samoan (Polynesian), English
CURRENCY Samoan dollar = 100 sene
MEDICAL Vaccination against polio and typhoid are recommended. Water is untreated and is unsafe to drink
TRAVEL Most visits are trouble-free, but traditional moral and religious codes are very important. Beachwear should not be worn outside resorts
WEATHER Tropical climate with cooler temperatures in the evenings. The rainy season is from Dec to Apr
BANKING 0900–1500 Mon to Fri; 0830–1130 Sat
EMERGENCY All services 999
TIME ZONE GMT –11
INTERNATIONAL DIALING CODE 685

SAUDI ARABIA

GOVERNMENT Absolute monarchy with consultative assembly
LANGUAGES Arabic (official)
CURRENCY Saudi riyal = 100 halalas
MEDICAL Cases of cerebral malaria have been reported in Jizan, southwest Saudi Arabia
TRAVEL Visitors should seek advice on recent developments. Islamic customs must be followed. Bombings have occurred in Riyadh and visitors should remain extremely vigilant
WEATHER Desert climate; extremely dry; May to Oct very hot; Nov to Feb mild
BANKING 0830–1200 and 1700–1900 Sat to Wed; 0830–1200 Thu
EMERGENCY Unavailable
TIME ZONE GMT +3
INTERNATIONAL DIALING CODE 966

SERBIA

GOVERNMENT Republic
LANGUAGES Serbian (official), Albanian
CURRENCY New dinar = 100 paras
MEDICAL The medical system is suffering from widespread shortages. Visitors should protect themselves against hepatitis and rabies.
TRAVEL The situation in Serbia is calm at present, though visitors should seek advice on developments before travelling. Travel to Kosovo is still inadvisable
WEATHER Serbia has a continental climate with a gradual transition between the four seasons. Nov to Mar very cold; Jun to Sep warm
BANKING 0700–1500 Mon to Fri; 0800-1400 Sat
EMERGENCY Police 92; Fire 93; Ambulance 94
TIME ZONE GMT +1
INTERNATIONAL DIALLING CODE 381

SEYCHELLES

GOVERNMENT Democratic republic
LANGUAGES English, French, French Creole
CURRENCY Seychelles rupee = 100 cents
MEDICAL There are no specific health risks
TRAVEL Crime is relatively rare, but incidents of theft do occur in tourist areas. Visitors, particularly women, should remain vigilant and avoid walking in quiet areas after dark. Roads often have sheer drops and no barriers
WEATHER Nov to Feb hot, humid monsoon; very warm temperatures all year round; May and Oct breezy at the start and finish of the trade winds
BANKING 0830–1430 Mon to Fri
EMERGENCY Unavailable
TIME ZONE GMT +4
INTERNATIONAL DIALLING CODE 248

SINGAPORE

GOVERNMENT Multiparty republic
LANGUAGES Chinese, Malay, Tamil and English (all official)
CURRENCY Singapore dollar = 100 cents
MEDICAL There are no specific health risks
TRAVEL The crime rate is very low in Singapore and most visits remain trouble-free. There are harsh penalties, including the death penalty, for all drug offences. Smoking is illegal in public places
WEATHER Hot and humid all year round; Nov to Jan low with most rainfall
BANKING 1000–1500 Mon to Fri; 1100-1600 Sat
EMERGENCY All Services 999
TIME ZONE GMT +8
INTERNATIONAL DIALLING CODE 65

SLOVAK REPUBLIC

GOVERNMENT Multiparty republic
LANGUAGES Slovak (official), Hungarian
CURRENCY Slovak koruna = 100 halierov
MEDICAL There is risk from rabies and tick-borne encephalitis in forested areas during summer months
TRAVEL Pickpockets operate around the main tourist areas, and foreigners are easily identified and targeted. Sensible precautions should be taken
WEATHER A temperate climate with cold winters and mild summers
BANKING 0800–1700 Mon to Fri
EMERGENCY Fire 150; Ambulance 155; Police 158
TIME ZONE GMT +1 in winter; GMT +2 in summer
INTERNATIONAL DIALLING CODE 42

SLOVENIA

GOVERNMENT Multiparty republic
LANGUAGES Slovene (official), Serbo-Croatian
CURRENCY Tolar = 100 stotin
MEDICAL Summer visitors to forested areas should seek advice about protection against tick-borne encephalitis
TRAVEL Harsh fines are given for traffic offences and jaywalking. Passports and international driving licences should be carried at all times
WEATHER Continental climate inland; Jun to Sep warm; Nov to Mar cold; Mediterranean climate in coastal areas; Sep is the best time for hiking and climbing
BANKING 0800–1800 Mon to Fri
EMERGENCY Police 92; Fire 93; Ambulance 94
TIME ZONE GMT +1
INTERNATIONAL DIALLING CODE 386

SOUTH AFRICA

GOVERNMENT Multiparty republic
LANGUAGES Afrikaans, English, Ndebele, Pedi, Sotho, Swazi, Tsonga, Tswana, Venda, Xhosa and Zulu (all official)
CURRENCY Rand = 100 cents
MEDICAL There is a high incidence of HIV/AIDS. Malaria is a risk in certain areas. Hygiene and water standards are high in tourist areas
TRAVEL Violent crime is high in the townships. There is a risk of car-jacking and armed robbery. Visitors should take valuables and seek advice about which areas to avoid
WEATHER Generally warm and sunny all year
BANKING 0830–1530 Mon to Fri
EMERGENCY Police 1011; Ambulance 10222
TIME ZONE GMT +2
INTERNATIONAL DIALLING CODE 27

SPAIN

GOVERNMENT Constitutional monarchy
LANGUAGES Castilian Spanish (official), Catalan, Galician, Basque
CURRENCY Euro = 100 cents
MEDICAL There are no specific health risks in Spain
TRAVEL Most visits to Spain are trouble-free. The country is rich in arts and culture
WEATHER Temperate in north; Apr to Oct hot and dry, particularly in the south; central plateau can by very cold during winter
BANKING 0900–1400 Mon to Fri; 0900–1300 Sat (but not during summer)
EMERGENCY Police 091; Fire/Ambulance 085; Emergency Services 112
TIME ZONE GMT +1
INTERNATIONAL DIALING CODE 34

SWEDEN

GOVERNMENT Constitutional monarchy
LANGUAGES Swedish (official), Finnish, Sami
CURRENCY Swedish krona = 100 öre
MEDICAL There are no specific health risks
TRAVEL Most visits to Sweden are generally trouble-free. Since devaluation of the Swedish currency, the country has become considerably more affordable
WEATHER May to Jul hot and dry, but Aug can be wet; the midnight sun can be seen from May to Jun above the Arctic Circle; Nov to Apr extremely cold, particularly in the north
BANKING 0930–1500 Mon to Fri
EMERGENCY Emergency Services 112; All Services 90 000/112
TIME ZONE GMT +1
INTERNATIONAL DIALING CODE 46

SYRIA

GOVERNMENT Multiparty republic
LANGUAGES Arabic (official), Kurdish, Armenian
CURRENCY Syrian pound = 100 piastres
MEDICAL Visitors should vaccinate against polio, hepatitis A and B, and tetanus
TRAVEL Visitors should keep informed of developments in the Middle East. They should dress modestly and avoid driving out of main cities at night. Harsh penalties exist for drug offences
WEATHER Apr to Jun mild and dry; Jun to Sep hot; Dec to Mar very cold, particularly in coastal and upland regions
BANKING 0800–1400 Sat and Thu
EMERGENCY Contact hotel operator
TIME ZONE GMT +2
INTERNATIONAL DIALING CODE 963

SRI LANKA

GOVERNMENT Multiparty republic
LANGUAGES Sinhala and Tamil (both official)
CURRENCY Sri Lankan rupee = 100 cents
MEDICAL There is a risk of cholera and malaria. Rabies is widespread
TRAVEL The northern region and the eastern coast remain heavily mined. A cease-fire between the Tamil Tigers and the government was signed in February 2002
WEATHER Tropical climate; May to Jul and Dec to Jan monsoon seasons; coastal regions are cool due to sea breezes
BANKING 0900–1300 Mon to Sat; 0900–1500 Tue to Fri
EMERGENCY All Services 1 691095/699935
TIME ZONE GMT +5.30
INTERNATIONAL DIALING CODE 94

SWITZERLAND

GOVERNMENT Federal republic
LANGUAGES French, German, Italian and Romansch (all official)
CURRENCY Swiss franc = 100 centimes
MEDICAL There is a risk of altitude sickness, sunburn and hypothermia in the Alps
TRAVEL Most visits to Switzerland remain trouble-free
WEATHER Climate varies from region to region; Alpine regions have lower temperatures; Jun to Sep warm and sunny; Nov to Apr cold with snow which starts to melt in Apr
BANKING 0830–1630 Mon to Fri
EMERGENCY Police 117; Fire 118; Ambulance 144
TIME ZONE GMT +1
INTERNATIONAL DIALING CODE 41

TAIWAN

GOVERNMENT Unitary multiparty republic
LANGUAGES Mandarin Chinese (official)
CURRENCY New Taiwan dollar = 100 cents
MEDICAL There are no specific health risks, but visitors should be vaccinated against hepatitis
TRAVEL Most visits to Taiwan are trouble-free. Petty crime exists, but is not common. Some roads in central and southern areas may still be blocked by landslides following the 1999 earthquake
WEATHER Subtropical climate with moderate temperatures in the north; Jun to Sep very hot and humid; Jun to Oct typhoon season
BANKING 0900–1530 Mon to Fri; 0900–1230 Sat
EMERGENCY Police 110
TIME ZONE GMT +8
INTERNATIONAL DIALING CODE 886

TANZANIA

GOVERNMENT Multiparty republic
LANGUAGES Swahili and English (both official)
CURRENCY Tanzanian shilling = 100 cents
MEDICAL There is a risk of yellow fever, malaria, cholera, and hepatitis. AIDS is widespread
TRAVEL Most visits are trouble-free, but crime does occur, particularly on public transport and in tourist areas. There are increased risks in Zanzibar where bomb explosions have occurred
WEATHER Tropical climate; Mar to May rainy season in coastal areas; Jan to Feb hot and dry; Nov to Dec and Feb to May rainy season in highland areas
BANKING 0830–1600 Mon to Fri
EMERGENCY Unavailable
TIME ZONE GMT +3
INTERNATIONAL DIALING CODE 255

THAILAND

GOVERNMENT Constitutional monarchy
LANGUAGES Thai (official), English, local dialects
CURRENCY Baht = 100 satang
MEDICAL Visitors should protect against malaria, dengue fever, AIDS, and cholera
TRAVEL Harsh penalties exist for drug offences. Tourists should use licensed taxis with yellow number plates. Visitors should seek advice before traveling to border areas with Burma or Cambodia. Riptides occur off the coast of Phuket
WEATHER Jun to Oct hot and rainy monsoon; Nov to Feb dry and pleasant; Mar to May hot; temperatures are more consistent in the south
BANKING 0830–1530 Mon to Fri
EMERGENCY Unavailable
TIME ZONE GMT +7
INTERNATIONAL DIALING CODE 66

TRINIDAD & TOBAGO

GOVERNMENT Parliamentary democracy
LANGUAGES English (official), Spanish
CURRENCY Trinidad & Tobago dollar = 100 cents
MEDICAL Dengue fever has become a problem in recent years. Medical facilities are basic and limited
TRAVEL While most visits are trouble-free, attacks on travelers are on the increase. Visitors should remain vigilant and alert at all times, and take sensible precautions
WEATHER Tropical climate with cooling trade winds. Hottest and wettest time is Jun to Nov
BANKING 0900–1400 Mon to Thu; 0900–1200 and 1500–1700 Fri
EMERGENCY Police 999; Ambulance/Fire 990
TIME ZONE GMT –4
INTERNATIONAL DIALING CODE 1 868

TUNISIA

GOVERNMENT Multiparty republic
LANGUAGES Arabic (official), French
CURRENCY Tunisian dinar = 1,000 millimes
MEDICAL There is a risk of yellow fever and malaria
TRAVEL Travel to Tunisia is generally trouble-free, but visitors to southern desert areas and to areas close to the Algerian border should exercise caution. Tunisian laws and customs should be respected. Drug offences carry harsh penalties
WEATHER Jun to Aug hot and humid; Jan to Feb. cooler; hotter inland; higher rainfall in winter
BANKING 0830–1200 and 1300–1700 Mon to Fri
EMERGENCY Unavailable
TIME ZONE GMT +1
INTERNATIONAL DIALING CODE 216

TURKEY

GOVERNMENT Multiparty republic
LANGUAGES Turkish (official), Kurdish, Arabic
CURRENCY New Turkish lira = 100 kurus
MEDICAL Contagious diseases are increasing and visitors should keep inoculations up-to-date
TRAVEL Most visits are trouble-free, but visitors should exercise caution, particularly in the tourist areas of Istanbul where street robbery is common, and seek recent advice before traveling
WEATHER Mediterranean climate; summers are hot and winters are mild
BANKING 0830–1200 and 1300–1700 Mon to Fri
EMERGENCY Police 155; Fire 111; Ambulance 112
TIME ZONE GMT +2
INTERNATIONAL DIALING CODE 90

UGANDA

GOVERNMENT Republic in transition
LANGUAGES English and Swahili (both official)
CURRENCY Ugandan shilling = 100 cents
MEDICAL There is a risk of AIDS, yellow fever, and malaria
TRAVEL Most visits to Uganda are trouble-free, but visitors should seek recent advice before traveling. It is inadvisable to travel to areas bordering the Democratic Republic of the Congo or Sudan, and visitors should remain cautious if traveling to areas bordering Rwanda
WEATHER Dec to Feb and Jun to Aug hot and dry; Mar to May and Oct to Nov heavy rain
BANKING 0830–1400 Mon to Fri
EMERGENCY Unavailable
TIME ZONE GMT +3
INTERNATIONAL DIALING CODE 256

UKRAINE

Government Multiparty republic
Languages Ukrainian (official), Russian
Currency Hryvnia = 100 kopiykas
Medical There is a risk of diptheria in western Ukraine. Tick-borne encephalitis is common in forested areas. Do not drink tap water without first boiling it
Travel Crime in the Ukraine remains low, but visitors should remain vigilant and keep valuables out of sight, particularly in crowded areas where pickpocketing and bag-snatching can occur
Weather Jun to Aug warm; Oct to Nov sunny but cold; Dec to Mar cold with snowfall
Banking 0900–1600 Mon to Fri
Emergency Unavailable
Time zone GMT +2
International dialing code 380

UNITED KINGDOM

Government Constitutional monarchy
Languages English (official), Welsh, Gaelic
Currency Pound sterling = 100 pence
Medical No vaccinations are required in the UK and citizens of all EU countries are entitled to free medical treatment at National Health Service hospitals
Travel Most visits are trouble-free, but visitors should exercise caution in urban areas after dark
Weather May to Aug warm and wet; Sep to Apr mild and wet
Banking 0900–1730 Mon to Fri. Some bank branches open on Saturday mornings
Emergency Police/Fire/Ambulance 999; Emergency Services 112
Time zone GMT
International dialing code 44

URUGUAY

Government Multiparty republic
Languages Spanish (official)
Currency Uruguayan peso = 100 centésimos
Medical There are no specific health risks, but medical treatment can be expensive
Travel Most visits to Uruguay are trouble-free, but street crime exists in urban areas, including Montevideo. It is, however, less common than in other Latin American countries
Weather Dec to Mar hot, but nights can be cool; Apr to Nov mild
Banking 1330–1730 Mon to Fri (summer); 1300–1700 Mon to Fri (winter)
Emergency Police 109; Fire 104; Ambulance 105; All Services 999
Time zone GMT −3
International dialing code 598

UNITED ARAB EMIRATES

Government Federation of seven emirates, each with its own government
Languages Arabic (official), English
Currency Dirham = 100 fils
Medical There is a risk of hepatitis A and B
Travel Visitors should remain informed of recent international developments before traveling. They should dress modestly and respect local customs. Penalties for all drug offences are harsh and can include the death penalty
Weather Jun to Sep very hot and dry; Oct to May cooler and is the best time to visit
Banking 0800–1200 Sat to Wed and 0800–1100 Thu
Emergency All Services 344 663
Time zone GMT +4
International dialing code 971

UNITED STATES OF AMERICA

Government Federal republic
Languages English (official), Spanish, more than 30 others
Currency US dollar = 100 cents
Medical There are no specific health risks, but medical treatment is expensive
Travel Most visits to the USA are trouble-free, but visitors should remain vigilant and avoid wearing valuable jewelry or walking through isolated urban areas after dark
Weather Varies considerably; check climate before traveling
Banking 0900–1500 Mon to Fri
Emergency Emergency Services 911
Time zone USA has six time zones from GMT −5 on East coast to −10 in Hawai'i
International dialing code 1

VENEZUELA

Government Federal republic
Languages Spanish (official), local dialects
Currency Bolívar = 100 céntimos
Medical There is a risk of yellow fever, cholera, dengue fever, and hepatitis
Travel The incidence of violent crime is high and the political situation is volatile. Visitors should take precautions. Terrorist and narcotic gangs are active in areas bordering Colombia, where there is the risk of kidnapping
Weather May to Dec rainy season; Jan to Apr pleasant temperatures
Banking 0830–1130 and 1400–1630 Mon to Fri
Emergency Doctor 02 483 7021; Ambulance 02 545 4545
Time zone GMT −4
International dialing code 58

VIETNAM

GOVERNMENT Socialist republic
LANGUAGES Vietnamese (official), English, Chinese
CURRENCY Dong = 10 hao = 100 xu
MEDICAL Malaria, dengue fever, and encephalitis are common throughout the country. Visitors should avoid mosquito bites. Typhoid is common in the Mekong Delta
TRAVEL Take care if traveling in border areas. Unexploded mines and bombs still exist in certain areas. Drug smuggling carries the death penalty. Serious flooding can occur in central areas
WEATHER May to Oct tropical monsoons; Nov to Apr hot and dry
BANKING 0800–1630 Mon to Fri
EMERGENCY Police 13; Fire 14; Ambulance 15
TIME ZONE GMT +7
INTERNATIONAL DIALING CODE 84

VIRGIN ISLANDS, BRITISH

GOVERNMENT UK overseas territory
LANGUAGES English (official)
CURRENCY US dollar = 100 cents
MEDICAL Medical facilities are limited. Precautions should be taken against polio, typhoid and dengue fever
TRAVEL There is a low crime rate, but sensible precautions should be taken. Backpacking is discouraged throughout the 60 islands
WEATHER Subtropical and humid climate moderated by trade winds. Hurricanes are a risk from Jul to Oct
BANKING 0900–1500 Mon to Thu; 0900–1700 Fri
EMERGENCY Police 114; Ambulance 112
TIME ZONE GMT –4
INTERNATIONAL DIALING CODE 1 284

VIRGIN ISLANDS, US

GOVERNMENT US overseas territory
LANGUAGES English, Spanish, French, Creole
CURRENCY US dollar = 100 cents
MEDICAL Visitors should protect against typhoid and polio. Water is generally considered drinkable
TRAVEL Most visit are trouble-free and normal precautions should be taken. There is a large selection of hotel accommodation available
WEATHER Hot climate with cool winds. Low humidity with little seasonal temperature variation. The rainy season is Sep to Nov
BANKING 0900–1430 Mon to Thu; 0900–1400 and 1530–1700 Fri
EMERGENCY All services 911
TIME ZONE GMT –4
INTERNATIONAL DIALING CODE 1 340

YEMEN

GOVERNMENT Multiparty republic
LANGUAGES Arabic (official)
CURRENCY Yemeni rial = 100 fils
MEDICAL Visitors should protect against hepatitis A and B
TRAVEL Most governments currently strongly advise against travel to Yemen. Random armed kidnapping is common, and foreigners remain targets for crime and terrorism
WEATHER Varies with altitude; Oct to Mar nights can be very cold in upland regions; Apr to Sep very hot; Oct to Apr cool, dry and dusty
BANKING 0800–1200 Sat to Wed; 0800–1100 Thu. Closed on Fridays
EMERGENCY Unavailable
TIME ZONE GMT +3
INTERNATIONAL DIALING CODE 967

ZAMBIA

GOVERNMENT Multiparty republic
LANGUAGES English (official), Bemba, Nyanja
CURRENCY Zambian kwacha = 100 ngwee
MEDICAL Outbreaks of cholera and dysentery are common. Malaria is endemic, and cases of AIDS and tuberculosis are very high
TRAVEL Visitors should avoid traveling to areas bordering Angola and the Democratic Republic of the Congo. Armed robbery, bag-snatching and mugging are increasing, particularly in downtown areas. Keep valuables out of sight
WEATHER May to Sep very cool and dry; Oct to Nov hot and dry; Dec to Apr hot and wet
BANKING 0815–1430 Mon to Fri
EMERGENCY All Services 1 2 25067/254798
TIME ZONE GMT +2
INTERNATIONAL DIALING CODE 260

ZIMBABWE

GOVERNMENT Multiparty republic
LANGUAGES English (official), Shona, Ndebele
CURRENCY Zimbabwean dollar = 100 cents
MEDICAL There is a risk of bilharzia, cholera, malaria, yellow fever, and rabies. Incidences of HIV/AIDS are very high
TRAVEL There is currently political and social unrest throughout the country, in both rural and urban areas. Visitors should exercise caution and avoid large crowds and demonstrations
WEATHER May to Oct warm and dry, but cold at night; Nov to Apr wet and hot
BANKING 0800–1500 Mon, Tue, Thu and Fri. 0800–1300 Wed and 0800–1130 Sat
EMERGENCY Police 995; Ambulance 994
TIME ZONE GMT +2
INTERNATIONAL DIALING CODE 263

World Maps — general reference

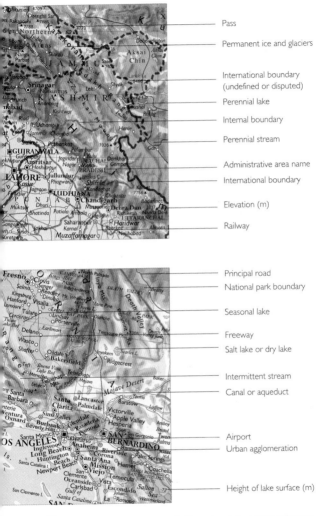

- Pass
- Permanent ice and glaciers
- International boundary (undefined or disputed)
- Perennial lake
- Internal boundary
- Perennial stream
- Administrative area name
- International boundary
- Elevation (m)
- Railway

- Principal road
- National park boundary
- Seasonal lake
- Freeway
- Salt lake or dry lake
- Intermittent stream
- Canal or aqueduct
- Airport
- Urban agglomeration
- Height of lake surface (m)

Settlements

Capital cities have red infills

Settlement symbols and type styles vary according to the scale of each map and indicate the importance of towns rather than specific population figures.

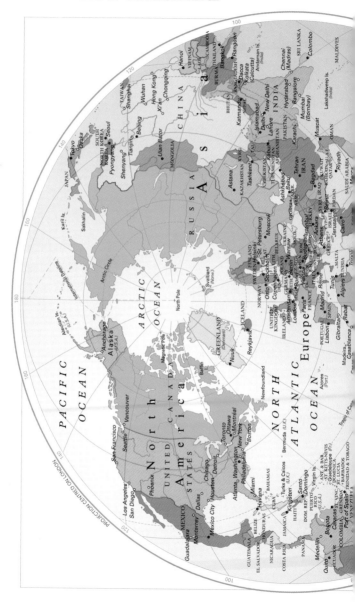

3

OCEAN

Chagos Arch. (U.K.)

SEYCHELLES

SOMALIA *Mogadishu*

DJIBOUTI
ETHIOPIA
Asmara ERITREA
Khartoum SUDAN

MAURITIUS

Réunion (Fr.) MADAGASCAR
Antananarivo

COMOROS
Mayotte (Fr.)
Dar es Salaam
TANZANIA *Dodoma*

MOZAMBIQUE
Lilongwe MALAWI
Harare ZIMBABWE

Maputo
SWAZILAND
Pretoria *Johannesburg*
LESOTHO

20 East from Greenwich 60 40

PROJECTION CENTRED ON TOKYO

Buenos Aires
Rio de Janeiro
New York
Lisbon
Los Angeles
Mexico City
Honolulu
Tokyo
Beijing
Paris London Rome
Cairo
Moscow
Mumbai (Bombay)
Hong Kong
Kolkata (Calcutta)
Singapore
Darwin
Sydney
Wellington
Nairobi
Johannesburg

Capital cities have red infills

The maps have been constructed on an Oblique
Azimuthal Equidistant projection, on which all
distances measured through the centre point are
true to scale. The green lines are drawn at 5,000,
10,000 and 15,000 km from the central city.

COPYRIGHT PHILIP'S

PROJECTION CENTRED ON MEXICO CITY

Nairobi
Lagos
Mumbai (Bombay)
Beijing
Kolkata (Calcutta)
Moscow
Berlin Copenhagen
Paris Rome
Lisbon
Tokyo
London Toronto
Chicago New York
Los Angeles
Caracas
Rio de Janeiro
Buenos Aires
Mexico City
Honolulu
Hong Kong
Singapore
Johannesburg
Darwin
Sydney
Wellington

Projection: Oblique Azimuthal Equidistant

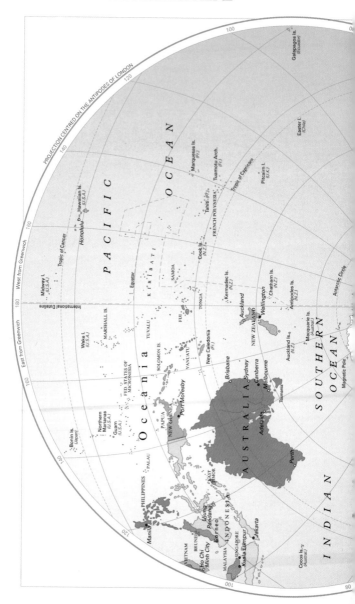

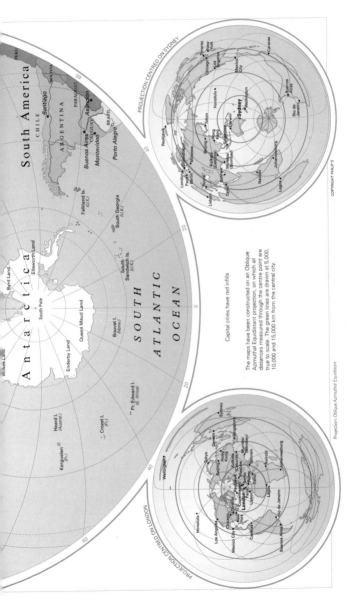

5

PROJECTION CENTRED ON SYDNEY

PROJECTION CENTRED ON LONDON

Capital cities have red infills

The maps have been constructed on an Oblique Azimuthal Equidistant projection, on which all distances measured through the centre point are true to scale. The green lines are drawn at 5,000, 10,000 and 15,000 km from the central city.

Projection: Oblique Azimuthal Equidistant

COPYRIGHT PHILIP'S

South America

CHILE

Santiago

ARGENTINA

PARAGUAY

Asunción

URUGUAY

BRAZIL

Buenos Aires

Montevideo

Porto Alegre

BOLIVIA

PERU

Falkland Is.
(U.K.)

South Georgia
(U.K.)

South
Sandwich Is.
(U.K.)

Bouvet I.
(Norw.)

Pr. Edward I.
(S. African)

Crozet I.
(Fr.)

Kerguelen
(Fr.)

Heard I.
(Austral.)

SOUTH

ATLANTIC

OCEAN

Antarctica

Byrd Land

Ellsworth Land

South Pole

Queen Maud Land

Enderby Land

Wilkes Land

Projection: Bonne · West from Greenwich · 0 · East from Greenwich

■ LONDON Capital Cities

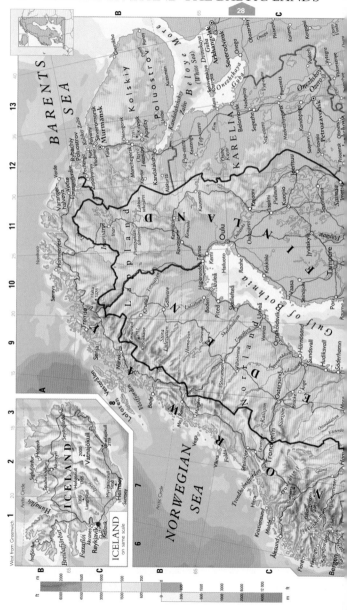

50 0 100 200 300 400 km

50 0 50 100 150 200 250 miles

COPYRIGHT PHILIP'S

D E F

RUSSIA

Cherepovets
Rybinsk
Res.
Tikhvin
Konoshlad
Borovichi
Bologoye
Vyshny Volochek
Tver
Rzhev
Zelenograd
MOSKVA
(Moscow)
Klin'y
Odintsovo
Kaluga
Belev
Orel
Kursk
Sumy
Okhtyrka
Poltava
Cherkasy
Konotop

12

ESTONIA
Espoo Helsinki
Gulf of Finland
SANKT
PETERBURG
(St. Petersburg)
Kohtla-Järve
Narva
Tartu
Pärnu
Kolpino
Novgorod
Dno
Staraya
Russa
Pskov
Ozero
Chudskoye
Ostrov
Velikiye
Luki
Smolensk
Vyazma
Roslavl
Bryansk
Chernihiv
Nizhyn
Pryluky
Pereyaslav-
Khmelnytskyy
Bila Tserkva
Berdychiv

LATVIA
Ventspils
Hiiumaa (Dago)
Saaremaa
Gulf of Riga
Riga
Jelgava
Rēzekne
Daugavpils
Polatsk
Vitsyebsk
Orsha
Mahilyow
Babruysk
Zhlobin
Homyel
Korosten
Zhytomyr

LITHUANIA
Liepāja
Šiauliai
Panevėžys
Klaipėda
Sovetsk
Kaliningrad
(Russia)
Kaunas
Vilnius
Hrodna
BELARUS
Baranavichy
Slutsk
Pinsk
Polesye
Marshes
Luninyets
Rivne
Lutsk

UKRAINE
KYÏV
(Kiev)
17 30

11

10

BALTIC SEA
STOCKHOLM
Uppsala
Solna
Eskilstuna
Norrköping
Linköping
Nyköping
Gotland
Visby
Öland
Kalmar
Karlskrona
Świnoujście
Szczecin
Gdynia
Gdańsk
Elbląg
Olsztyn
Suwałki
Białystok
Augustów
Soldau
Łomża
Brest

Sveland
Karlstad
Örebro
Västerås
Borås
Jönköping
Trollhättan
Göteborg
(Gothenburg)
Halmstad
Helsingborg
Lund
Malmö
KØBENHAVN
(Copenhagen)
Bornholm
Koszalin
Słupsk
Toruń
Bydgoszcz
Płock
WARSZAWA
(Warsaw)
Radom
Lublin
Rzeszów
Przemyśl

Götaland

DENMARK
Ålborg
Randers
Århus
Esbjerg
Odense
Svendborg
Fyn
Storebælt
Sjælland
Rügen
Stralsund
Rostock
Lübeck
Kiel
Flensburg
Holstebro
Schleswig

POLAND
Poznań
Kalisz
Łódź
Wrocław
Legnica
Wałbrzych
Opole
Częstochowa
Katowice
Kraków
Tarnów

9

GERMANY
HAMBURG
BERLIN
Potsdam
Magdeburg
Hannover
Braunschweig
Halle
Leipzig
Dresden
Erfurt
Chemnitz
Cottbus
Görlitz
Zwickau
Bremen
Osnabrück
Münster
Dortmund
Emden
Helgoland
Kassel
Fulda
Würzburg
Frankfurt
Darmstadt
Mannheim
Heidelberg
Nürnberg

CZECH REP.
PRAHA
(Prague)
Liberec
Hradec
Králové
Ostrava
Žilina

16

8

7

Projection: Conical with two standard parallels

20 East from Greenwich

15

55

50

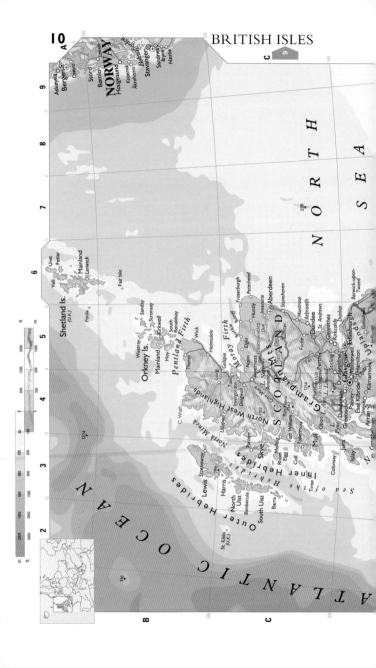

ATLANTIC OCEAN

NORTH SEA

NORWAY

Bergen
Askøyna
Osøyro
Stord
Bømlo
Haugesund
Kopervik
Åkrehamn
Stavanger
Sandnes
Bryne
Nærbø
Lenvik

Shetland Is.
(U.K.)
Unst
Yell
Fetlar
Mainland
Lerwick
Foula

Fair Isle

Orkney Is.
Mainland
Hoy
Kirkwall
Sanday
Stronsay
South Ronaldsay
Westray

St Kilda
(U.K.)

Outer Hebrides
Lewis
Harris
North Uist
Benbecula
South Uist
Barra
Stornoway

Inner Hebrides
Skye
Rùm
Eigg
Coll
Tiree
Mull
Colonsay
Jura
Islay

Sea of the Hebrides

North West Highlands
C. Wrath
Ullapool
Portree
Fort William
Ben Nevis
1344
Oban
Tobermory

North Minch

Thurso
Wick
Helmsdale
Golspie
Tain
Lairg
Invergordon
Dingwall
Inverness
Loch Ness
Nairn
Elgin
Aviemore
Glen More
SCOTLAND
GRAMPIAN Mts.
Buckie
Huntly
Banff
Fraserburgh
Peterhead
Aberdeen
Stonehaven

Pentland Firth
Moray Firth

GRAMPIANS
Braemar
1309

Ben Macdui
1309

Montrose
Arbroath
Forfar
Dundee
Perth
St. Andrews
Stirling
Glenrothes
Kirkcaldy
Dunfermline
Dunbar
Edinburgh
Berwick-upon-Tweed

Loch Lomond
L. Fyne
Arran
Campbeltown
Dumbarton
Glasgow
Paisley
Greenock
Kilmarnock
East Kilbride
Hamilton
Motherwell

Uplands

NORTH

SEA

N

O

R

T

H

Hatton

1224

1224

789

816

336

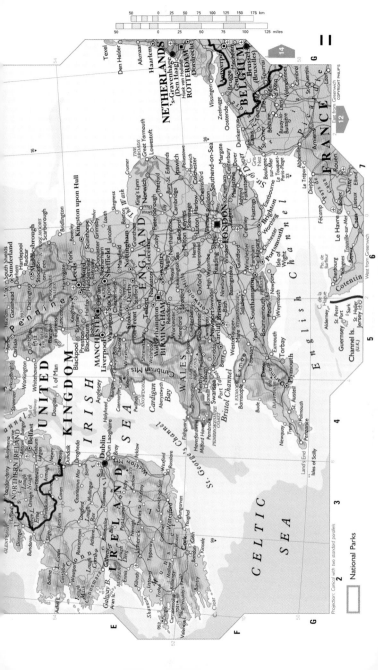

National Parks

Projection: Conical with two standard parallels

COPYRIGHT PHILIP'S

East from Greenwich

West from Greenwich

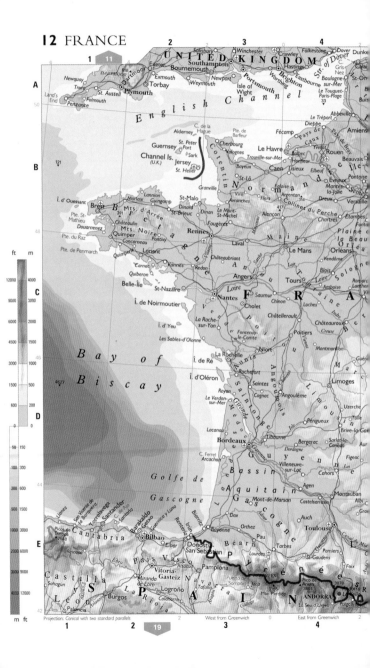

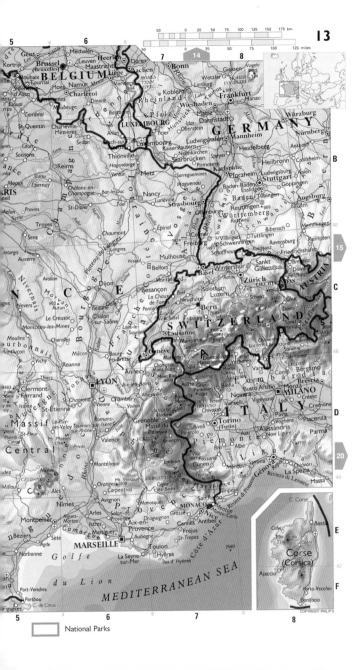

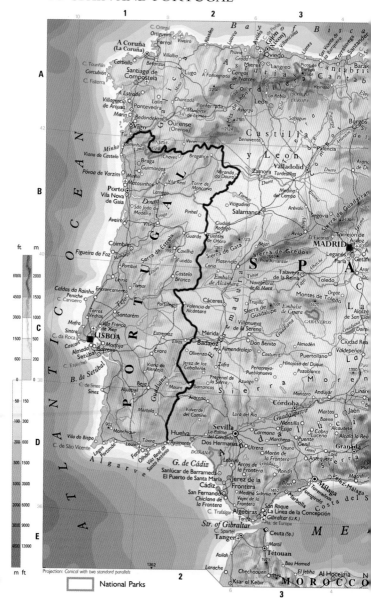

National Parks

Projection: Conical with two standard parallels

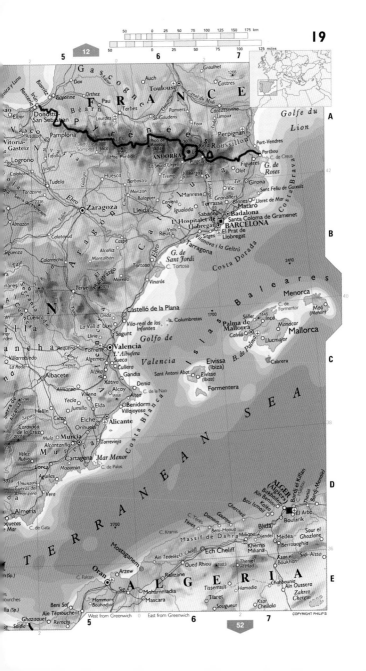

ITALY AND THE ADRIATIC

21

50 0 25 50 75 100 125 150 175 km
50 0 25 50 75 100 125 miles

East from Greenwich

COPYRIGHT PHILIP'S

National Parks

m 4000 3000 2000 1000 500 200 100 0
ft 12000 9000 6000 3000 1500 600 300 0

Projection: Conical with two standard parallels

IONIAN SEA

TYRRHENIAN SEA

MEDITERRANEAN SEA

Golfo di Táranto

Stretto di Messina

Golfe de Tunis

Golfe de Hammamet

Brindisi
Ostuni
Lecce
Gallipoli
Otranto
Nardò
Fontcoula
Táranto
Martina
Matera
Potenza
Náploi
Ischia
Capri
Castellammare
Torre del Greco
Napoli
Salerno
Sapri
Lágonegro
Cosenza
Crotone
Catanzaro
Rossano
Nicastro
Vibo Valéntia
Reggio di Calábria
Messina
Milazzo
Catánia
Siracusa
Augusta
Ávola
Módica
Ragusa
Gela
Vittória
Licata
Agrigento
Sciacca
Marsala
Mazara del Vallo
Trápani
Erice
Palermo
Castelvetrano
Bagheria
Isole Eólie
Lípari
Vulcano
Salina
Strómboli
Pantelleria (Italy)
Lampedusa
Isole Pelagie (Italy)
Lampione
Linosa
Malta
Valletta
Gozo
Rabat
Sardegna (Sardinia)
C. Cómino
Núoro
Oristano
Quartu Sant' Elena
Cágliari
G. di Cágliari
G. di Oristano
Iglésias
Carbónia
San Pietro
Sant' António
C. Spartivento
Carloforte
TUNISIA
TUNIS
Bizerte
Menzel-Bourguiba
Béja
Tébourba
Nabeul
Hammamet
Sousse
Monastir
Mahdia
Kairouan
ALGERIA
El Kef
Tébessa
Ain Beida
Souk-Ahras
Guelma

Isole Égadi
Favignana
Marética
Favorita

Str. di Messina

50 0   100   200   300   400 km
50   0   50   100   150   200   250 miles

D **E** **F**

CASPIAN SEA

CASPIAN

Depression

Astrakhan

KALMYKIA

Vozrozhdeniya

Volga

Elista

Ozero Manych-Gudilo

Makhachkala

DAGESTAN

Derbent

Sumqayıt

Baku

Lənkəran

Astara

Ardabīl

İRAN

TABRĪZ

AZERBAIJAN

ARMENIA

YEREVAN

GEORGIA

TBILISI

Kutaisi

Batumi

Sochi

Sokhumi

CHECHENIA

Grozny

Rostov

Y U Z H N Y

ROSTOV

Tsimlyansk Vdkhr.

Don

Volgodonsk

Salsk

Tikhoretsk

Krasnodar

Armavir

Labinsk

Nevinnomysk

Stavropol

Budennovsk

Blagodarnyy

Georgiyevsk

Mineralnyye Vody

Cherkessk

KARACHAY-CHERKESSIA

KABARDINO-BALKARIA

Nalchik

Nazran

NORTH OSSETIA

INGUSHETIA

Vladikavkaz

C A U C A S U S

Elbrus

Maykop

Tuapse

Novorossiysk

Gelendzhik

Anapa

Temryuk

Kerch

Feodosiya

Yalta

Sevastopol

Simferopol

Yevpatoriya

C R I M E A

Dzhankoy

Mys Tarkhankut

Skadovsk

Kherson

Kakhovka

Nova Kakhovka

Melitopol

Berdyansk

Mariupol

Taganrog

Yeysk

Azov

Sea of Azov

Krasnodar

B L A C K   S E A

Constanța

Varna

Burgas

BULGARIA

Silven

Khaskovo

Edirne

İSTANBUL

Tekirdağ

Marmara Denizi

Bandırma

BURSA

İZMIR (Smyrna)

Balıkesir

Manisa

Aydın

Uşak

Eskişehir

ANKARA

T U R K E Y

A n a d o l u

Kütahya

Afyon

Konya

Kayseri

Kırşehir

Kırıkkale

Aksaray

Çorum

Tokat

Amasya

Sivas

Malatya

Samsun

Ordu

Giresun

Trabzon

Kuzey Anadolu Dağları

Erzurum

Erzincan

Ağrı

Van

Van Gölü

Batman

Tunceli

Bingöl

Muş

Bitlis

Zonguldak

Ereğli

Sakarya

Kocaeli (İzmit)

Gebze

Kastamonu

Karabük

Bolu

Bafra

Sinop

East from Greenwich

Projection: Conical with two standard parallels

COPYRIGHT PHILIP'S

2 **3** **4** **5** **6**

D **E** **F**

ROMANIA

MOLDOVA

Chișinău

București (Bucharest)

Ploiești

Brăila

Galați

Focșani

Bacău

Iași

Botoșani

Brașov

ODESA

100 0 200 400 600 800 1000 1200 1400 km
100 0 200 400 600 800 1000 miles

C   B   A

Barents Sea   Novaya Zemlya   Kara Sea

D

North Sea   NORWAY   Murmansk   Naryan Mar   Vorkuta   Novyy Port   Nore
UNITED KINGDOM   LONDON   SWEDEN   FINLAND   ST. PETERSBURG   KARELIA   Arkhangelsk   Ukhta   Novvy Port   Salekhard   R   U
PARIS   GERMANY   Berlin   Warsaw   ESTONIA   LATVIA   Pskov   KOMI   Syktyvkar   Surgut
E.   Warsaw   LITH.   Kaliningrad   BELARUS   MOSCOW   Nizhniy Novgorod   Glazov   Perm   Serov   Irbit   Tyumen
UKRAINE   Kiev   Smolensk   Tula   Ryazan   Vologda   Yaroslavl   Kazan   Izhevsk   Nizhniy Tagil   Tobolsk   Omsk
ROMANIA   Belgrade   Odessa   Rostov   Voronezh   Samara   BASHKORTOSTAN   Ufa   Chelyabinsk   Yekaterinburg   Magnitogorsk   Novosibirsk
BULGARIA   GREECE   Black Sea   Krasnodar   Don   Volgograd   Volga   Saratov   Orenburg   Kustanay   Pavlodar   Astana   Karaganda   Semey   Novokuznetsk
ISTANBUL   Bursa   Izmir   Ankara   Samsun   GEORGIA   Aral   Aqtöbe   Tsyl   KAZAKHSTAN   Ekibastuz   GORNO ALTAY
TURKEY   ARMENIA   AZER.   Baku   ARAL SEA   KARA-KALPAKSTAN   L. Balkhash   Ömken   ALTAY
CYPRUS   Adana   Aleppo   Yerevan   Caspian Sea   Astrakhan   Aral   Aral Sea   Syr   Taraz   Alma Ata   Ürümqi   SINKIANG
Mediterranean Sea   SYRIA   Mosul   Tabriz   TURKMENISTAN   Urgench   UZBEKISTAN   Tashkent   Samarkand   KYRGYZSTAN   Bishkek   Kashi   Tarim   Hotan
Alexandria   ISRAEL   Tel Aviv   Damascus   Baghdad   TEHRAN   Mashhad   Ashkhabad   TAJIKISTAN   Dushanbe
CAIRO   JORDAN   Amman   IRAQ   Kermanshah   Esfahan   IRAN   Herat   Kabul   Islamabad   Rawalpindi   T   I   B
Suez   Basra   Ahvaz   Yazd   AFGHANISTAN   Kandahar   LAHORE
EGYPT   KUWAIT   Kerman   Shiraz   Zahedan   Quetta   Faisalabad   Multan
Medina   BAHRAIN   Bandar Abbas   PAKISTAN   DELHI   Bareilly   NEPAL   Katmandu
SAUDI   Riyadh   QATAR   Doha   Abu Dhabi   Gulf of Oman   KARACHI   New Delhi   Agra   Lucknow   Patna   Kanpur   Varanasi   BA   DA
ARABIA   Mecca   UNITED ARAB EMIRATES   Muscat   Hyderabad   Jaipur   Jodhpur   Allahabad   Jabalpur   Jamshedpur   KOLKA
Red Sea   Port Sudan   Abha   OMAN   Ahmadabad   Vadodara   Indore   Bhopal   Nagpur   INDIA   Vishakhapat
Sana'   G. of Aden   Surat   MUMBAI   Pune   HYDERABAD   Kakinada   Bem
ETHIOPIA   YEMEN   Aden   Socotra (Yemen)   Arabian Sea   Panaji   Vijayawada
Addis Ababa   DJIBOUTI   SOMALI REP.   Mangalore   Nellore   A
Africa   Hargeisa   Lakshadweep Is. (India)   BANGALORE   CHENNAI   Pondicherry
KENYA   Mogadishu   Cochin   Coimbatore   Madurai   Jaffna
Mombasa   Trivandrum   Colombo   SRI LANKA
MALDIVES   Malé   Equator   INDIAN   OCE
Dar es Salaam   SEYCHELLES   Victoria
TANZANIA   Aldabra (Seychelles)   COMOROS   Chagos Arch. (UK)

m ft
0
200 600
1000 3000
2000 6000
4000 12000
6000 18000
8000 24000

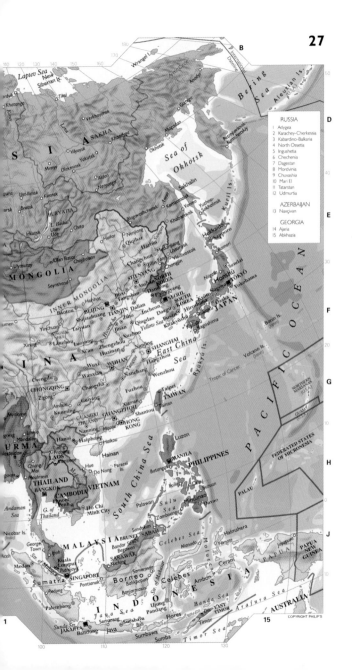

27

RUSSIA
1 Adygea
2 Karachey-Cherkessia
3 Kabardino-Balkaria
4 North Ossetia
5 Ingushetia
6 Chechenia
7 Dagestan
8 Mordvinia
9 Chuvashia
10 Mari El
11 Tatarstan
12 Udmurtia

AZERBAIJAN
13 Naxçivan

GEORGIA
14 Ajaria
15 Abkhazia

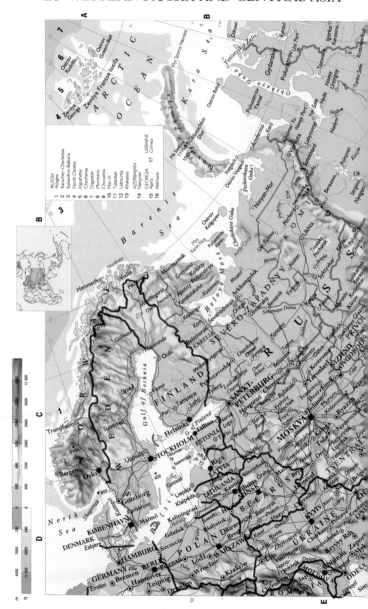

RUSSIA
1 Karachay-Cherkessia
2 Kabardino-Balkaria
3 North Ossetia
4 Ingushetia
5 Chechenia
6 Dagestan
7 Mordovia
8 Chuvashia
9 Mari El
10 Tatarstan
11 Udmurtia
12 Khakassia

AZERBAIJAN
14 Nakhichevan

GEORGIA
15 Ajaria
16 Abkhazia

UKRAINE
17 Crimea

29

Projection: Conical Orthomorphic with two standard parallels

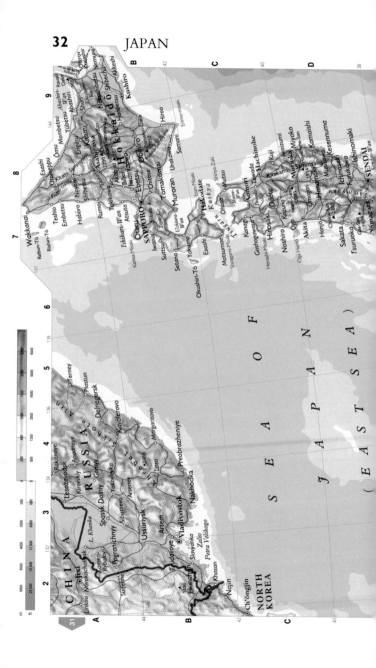

31

A B C D

9
8
7
6
5
4
3
2

Ostrov Kunashir
Rausu
Shari
Abashiri
Nokkemappu
Nemuro
Shibecha
Akkeshi
Kushiro
Hiroo
Erimo-misaki

Esashi
Ōmu
Mombetsu
Kitami
Engaru
Otaneppu
HOKKAIDŌ
Asahigawa
Kutchan
Ō-dake
2290
Obihiro
Kamui-Dake
Samani

Wakkanai
Teshio
Haboro
Rumoi
Ishikari-Wan
SAPPORO
Otaru
Ebetsu
Bibai
Iwamizawa
Chitose
Tomakomai
Urakawa

Rebun-Tō
Embetsu
Shibetsu
Atsuta
Suttsu
Setana
Yokatsu
Uchiura Wan
Muroran

Okushiri-Tō
Esashi
Matsumae
Shirakami-Misaki

Kamui-Misaki

Hakodate
Tsugaru Kaikyō
Ōhata
Mutsu
Shiriya-Zaki

Kanagi
Goshogawara
Hirosaki
Noshiro
Ogi-Hantō
Akita
Honjō
Sakata
Tsuruoka

Aomori
Towada
Hachinohe
Kuji
Morioka
Iwate-San 2041
Kitakami
Miyako
Kamaishi
Kesennuma
Ishinomaki
Ichinoseki
Furukawa
SENDAI

RUSSIA
Roki tnoye
Kirovskiy
Ariadnoye
Terney
Plastun

Dalnegorsk
Kavalerovo
Margaritovo
Preobrazheniye

Tissozavodsk
Gornyy
Yakovlevka
Arsenev
Izzo

Spassk Dalniy
Ussuriysk
Pogranichnyy
Sibirtsevo
Artem
Vladivostok
Nakhodka

Lesozavodsk
Kirovskiy

CHINA
Linkou
Jixi
Novokachalinsk
L. Khanka
Kamen Rybolov

Suifenhe

Razdolnoye
Slavyanka
Zaliv Petra Velikogo

Khasan

NORTH KOREA
Najin
Ch'ŏngjin
Hunchun
1498

SEA OF JAPAN
(E A S T S E A)

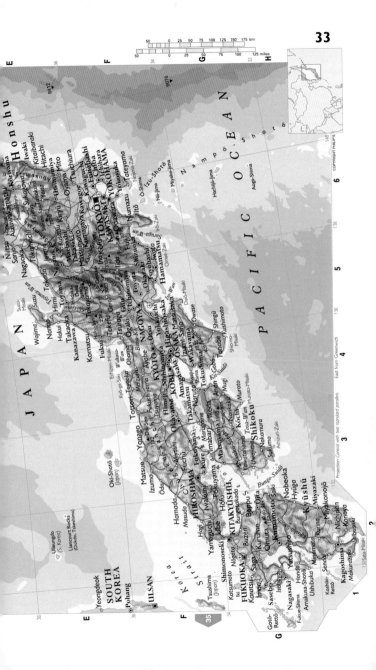

33

E 36 F G 34 H

50   0   25 50 75 100 125 150 175 km
50   0   25   50   75   100 125 miles

H o n s h u

8112

9076

JAPAN

SOUTH KOREA

Ulleungdo (S. Korea)

Liancourt Rocks (Dokdo, Takeshima)

Yeongdeok

Pohang

ULSAN

Oki-Shotō (Japan)

Tsushima (Japan)

Matsue
Izumo
Yonago
Tottori
Toyooka

Hamada
Masuda
Hagi
Ōda
Fuchū
Takahashi
Tsuyama
Himeji

Yamaguchi
Ube
Tokuyama
Hōfu
HIROSHIMA
Iwakuni
Kure
Fukuyama
Okayama
Kurashiki

Shimonoseki
KITAKYŪSHŪ
Buzen
Ōita
Kōbe
OSAKA
KYŌTO

FUKUOKA
Nōgata
Iizuka
Saga
Kurume
Ōmuta
Bungo S.
Beppu

Karatsu
Imari
Sasebo
Isahaya
Honda
Yatsushiro
Kumamoto
Nobeoka
Hyūga

Nagasaki
Amakusa-Shotō
Minamata
Kuma
Miyazaki

Gotō-Rettō
Fukue-Shima
Koshiki-Rettō
Ushibuka
Sendai
Miyakonojō
Nichinan
Kanoya

Kagoshima
Mokurazaki
Ibusuki
Sata-Misaki

Kōchi
Shikoku
Nakamura
Sukumo
Ashizuri-Zaki

PACIFIC OCEAN

Zampō-shotō

Hachijō-jima
Aoga-Shima

Miyake-jima
Ō-Shima
Izu-Shotō
Nii-jima

Iwo-Tori-Shima

140

138

136

134

East from Greenwich

Projection: Conical with two standard parallels

COPYRIGHT PHILIP'S

2   1   G   2

6   5   4   3

35

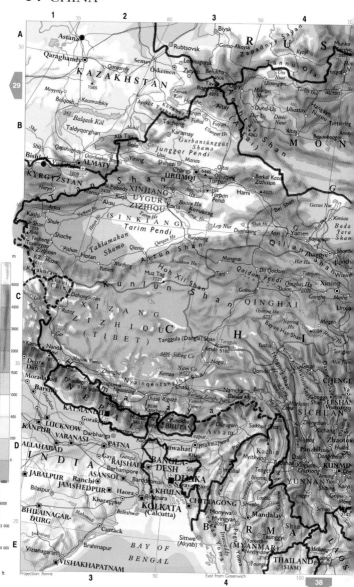

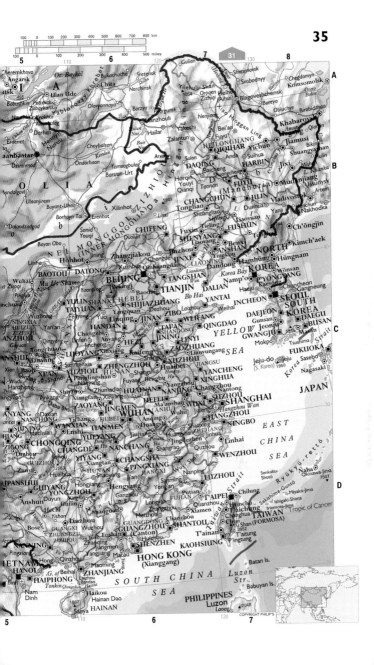

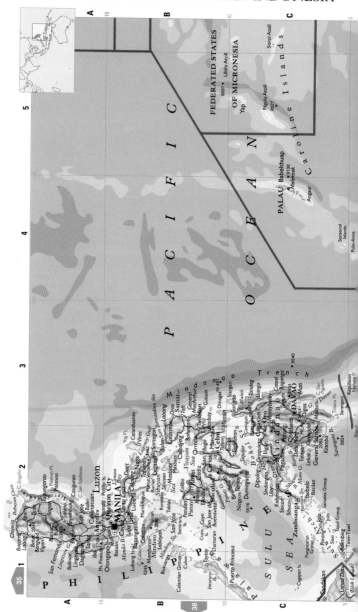

PHILIPPINE

P A C I F I C   O C E A N

FEDERATED STATES
OF MICRONESIA

Yap

Caroline Islands

PALAU   Babelthuap
Melekeok

Ngulu Atoll
8527

Ulithi Atoll
8597

Sorol Atoll

Angaur

Sonsorol
Islands

Pulo-Anna

Luzon
MANILA
Quezon City

Mindoro

Panay
Negros
Cebu
Bohol
Leyte
Samar
Masbate
Mindanao

DAVAO
General Santos

Zamboanga

S U L U   S E A

Basilan

Puerto Princesa

Palawan

Kepulauan Nanusa

Sangihe

Mindanao Trench

9540

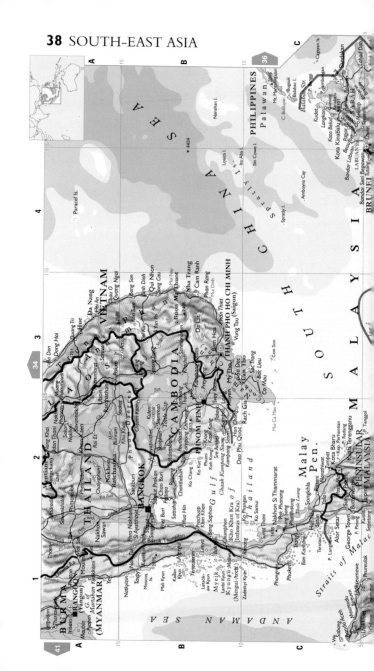

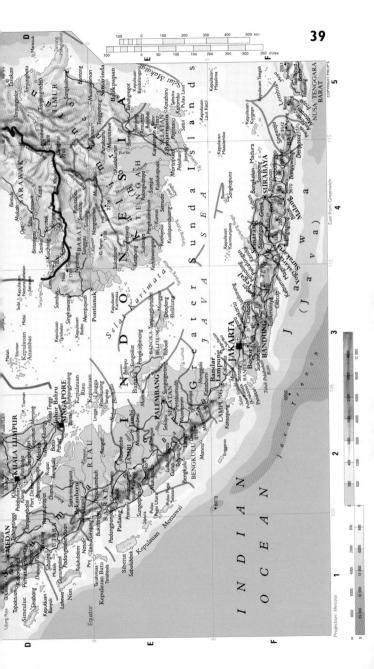

39

Projection: Mercator

COPYRIGHT PHILIPS

East from Greenwich

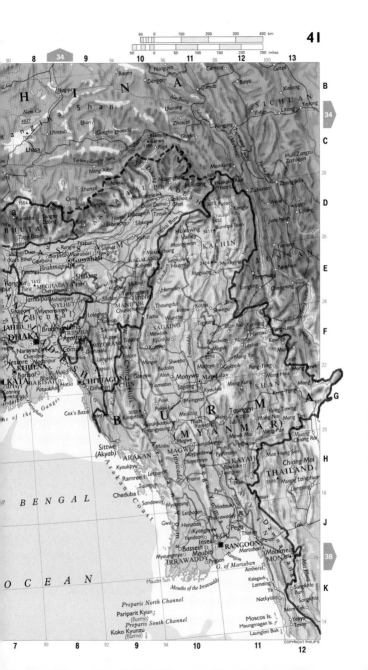

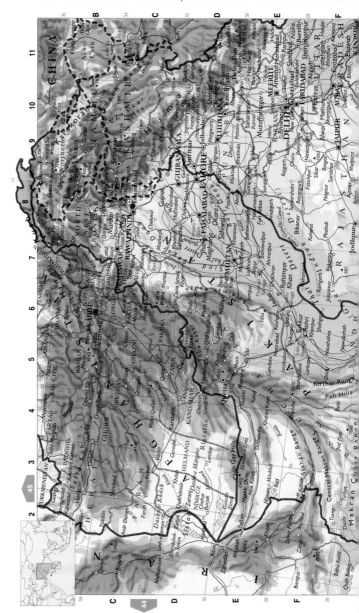

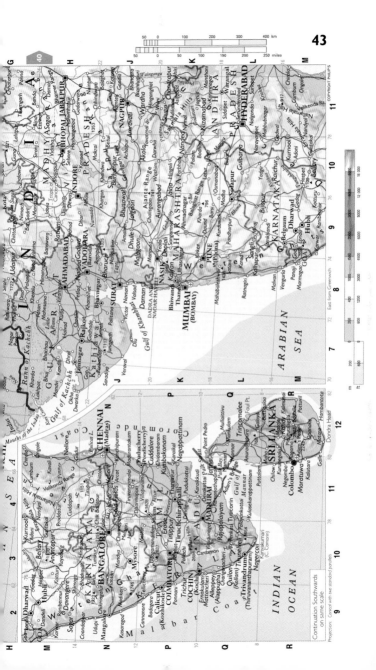

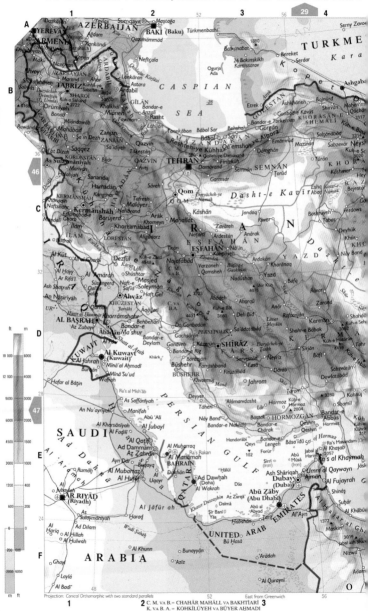

East from Greenwich

2 C. M. va B. = CHAHĀR MAHĀLL va BAKHTĪĀRI
K. va B. A. = KOHKĪLŪYEH va BŪYER AḤMADĪ

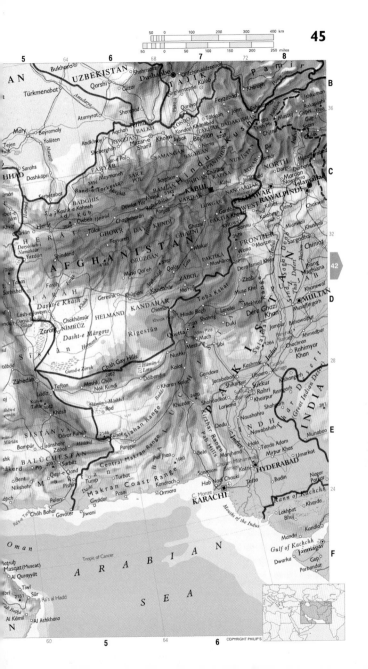

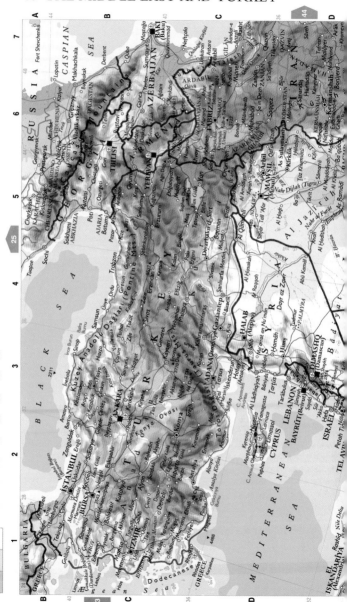

50 0 100 200 300 400 km
50 0 50 100 150 200 250 miles

PERSIAN GULF

Ahvāz · KHUZESTAN · Bandar-e Deylam · Shadegān · Neft-e Soleymān · Soffid ve-Heft Gel

Al Kuwayt (Kuwait) · KUWAIT · Al Ahmadī · Mīnā' al Ahmadī · Mīnā' Su'ūd

Abū 'Alī · Al Jubayl · Az Zuhrān · Al Khafjī · Al Mishāb · Manīfah · Al Qatīf · Ad Dammām · Al Hufūf · Al Jubayl

Ra's al Mish'āb · Ra's Tanūrah · Al Khaffī

Al Baṣrah · AL BAṢRAH · Az Zubayr · Umm Qaṣr · Khawr al Ḥammār

An Nāşirīyah · Al 'Amārah · Al Kūt · Al Qurnah · Ar Rifa'ī

AR RIYĀD (Riyadh) · Ad Dilam · Al Hillah · Al Hāriq · Al Hufūf · Al Hawtah · Laylā · Al Bādi' · Al Kharj · As Sulayyil

Ad Dahnā' · Rumāh · Al 'Uwaynah · Ghaţ · Majma'ah · Shaqrā' · Az Zilfi · Al Majma'ah · Al 'Uwayqīlah

Al 'Irq · Ar Ruwaydah · Ad Dawādimī · Al Quway'īyah · Afīf · 'Aţţūd · Wādī ad Dawāsir

An Najaf · An Nukhayb · As Salmān · As Samāwah · Ash Shabakah · Ash Shabicah · Najaf

As Sulaymānīyah · Hafar al Bāṭin · An Nu'ayrīyah

Nukhayb · Ar Rutbah · Ar Ruţbah · Rafḥā' · Ash Shu'bah · Ţurabah · Rafḥā' · Badanah

An Nafūd · Sakākah · Al Jawf · Jubbah · Haditha

Jabal Shammar · Hā'il · Fayd · Al 'Ulā · Mada'in Ṣāliḥ

Ṣafājah · Ḥarrat Khaybar

Al Wajh · 'Umm Lajj · Tabūk · Al Bad' · Duba · Al Muwaylih · Sharmah · Haqi · 'Ajā Qurayn

RED SEA

Buraydah · 'Unayzah · Ar Rass · Al Midhnab · Al Mulaydah · Ad Dawādimī

Al Madīnah (Medina) · As Suwayrqiyah · Al Hanākīyah · Mahd adh Dhahab

Yanbu' al Baḥr · Rābigh · Maṣţūrah · Al Ḥamrā' · Badr Ḥunayn

SAUDI ARABIA

HIJAZ · Makkah (Mecca) · 2641 · Aṭ Ṭā'if · Zaymah · Al Qunfudhah · Al Līth

JIDDAH (Jedda) · Al Qaḍīmah · Ra's al Qaṭīf · Ra's Banās

SUDAN · Es Sahrā' en Nūbīya · HALAIB TRIANGLE · Wadi Halfa · Ras Hadarba · Muhammad Qol · Gebeit · Halaib

EGYPT · EL QÂHIRA (Cairo) · Es Sahrâ' esh Sharqîya · Es Suweis (Suez) · Helwân · Beni Suef · El Faiyûm · El Minyâ · Mallawî · Asyûţ · Sôhâg · Qena · THEBES · Idfu · Kôm Ombo · Aswân · (Aswan High Dam) · El Kharga · Baris

El Gîza · PYRAMIDS · Bûsh · Beni Mazâr

Khalîg el Suweis · Gebel Shâyib el Banât 2187 · Bûr Safâga · Hurghada · Râs Ghârib

Jazâ'ir Farasân

El Gezîra

Tropic of Cancer

East from Greenwich

Projection: Conical Orthomorphic with two standard parallels

44 · 48 · 54

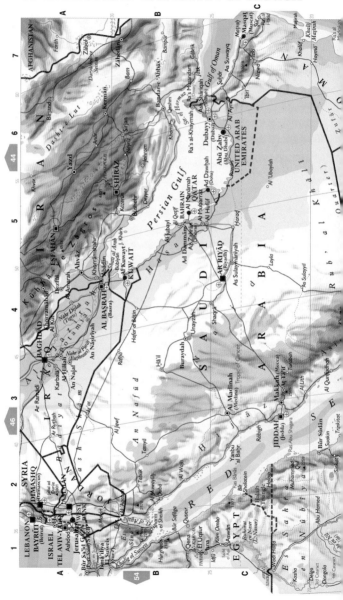

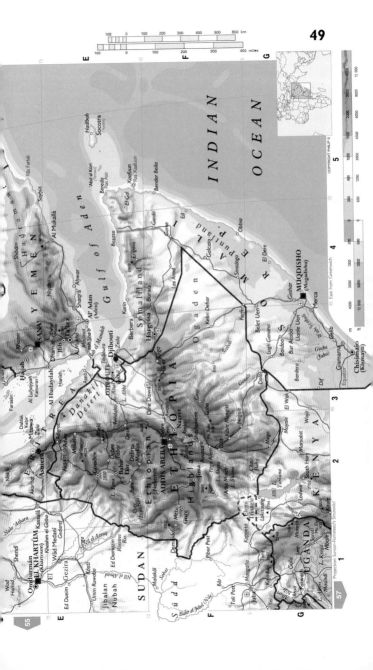

49

NORTH ATLANTIC OCEAN

RUSSIA
KAZAKHSTAN
TURKMEN.
Caspian Sea
Volgograd
Kiev
UKRAINE
GEORGIA
AZER.
ARM.
TEHRAN
Isfahan
IRAN
Warsaw
POLAND
GERMANY
Prague
CZECH REP.
SLOVAK REP.
Vienna
AUSTRIA
HUNGARY
SWITZ.
SLOVENIA
CROATIA
BOS. HERZ.
SERBIA
ROMANIA
BULGARIA
MAC.
ALB.
Adriatic Sea
Black Sea
Odesa
Ankara
TURKEY
Mosul
Baghdad
Tigris
Euphrates
IRAQ
Basra
KUWAIT
Persian Gulf
Bahrain
Qatar
Riyadh
SAUDI ARABIA
Medina
Mecca
YEMEN
G. of Aden
Socotra
Ras Asir
DJIBOUTI
Djibouti
Berbera
Hargeysa
Aleppo
SYRIA
Damascus
LEBANON
Beirut
Tel Aviv
ISRAEL
Jerusalem
Amman
JORDAN
Suez
Port Said
Aswan
Red Sea
Port Sudan
Atbara
Khartoum
Omdurman
White Nile
Blue Nile
ETHIOPIA
Addis Ababa
UNITED KINGDOM
LONDON
NETH.
BELG.
PARIS
FRANCE
GREECE
Athens
Crete
CYPRUS
Mediterranean Sea
Alexandria
CAIRO
El Faiyûm
EGYPT
Asyût
Nile
Wâdi Halfa
Wâd Medani
El Obeid
El Fasher
Nyala
SUDAN
Malakal
Sobat
Madrid
SPAIN
PORTUGAL
Lisbon
B. of Biscay
Azores
(Port.)
Ponta Delgada
Madeira
(Port.)
Funchal
Santa Cruz de Tenerife
Canary Is.
(Sp.)
Las Palmas
Corsica
Sardinia
Rome
ITALY
Sicily
MALTA
Tripoli
Misrâtah
Sfax
Tunis
TUNISIA
Constantine
Annaba
Algiers
Oran
Tetouan
Fès
Rabat
Casablanca
MOROCCO
Marrakech
Sahara
Tropic of Cancer
WESTERN SAHARA
Dakhla
Ras Nouâdhibou
Nouâdhibou
Nouakchott
MAURITANIA
Tombouctou
MALI
Bamako
Senegal
St-Louis
Dakar
SENEGAL
GAMBIA
GUINEA-BISSAU
GUINEA
SIERRA LEONE
Conakry
C. Vert
CAPE VERDE IS.
Praia
Ghadâmes
Ghât
In Salah
Ghardaïa
Sebha
Marzûq
ALGERIA
LIBYA
Benghazi
Al Jawf
Al Kufra
Adrar
CHAD
L. Chad
Abéché
Ndjamena
Maiduguri
Agadez
NIGER
Zinder
Kano
NIGERIA
Niger
Tahoua
BURKINA FASO
Ouagadougou
Bobo-Dioulasso
BENIN
GHANA
TOGO
IVORY COAST
Black Sea

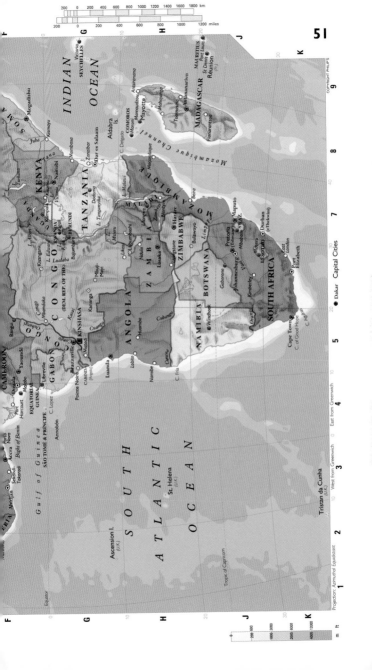

51

INDIAN OCEAN

SOMALIA
Mogadishu
Kismayu

KENYA
Nairobi
L. Turkana
Eldoret
Nakuru
Mombasa
Zanzibar
Dar es Salaam

UGANDA
Kampala
L. Victoria

L. Albert
RWANDA
Kigali
BURUNDI
Bujumbura

TANZANIA
Dodoma
L. Tanganyika
L. Rukwa

SEYCHELLES
Victoria

COMOROS
Moroni
Mayotte
Mamoudzou
Aldabra Is.
C. Delgado

CONGO
(DEM. REP. OF THE)
KINSHASA
Kananga
Mbuji-
Mayi
L. Edward
L. Kivu
Kisangani
L. Mweru
Lualaba
Lukuga
Kasai
Kwango
Kwilu

CAMEROUN
Yaoundé
Douala

NIGERIA
Abuja
Port
Harcourt

EQUATORIAL
GUINEA
Malabo

GABON
Libreville
Port
Gentil
C. Lopez

CONGO
Brazzaville
Pointe Noire
CABINDA
(Angola)
Matadi

SÃO TOMÉ & PRÍNCIPE
Annobón

Gulf of Guinea
Bight of Benin

Accra
Sekondi-
Takoradi
Abidjan

MADAGASCAR
Antananarivo
Antsiranana
Toamasina
Fianarantsoa
Toliara

MAURITIUS
Port Louis
Réunion (Fr.)
St Denis

MALAWI
Lilongwe
L. Malawi
Blantyre

MOZAMBIQUE
Mozambique
Nampula
Zambezi
Beira

Mozambique Channel

ZAMBIA
Lusaka
Ndola
Kitwe
Luangwa

ZIMBABWE
Harare
Bulawayo
Mutare

ANGOLA
Luanda
Huambo
Lobito
Namibe
Cuando
Cubango
Cuanza
C. Fria

NAMIBIA
Windhoek

BOTSWANA
Gaborone
Okavango

SOUTH AFRICA
Pretoria
Johannesburg
Kimberley
Bloemfontein
East London
Port Elizabeth
Cape Town
C. of Good Hope
Orange
Durban
(eThekwini)
SWAZILAND
(eSwatini)
LESOTHO
Maseru
Mbabane
Maputo
Limpopo

SOUTH ATLANTIC OCEAN

Ascension I. (U.K.)

St. Helena (U.K.)

Tristan da Cunha (U.K.)

Tropic of Capricorn

Equator

● Dakar Capital Cities

West from Greenwich East from Greenwich

Projection: Azimuthal Equidistant

200 0 200 400 600 800 1000 1200 1400 1600 1800 km
200 0 200 400 600 800 1000 1200 miles

m ft

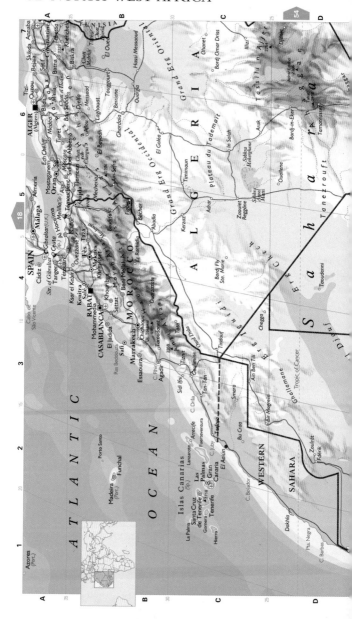

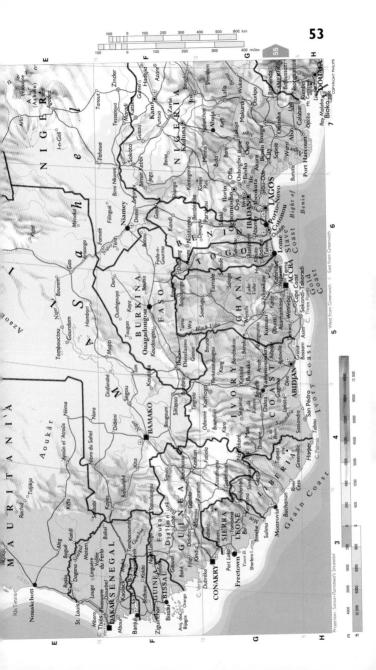

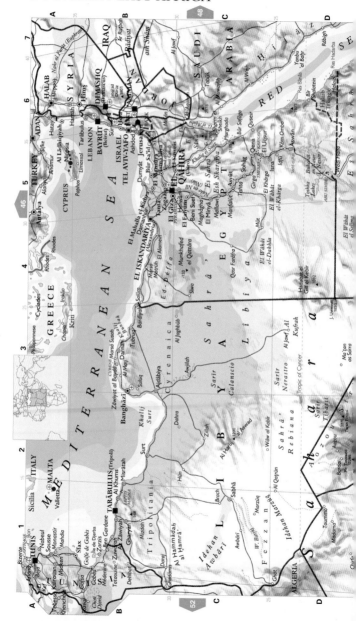

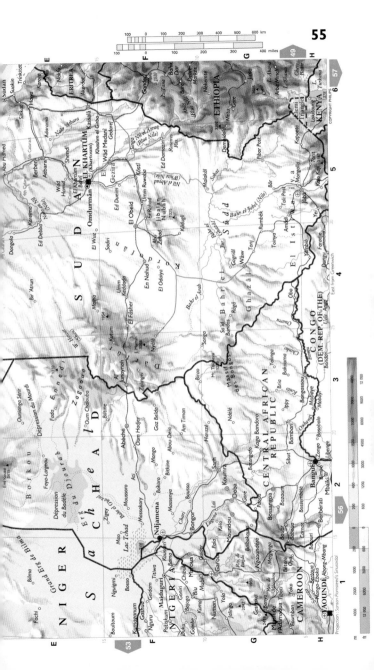

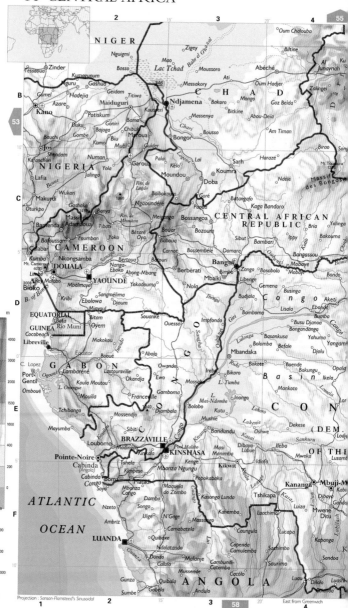

NIGER

Tessaoua   Zinder
Kumagunum
Nguigmi   Zigey   Oum Chalouba
Nguru   Gashua   Bosso   Mao   Lac Tchad   Moussoro   Biltine
Gumel   Hadejia   Bahr el Ghazal   Abéché   Junaynah
Kano   Azare   Maiduguri   Titiwa   Massakory   Ati   Oum Hadjer   Zalingei
Duku   Patiskum   Goniri   Kousseri   **CHAD**   Monga   Goz Beïda
Bauchi   Gombe   Bajoga   Chibuk   Bama   Maroua   Bokoro   Bitkine   Am Timan
Kumo   Biu   Mubi   346   Ndjamena   Massenya   Harazé   Birao
Jos   Shendam   Numan   Chari   Bongor   Bousso   Massif
Kafanchan   Yola   Guider   Lere   Bongor   des Bongos
NIGERIA   Jalingo   Garoua   Kélo   Lai   Sarh   Koumra   Ndélé   Mt Toussidé
Lafia   Wukari   Moundou   Doba   Batangafo   Kaga Bandoro
Makurdi   Gashaka   Banyo   Reï de   Goré   Poala
Oturkpo   Massif   Adamaoua   Lao   **CENTRAL AFRICAN**   Bria   Yalinga
Bamenda   Tibati   Meiganga   Bossangoa   **REPUBLIC**   Ippy   Bakouma
Bafoussam   Foumban   Yoko   Bétaré   Bouar   Bozoum   Sibut   Bambari   Bangassou
Calabar   **CAMEROON**   Oya   Baboua   Carnot   Bossembélé   Damara   Obangui   Bondo
Kumba   Nkongsamba   Bertoua   Bossembélé   Bangui   Zongo   Bosobolo   Mobaye
Mt Cameroon   Nanga-   Abong-Mbang   Berbérati   Bimbo   Mobayi   Aketi
DOUALA   Eboko   Mbaïki   Libenge   Gemena   Busunga   **Congo**
Limbe   **YAOUNDÉ**   Yokadouma   Nola   Ibenga   Budjala   Lisala   Ebonda
Bioko   Mbalmayo   Ngoumou   Sangmélima   Djoum   Bombomo   Busu Djanoa   Bumba
B. of Bon.   Kribi   Ebolowa   Souanke   Ouesso   Impfondo   Girl   Bolomba   Bongandanga   Congo
        Minvoul   Abolo   Lalonga   Basankusu   Yahuma   Yangam
EQUATORIAL   Bitam   Mbandaka   Befale   Djolu
GUINEA   Bata   Oyem   Boende   Bakungu   Opal
Rio Muni   Makokou   Owando   Irebu   Bikoro   Boende   Ikela
Cocobeach   Équator   Ouandja   Ewo   Mossaka   L. Tumba   Monkoto
Libreville   Booué   **B a s i n**
C. Lopez   **G A B O N**   Lambaréné   Lastoursville   Okandja   Gamboma   Inongo   Lokoro   Dekese   Lomela   **C O N**
Port-   Ogooué   Koula Moutou   Franceville   Djambala   Mai-Ndombe   Kutu   Lukenie   Oshwe   **(DEM.**
Gentil   L. Onangue   Mouila   Bolobo   Mushie   Bandundu   Kasai   Ilebo   Lodja
Omboué   Tchibanga   Mossendjo   Sibiti   Madingou   Kinkala   Masi   Dibaya   Lusamt   **OF TH**
        Mayumba   Loubomo   **BRAZZAVILLE**   Kenge   Manimba   Lubue   Idiofa   Mweka
Pointe-Noire   Tshela   Kimpese   **KINSHASA**   Kikwit   Tshikapa   **Kananga**   Mbuji-M   Kabi
Cabinda   Kimpese   Mbanza Ngungu   Popokabaka   Loange   Luiza   Dibaya   Gand
Cabinda   Boma   Matadi   Maquela   Kasongo Lunda   Kahemba   Luachimo   Mwene   Kapanga
(Angola)   Soyo   Mbanza   do Zombo   Kasongo Lunda   Dítu   Sachimbo   K
Congo   Nzeto   Congo   Songo   Uíge   N'Gage   Massango   Camabatela   Caungula   Lucapa   Saurimo   Sandoa
ATLANTIC   Ambriz   Quibaxe   Capenda   Camulemba
        Dondo   Malanje   Cambundi-   Cacólo
OCEAN   **LUANDA**   Ndalatando   Quibala   Catembo   Luau   Luash
Gunza   Quibala   Calulo   Mussende   Andulo   **ANGOLA**   Dilolo   Luashi
Sumbe   Gabela   Gunza

ft   m
12 000   4000
9000   3000
6000   2000
4500   1500
3000   1000
1200   400
600   200
0   0
200   600
1000   3000
2000   6000
4000   12 000
m   ft

Projection : Sanson-Flamsteed's Sinusoidal

East from Greenwich

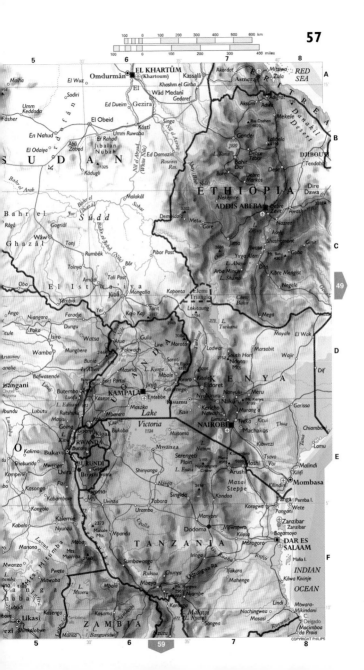

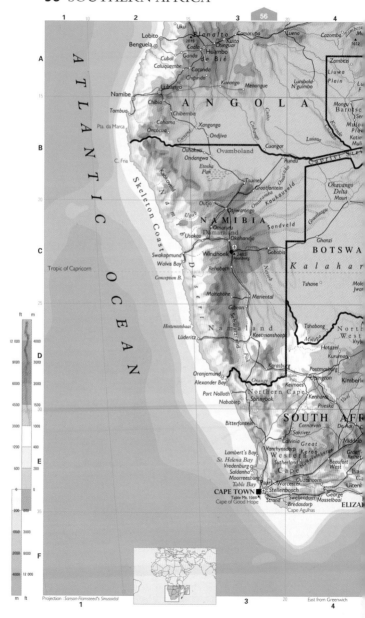

ATLANTIC

OCEAN

Tropic of Capricorn

ANGOLA

Lobito
Benguela
Cubal
Caluquembe
Ganda
Huambo
Coala
Chinguar
Kuito
Camacupa
Lueno
Cazomba
Zambeze
Uku
Planalto de Bié
Chipindo
Kuvango
Menongue
Lumbala N'guimbo

Namibe
Tombua
Pta. da Marca
Chibia
Chibemba
Cahama
Oncócua
Cunene
Xangongo
Ondjiva
Luana
Zambezi
Liuwa Plain
Mongu
Barotse
Plain
Kasaba
Lu
F

C. Fria
Oshakati
Ondangwa
Ovamboland
Cuangar
Rundu
Caprivi Strip
Katir
Muli

Skeleton Coast
Kaokoveld
Etosha Pan
Tsumeb
Grootfontein
Koukauveld
Okavango Delta
Maun
Okaulagte

Outjo
Otjiwarongo
Omaruru
Damaraland
Okahandja
Omaruru
Onaramoru
Sandveld
Ghanzi
BOTSWANA

Swakopmund
Walvis Bay
Conception B.
Windhoek
2483
Auasberge
Rehoboth
Gobabis
Nossob
Tshane
Molopo
Jwar
Kalahari

Maltahöhe
Mariental
Gibeon

Hottentotbaai
Namaland
Keetmanshoop
Tshabong
Molopo
Hotazel
Kuruman
North
West
Vryb

Lüderitz
Fish
Karasburg
Postmasburg
Upington
Kimber

Oranjemund
Alexander Bay
Port Nolloth
Nababiep
Springbok
Orange
Augrabies
Keimoes
Kenhardt
Prieska
Vaal
Northern Cape

Bitterfontein
Carnarvon
De Aar
Middel
SOUTH AFRICA

Sakriver
Calvinia
Great
Vanrhynsdorp
Karoo
Sutherland
Graaff-
Reinet
Beaufort West
Bas
Lambert's Bay
St. Helena Bay
Vredenburg
Saldanha
Moorreesburg
Western
Cape
Oudtshoorn
George
Uiten
Paarl
Worcester
Stellenbosch
CAPE TOWN
Table Mt. 1086
Cape of Good Hope
Table Bay
Strand
Swellendam
Mosselbaai
Bredasdorp
Cape Agulhas
ELIZ

Projection : Sanson-Flamsteed's Sinusoidal

East from Greenwich

ft   m
12 000 4000
9000   3000
6000   2000
4500   1500
3000   1000
1200   400
600   200
0   0
200   600
1000   3000
2000   6000
4000   12 000
m   ft

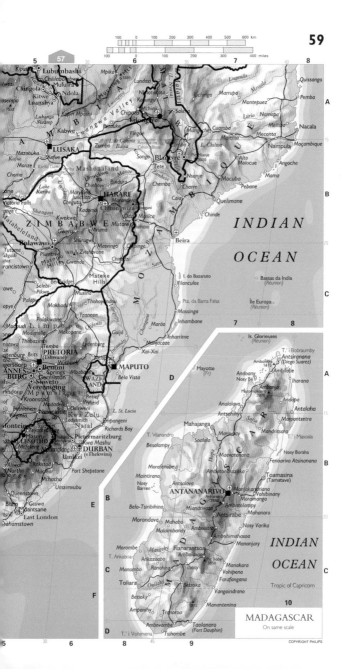

100 0 100 200 300 400 500 600 km
100 0 100 200 300 400 miles

57

5 Lubumbashi   Mpika   Lundazi   Lagenda   Quissanga
Kipushi   Chililabombwe   Mufulira   Nchotokota   Uchinga   Marrupa   Mesalo   **A**
Chingola   Kitwe   Ndola   Nchinji   Lichinga   Namapo   Pemba
Iuwezi   Luanshya   Kalamba   Petauke   Lilongwe   Mangoche   Cuamba   Montepuez   Lirio
Iasempa   Kapiri Mposhi   Chipata   Zumbo   L. de Cahora   Tete   Malema   Meconta   Nacala
   Kabwe   Luangwa Valley   Bassa   Blantyre   Moçambique
   Z A M B I A   Songo   L. Chilwa   Alto Molocue   Nampula
   A   LUSAKA   Kafue   Monze   Chinhoyi   Chemba   Caia   Quelimane   Mocuba   Moma   Angoche   Pebane
Mazabuka   Mashonaland   Bindura   Charre   Nsanje
Choma   Lake Kariba   Moxico Junction   HARARE   Marondera   Chinde   **B**
Victoria Falls   Shangani   Chegutu   Kadoma   Odzi   Mutare   Quelimane
range   Kwekwe   Chakari   Chitungwiza   Manica   Beira
   Z I M B A B W E   Gweru   Mvuma   Chimoio
Matabeleland   Bulawayo   Masvingo   Chipinge   **I N D I A N**
   Plumtree   Zvishavane   Chiredzi   **B**
Tuttume   Matobo Hills   Mateke Hills   I. do Bazaruto   **O C E A N**
Francistown   Beitbridge   Hills   Vilanculos   Bassas da India (Réunion)
   Selebi-Pikwe   Musina   Thohoyandou   Pta. da Barra Falsa   Île Europa (Réunion)   **C**
   Palapye   Makhado   Tzaneen   Massinga
   Polokwane   L i m p o p o   Giyani   Marão   Inhambane
Magudi   Modjadjiskloof   Mopane   Guijá   Inharrime
Thabazimbi   Temba   Lydenburg   Xai-Xai   Manjacaze   **D**
   Rustenburg   Brits   Witbank   **MAPUTO**
   JOHANNESBURG   Benoni   Mbabane   Bela Vista
   Soweto   Germiston   Springs   SWAZILAND
Klerksdorp   Vereeniging   Ermelo   Vryheid
   Kroonstad   Mpumalanga   L. St. Lucia
   Bethlehem   Newcastle   Empangeni
Virginia   Harrismith   Ladysmith   Richards Bay
Frankfort   Greytown   Kwa Zulu   Natal   Port Shepstone
   LESOTHO   Maseru   Pietermaritzburg
   Mafeteng   Pmlanga   Kwa Mashu   DURBAN (eThekwini)   **E**
Aliwal North   Kokstad   Umlazi
   Maclear   Mthatha   Umzimvubu
Queenstown   Port St Johns
   Ncuwa   Qoboqobo   East London
Grahamstown   **F**

5   6   7   8

INDIAN OCEAN inset (MADAGASCAR)

Is. Glorieuses (Réunion)   T.i Bobraumby   **A**
Mayotte (Fr)   Antsiranana (Diego Suarez)
   Ambolobozo   Ambilobe
   Andoany   Nosy Be   Iharana
   Ambanja   Marromokotra 2876   Andapa
Analalava   Antsohihy   Antalaha
Mahajanga   Sofia   Maroantsetra
   Marovoay   Mandritsara   T.i Masoala   **B**
T. Vilanandro   Soalala   Nosy Boraha
Besalampy   Maevatanana   Fenoarivo Atsinanana
Morafenobe   Ambatondrazaka   Toamasina (Tamatave)
Maintirano   Antsalova   Moramanga
   Nosy Barren   **ANTANANARIVO**   Vohibinany   **B**
Belo-Tsiribihina   Miandrivazo   Ambatolampy   Mahanoro
   Morondava   Mahabo   Antsirabe   Nosy Varika
   Malaimbandy   Ambohimahasoa   Mananjary
Morombe   Mankely   Fianarantsoa   Ambalavao   Makanara
T. Ankaboa   Ankazoabo   Ranohira   Ihosy   Vohipeno   **C**
Manombo   Omilahy   Betroka   Farafangana
Toliara   Vangaindrano
   Bétioky   Manantenina
   Ampanihy   Tranoroa   Tropic of Capricorn
   Amboyombe   Taolanaro (Fort Dauphin)
T.i Vohimena   Tsihombe   **D**

INDIAN OCEAN

MADAGASCAR On same scale

COPYRIGHT PHILIPS

8   9   10

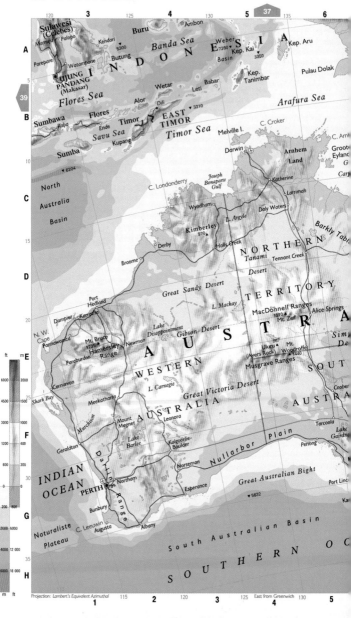

INDONESIA

Sulawesi (Celebes)
Mamuju · Palopo
Parepare · Watampone
UJUNG PANDANG (Makasar)
Kendari
Buru
Ambon
Banda Sea
Weber Basin
Kep. Kai
Kep. Aru
Pulau Dolak
Butung
8300
7290
3350
Flores Sea
Wetar
Leti Babar
Kep. Tanimbar
Arafura Sea
Alor Dili
Sumbawa
Flores
Raba
Ende
Timor
Savu Sea
Kupang
EAST TIMOR
3310
Timor Sea
Melville I.
C. Croker
C. Arnh
Sumba
Darwin
Arnhem Land
Groot Eyland
G
Cart
North Australia Basin
6204
C. Londonderry
Joseph Bonaparte Gulf
Katherine
Larrimah
Daly Waters
Barkly Tabl
Wyndham
L. Argyle
Kimberley
970
Halls Creek
NORTHERN
Tanami Desert
Tennant Creek
Derby
Broome
Port Hedland
Great Sandy Desert
TERRITORY
L. Mackay
MacDonnell Ranges
Alice Springs
Dampier · Karratha
N.W. Cape
Pannawonica
Lake Disappointment
Gibson Desert
Mt. Zeil
AUSTRA
Mt. Bruce
1235
Hamersley Range
Newman
Uluru Mt.
(Ayers Rock) Woodroffe
867
Sim De
Paraburdoo
WESTERN
1440
Musgrave Ranges
SOUT
Carnarvon
L. Carnegie
Great Victoria Desert
AUSTRA
Shark Bay
Meekatharra
AUSTRALIA
Coober
Mount Magnet
Leonora
Tarcoola
Lake Gairdne
Geraldton
Lake Barlee
Kalgoorlie-Boulder
Penong
Murchison
Nullarbor Plain
Norseman
Port Lin
Northam
PERTH
Great Australian Bight
INDIAN OCEAN
Darling Range
Esperance
Bunbury
5632
Kai
Naturaliste Plateau
C. Leeuwin
Augusta
Albany
South Australian Basin
SOUTHERN
OC

ft m
6000 2000
4500 1500
3000 1000
1200 400
600 200
0 0
200 600
2000 6000
4000 12 000
6000 18 000
m ft

Projection: Lambert's Equivalent Azimuthal   East from Greenwich

100 0 100 200 300 400 500 600 700 800 km
100 0 100 200 300 400 500 miles

7 145 **8** 155 **10** 160 **11**

W

Mount Hagen 4668 ▲ Mt. Wilhelm
Lae
●Eae

New Britain

New Britain Trench 274m ▲Mt. Balbi Bougainville
●Shortland I. 9140 ● Choiseul

SOLOMON ISLANDS
Santa Isabel

PAPUA NEW GUINEA

uinea

Fly

Gulf of Papua

Solomon Sea

Vella Lavella

Port Moresby

Owen Stanley Range

New Georgia Is.

Vangunu
Russell Is. Florida Is.
Honiara ▲2439
Guadalcanal

Malaita

San Cristóbal
(Makira)

B

10

D'Entrecasteaux Islands

Torres Strait
Badu I. Moa I.
Prince of
Wales I. C. York

Louisiade Archipelago

Pocklington Reef

Bellona

Rennell

Weipa Cape York Peninsula

Great Barrier Reef

Coral Sea Basin

C o r a l   S e a

C

64

15

ellesley Is. Mitchell

Normanton
Forsayth

Cooktown

Cairns 1622

Queensland Plateau

P A C I F I C

CORAL SEA ISLANDS TERRITORY

Îles D'Entrecasteaux (Fr.)

D

20

Townsville
Charters Towers

sq Cloncurry Hughenden
Winton

Whitsunday Is.
Mackay

Îles Chesterfield (Fr.)

L. Dalrymple

O C E A N

E

arr ny sert

Longreach
Yaraka

Rockhampton
Gladstone

Emerald

Tropic of Capricorn

25

Diamantina
Creek

Thargomindah

Charleville
Quilpie

216

Grey Range

Bundaberg

Maryborough
Gympie Sunshine Coast

Roma

Toowoomba BRISBANE
Ipswich Gold Coast
Lismore

Q U E E N S L A N D
I A

1312

Lord Howe Seamount Chain

F

Eyre

Cunnamulla

Dirranbandi

Moree

Grafton

Bourke Walgett

Round Mt.

arree

NEW SOUTH

Cobar

Tamworth

Port Macquarie
Taree

Lord Howe I. (Austral.)
▼734

G

30

Broken Hill
Port Pirie

Flinders Ranges

Darling

WALES

Dubbo

Newcastle

SYDNEY
Wollongong

35

Menindee

Mildura

Griffith

Orange Bathurst

Goulburn
Canberra
A.C.T.

Murray

Hay

Wagga Wagga
Albury

Mt. Kosciuszko 2228▲

T a s m a n   S e a

ADELAIDE

Swan Hill Shepparton
Bendigo

Wodonga Snowy
Bombala

C. Howe

H

Murray

Horsham

VICTORIA

Ballarat MELBOURNE
Geelong Sale

Mount Gambier
Warrnambool

N

Bass Strait Flinders I.
Furneaux Group

King I.

Tasman Abyssal Plain

▼5267

1

Burnie

Launceston

6 145 **7** **8** 150 S.E. Cape **9** 155 **10**

TASMANIA

1617 ▲Mt. Ossa

Hobart

COPYRIGHT PHILIP'S

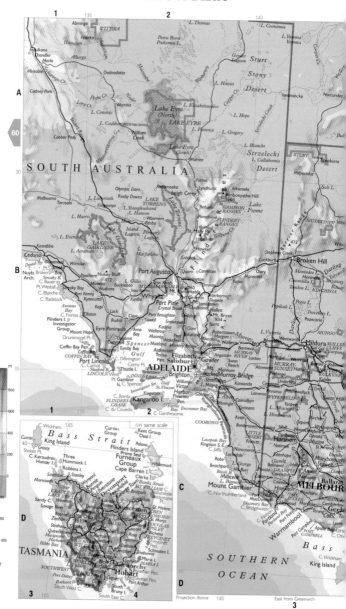

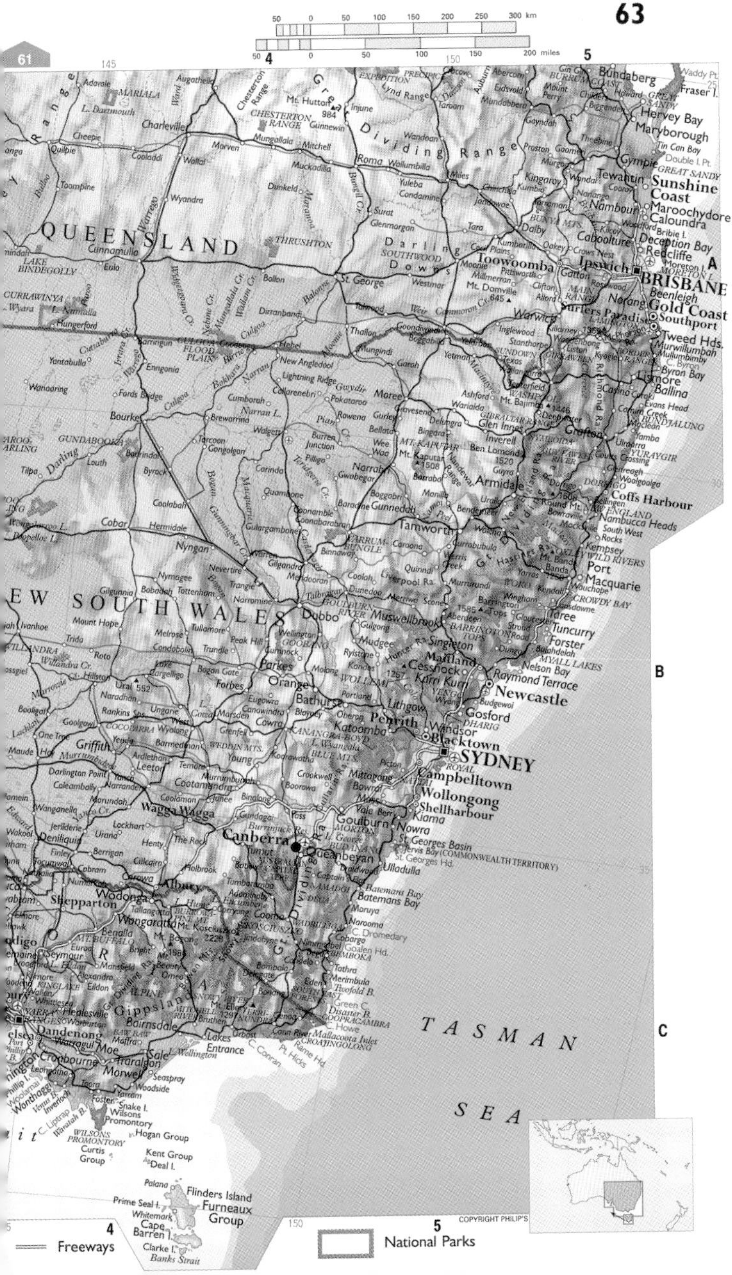

50 0 50 100 150 200 250 300 km
50 0 50 100 150 200 miles

4   5

QUEENSLAND

Adavale
Augathella
Adavale
L. Dartmouth
MARALA
Ward
Mt. Hutton 984
Injune
Charleville
CHESTERTON RANGE
Gunnewin
Cheepie
Mungallala
Mitchell
Roma
Miles
Chinchilla
Condamine
Tara
Dalby
Kingaroy
Toowoomba
Gatton
Ipswich
Surat
Glenmorgan
Darling
SOUTHWOOD
Downs
Moonie
St. George
Westmar
Warwick
Goondiwindi
Stanthorpe
Dirranbandi
Thallon
Mungindi
Boggabilla
Inglewood
Texas
Tenterfield
Casino
Lismore
Ballina

Cunnamulla
Eulo
LAKE BINDEGOLLY
Thargomindah
CURRAWINYA
Hungerford
Bourke
Brewarrina
Lightning Ridge
Walgett
Collarenebri
Moree
Warialda
Inverell
Glen Innes
Grafton
Coffs Harbour

NEW SOUTH WALES

Louth
Coolabah
Nyngan
Gilgandra
Coonamble
Coonabarabran
Gunnedah
Tamworth
Armidale
Nambucca Heads
Kempsey
Port Macquarie

Cobar
Nymagee
Condobolin
Dubbo
Mudgee
Muswellbrook
Singleton
Maitland
Newcastle
Gosford

Forbes
Parkes
Orange
Bathurst
Katoomba
Penrith
Blacktown
SYDNEY
Campbelltown
Wollongong
Shellharbour
Kiama

Griffith
Leeton
Young
Goulburn
Nowra
Ulladulla

Wagga Wagga
Canberra
Queanbeyan
Batemans Bay
Moruya
Narooma

Albury
Wodonga
Wangaratta
Cooma
Bega
Merimbula
Eden

Shepparton
Benalla
Bairnsdale
Sale
Morwell
Traralgon

WILSONS PROMONTORY
Curtis Group
Hogan Group
Deal I.
Flinders Island
Furneaux Group
Cape Barren
Banks Strait

BRISBANE
Redcliffe
Caboolture
Gympie
Sunshine Coast
Maroochydore
Caloundra
Bribie I.
Deception Bay
Gold Coast
Southport
Surfers Paradise
Tweed Heads
Byron Bay
Evans Head

Hervey Bay
Maryborough
Bundaberg
Fraser I.
GREAT SANDY

GREAT DIVIDING RANGE

TASMAN SEA

COPYRIGHT PHILIP'S

Freeways

National Parks

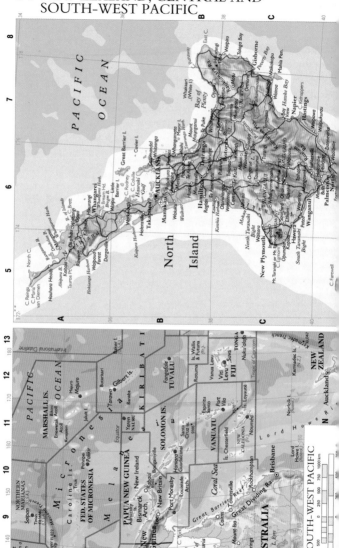

m
ft

PACIFIC OCEAN

North C.

C. Reinga
C. Maria
van Diemen
Houhora Heads
North C.
Rangaunu B.
Taura Pt.
Ahipara B.
Kaitaia
Kohukohu
Hokianga Harbour
Waipoua
Forest
Dargaville

Kaipara Harbour
Helensville
Takapuna
Manukau
Harbour

Whangarei
Whangaruru Hd.
Bay of Is.
Brynderwyn
Brynderwyn Bank
Little
Barrier I.
C. Rodney
C. Colville
Hauraki
Gulf
Coromandel

Great Barrier I.

Cuvier I.

Whakatane (White I.)
Bay of Plenty
Opotiki
Te Puke
Whakatane
Tauranga
Rotorua
Te Kuiti

AUCKLAND
Hamilton

Whangamata
Morrinsville

North
Island

New Plymouth
Mt. Taranaki or Mt.
Egmont
Opunake

Waikato R.
Cambridge
Te Awamutu
Kawhia Harbour
Kawhia
Te Kuiti

Taumarunui

Wanganui

North Taranaki
Bight
South Taranaki
Bight
Kapiti I.

Hawera
Patea
Foxton
Levin

Ruapehu
Taupo
L. Taupo
Turangi

Tokaanu

Taihape

Napier
Hastings
Cape Kidnappers

Waipukurau
Dannevirke

Feilding
Palmerston
North

C. Farewell

Whakatane
Gisborne
Poverty Bay
Mahia Pen.
Wairoa
Waikaremoana

Kaikohe

East C.

Tolaga Bay

PACIFIC

OCEAN

SOUTH-WEST PACIFIC

NORTHERN
MARIANAS
(U.S.A.)
Saipan
Tinian
Rota
Guam

PALAU
Koror

West
Mariana
Basin

Challenger Deep 11,022

Yap

FED. STATES
OF MICRONESIA
Palikir
Pohnpei

Caroline Is.

Micronesia

MARSHALL IS.
Bikini
Enewetak Atoll
Kwajalein
Majuro
Jaluit I.

KIRIBATI
Banaba
Tarawa
Yaren
NAURU
Butaritari

Baker I.

Gilbert Is.

TUVALU
Funafuti

Rotuma
FIJI
Vanua Levu
Viti
Levu
Suva

Is. Wallis &
Futuna
(Fr.)

TONGA
Nuku'alofa

International Dateline

PAPUA NEW GUINEA
Admiralty Is.
Manus
New Hanover
New Ireland
Rabaul
New Britain
Bismarck Arch.
Bougainville
Lae
Port Moresby

New
Guinea
Gulf of
Papua

C. York
Gulf of
Carpentaria
Arnhem
Land

SOLOMON IS.
Honiara
Guadalcanal
Santa
Cruz Is.

VANUATU
Espiritu
Santo
Port
Vila

Mt. Tabwemasana 1879

NEW CALEDONIA
(Fr.)
Is. Chesterfield
Nouméa
Is. Loyauté

Norfolk I.
(Austr.)

Lord
Howe
Rise

Lord
Howe I.
(Austr.)

Kermadec Is.
(N.Z.)

NEW
ZEALAND
Auckland

Kermadec Trench

AUSTRALIA
Alice Springs
L. Eyre
Mount Isa
Townsville
Cairns
Great Barrier Reef
Rockhampton
Brisbane
Great Dividing Ra.
Coral Sea
Tropic of Capricorn

Equator

Melanesia

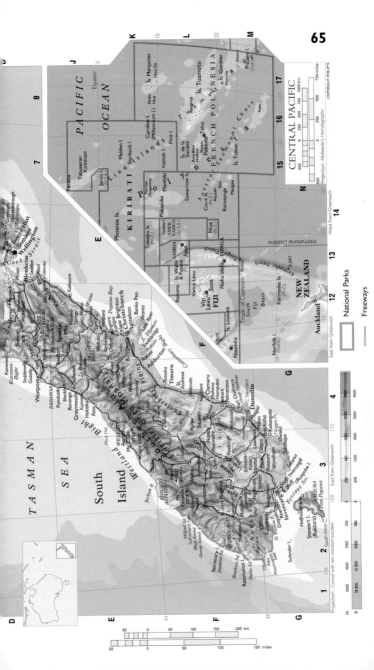

65

PACIFIC

OCEAN

Equator

CENTRAL PACIFIC

National Parks

Freeways

COPYRIGHT PHILIP'S

Ks. Marquises

Ks. Tuamotu

FRENCH POLYNESIA

Ks. Gambier

Pitcairn I. (U.K.)

Caroline I. (Millennium I.)

Starbuck I.

Flint I.

Vostok I.

Malden I.

Jarvis I. (U.S.A.)

Tabuaeran Kiritimati

Teraina

KIRIBATI

Line Islands

Phoenix Is.

Manihiki

Pukapuka

Suwarrow I.

Cook Is. (N.Z.)

Rarotonga

Mangaia

Tokelau Is. (N.Z.)

AMERICAN SAMOA (U.S.A.)

Swains I.

SAMOA

Apia

Niue (N.Z.)

Is. Wallis & Futuna (Fr.)

Rotuma

Vanua Levu

Viti Levu

FIJI

Suva

TONGA

Nuku'alofa

Tongatapu

Is. Société

Bora Bora

Tahiti

Papeete

Is. Tubuai

Society Seamount Chain

Rarotonga

Tropic of Capricorn

South Fiji Basin

Is. Loyauté

Nouméa

Norfolk I. (Aust.)

Kermadec Is. (N.Z.)

Kermadec Trench

NEW ZEALAND

Auckland

International Dateline

West from Greenwich

East from Greenwich

TASMAN SEA

South Island

Southern Alps

Canterbury Plains

Christchurch

Wellington

Cook Strait

Blenheim

Picton

Nelson

Westport

Greymouth

Hokitika

Ross

Timaru

Oamaru

Dunedin

Invercargill

Stewart I. (Rakiura)

FIORDLAND

Queenstown

Projection: Conical with two standard parallels

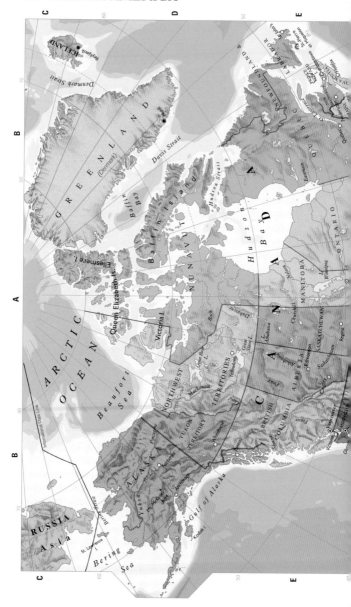

ICELAND
Reykjavik

Denmark Strait

G R E E N L A N D
(Denmark)

Davis Strait

Baffin Bay

Hudson Strait

LABRADOR

NEWFOUNDLAND

QUEBEC

ONTARIO

Ellesmere Is.

Baffin Island

Queen Elizabeth Is.

NUNAVUT

Hudson Bay

MANITOBA

C A N A D A

A R C T I C

O C E A N

Victoria I.

Beaufort
Sea

Great Bear
L.

Great
Slave L.

Yellowknife

NORTHWEST
TERRITORIES

Mackenzie

SASKATCHEWAN

ALBERTA

Edmonton

Calgary

Saskatoon

Regina

International Date Line

YUKON
TERRITORY

Whitehorse

BRITISH
COLUMBIA

Vancouver

A L A S K A

Yukon

Anchorage

Gulf of Alaska

Kodiak I.

RUSSIA
Asia

Bering Strait

St. Lawrence
I.

Bering
Sea

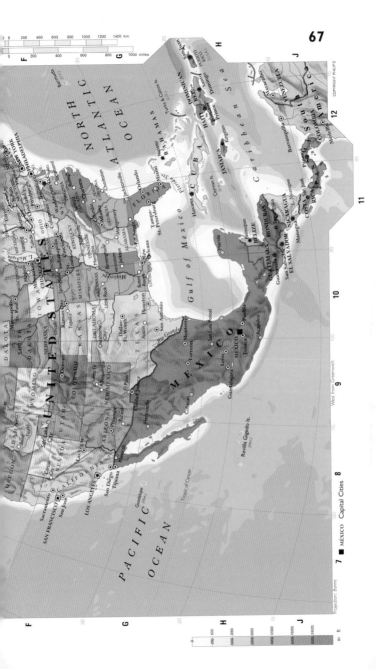

67

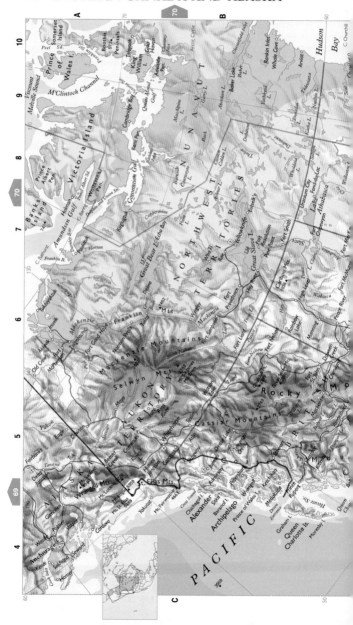

69

100 0 100 200 300 400 500 600 km
100 0 100 200 300 400 miles

C · D

71

74

31

ONTARIO
MANITOBA
SASKATCHEWAN
ALBERTA

Sioux Lookout
Lac Seul
Red Lake
Fort Frances
Dryden
Kenora
L. of the Woods
Rainy L.

Duluth
Superior
WISCONSIN
La Crosse
IOWA
Rochester
Austin
Mason City
Waterloo
Dubuque
Cedar Rapids
Des Moines
Fort Dodge
Omaha

ST. PAUL
MINNEAPOLIS
MINNESOTA
St. Cloud
Mankato
Bemidji
Brainerd
Moorhead
Fargo

Winnipeg
Portage la Prairie
Morden
Winkler
Selkirk
Hodgson
Dauphin
Neepawa
Brandon

NORTH DAKOTA
Grand Forks
Devils Lake
Jamestown
Bismarck
Minot
Dickinson

Thompson
Norway House
Gypsum
Cedar L.
Grand Rapids
Flin Flon
The Pas
Lake Winnipeg
Lake Manitoba

UNITED STATES

SOUTH DAKOTA
Aberdeen
Huron
Pierre
Mitchell
Yankton
Sioux Falls
Rapid City
Hot Springs

NEBRASKA
North Platte
Chadron
Alliance
Sterling

MONTANA
Great Falls
Lewistown
Miles City
Glendive
Glasgow
Havre
Fort Peck L.

Regina
Moose Jaw
Weyburn
Estevan
Swift Current
Medicine Hat
Melville
Yorkton

Saskatoon
Prince Albert
North Battleford
Lloydminster
Meadow Lake
La Ronge

Edmonton
Calgary
Red Deer
Lethbridge
Medicine Hat
Banff
Jasper

BRITISH COLUMBIA

Vancouver I.
VANCOUVER
Victoria
Port Alberni
Nanaimo

WASHINGTON
SEATTLE
Spokane
Olympia
Aberdeen

OCEAN

ALASKA
Prudhoe Bay
Barrow
Point Hope
Kotzebue
Nome
Fairbanks
ANCHORAGE
Mt. McKinley 6194
Valdez
Seward
Kodiak
Kodiak I.
Cordova
Juneau
Sitka
GULF OF ALASKA
Alexander Archipelago
Queen Charlotte Is.

Brooks Range
Yukon
Koyukuk
Tanana
Bethel
Dillingham
Bristol Bay

CHUKCHI SEA
BERING SEA
St. Lawrence I.
Nunivak I.
St. Matthew I.
Pribilof Is.
Nelson I.

RUSSIA

PACIFIC OCEAN

Aleutian Is.
Unimak I.
Dutch Harbor
Unalaska I.
Umnak I.
Andreanof Is.
Adak I.
Rat Is.
Near Is.
Attu
Amchitka
Kiska

Shumagin Is.
Alaska Pen.

ALASKA
Projection: Bonne
100 0 100 200 300 400 500 600 700 800 900 km
100 0 100 200 300 400 miles

m 6000 4000 2000 1000 400 200 0
ft 18000 12000 6000 3000 1500 600 0

West from Greenwich

COPYRIGHT PHILIP'S

1 · 2 · 3 · 4 · 5 · 6 · 9 · 10

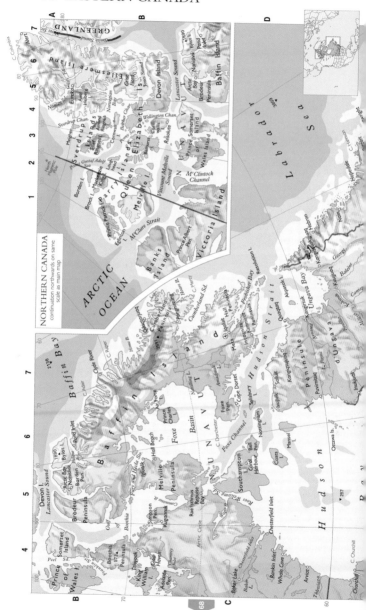

NORTHERN CANADA
continuation northwards on same
scale as main map

GREENLAND
(Denmark)

ARCTIC OCEAN

Ellesmere Island

Queen Elizabeth Islands

Sverdrup Islands

Parry Islands

Baffin Island

Baffin Bay

Labrador Sea

Devon I.

Banks Island

Victoria Island

NUNAVUT

Boothia Peninsula

Melville Peninsula

Foxe Basin

Southampton I.

Hudson Bay

Ungava Peninsula

Hudson Strait

Prince of Wales I.

Somerset Island

Broadeur Peninsula

Lancaster Sound

Cumberland Sd.

68

1 2 3 120 4 118 5

VANCOUVER
Nanaimo
Vancouver
Island Duncan
Juan de Fuca Strait
Sooke
Flattery
Neah Bay

PACIFIC RAIL
NAT. REC.
AREA
Surrey New
Westminster
Coquitlam
Chilliwack
Mt. Baker
NORTH
CASCADES
NAT. PARK

BRITISH C

B

Victoria
Esquimalt
Oak Har.
Port Townsend
Port Angeles
La Push
OLYMPIC
NAT. PARK
4428

Anacortes
Burlington
Sedro-Woolley
Mount Vernon
Arlington
Concrete
Glacier Peak
3329
Winthrop
Oroville
Tonasket
Republic
Curlew
Franklin D.
Roosevelt L.
Kettle Falls
Colville
Trail

Bellingham

PACIFIC OCEAN

C

Moclips
Neilton
Hoodsport
Shelton

Everett
Snohomish
SEATTLE
Bremerton
Bellevue
Tacoma
Renton
Olympia
Lacey
Puyallup
Enumclaw

Chelan
Waterville
WASHINGTON
Wenatchee
Grand Coulee
Coulee City
Moses Lake

Spokane
Davenport
Cheney
Opportunity
Post Falls
Coeu
d'Ale

46

Hoquiam
Aberdeen
Grays Harbor
Montesano
Raymond
Willapa B.
Ocean Park
Long Beach
Ocean City

Centralia
Chehalis
MOUNT RAINIER
NAT. PARK
4392
Morton
Yakima
Ellensburg
Quincy
HANFORD REACH
NAT. MON.
Othello
Lind
Ritzville
Columbia
Basin
Garfield
Oakesdale
Rosalia
Pullman
Moscow

D

Seaside
Cannon Beach
Warrenton
Astoria
Wheeler
Tillamook

Longview
Kelso
St. Helens
Kalama
MOUNT ST. HELENS
NAT. MON.
2551
Battle Ground
PORTLAND
Vancouver
Camas
Cascade Locks
Hood River
3427
Goldendale
Columbia
Toppenish
Sunnyside
Grandview
Prosser
Kennewick
Richland
Pasco
Walla Walla
Milton-Freewater
Weston
Waitsburg
Dayton
Pomeroy
HELLS CANYON
NAT. REC. AREA
Lewiston
Clarkston

Hillsboro
Beaverton
Milwaukie
Gresham
Oregon City
Canby
Union Gap
Naches
Wapato

Tillamook
Meares
Lincoln City
McMinnville
Newberg
Woodburn
Salem
Keizer
Dallas
Monmouth
Stayton

The Dalles
Wasco
Arlington
Grass
Valley
Fossil
Hermiston
Pilot Rock
Pendleton
Elgin
La Grande
North Powder
Wallowa
Enterprise
Joseph
White
Riggins

Newport
Toledo
Philomath
Corvallis
Albany
Lebanon
Sweet Home

Madras
JOHN DAY FOSSIL
BEDS NAT. MON.
Mitchell
John Day
Spray
Prairie City
Baker City
Haines
Council
McCall
New
Meadows

Waldport
Mapleton
Florence
OREGON DUNES
NAT. REC. AREA
Reedsport

Eugene
Springfield
3186
McKenzie
Redmond
Prineville
Dayville

Mountains

Huntington
Ontario
Payette
New Plymouth
Emmett
Fruitland
Parma
Nampa
Caldwell
Garden City
Meridian
Eagle
BOISE
Mountain H

E

North Bend
Coos Bay
Coquille
Myrtle Point
Bandon
Pt. Blanco
Port Orford
Gold Beach

Cottage
Grove
Sutherlin
Roseburg
Myrtle Creek
Canyonville

Bend
NEWBERRY
NAT. VOLCANIC MON.
La Pine
Chemult
Silver Lake
Summer
L.

OREGON
Brothers
Burns
Junction

Harney Basin
Harney L.
Malheur L.
Crane
Riley
Juntura
Vale
Homedale
Murphy

OWYHEE Res.
Jordan
Valley
Bruneau

Brookings
SMITH RIVER
NAT. REC. AREA

Grants Pass
Gold
Hill
Central
Point
Medford
White Mt.
City McLoughlin
2894
Fort Klamath
Rajneesh
Abert
L.
Valley Falls

Steens Mountain
2962
Alvord
Desert

HAGERMA
FOSSIL-A
NAT. REC.
AREA

44

REDWOOD
NAT. PARK
Crescent
City

Cave Jct.
CRATER LAKE
NAT. PARK

Klamath
Falls
Altamont
Clear Lake
Lakeview
LAVA BEDS
NAT. MON.

Warner Mts.

McDermitt

Plateau

F

Klamath
Hoopa
Hornbrook
Yreka
Mt. Shasta
4317
Ashland
Talent
Dorris
Canby
Altamont
Goose
L.

Winnemucca
Paradise
Valley
Golconda
Battle
Mountain
Elko
Spring
Creek

McKinleyville
Arcata
Eureka
Fortuna
Scotia
Weott
Cape
Mendocino
Garberville

Mt. Shasta
McCloud
Weaverville
KLAMATH
MTS.
TRINITY ALPS
WILDERNESS
Burney
Bieber
Middle
Alkali L.
Lower
Alkali L.

Santa Rosa Range
Little Humboldt R.

Independence Mts.
Mountain City

124

CALIFORNIA

Redding
Anderson
Red Bluff
Shasta L.
3187
Lassen Pk.
LASSEN
VOLCANIC
NAT. PARK
Chester
Westwood
Eagle
L.

Lovelock
Humboldt R.

Ruby
L.
Ruby
Mts.
Franklin
L.

Leggett
Laytonville
Willits

Corning
Orland
Chico
Paradise
Oroville
Portola

Gerlach
Rye Patch
Res.
Honey
L.

Trinity
Range

Smith Creek
Dunphy

G

Ft. Bragg
Mendocino
Pt. Arena
Ukiah
Hopland
Cloverdale
Healdsburg
Windsor
Santa Rosa
Petaluma
Calistoga
St.
Helena
Napa
Sonoma
Vallejo
San Rafael
Berkeley
POINT REYES
NAT. SEASHORE
Golden Gate

Clearlake
Willows
Williams
Colusa
Arbuckle
Clear
Lake
Lower
Lake
Upper
Lake
Woodland
Davis
Vacaville
Fairfield
Richmond
Concord

Yuba City
Marysville
Grass
Valley
Roseville
SACRAMENTO
Arden
Elk Grove
Lodi
Galt
San Andreas
Ione
Olivehurst
Auburn
Camino

Wadsworth
Sparks
RENO
Fernley
Carson
Sink
Stillwater
Ra.
Fallon
Carson City
Virginia
City
Schurz
Walker L.
Mt. Jefferson
3626
Luning
Hot
Springs
Range
Currant

Sierra
Truckee
Nevada
Lake
Tahoe

NEVADA
Toiyabe
Shoshone Mountains

McGil

Projection: Albers' Equal Area with two standard parallels

1 2 3 120 4 118 78 5 116 6

===== Freeways   ⊠ ⊛ State Capitals   ☐ National Parks

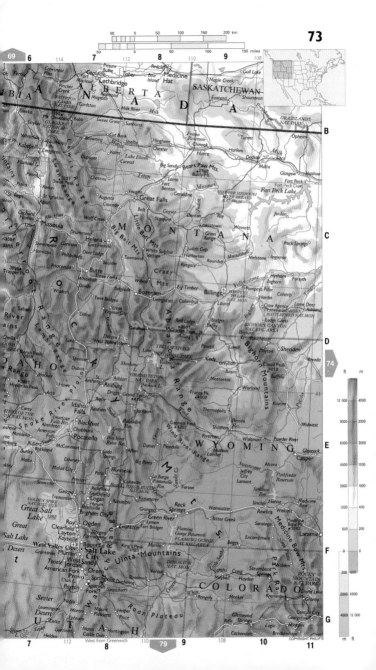

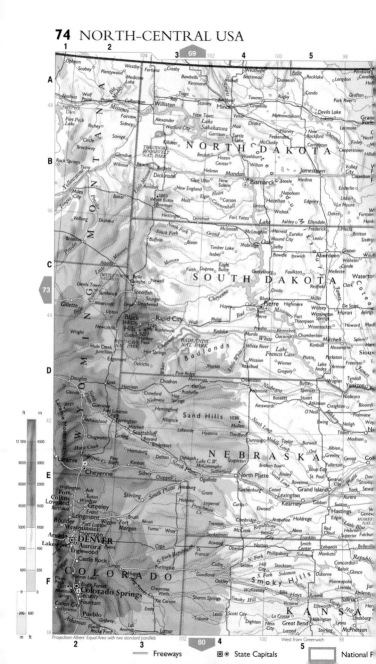

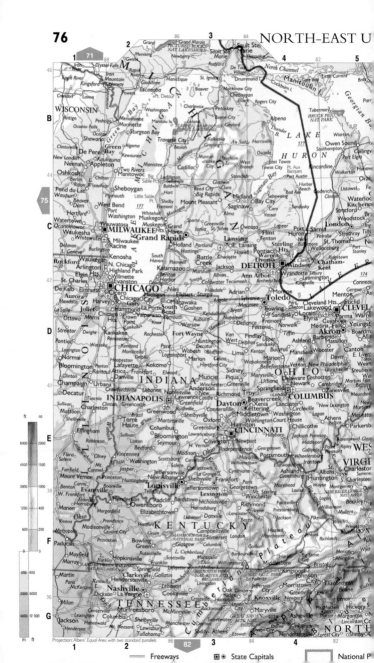

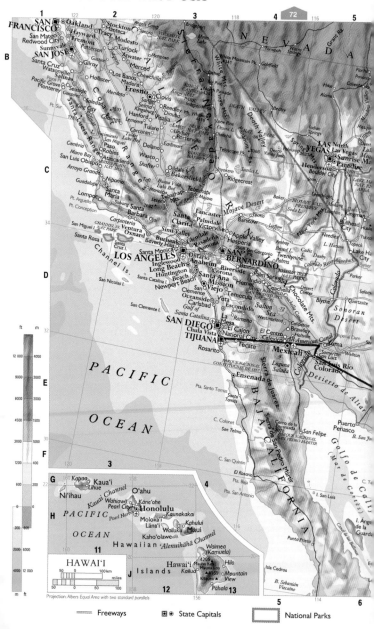

Freeways ⌗ ✦ State Capitals ▭ National Parks

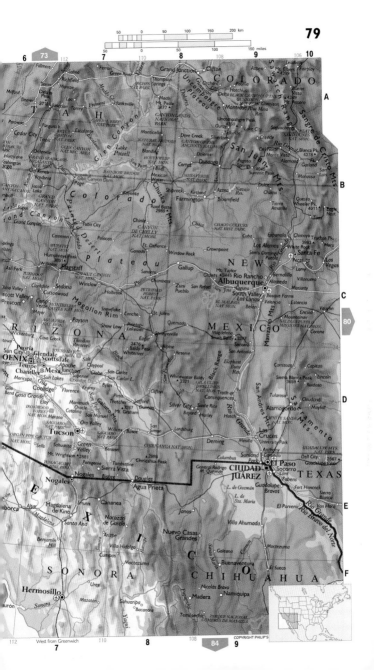

50 0 50 100 150 200 km
50 0 50 100 150 miles

COLORADO

Fillmore Ferron Green River Grand Junction Clifton
Orchard Hotchkiss Aspen Leadville Fairplay
Richfield Thompson Delta Gunnison Buena Vista
Monroe Mt. Peale BLACK CANYON OF THE Mt. Elbert A
Milford Beaver ARCHES 3877 GUNNISON 4399 Salida
Junction Torrey Hanksville CANYONLANDS Montrose Blue Mesa Mt. Antero
Delta 3718 NATIONAL Uncompahgre Peak 4349
Marysvale PARK 4359

U T A H CAPITOL REEF Monticello Dove Creek Silverton Lake City Creede SAN de CRISTO Mts
NAT. PARK Telluride Rio Grande Blanca Pk.
Cedar City Escalante NATURAL BRIDGES Monte Vista 4378 Garland
BRYCE GLEN NAT. MON. Blanding HOVENWEEP Dolores Pagosa Summit Peak Alamosa Monassa
CANYON CANYON Lake NAT. MON. Cortez Durango Springs
NAT. PARK Powell MESA VERDE
Hurricane GLEN CANYON Mexican NAT. PARK B
Washington Kanab RAINBOW BRIDGE Waters Shiprock Kirtland Navajo Dulce Chama
Gorge Fredonia NAT. MON. Aztec Res. Tierra Questa Eagle
Jacob Page Amarilla Wheeler Pk. Nest
Kaibab Glen Canyon Kayenta C o l o r a d o Farmington Bloomfield 4011 Taos
GRAND Supai Root Butte CHACO CULTURE Española Chimayó Truchas Pk. Mora
CANYON 2989 NAT. HIST. PARK Cuba Los Alamos 3993
Grand Canyon Tuba City Chinle Chuze White Rock Santa Fe
Cameron CANYON Ft. Defiance San Domingo Las
DE CHELLY Crownpoint Pueblo Lamy Vegas
Supai NAT. MON. Window Rock N E W Rio Rancho Villanueva C
Ash Fork Williams Polacca Ganado Mt. Taylor Bernalillo Moriarty
TUZIGOOT WUPATKI 3445 Rio Rancho
Seligman NAT. MON. NAT. MON. Gallup Alameda Estancia
Flagstaff SUNSET CRATER Sanders Zuni San Rafael Albuquerque Encino
Pine Valley Clarkdale Cottonwood NAT. MON. Chambers Pueblo South Valley Vaughn
Scott Valley Sedona Winslow PETRIFIED Los Lunas Valencia
Mayer Humphreys Peak Holbrook FOREST EL MALPAIS Belén
Prescott 3851 NAT. PARK NAT. MON. Manzano Mts Corona
Camp MONTEZUMA M o g o l l o n St. Johns SALINAS PUEBLO
Verde CASTLE NAT. MON. Snowflake Concho MISSIONS NAT. MON. Mountainair

A R I Z O N A Show Low R i m Quemado Magdalena M E X I C O Vaughn
Payson Pinetop- South Baldy Socorro 342
Wickenburg TONTO NAT. Lakeside 3445 San Antonio Corona
Cave Creek MON. Theodore Baldy Peak Alpine Reserve
Peoria Glendale Roosevelt 3476 Whiteriver Elephant Corizozo Capitan
Scottsdale Salt Butte Res. Lincoln
PHOENIX Mesa Apache Sierra Blanca Peak Ruidoso
Tempe Junction Globe San Carlos GILA CLIFF 3659 D
Chandler Superior Claypool San Carlos L. Whitewater Baldy DWELLINGS Truth or Cloudcroft
Sun Lakes 3321 NAT. MON. Consequences Tularosa
Maricopa Gila Goodyear Florence Kearny Clifton Silver City Santa Rita Hatch Alamogordo Mayhill
Bend Casa Grande Miami Bayard Harley WHITE SANDS Sacramento Mts
Eloy Mammoth Oracle Thatcher Safford Las NAT. MON.
IRONWOOD Catalina San Manuel Mt. Graham Lordsburg Cruces
FOREST NAT. MON. Morano 3267 Deming Mesilla E
Oro Valley San Simon University Park GUADALUPE Mts
ORGAN PIPE CACTUS Tucson Bowie Anthony NAT. PARK
NAT. MON. SAGUARO Willcox Dell City 2667
Sells Mt. Wrightson NAT. PARK Benson CHIRICAHUA NAT. MON. Columbus Sunland Guadalupe Peak
2881 Park El Paso TEXAS
Sahuarita Green Tombstone General Rodrigo CIUDAD Socorro Fabens
Tubac Valley Sierra M. Quevedo JUÁREZ Clint
Nogales Patagonia Vista Bisbee Chiricahua Peak Fort Hancock
TUMACÁCORI Douglas 2986 Guadalupe Sierra
NAT. HIST. PARK Agua Prieta Bravos Blanca
Nogales El Porvenir Rio Grande
M Cananea Janos L. de Guzmán Van Horn
E Imuris L. de El Porvenir Rio Bravo del Norte E
Magdalena Santa Ana Sta. María
de Kino Nacozari Moctezuma
Tiborca Santa Ana de García Villa Ahumada
Benjamín Arizpe Nuevo Casas Galeana
Hill Villa Hidalgo Grandes Buenaventura F
C O El Sueco
Cumpas Moctezuma
S O N O R A C H I H U A H U A
Hermosillo Ures Nicolás Bravo
Sonora Namiquipa
Aurón Mazatán Sahuaripa Madera PARQUE NACIONAL
Bacanora Temósachic CUMBRES DE MAJALCA

Yaqui

COPYRIGHT PHILIP'S

80

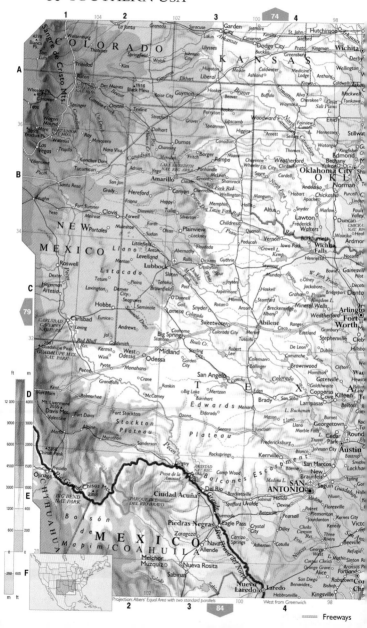

West from Greenwich

Freeways

Freeways   ⊠ ⊛ State Capitals   National Parks

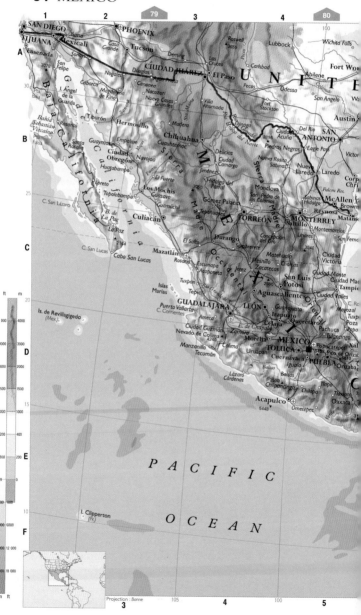

PACIFIC

OCEAN

Projection : Bonne

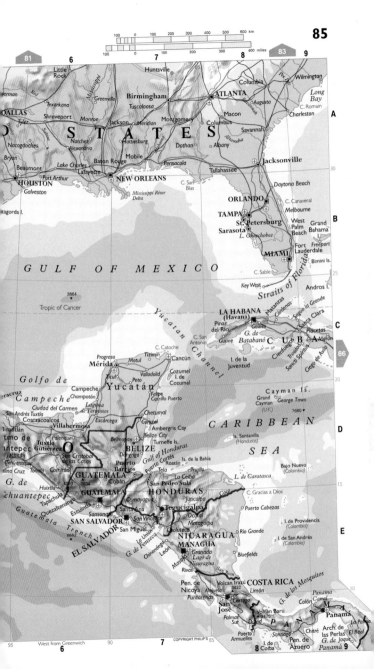

100   0   100   200   300   400   500   600 km
100   0   100   200   300   400 miles

Little Rock
Huntsville
Columbia
Wilmington
erman   Red
Greenville
Birmingham   ATLANTA   Augusta   Long Bay
Texarkana   Tuscaloosa   Charleston   C. Romain
DALLAS   Shreveport   Jackson   Meridian   Montgomery   Columbus   Macon   Savannah   **A**
Tyler   Monroe
Nacogdoches   Natchez   Alexandria   Hattiesburg   Dothan   Albany   Altamaha
Bryan   Lafayette   Mobile   Pensacola   Tallahassee   Jacksonville
Beaumont   Lake Charles   Baton Rouge
HOUSTON   Port Arthur   NEW ORLEANS   C. San   Daytona Beach   30
Galveston   Blas
atagorda I.   Mississippi River Delta   ORLANDO   C. Canaveral   **B**
Melbourne
TAMPA   West   Grand
St. Petersburg   Palm   Bahama
Sarasota   L. Okeechobee   Beach   Freeport
Fort   Bimini Is.
Lauderdale
MIAMI
G U L F   O F   M E X I C O   C. Sable   25
Key West   Straits of Florida   Andros I.
3664
Tropic of Cancer   LA HABANA   Matanzas   Sagua la Grande
Yucatan   (Havana)   Santa Clara
Pinar   Cárdenas
del Río   G. de   Colón   Placetas   **C**
Progreso   Güines   Batabanó   C U B A
C. Catoche   Cienfuegos   Trinidad   Sancti Spíritus   Ciego de Ávila
Mérida   Motul   Cancún   I. de Pinos   I. de la   20
Tizimín   Cozumel   Juventud
Ticul   Valladolid   I. de
Campeche   Peto   Cozumel
racruz   Champotón   Felipe   Cayman Is.   **D**
Campeche   Carrillo Puerto   Grand   George Town
Ciudad del Carmen   Chetumal   Cayman   7680
San Andrés Tuxtla   Laguna   (UK)
Coatzacoalcos   de Términos   Escárcega   Corozal   *C A R I B B E A N*
limantlán   Villahermosa   Ambergris Cay
timo de   Palenque   Belmopan   Turneffe Is.   Is. Santanilla
ntepec   BELIZE   (Honduras)   *S E A*
Jalapa   Tuxtla   San Cristóbal   Dangriga   Gulf of Honduras   Bajo Nuevo   15
Gutiérrez   de las Casas   Belize City   Is. de la Bahía   (Colombia)
lina Cruz   Tonalá   Comitán   Puerto   Roatán   L. de Caratasca
Huixtla   GUATEMALA   Barrios   Tela   La Ceiba   Trujillo
G. de   Cobán   Puerto Cortés
huantepec   Quetzaltenango   San Pedro Sula   HONDURAS   C. Gracias a Dios
Tapachula   GUATEMALA   Comayagua   Juticalpa
Guatemala   Escuintla   Santa Ana   TEGUCIGALPA   Ocotal   Puerto Cabezas
Trench   Sonsonate   San Vicente   Matagalpa   I. de Providencia   **E**
6662   SAN SALVADOR   San Miguel   Choluteca   (Colombia)
EL SALVADOR   G. de Fonseca   NICARAGUA   Río Grande   I. de San Andrés
León   MANAGUA   (Colombia)
Chinandega   Granada   Lago de   Bluefields
Masaya   Nicaragua
Rivas   San Juan
Pen. de   Volcán Irazú   COSTA RICA   G. de los Mosquitos
Nicoya   3432   Limón   Colón   Canal
Puntarenas   Alajuela   Cartago   PANAMÁ   Panama
SAN JOSÉ   David   Volcán Barú   Chitré   Arch. de
Palmar   3475   P A N A M Á   las Perlas   El Real
Sur   La Palma
Puerto   G. de Jaqué
Armuelles   I. de   Pen. de   Panamá   10
Coiba   Azuero
95   West from Greenwich   90   7   COPYRIGHT PHILIP'S   85
6   8   9

85

ft   m
12 000   4000
9000   3000
6000   2000
4500   1500
3000   1000
1200   400
600   200
0   0
200   600
2000   6000
4000   12 000
6000   18 000
m   ft

Projection : Bonne

West from Greenwich

100 0 100 200 300 400 500 600 km
100 0 100 200 300 400 miles

6   65   **7**   60   **8**   55

A

SARGASSO
SEA

ATLANTIC OCEAN

B

Tropic of Cancer

Guana I.
Turks & Caicos Is.
Cockburn (U.K.)
Town
de-Paix
Cap-Haïtien
Monte Christi
Fort-de-Paix
Santiago de
Plata
Los Caballeros
Ile San Francisco
de Macorís
Gonaïves
La Vega
DOMINICAN La Romana
REP.
San Pedro de Macorís
San Juan
SANTO DOMINGO
Barahona
Hispaniola
tilles

9200 Puerto Rico Trench

Mona
Passage
Arecibo SAN JUAN
Charlotte
Amalie Virgin Is.
(U.S.A./U.K.)
Caguas (U.S.A.)
Ponce St. Croix St-Eustatius
PUERTO RICO (Neth.)
(U.S.A.)
Mayagüez
Basseterre

C

Anguilla (U.K.)
St-Martin (Neth./Fr.)
St-Barthélemy (Fr.)
ST. KITTS & NEVIS
ANTIGUA &
BARBUDA
St. John's
Montserrat(U.K.)
GUADELOUPE(Fr.)
Pointe-à-Pitre
Basse-Terre
DOMINICA
Roseau
MARTINIQUE(Fr.)
Fort-de-France
Castries
ST. LUCIA
Kingstown
BARBADOS
Bridgetown
GRENADA
St George's

Leeward
Islands
Lesser
Antilles
BEAN SEA
ST. VINCENT &
THE GRENADINES
Windward
Islands

D

La Blanquilla
(Ven.)
Aruba (Neth.)
Pta. Gallinas
en. de la
Oranjestad
Guajira
Curaçao
Willemstad
Bonaire
NETH.
 ANTILLES
Punto
Fijo
Coro
La Tortuga
San
Felipe
Puerto Cabello
MARACAY
I. de Margarita
Porlamar
Tobago
Port of Spain
TRINIDAD & TOBAGO
San Fernando

nacha
ra Nevada
Santa Marta
Valledupar
MARACAIBO
Cabimas
Barquisimeto VALENCIA Barcelona
L. de
Maracaibo
Valera
Mérida
65074
Acarigua
Barinas
San Fernando
de Apure
Cumaná
Carúpano
Puerto La Cruz
2596
Maturin
El Tigre
Orinoco
Tucupita
G. de
Paria
Guiria

E

o Ciudad
Ciudad
Guayana
Bolívar
Embalse de Guri
Tumeremo
Georgetown
Bartica
New Amsterdam
Linden
Wismar

GUYANA

Bucaramanga
enta
to W
San Cristóbal
Sogamoso
unja
OGOTÁ
Villavicencio
L de
VENEZUELA
Puerto Carreño
Arauca
Meta
Caicara
Puerto Ayacucho
Orinoco
Mt. Roraima
Caroni
Cuyuni
Essequibo
SURINAME

F

Puerto Inírida
Guaviare
BIA
Sierra Pacaraima
Parima
Sierra
Parima
Casiquiare
Boa Vista
Equator

BRAZIL

92

5   70   **90**   **6**   65   **7**   60   **8**

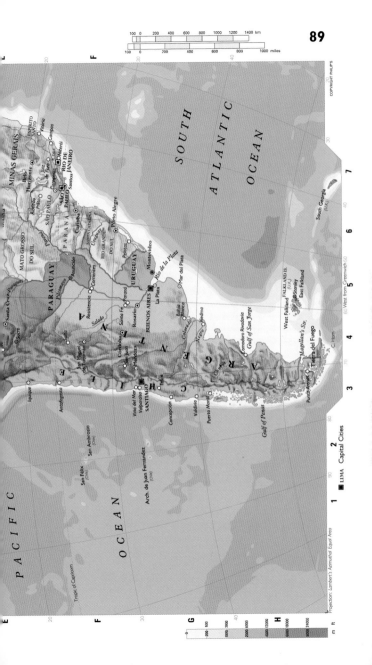

89

100 0 200 400 600 800 1000 1200 1400 km
100 0 200 400 600 800 1000 miles

COPYRIGHT PHILIPS

PACIFIC

OCEAN

Tropic of Capricorn

San Félix (Chile)   San Ambrosio (Chile)

Arch. de Juan Fernández (Chile)

Iquique

Antofagasta

Viña del Mar
Valparaíso
SANTIAGO
Talca

Concepción

Valdivia

Puerto Montt

Gulf of Penas

Punta Arenas

C. Horn

MINAS GERAIS
Victoria
ESPÍRITO SANTO

Belo Horizonte

Campos

Ouro Prêto
Juiz de Fora

MATO GROSSO DO SUL

Ribeirão Prêto

SÃO PAULO

RIO DE JANEIRO
Santos
Baía de Santos

PARANÁ

Curitiba

SANTA CATARINA

RIO GRANDE DO SUL

Uruguai

Pôrto Alegre

Pelotas

Santa Cruz

Sucre

Iberá

San Miguel de Tucumán

San Juan

Mendoza

Córdoba

PARAGUAY

Asunción

Pilcomayo

Paraguay

Resistencia

Corrientes

Salado

Santa Fé

Paraná

Rosario

URUGUAY

Montevideo

Río de la Plata

BUENOS AIRES

La Plata

Mar del Plata

Salado

Bahía Blanca

Colorado

Negro

Neuquén

Chubut

Comodoro Rivadavia

Gulf of San Jorge

Magellan's Str.

Tierra del Fuego

West Falland   FALKLAND IS. (U.K.)

Stanley

East Falkland

South Georgia (U.K.)

SOUTH

ATLANTIC

OCEAN

60 West from Greenwich (V)

Projection: Lambert's Azimuthal Equal Area

■ LIMA Capital Cities

m   ft
0
200   600
1000 3000
2000 6000
4000 12000
6000 18000
8000 24000

G   H

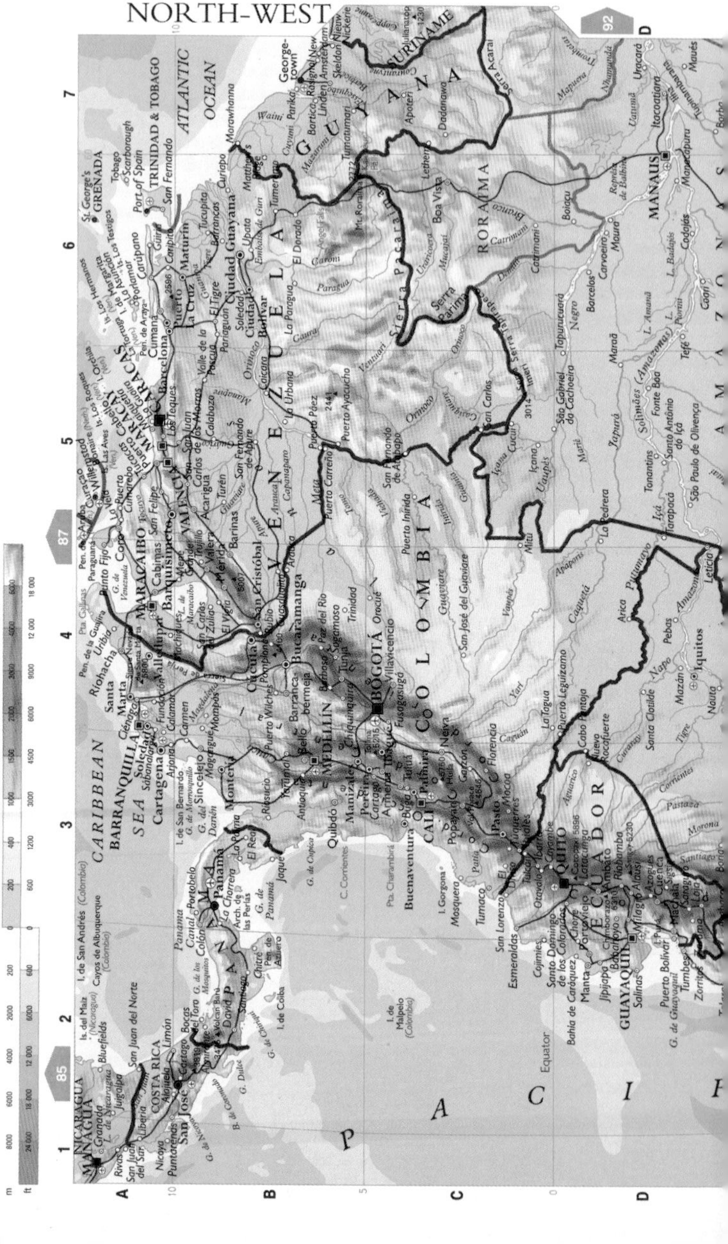
CARIBBEAN SEA
ATLANTIC OCEAN
PACIFIC
VENEZUELA
COLOMBIA
ECUADOR
PANAMA
COSTA RICA
NICARAGUA
GUYANA
SURINAME
TRINIDAD & TOBAGO
GRENADA
RORAIMA
AMAZONAS
CARACAS
BOGOTÁ
QUITO
GUAYAQUIL
MEDELLÍN
CALI
BARRANQUILLA
MARACAIBO
VALENCIA
MANAUS
Panamá
San José
Managua
Georgetown
Port of Spain
Cartagena
Barquisimeto
Ciudad Guayana
Cúcuta
Bucaramanga
Iquitos
Leticia
Cuenca
Equator
85
87
92

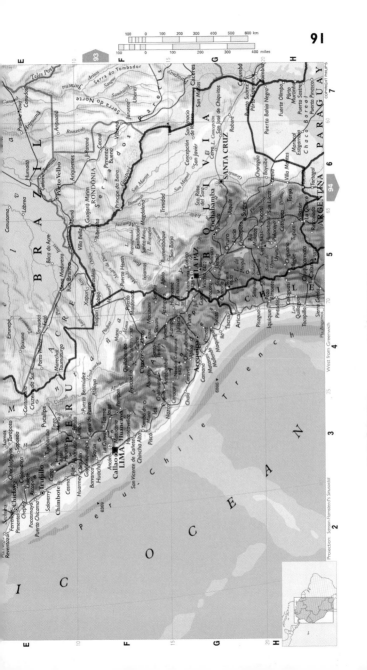

100   0   100   200   300   400   500   600 km
100   0   100   200   300   400 miles

Projection: Sanson-Flamsteed's Sinusoidal

West from Greenwich

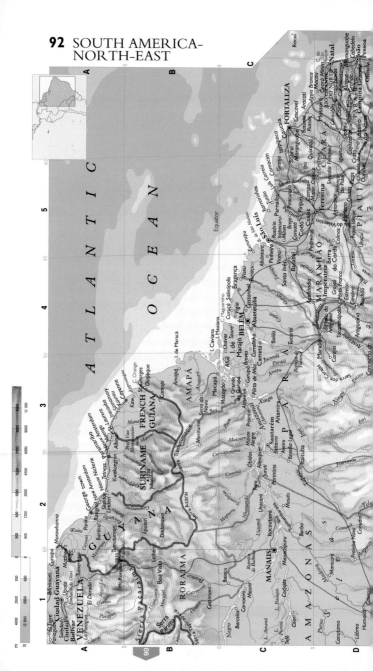

A T L A N T I C   O C E A N

VENEZUELA

GUYANA

SURINAME

FRENCH GUIANA

RORAIMA

AMAPÁ

P A R Á

MARANHÃO

PIAUÍ

CEARÁ

RIO GRANDE DO NORTE

A M A Z O N A S

MANAUS

BELÉM

São Luís

FORTALEZA

Boa Vista

Teresina

Equator

Serra Pacaraima

Serra Parima

90

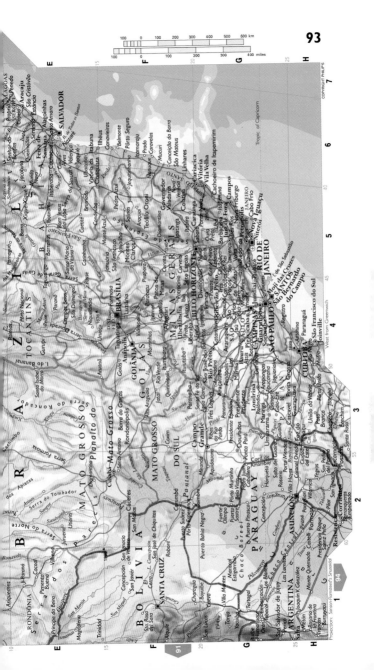

100 0 100 200 300 400 500 600 km
100 0 100 200 300 400 miles

Tropic of Capricorn

West from Greenwich

Projection: Sanson-Flamsteed's Sinusoidal

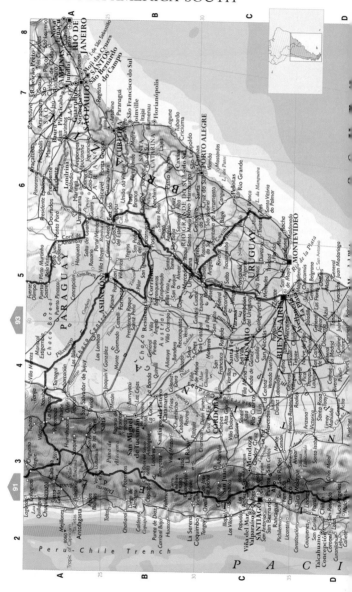

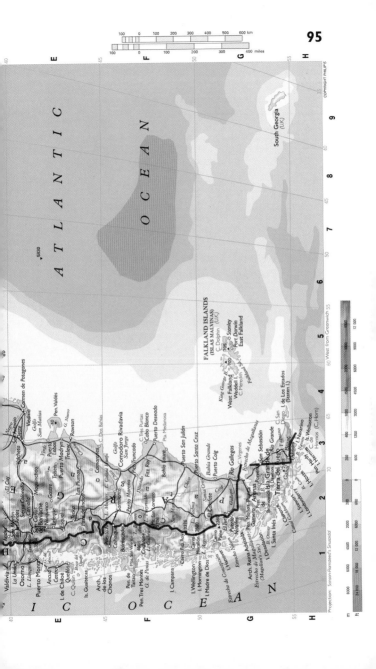

100 0 100 200 300 400 500 600 km
100 0 100 200 300 400 miles

COPYRIGHT PHILIPS

A T L A N T I C

O C E A N

South Georgia
(UK)

•5830

Carmen de Patagones
Viedma
Golfo
San Matías
Pen. Valdés
G. Nuevo
Rawson

Trelew
Puerto Madryn

Tecka
Tres Lagunas

Camarones
Golfo
San Jorge
C. Dos Bahías

Comodoro Rivadavia
C. Tres Puntas
Cabo Blanco

Fitz Roy
Deseado
Puerto Deseado
Pta. Medanosa

Perito Moreno

Puerto Santa Cruz
Puerto San Julián

Bahía Grande
Puerto Coig

Río Gallegos
C. Vírgenes

FALKLAND ISLANDS
(ISLAS MALVINAS)
(UK)

C. Dolphin
King George B.
West Fal---Stanley
land   Goose G.
C. Meredith Port Darwin
Falkland Sd. East Falkland

Valdivia
La Unión
Osorno
Puerto Montt
L. Llanquihue
Bariloche
Esquel
I. de Chiloé
Quellón
Chonos

Pen. de
Taitao
Pen. Tres Montes
G. de Penas

I. Campana
I. Wellington
I. Mornington
I. Madre de Dios

Estrecho de Magallanes
Punta Arenas
I. Dawson
B. Inútil
I. Santa Inés

Tierra del
Fuego
Río Grande
San Sebastián

I. de Los Estados
(Staten I.)
C. San
Diego

C. Hoorn
(C. Horn)

Projection: Sanson-Flamsteed's Sinusoidal

55 50 60 West from Greenwich 55

m 8000 6000 4000 2000 0
ft 24 000 18 000 12 000 6000 0

200 400 600 800 1000 1200 1500 3000 4500 6000 9000 12 000
600 1200 3000 4500 6000 9000 12 000

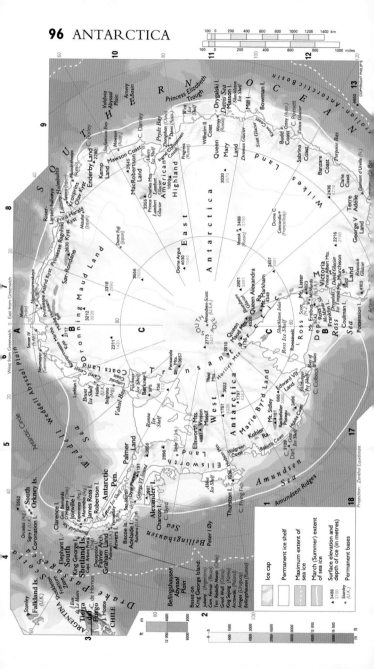

100 0 200 400 600 800 1000 1200 1400 km
100 0 200 400 600 800 1000 miles

COPYRIGHT PHILIP'S

S O U T H E R N

Riiser-Larsen-Halvøya

Amery E. Basin

Princess Elizabeth Trough

Drygalski I.
Davis Sea
Masson I.
Shackleton Ice Shelf
Mill I.
Bowman I.

Victoria E. Plain

O C E A N

Australian—Antarctic Basin

-4650 4521

13

12

9

Syowa (Japan)
Lazarev (Russia)
Novolazarevskaya
Maitri (India)

Sanae IV
(S. Africa)

Neumayer (Germany)

C. Darnley
Mawson (Austr.)

Kemp
Land

Enderby Land
2280

MacRobertson
Land

Prince Charles Mts.
3355
Lambert Glacier
Amery Ice Shelf

Ingrid Christensen Coast
Zhongshan (China)
Progress (Russia)

American Highland
1800

Mawson Coast
2645

Mirnyy (Russia)

Wilhelm II
Coast

Queen Mary Land

C. Filchner
Davis (Austr.)
Poynduu Bay

Shackleton Ice Shelf

Budd
Coast
Casey (Austr.)
Sabrina Coast
Banzare Coast
Clarie Coast

Knox Coast
Scott Glacier
Totten Glacier
Drewsen Glacier

Wilkes Land

Sabrina
Coast

Terre Adélie
Dumont d'Urville (Fr.)
Commonwealth Bay

George V Land

3030 2970

2436 4476

2216 2798

Prince Olav Coast
Prince Harald Kyst
Prinsesse Ragnhild Kyst
Princesse Astrid Kyst

Dome Fuji (Japan)

Dronning Maud Land

Sør-Rondane

3656 3202

3318 2990

3212 3039

Dome Argus 4030
4091

Vostok ▲ 3488
(Russia) 3700

Dome C
Concordia
(France/Italy)

East

Antarctica

2311 1431

2407
3587

C

2773
2407

SOUTH POLE
Amundsen-Scott (U.S.A.)

Mt. Markham 4351
2801

Mt. Lister 4025
Mt. Minto 4165

Victoria
Land

Prince Albert Mts.
Mt. Murchison 4163

Coulman I.

Possession I.

Cape Adare

R o s s

S e a

B

Mt. Erebus
McMurdo (U.S.A.)
Scott (N.Z.)
Ross I.
Mt. Terror

Queen Alexandra Ra. 4529
4709

Queen Maud Mts. 2773
4116

Beardmore Glacier
4810

Shackleton Inlet

Ross Ice Shelf

Roosevelt I.

Bay of Whales

Edward VII
Land

C. Colbeck

Sulzberger Bay
Sulzberger Ice Shelf

Marie Byrd Land

Mt. Sidley 4181

Kohler Ra.

Executive Committee Ra. 3080

Toney Mt.

David Glacier
Priestley Glacier
Mt. Franklin 4349

Lyddan I. (U.K.)

Maudheim

Halley (U.K.)

Brunt Ice Shelf

Coats Land

Belgrano II (Arg.)

Filchner Ice Shelf
Berkner I.
975

Ronne Ice Shelf

Vahsel Coast

Pensacola Mts. 3657

Thiel Mts.

Horlick Mts.
3022

West Antarctica

Ellsworth Land

Ellsworth Mts.
Vinson Massif 4897

2896

Byrd (U.S.A.)

Walgreen Coast

Bakutis Coast

C. Flying Fish

Thurston I.

Peter I Øy (Nor.)

Bellingshausen
Abyssal Plain

Bellingshausen Sea

Eights Coast

Abbot Ice Shelf

C. Dart
Getz Ice Shelf
Grant I. 3109

A m u n d s e n S e a

Amundsen Ridges

Charcot I.

Alexander I.

Palmer Land

Robertson I.

Antarctic Pen.

Graham Land

Palmer Arch.
Anvers I.
Adelaide I.
Rothera (U.K.)
Biscoe Is.

Marguerite Bay
Bellingshausen (Russia)

George VI Sound

Fletcher Peninsula

Larsen Ice Shelf

Seal Nunataks 1191

Dyer Plateau

James Ross I.
Joinville I.
Clarence I.
Elephant I.

King George I.
South Shetland Is.
Deception I.
Livingston I.

Esperanza (Arg.)
Capt. Arturo Prat (Chile)
O'Higgins (Chile)
Gen. Bernardo

South Orkney Is.
Coronation I.
Signy I. (U.K.)
Laurie I.
Orcadas (Arg.) ▲5552

Clarence I.

S c o t i a   R i d g e s

South Georgia

Shag Rocks

Falkland Is. (U.K.)
Stanley

Tierra del Fuego
C. de Hornos
Hoste I.

ARGENTINA
CHILE

Weddell Abyssal Plain

Antarctic Circle

W e d d e l l

S e a

Drake Passage

Antarctic Circle

Projection: Zenithal Equidistant

Bases on King George Island	
Jubany (Argentina)	
Teniente Marsh (Chile)	
Great Wall (China)	
King Sejong (Korea)	
Arctowski (Poland)	
Artigas (Uruguay)	
Bellingshausen (Russia)	

Ice cap

Permanent ice shelf

Maximum extent of sea ice

March (Summer) extent of sea ice

Surface elevation and depth of ice (in metres)
▲ 3488
= 3700

▲ Permanent bases

ft
15 000
12 000
9000
6000
3000
1500
0
m
5000
4000
3000
2000
1000
500
0

Index to Map Pages

The index contains the names of all the principal places and features shown on the world maps. Physical features composed of a proper name (Erie) and a description (Lake) are positioned alphabetically by the proper name. The description is positioned after the proper name and is usually abbreviated:

Erie, L. 76 C5

Where a description forms part of a settlement or administrative name, however, it is always written in full and put in its true alphabetical position:

Lake Charles 81 D7

Names beginning St. are alphabetized under Saint, but Sankt, Sant, Santa and San are all spelt in full and are alphabetized accordingly.

The number in bold type which follows each name in the index refers to the number of the map page where that feature or place will be found. This is usually the largest scale at which the place or feature appears.

The letter and figure which are in bold type immediately after the page number give the grid square on the map page, within which the feature is situated.

Rivers are indexed to their mouths or confluences, and carry the symbol → after their names. The following symbols are also used in the index: ■ country, ☑ overseas territory or dependency, □ first order administrative area, △ national park.

A

A Coruña **18 A1**
A Estrada **18 A1**
A Fonsagrada **18 A2**
Aachen **14 C4**
Aalborg **9 D7**
Aalen **14 D6**
Aarhus = Århus **9 D8**
Aba **53 G7**
Abaco I. **86 A4**
Ābādān **47 E7**
Ābādeh **44 D3**
Abadla **52 B5**
Abaetetuba **92 C4**
Abakan **30 D7**
Abancay **91 F4**
Abarqū **44 D3**
Abashiri **32 A9**
Abashiri-Wan **32 B9**
Ābay = Nîl el Azraq → **55 E5**
Abay **29 E8**
Abaya, L. **55 E5**
Abaya, L. **55 G6**
Abbay = Nîl el Azraq → **55 E5**
Abbeville **12 A4**
Abbieglassie **63 A4**
Abbot Ice Shelf **96 B2**
ABC Islands = Netherlands Antilles ☑ **87 D6**
Abd al Kūrī **49 E5**
Abéché **55 F3**
Abel Tasman △ **64 D5**
Abeokuta **53 G6**
Abercorn **63 A5**

Aberdeen *Australia* **63 B5**
Aberdeen *U.K.* **10 C5**
Aberdeen *S. Dak., U.S.A.* **74 C5**
Aberdeen *Wash., U.S.A.* **72 C2**
Aberystwyth **11 E4**
Abidjan **53 G5**
Abilene **80 C4**
Abitibi, L. **71 E6**
Abkhaz Republic = Abkhazia □ **25 E5**
Abkhazia □ **25 E5**
Abminga **62 A1**
Åbo = Turku **9 C10**
Abohar **42 D9**
Abomey **53 G6**
Abong-Mbang **56 D2**
Abou-Deïa **55 F2**
Absaroka Range **73 D9**
Abū 'Alī **47 F7**
Abu Dhabi = Abū Ȥaby **44 E3**
Abu Hamed **55 E5**
Abū Kamāl **46 D5**
Abū Madd, Ra's **47 F4**
Abu Rudeis **47 E3**
Abū Zabad **55 F4**
Abū Ȥaby **44 E3**
Abuja **53 G7**
Abunã **91 E5**
Abunã → **91 E5**
Abut Hd. **65 E4**
Acaponeta **84 C3**
Acapulco **84 D5**
Acarigua **90 B5**
Accra **53 G5**

Aceh □ **38 D1**
Achalpur **43 J10**
Acharnes **23 E4**
Acheloos → **23 E3**
Achill I. **11 E1**
Achinsk **30 D7**
Acireale **21 F5**
Acklins I. **86 B5**
Aconcagua, Cerro **94 C3**
Aconquija, Mt. **94 B3**
Açores, Is. dos **50 C1**
Acraman, L. **62 B2**
Acre = 'Akko **46 D3**
Acre □ **91 E4**
Acre → **91 E5**
Ad Dahnā **47 F7**
Ad Dammām **47 F7**
Ad Dawādimī **47 F6**
Ad Dawḩah **44 E2**
Ad Dilam **47 G6**
Ad Dīwānīyah **47 E6**
Ada **81 B5**
Adair, C. **70 B6**
Adaja → **18 B3**
Adam **44 F4**
Adamaoua, Massif de l' **55 G1**
Adamawa Highlands = Adamaoua, Massif de l' **55 G1**
Adamello, Mte. **13 C9**
Adaminaby **63 C4**
Adams, Mt. **72 C3**
Adam's Bridge **43 Q11**
Adana **46 C3**
Adapazarı = Sakarya **25 E3**

Adarama **55 E5**
Adare, C. **96 B15**
Adaut **37 F4**
Adavale **63 A3**
Adda → **13 D8**
Addis Ababa = Addis Abeba **49 F2**
Addis Abeba **49 F2**
Adelaide **62 B2**
Adelaide I. **96 A3**
Adelaide Pen. **68 B10**
Adélie, Terre **96 A14**
Adelie Land = Adélie, Terre **96 A14**
Aden = Al 'Adan **49 E4**
Aden, G. of **49 E4**
Adi **37 E4**
Adige → **20 B4**
Adilabad **43 K11**
Adirondack Mts. **77 C8**
Adis Abeba = Addis Abeba **49 F2**
Admiralty I. **68 C6**
Admiralty Is. **64 K9**
Adonara **37 F2**
Adoni **43 M10**
Adour → **12 E3**
Adra **18 D4**
Adrano **21 F5**
Adrar **52 D6**
Adrar des Iforas **52 E6**
Adriatic Sea **20 C5**
Adua **37 E3**
Adzhar Republic = Ajaria □ **25 E5**
Ægean Sea **23 E5**
Aerhtai Shan **34 B4**

Afghanistan ■ 45 C6
'Afīf 47 G5
Afuá 92 C3
Afyon 46 C2
Afyonkarahisar = Afyon
46 C2
Agadès = Agadez 53 E7
Agadez 53 E7
Agadir 52 B4
Agapa 30 B6
Agartala 41 F8
Agats 37 F5
Agboville 53 G5
Agde 13 E5
Agen 12 D4
Aghaggar 52 D2
Ahar 46 C6
Ahipara B. 64 A5
Ahiri 43 K12
Ahmadabad 43 H8
Ahmadnagar 43 K9
Ahmadpur 42 E7
Ahmedabad = Ahmadabad
43 H8
Ahmednagar =
Ahmadnagar 43 K9
Ahvāz 47 E7
Ahvenanmaa = Åland
9 C10
Aḥwar 49 E4
Aigues-Mortes 13 E6
Aihui = Heihe 35 A7
Aija 91 E3
Aikawa 33 D6
Aiken 83 C7
Aimere 37 F2
Ain Banaiyan 44 F2
Aïn Ben Tili 52 D3
Aïn Sefra 52 B5
Aïr 53 E7
Air Force I. 70 C6
Aisne → 13 B5
Aitutaki 65 L14
Aix-en-Provence 13 E6
Aix-la-Chapelle = Aachen
14 C4
Aix-les-Bains 13 D6
Aizawl 41 F9
Aizuwakamatsu 33 E6
Ajaccio 13 F8

Ajanta Ra. 43 J9
Ajari Rep. = Ajaria □
25 E5
Ajaria □ 25 E5
Ajdābiyā 54 B3
Ajka 16 E3
'Ajmān 44 E3
Ajmer 42 F9
Ajo, C. de 18 A4
Akaroa 65 E5
Akelamo 37 D3
Aketi 56 D4
Akhisar 23 E6
Akimiski I. 71 D5
Akita 32 D7
Akjoujt 53 E3
Akkeshi 32 B9
'Akko 46 D3
Akkol = Aqköl 29 E8
Aklavik 68 B6
Akola 43 J10
Akordat 57 A7
Akpatok I. 70 C7
Akranes 8 C1
Akron 76 D5
Aksai Chin 42 B11
Aksaray 46 C3
Aksarka 28 C7
Akşehir 46 C2
Aksu 34 B3
Aktsyabrski 17 B9
Aktyubinsk = Aqtöbe
29 D6
Akure 53 G7
Akureyri 8 B2
Akyab = Sittwe 41 G9
Al 'Adan 49 E4
Al Aḥsā = Hasa 47 F7
Al Amādīyah 46 C5
Al 'Amārah 47 E6
Al 'Aqabah 47 E3
Al 'Aramah 47 F6
Al Ashkhara 45 F4
Al Badī' 47 G6
Al Baḥral Mayyit = Dead
Sea 47 E3
Al Başrah 47 E6
Al Batinah 44 F3
Al Baydā 54 B3
Al Faḍilī 47 F7
Al Fallūjah 46 D5
Al Fāw 47 E7
Al Fujayrah 44 E4
Al Hābah 47 F6
Al Ḥaddār 47 G6
Al Ḥāmad 47 E4
Al Ḥamar 47 G6
Al Ḥamrā' 47 F4
Al Ḥarīq 47 G6
Al Ḥasakah 46 C5
Al Ḥayy 47 D6
Al Ḥillah Iraq 47 D6
Al Ḥillah Si. Arabia 47 G6
Al Hoceïma 52 A5
Al Ḥudaydah 49 E3
Al Hufūf 47 F6
Al Jāfūrah 47 F7
Al Jaghbūb 54 C3
Al Jahrah 47 E6

Al Jalāmīd 47 E4
Al Jawf Libya 54 D3
Al Jawf Si. Arabia 47 E4
Al Jazair = Algeria ■
52 C6
Al Jazirah 46 D5
Al Jubayl 47 F6
Al Jubaylah 47 F6
Al Junaynah 55 F3
Al Khābūra 44 F4
Al Khalīl 47 E3
Al Kharfah 47 G6
Al Kharsānīyah 47 F7
Al Khaṣab 44 E4
Al Kufrah 54 D3
Al Küt 47 D6
Al Kuwayt 47 E7
Al Lādhiqīyah 46 D3
Al Luḥayyah 49 D3
Al Madīnah 47 F4
Al Maghreb = Morocco ■
52 B4
Al Majma'ah 47 F6
Al Manāmah 44 E2
Al Marj 54 B3
Al Mawşil 46 C5
Al Midhnab 47 F6
Al Mish'āb 47 E7
Al Mubarraz 47 F7
Al Muḥarraq 44 E2
Al Mukallā 49 E4
Al Mukhā 49 E3
Al Musayyib 47 D6
Al Muwayliḥ 47 F3
Al Qaḍīmah 47 G4
Al Qā'iyah 47 F5
Al Qāmishlī 46 C5
Al Qaşīm □ 47 F5
Al Qaţīf 47 F7
Al Qaţrūn 54 D2
Al Quaisūmah 47 E6
Al Qurnah 47 E6
Al 'Ulā 47 F4
Al 'Uqayr 47 F7
Al 'Uthmānīyah 47 F7
Al Uwaynid 47 F6
Al 'Uwayqīlah 47 E5
Al 'Uyūn 47 F5
Al Wakrah 44 E2
Al Yamāmah 47 F6
Al Yaman = Yemen ■
49 D4
Alabama □ 82 C4
Alabama → 82 D4
Alaçam Dağları 23 E7
Alacant = Alicante 19 C5
Alagoa Grande 92 D6
Alagoas □ 93 D6
Alagoinhas 93 E6
Alajuela 86 D3
Alamosa 79 B10
Åland 9 C10
Alania = North Ossetia □
25 E5
Alanya 46 C2
Alapayevsk 29 D7
Alappuzha = Alleppey
43 Q10

Alaşehir 23 E7
Alaska □ 69 B4
Alaska, G. of 69 C5
Alaska Peninsula 69 C4
Alaska Range 69 C4
Alataw Shankou 34 B3
Alatyr 24 C6
Alausi 90 D3
Alawoona 62 B3
Alba 13 D8
Albacete 19 C5
Albacutya, L. 62 C3
Albanel, L. 71 D6
Albania ■ 23 D3
Albany Australia 60 H2
Albany Ga., U.S.A. 83 D5
Albany N.Y., U.S.A. 77 C9
Albany Oreg., U.S.A.
72 D2
Albany → 71 D5
Albardón 94 C2
Albemarle 83 B7
Alberche → 18 C3
Alberga → 62 A2
Albert, L. Africa 57 D6
Albert, L. Australia 62 C2
Albert Nile → 57 D6
Albertville 13 D7
Albi 12 E5
Albina 92 A3
Alborán 18 E4
Ålborg = Aalborg 9 D7
Alborz, Reshteh-ye
Kühhā-ye 44 B3
Albuquerque 79 C9
Albury 63 C4
Alcalá de Henares 18 B4
Alcalá la Real 18 D4
Álcamo 21 F4
Alcañiz 19 B5
Alcántara 92 C5
Alcántara, Embalse de
18 C2
Alcantarilla 19 D5
Alcaraz, Sierra de 19 C4
Alcaudete 18 D3
Alcázar de San Juan
18 C4
Alchevsk 25 D4
Alcira = Alzira 19 C5
Alcoy 19 C5
Aldabra Is. 51 G8
Aldan → 31 C10
Alderney 11 G5
Aleg 53 E3
Alegrete 94 B5
Aleksandriya =
Oleksandriya 17 C8
Aleksandrovskoye 29 C8
Alençon 12 B4
Aleppo = Ḥalab 46 C4
Alert 70 A7
Alès 13 D6
Alessándria 13 D8
Ålesund 8 C7
Aleutian Is. 69 C2
Alexander Arch. 69 C6
Alexander I. 96 A3
Alexandra Australia 63 C4
Alexandra N.Z. 65 F3

Alexandria = El Iskandarîya 54 B4
Alexandria *Romania* 22 C5
Alexandria *La., U.S.A.* 81 D7
Alexandria *Va., U.S.A.* 77 E7
Alexandrina, L. 62 C2
Alexandroupoli 22 D5
Aleysk 29 D9
Alga 29 E6
Algarve 18 D1
Algeciras 18 D3
Algemesí 19 C5
Alger 52 A6
Algeria ■ 52 C6
Alghero 21 D2
Algiers = Alger 52 A6
Alhucemas = Al Hoceïma 52 A5
'Alî al Gharbî 47 D6
'Alî Khêl 42 C6
Aliağa 23 E6
Alicante 19 C5
Alice Springs 60 E5
Aligarh 42 F11
Alīgūdarz 46 D7
Alipur 42 E7
Alipur Duar 41 D7
Aliwal North 59 E5
Aljustrel 18 D1
Alkmaar 14 B3
All American Canal 78 D5
Allahabad 40 E3
Alleghany → 77 D5
Allegheny Mts. 77 F5
Allentown 77 D8
Alleppey 43 Q10
Aller → 14 B5
Allier → 13 C5
Allora 63 A5
Alma Ata = Almaty 29 E8
Almada 18 C1
Almadén 18 C3
Almansa 19 C5
Almanzor, Pico 18 B3
Almanzora → 19 D5
Almaty 29 E8
Almazán 19 B4
Almelo 14 B4
Almeirim 92 C3
Almendralejo 18 C2
Almería 19 D4
Almora 42 E11
Alnwick 10 D6
Alon 41 F10
Alor 37 F2
Alor Setar 38 C2
Alps 14 E5
Alsace □ 13 B7
Alsask 69 C9
Alsasua 19 A4
Alta Gracia 94 C4
Altai = Aerhtai Shan 34 B4
Altai = Gorno-Altay □ 29 D9
Altamira 92 C3
Altamura 21 D6
Altanbulag 35 A5
Altay 34 B3

Altea 19 C5
Alto Araguaia 93 F3
Alto Molocue 59 B7
Alton 75 F9
Alton Downs 62 A2
Altoona 77 D6
Altun Shan 34 C3
Alusi 37 F4
Alvear 94 B5
Alvie 62 C3
Alwar 42 F10
Alxa Zuoqi 35 C5
Alzira 19 C5
Am Timan 55 F3
Amâdi 55 G5
Amadjuak 70 C6
Amadjuak L. 70 C6
Amagasaki 33 F4
Amahai 37 E3
Amakusa-Shotō 33 G2
Amaliada 23 F3
Amalner 43 J9
Amambay, Cordillera de 94 A5
Amankeldi 29 D7
Amapá 92 B3
Amapá □ 92 B3
Amarante 92 D5
Amarillo 80 B3
Amaro, Mte. 20 C5
Amasra 46 B3
Amazon = Amazonas → 92 C3
Amazonas □ 90 D6
Amazonas → 92 C3
Ambala 42 D10
Ambalavao 59 C9
Ambanja 59 A9
Ambato 90 D3
Ambatolampy 59 B9
Ambatondrazaka 59 B9
Amberg 15 D6
Ambergris Cay 85 D7
Amberley 65 E5
Ambikapur 40 F4
Ambilobé 59 A9
Ambo 91 F3
Amboise 12 C4
Ambon 37 E3
Ambositra 59 C9
Ambovombe 59 D9
Amboyna Cay 38 C4
Ambriz 56 F2
Amby 63 A4
Amchitka I. 69 C1
Amderma 28 C7
Ameca 84 C4
Ameland 14 B3
American Highland 96 B10
American Samoa ☑ 65 L13
Americus 83 C5
Amery 69 C10
Amery Ice Shelf 96 A10
Ames 75 D8
Amherst *Burma* 41 J11
Amherst *Canada* 71 E7
Amiata, Mte. 20 C3

Amiens 12 B5
Amirante Is. 26 K9
'Ammān 47 E3
Ammochostos = Famagusta 46 D3
Amorgós 23 F5
Amos 71 E5
Amoy = Xiamen 35 D6
Ampanihy 59 C8
Ampenan 39 F5
Amper → 15 D6
Amravati 43 J10
Amreli 43 J7
Amritsar 42 D9
Amroha 42 E11
Amsterdam 14 B3
Amstetten 15 D8
Amudarya → 29 E6
Amund Ringnes I. 70 B4
Amundsen Gulf 68 A7
Amundsen Sea 96 B1
Amuntai 39 E5
Amur → 31 D12
Amurang 37 D2
Amyderya = Amudarya → 29 E6
An Nafūd 47 E5
An Najaf 47 D6
An Nhon 38 B3
An Nu'ayrīyah 47 F7
Anabar → 30 B9
Anaconda 73 C7
Anadolu 25 F3
'Ānah 46 D5
Anaheim 78 D4
Anakapalle 40 J4
Anambas, Kepulauan 39 D3
Anambas Is. = Anambas, Kepulauan 39 D3
Anamur 46 C3
Anan 33 G4
Anantnag 42 C9
Ananyiv 17 E9
Anápolis 93 F4
Anār 44 D3
Anārak 44 C3
Anatolia = Anadolu 25 F3
Añatuya 94 B4
Anchorage 69 B5
Ancohuma, Nevado 91 G5
Ancón 91 F3
Ancona 20 C4
Ancud 95 E2
Ancud, G. de 95 E2
Andalgalá 94 B3
Andalucía □ 18 D3
Andalusia = Andalucía □ 18 D3
Andalusia 82 D4
Andaman Is. 27 G11
Andaman Sea 38 B1
Andapa 59 A9
Anderson 76 D3
Anderson → 68 B7
Andes, Cord. de los 91 G4
Andhra Pradesh □ 43 L11
Andijon 29 E8
Andikíthira = Antikythira 23 G4

Andizhan = Andijon 29 E8
Andkhvoy 45 B6
Andoany 59 A9
Andorra ■ 19 A6
Andorra La Vella 12 E4
Andreanof Is. 69 C2
Andrewilla 62 A2
Ándria 20 D6
Andros 23 F5
Andros I. 86 B4
Andújar 18 C3
Andulo 56 G3
Aneto, Pico de 19 A6
Ang'angxi 35 B7
Angara → 30 D7
Angarsk 30 D8
Angaston 62 B2
Ånge 8 C9
Angeles 36 A2
Angellala 63 A4
Ångermanälven → 8 C9
Angers 12 C3
Anglesey 11 E4
Ango 57 D5
Angoche 59 B7
Angol 94 D1
Angola ■ 58 A3
Angoulême 12 D4
Angoumois 12 D4
Angren 29 E8
Anguilla ☑ 87 C7
Anhui □ 35 C6
Anhwei = Anhui □ 35 C6
Anjou 12 C3
Ankaboa, Tanjona 59 C8
Ankang 35 C5
Ankara 25 F3
Ankaratra 59 B9
Ann Arbor 76 C4
Annaba 52 A7
Annan 11 D5
Annapolis 77 E7
Annecy 13 D7
Anning 34 D5
Anniston 82 C5
Annobón 51 G4
Annuello 62 B3
Anqing 35 C6
Ansbach 14 D6
Anshan 35 B7
Anshun 35 D5
Ansongo 53 E6
Ansudu 37 E5
Antabamba 91 F4
Antakya = Hatay 46 C4
Antalaha 59 A10
Antalya 46 C2
Antalya Körfezi 46 C2
Antananarivo 59 B9
Antarctic Pen. 96 A4
Antarctica 96 C
Antequera 18 D3
Anti Atlas 52 C4
Antibes 13 E7
Anticosti, Î. d' 71 E7
Antigonish 71 E7
Antigua & Barbuda ■ 87 C7
Antikythira 23 G4
Antioquia 90 B3
Antofagasta 94 A2

Antonina 94 B7
Antrim 11 D3
Antsirabe 59 B9
Antsiranana 59 A9
Antsohihy 59 A9
Antwerp = Antwerpen
14 C3
Antwerpen 14 C3
Anupgarh 42 E8
Anvers = Antwerpen
14 C3
Anvers I. 96 A3
Anxi 34 B4
Anxious B. 62 B1
Anyang 35 C6
Anzhero-Sudzhensk
29 D9
Ánzio 20 D4
Aoga-Shima 33 G6
Aomen = Macau 35 D6
Aomori 32 C7
Aoraki Mount Cook 65 E4
Aosta 13 D7
Aotearoa = New
Zealand ■ 64 D7
Aouk, Bahr → 56 C3
Apalachicola → 82 E5
Apaporis → 90 D5
Aparri 36 A2
Apeldoorn 14 B3
Apennines = Appennini
20 B3
Apia 65 L13
Apiacás, Serra dos 91 E7
Aplao 91 G4
Apo, Mt. 36 C3
Apolo 91 F5
Apoteri 90 C7
Appalachian Mts. 77 F5
Appennini 20 B3
Appleton 76 B1
Aprília 20 D4
Apucarana 94 A6
Apure → 90 B5
Apurímac → 91 F4
Aqaba = Al 'Aqabah 47 E3
Aqaba, G. of 47 E3
'Aqabah, Khalīj al = Aqaba,
G. of 47 E3
Āqchah 45 B6
Aqköl 29 E8
'Aqrah 46 C5
Aqtöbe 29 E6
Aqtoghay 29 E8
Aquidauana 93 G2
Aquitain, Bassin 12 D3
Ar Rachidiya = Er Rachidia
52 B5
Ar Ramādī 46 D5
Ar Raqqah 46 D4
Ar Rass 47 F5
Ar Rifā'ī 47 E6
Ar Riyāḍ 47 F6
Ar Ruṭbah 46 D5
Ar Ruwaydah 47 G6
Ara 40 E5
'Arab, Bahr el → 55 G4
Arab, Shatt al → 47 E7
Arabian Desert = Es Sahrâ'
Esh Sharqîya 54 C5

Arabian Gulf = Persian Gulf
44 E2
Arabian Sea 26 G8
Araç 46 B3
Aracaju 93 E6
Aracati 92 C6
Araçatuba 93 G3
Aracena 18 D2
Araçuaí 93 F5
Arad 16 E5
Arafura Sea 37 F4
Aragón □ 19 B5
Aragón → 19 A5
Araguacema 92 D4
Araguaia → 92 D4
Araguari 93 F4
Araguari → 92 B4
Arak 52 C6
Arakan Coast 41 H9
Arakan Yoma 41 H10
Araks = Aras, Rūd-e →
46 B7
Aral 29 E7
Aral Sea 29 E6
Aral Tengizi = Aral Sea
29 E6
Aralsk = Aral 29 E7
Aralskoye More = Aral Sea
29 E6
Aran I. 10 D2
Aran Is. 11 E2
Aranda de Duero 18 B4
Aranjuez 18 B4
Arapgir 46 C4
Arapiraca 93 D6
Arapongas 94 A6
Araraquara 93 G4
Ararat 62 C3
Ararat, Mt. = Ağrı Dağı
25 F5
Araripe, Chapada do
92 D6
Aras, Rūd-e → 46 B7
Arauca 90 B4
Arauca → 90 B5
Araxá 93 F4
Araya, Pen. de 90 A6
Árbatax 21 E2
Arbīl 46 C6
Arbroath 10 C5
Arcachon 12 D3
Archangel = Arkhangelsk
28 C5
Arckaringa 62 A1
Arckaringa Cr. → 62 A2
Arcos de la Frontera
18 D3
Arcot 43 N11
Arctic Bay 70 B5
Arctic Red River =
Tsiigehtchic 68 B6
Arda → 22 D6
Ardabīl 46 C7
Ardahan 46 B5
Ardennes = Ardenne
14 D3
Ardestān 44 C3
Ardlethan 63 B4
Ardmore 80 B5

Ardrossan 62 B2
Arecibo 87 C6
Areia Branca 92 C6
Arendal 9 D7
Arequipa 91 G4
Arévalo 18 B3
Arezzo 20 C3
Arganda 18 B4
Argentan 12 B3
Argentário, Mte. 20 C3
Argentina ■ 94 D3
Argentina Is. 96 A3
Argentino, L. 95 G2
Argeş → 22 B6
Arghandab → 42 D4
Argolikos Kolpos 23 F4
Argos 23 F4
Argostoli 23 E3
Århus 9 D8
Ariadnoye 32 A4
Arica Chile 91 G4
Arica Colombia 90 D4
Aridh 47 F6
Arinos → 91 F7
Aripuanã 91 E6
Aripuanã → 90 E6
Ariquemes 91 E6
Arizona 94 D3
Arizona □ 79 C7
Arjona 90 A3
Arkalyk = Arqalyk 29 D7
Arkansas → 81 C8
Arkansas □ 81 B7
Arkansas City 80 A5
Arkhangelsk 28 C5
Arklow 11 E3
Arktícheskiy, Mys 30 A7
Arlanzón → 18 A3
Arlberpass 14 E4
Arles 13 E6
Arlington Va., U.S.A. 77 E7
Arlington Wash., U.S.A.
72 B2
Arlon 14 D3
Armagh 11 D3
Armavir 25 D5
Armenia 90 C3
Armenia ■ 25 F7
Armidale 63 B5
Arnaud → 70 C6
Arnauti, C. 46 D3
Arnhem 14 C3
Arnhem, C. 60 C5
Arnhem Land 60 C5
Arno → 20 C3
Arno Bay 62 B2
Arnsberg 14 C5
Arqalyk 29 D7
Arrabury 62 A3
Arrah = Ara 40 E5
Arran 10 D4
Arras 13 A5
Arrecife 52 C3
Arrée, Mts. d' 12 B2
Arrowtown 65 F3
Arthur → 62 D3
Arthur's Pass 65 E4

Arthur's Pass △ 65 E4
Artigas 94 C5
Artois 12 A5
Artsyz 17 E9
Artvin 25 E5
Aru, Kepulauan 37 F4
Aru Is. = Aru, Kepulauan
37 F4
Arua 57 D6
Aruanã 93 E3
Aruba ☑ 87 D6
Arunachal Pradesh □
41 C10
Arusha 57 E7
Aruwimi → 56 D4
Arviat 68 B10
Arxan 35 B6
Arys 29 E7
Arzamas 24 B5
As Saffānīyah 47 E7
As Samāwah 47 E6
As Sohar = Şuḥār 44 E4
As Sulaymānīyah Iraq
46 D6
As Sulaymānīyah
Si. Arabia 47 F6
As Summān 47 F6
As Sūq 47 G5
As Suwaydā' 46 D4
As Suwayḥ 45 F4
Aş Şuwayrah 47 D6
Asahigawa 32 B8
Asansol 40 F6
Ascension I. 51 G2
Aschaffenburg 14 D5
Aschersleben 15 C6
Áscoli Piceno 20 C4
Ascope 91 E3
Aseb 49 E3
Asenovgrad 22 C5
Aşgabat = Ashgabat 29 F6
Ash Shāmīyah 47 E6
Ash Shāriqah 44 E3
Ash Shaṭrah 47 E6
Ash Shu'aybah 47 F6
Ash Shu'bah 47 E6
Ashburton 65 E4
Asheville 83 B6
Ashford Australia 63 A5
Ashford U.K. 11 F7
Ashgabat 29 F6
Ashizuri-Zaki 33 G3
Ashkhabad = Ashgabat
29 F6
Ashmyany 17 A7
Ashqelon 47 E3
Ashtabula 76 D5
Ashuanipi, L. 71 D7
Asia, Kepulauan 37 D4
Asifabad 43 K11
Asinara 20 D2
Asinara, G. dell' 20 D2
Asino 29 D9
Asipovichy 17 B9
'Asīr 48 D3
Asir, Ras 49 E5
Asmara = Asmera 57 A7
Asmera 57 A7
Aspiring, Mt. 65 F3
Assab = Aseb 49 E3

Assam □ **41 D9**
Assen **14 B4**
Assiniboia **69 D9**
Assiniboine ➤ **69 D10**
Assis **94 A6**
Assisi **20 C4**
Astana **29 D8**
Asti **13 D8**
Astipalea **23 F6**
Astorga **18 A2**
Astoria **72 C2**
Astrakhan **25 D6**
Astrakhan-Bazâr **25 F6**
Asturias □ **18 A3**
Asunción **94 B5**
Aswân **54 D5**
Aswan Dam = Sadd el Aali **54 D5**
Asyût **54 C5**
At Ţafilah **47 E3**
Aţ Ţâ'if **48 C3**
Atacama, Desierto de **94 A3**
Atacama, Salar de **94 A3**
Atalaya **91 F4**
Atamyrat **29 F7**
Atapupu **37 F2**
Atâr **52 D3**
Atasū **29 E8**
Atauro **37 F3**
Atbara **55 E5**
'Atbara, Nahr ➤ **55 E5**
Atbasar **29 D7**
Athabasca **69 C8**
Athabasca ➤ **68 C8**
Athabasca, L. **68 C8**
Athens = Athína **23 F4**
Athens Ala., U.S.A. **82 B4**
Athens Ga., U.S.A. **83 C6**
Athína **23 F4**
Athínai = Athína **23 F4**
Athlone **11 E3**
Athos **23 D5**
Athy **11 E3**
Ati **55 F2**
Atlanta **83 C5**
Atlantic City **77 E8**
Atlas Mts. = Haut Atlas **52 B4**
Atrak = Atrek ➤ **44 B3**
Atrek ➤ **44 B3**
Atsuta **32 B7**
Attapu **38 E6**
Attawapiskat **71 D5**
Attawapiskat ➤ **71 D5**
Attock **42 C8**
Attopeu = Attapu **38 B3**
Attur **43 P11**
Atuel ➤ **94 D3**
Atyraū **29 E6**
Aubagne **13 E6**
Aube ➤ **13 B5**
Aubenas **13 D6**
Auburn **82 C5**
Auburn Ra. **63 A5**
Aubusson **12 D5**
Auch **12 E4**
Auckland **64 B6**
Aude ➤ **13 E5**
Augathella **63 A4**
Augsburg **14 D6**

Augusta Italy **21 F5**
Augusta Ga., U.S.A. **83 C7**
Augusta Maine, U.S.A. **77 B11**
Aujuittuq = Grise Fiord **70 B5**
Aunis **12 C3**
Auponhia **37 E3**
Aurangabad Bihar, India **40 E5**
Aurangabad Maharashtra, India **43 K9**
Aurich **14 B4**
Aurillac **12 D5**
Aurora Colo., U.S.A. **74 F2**
Aurora Ill., U.S.A. **76 D1**
Austin Minn., U.S.A. **75 D8**
Austin Tex., U.S.A. **80 D5**
Austral Is. = Tubuaï, Îs. **65 M16**
Austral Seamount Chain **65 M16**
Australia ■ **60 E6**
Australian Alps **63 C4**
Australian Capital Territory □ **63 C4**
Austria ■ **15 E8**
Autun **13 C6**
Auvergne □ **13 D5**
Auvergne, Mts. d' **13 D5**
Auxerre **13 C5**
Avallon **13 C5**
Aveiro Brazil **92 C2**
Aveiro Portugal **18 B1**
Ävej **46 D7**
Avellaneda **94 C5**
Avellino **21 D5**
Aversa **21 D5**
Avesta **9 C9**
Avezzano **20 C5**
Aviemore **10 C5**
Avignon **13 E6**
Ávila **18 B3**
Avilés **18 A3**
Avoca ➤ **62 C3**
Avola **21 F5**
Avranches **12 B3**
Awaji-Shima **33 F4**
Awash **49 E3**
Awatere ➤ **65 D6**
Awbārī **54 C1**
Awbārī, Idehan **54 C1**
Awjilah **54 C3**
Axel Heiberg I. **70 B5**
Axim **53 H5**
Axios ➤ **23 D4**
Ayabaca **90 D3**
Ayabe **33 F4**
Ayacucho Argentina **94 D5**
Ayacucho Peru **91 F4**
Ayaguz = Ayaköz **29 E9**
Ayaköz **29 E9**
Ayamonte **18 D2**
Ayaviri **91 F4**
Âybak **45 B7**
Aydın **23 F6**
Ayers Rock = Uluru **60 F5**
Ayeyarwady = Irrawaddy ➤ **41 K10**
Aylmer, L. **68 B8**

Ayn Dār **47 F7**
Ayr **10 D4**
Aytos **22 C6**
Ayu, Kepulauan **37 D4**
Ayvacık **23 E6**
Ayvalık **23 E6**
Aẕ Ẕahrān **47 F7**
Az Zilfi **47 F6**
Az Zarqā **46 D4**
Az Zubayr **47 E6**
Azamgarh **40 D4**
Azärbaycan = Azerbaijan ■ **25 E6**
Āzārbāyjān-e Gharbī □ **46 C6**
Āzārbāyjān-e Sharqī □ **46 C6**
Azare **53 F8**
Azbine = Aïr **53 E7**
Azerbaijan ■ **25 E6**
Azogues **90 D3**
Azores = Açores, Is. dos **50 C1**
Azov **25 D4**
Azov, Sea of **25 D4**
Azovskoye More = Azov, Sea of **25 D4**
Azovy **28 C7**
Azuaga **18 C3**
Azuero, Pen. de **86 E3**
Azul **94 D5**

B

Ba Don **38 A3**
Ba Ria **38 B3**
Baardeere = Bardera **49 G3**
Bab el Mandeb **49 E3**
Bābā, Koh-i- **42 B5**
Baba Burnu **23 E6**
Babadag **22 B7**
Babadayhan **29 F7**
Babaeski **22 D6**
Babahoyo **90 D3**
Babar **37 F3**
Babo **37 E4**
Bābol **44 B3**
Bābol Sar **44 B3**
Babruysk **17 B9**
Babuyan Chan. **36 A2**
Babylon **47 D6**
Bacabal **92 C5**
Bacan, Kepulauan **37 E3**
Bacarra **36 A2**
Bacău **17 E8**
Bachelina **29 D7**
Back ➤ **68 B9**
Bacolod **36 B2**
Bad Ischl **15 E7**
Bad Kissingen **14 C6**
Badagara **43 P9**
Badajoz **18 C2**
Badalona **19 B7**
Badampahar **40 F6**
Badanah **47 E5**
Badas **38 D4**
Badas, Kepulauan **39 D3**
Baddo ➤ **42 E4**

Bade **37 F5**
Baden **15 D9**
Baden-Baden **14 D5**
Baden-Württemberg □ **14 D5**
Badgastein **15 E7**
Bādghīs □ **42 B3**
Badin **43 G6**
Badlands **74 D3**
Baena **18 D3**
Baeza **18 D4**
Baffin B. **70 B7**
Baffin I. **70 C6**
Bafia **53 H8**
Bafing ➤ **53 F3**
Bafoulabé **53 F3**
Bäfq **44 D3**
Bäft **44 D4**
Bafwasende **57 D5**
Bagamoyo **57 F7**
Baganga **36 C3**
Bagansiapiapi **39 D2**
Bagdarin **30 D9**
Bagé **94 C6**
Baghdād **46 D6**
Bagheria **21 E4**
Baghlān **42 A6**
Baghlān □ **45 C7**
Bago = Pegu **41 J11**
Baguio **36 A2**
Bahamas ■ **86 A4**
Baharampur **40 E7**
Bahawalpur **42 E7**
Bahía = Salvador **93 E6**
Bahía □ **93 E5**
Bahía Blanca **94 D4**
Bahía de Caráquez **90 D2**
Bahía Laura **95 F3**
Bahía Negra **91 H7**
Bahraich **40 D3**
Bahrain ■ **44 E2**
Baia Mare **17 E6**
Baïbokoum **55 G2**
Baidoa **49 G3**
Baie-Comeau **71 E7**
Baie Verte **71 E8**
Ba'ījī **46 D5**
Baikal, L. = Baykal, Oz. **30 D8**
Baikonur = Bayqongyr **29 E7**
Baile Atha Cliath = Dublin **11 E3**
Bälești **22 B4**
Bā'ir **47 E4**
Bairiki = Tarawa **64 J12**
Bairnsdale **63 C4**
Baitadi **40 C3**
Baiyin **35 C5**
Baja **16 E4**
Baja, Pta. **84 B1**
Baja California **84 A1**
Bajimba, Mt. **63 A5**
Bakala **55 G3**
Bakchar **29 D9**
Bakel **53 F3**
Baker, L. **68 B10**
Baker, Mt. **72 B3**
Baker I. **64 J13**
Baker Lake **68 B10**

Bakers Dozen Is. **71 D6**
Bakersfield **78 C3**
Bākhtarān = Kermānshāh **46 D6**
Bakı **25 E6**
Bakony **16 E3**
Bakony Forest = Bakony **16 E3**
Bakouma **56 A3**
Baku = Bakı **25 E6**
Bakutis Coast **96 B1**
Baky = Bakı **25 E6**
Balabac I. **38 C5**
Balabac Str. **38 C5**
Balabalangan, Kepulauan **39 E5**
Balaghat Ra. **43 K10**
Balaguer **19 B6**
Balaklava **25 E3**
Balakovo **24 C6**
Balashov **24 C5**
Balasore = Baleshwar **40 G6**
Balaton **16 E3**
Balbina, Reprêsa de **90 D7**
Balchik **22 C7**
Balclutha **65 G3**
Baleares, Is. **19 C7**
Balearic Is. = Baleares, Is. **19 C7**
Baleine = Whale → **70 D7**
Baler **36 A2**
Baleshwar **40 G6**
Bali **39 F5**
Bali □ **39 F5**
Baliem → **37 F5**
Balıkeşir **23 E6**
Balikpapan **39 E5**
Balimbing **36 C1**
Balipara **41 D9**
Balkan Mts. = Stara Planina **22 C4**
Balkanabat **29 F6**
Balkh **45 B6**
Balkhash = Balqash **29 E8**
Balkhash, Ozero = Balqash Köli **29 E8**
Balla **41 E8**
Ballarat **62 C3**
Ballater **10 C5**
Ballina *Australia* **63 A5**
Ballina *Ireland* **11 D2**
Ballinasloe **11 E2**
Balmaceda **95 F2**
Balmoral **62 C3**
Balochistan = Baluchistan □ **42 F4**
Balonne → **63 A4**
Balqash **29 E8**
Balqash Köli **29 E8**
Balrampur **40 D4**
Balranald **62 B3**
Balsas → **84 D4**
Balta **17 D9**
Bălți **17 E8**
Baltic Sea **9 D9**
Baltimore **77 E7**
Baluchistan □ **42 F4**

Balya **23 E6**
Bam **44 D4**
Bama **55 F1**
Bamako **53 F4**
Bambari **55 G3**
Bamberg **14 D6**
Bamenda **53 G8**
Bāmīān □ **42 B5**
Bampūr **45 E5**
Ban Don = Surat Thani **38 C1**
Ban Kantang **38 C1**
Ban Mê Thuôt = Buon Ma Thuot **38 B3**
Banaba **64 K11**
Banalia **57 D5**
Bananal, I. do **93 E3**
Banaras = Varanasi **40 E4**
Bânâs, Ras **54 D6**
Band-e Torkestan **45 C6**
Banda, Kepulauan **37 E3**
Banda Aceh **38 C1**
Banda Banda, Mt. **63 B5**
Banda Elat **37 F4**
Banda Is. = Banda, Kepulauan **37 E3**
Banda Sea **37 F3**
Bandanaira **37 E3**
Bandar = Machilipatnam **40 J3**
Bandar-e Abbās **44 E4**
Bandar-e Anzalī **46 C7**
Bandar-e Bushehr = Būshehr **44 D2**
Bandar-e Chārak **44 E3**
Bandar-e Deylam **47 E7**
Bandar-e Emām Khomeynī **47 E7**
Bandar-e Lengeh **44 E4**
Bandar-e Nakhīlū **44 E3**
Bandar-e Rīg **44 D2**
Bandar-e Torkeman **44 B3**
Bandar Lampung **39 F3**
Bandar Maharani = Muar **39 D2**
Bandar Penggaram = Batu Pahat **39 D2**
Bandar Seri Begawan **38 D5**
Bandar Sri Aman = Sri Aman **39 D4**
Bandera **94 B4**
Bandırma **23 D7**
Bandjarmasin = Banjarmasin **39 E4**
Bandon **11 F2**
Bandundu **56 E3**
Bandung **39 F3**
Banff *Canada* **69 C8**
Banff *U.K.* **10 C5**
Bang Saphan **38 B1**
Bangalore **43 N10**
Bangassou **54 G8**
Banggai, Kepulauan **37 E2**
Banggai Arch. = Banggai, Kepulauan **37 E2**
Banggi, Pulau **38 C5**
Banghāzī **54 B3**
Bangka *Sulawesi, Indonesia* **37 D3**

Bangka *Sumatera, Indonesia* **39 E3**
Bangka, Selat **39 E3**
Bangkinang **39 D2**
Bangko **39 E2**
Bangkok **38 B2**
Bangladesh ■ **41 E7**
Bangong Co **42 B11**
Bangor *Down, U.K.* **11 D4**
Bangor *Gwynedd, U.K.* **11 E4**
Bangor *U.S.A.* **77 B11**
Bangued **36 A2**
Bangui **56 D3**
Bangweulu, L. **57 G6**
Banī **87 C5**
Banī Walīd **54 B1**
Bāniyās **46 D3**
Banja Luka **20 B6**
Banjarmasin **39 E4**
Banjul **53 F2**
Bankipore **40 E5**
Banks I. **68 A7**
Banks Pen. **65 E5**
Banks Str. **62 D4**
Bankura **40 F6**
Bannu **42 C7**
Banswara **43 H9**
Bantry **11 F2**
Banu **42 B6**
Banyak, Kepulauan **39 D1**
Banzare Coast **96 A13**
Baoding **35 C6**
Baoshan **34 D4**
Baoji **35 C5**
Baotou **35 B6**
Bapatla **40 K3**
Ba'qūbah **46 D6**
Bar *Montenegro* **22 C2**
Bar *Ukraine* **17 D8**
Bar-le-Duc **13 B6**
Barabai **39 E5**
Barabinsk **29 D8**
Baracoa **86 B5**
Barahona **87 C5**
Barail Range **41 E9**
Barakaldo **19 A4**
Barakhola **41 E9**
Barakpur **41 F7**
Barakula **63 A5**
Baramula **42 B9**
Baran **43 G10**
Baranavichy **17 B8**
Baranof I. **69 C6**
Barapasi **37 E5**
Barat Daya, Kepulauan **37 F3**
Barbacena **93 G5**
Barbados ■ **87 D8**
Barbastro **19 A6**
Barcellona Pozzo di Gotto **21 E5**
Barcelona *Spain* **19 B7**
Barcelona *Venezuela* **90 A6**
Barcelos **90 D6**
Bardaï **54 D2**
Barddhaman **40 F6**
Bardera **49 G3**
Bardīyah **54 B4**

Bareilly **42 E11**
Barfleur, Pte. de **12 B3**
Barga **34 C3**
Barhi **40 F5**
Bari **20 D6**
Bari Doab **42 D8**
Barīdī, Ra's **47 F4**
Barinas **90 B4**
Baring, C. **68 B8**
Barisal **41 F8**
Barisan, Pegunungan **39 E2**
Barito → **39 E4**
Barkly Tableland **60 D6**
Bârlad → **17 F8**
Barlee, L. **60 F2**
Barletta **20 D6**
Barmedman **63 B4**
Barmer **42 G7**
Barmera **62 B3**
Barnaul **29 D9**
Barnsley **11 E6**
Barnstaple **11 F4**
Baro **53 G7**
Baroda = Vadodara **43 H8**
Barotseland **58 B4**
Barpeta **41 D8**
Barquísimeto **90 A5**
Barra *Brazil* **93 E5**
Barra *U.K.* **10 C3**
Barra do Corda **92 D4**
Barra Falsa, Pta. da **59 C7**
Barraba **63 B5**
Barrackpur = Barakpur **41 F7**
Barraigh = Barra **10 C3**
Barranca *Lima, Peru* **91 F3**
Barranca *Loreto, Peru* **90 D3**
Barrancabermeja **90 B4**
Barrancas **90 B6**
Barrancos **18 C2**
Barranqueras **94 B5**
Barranquilla **90 A4**
Barreiras **93 E5**
Barreirinhas **92 C5**
Barreiro **18 C1**
Barretos **93 G4**
Barrie **71 E6**
Barrier Ra. **62 B3**
Barrington Tops **63 B5**
Barringun **63 A4**
Barrow **69 A4**
Barrow-in-Furness **11 D5**
Barry **11 F5**
Barsi **43 K9**
Barsoi **40 E6**
Barstow **78 C4**
Bartica **90 B7**
Bartin **46 B3**
Bartlesville **81 A6**
Barysaw **17 A9**
Bāsa'idū **44 E3**
Basankusa **56 D3**
Basarabeasca **17 E9**
Basarabia = Bessarabiya **17 E9**
Basel **14 E4**
Bashkir Republic = Bashkortostan □ **29 D6**

Bashkortostan □ **29 D6**
Basilan **36 C2**
Basilan Str. **36 C2**
Basildon **11 F7**
Basim = Washim **43 J10**
Basingstoke **11 F6**
Basle = Basel **14 E4**
Basoko **56 D4**
Basque Provinces = País
Vasco □ **19 A4**
Basra = Al Başrah **47 E6**
Bass Str. **61 H8**
Bassano del Grappa
20 B3
Bassas da India **59 C7**
Basse-Terre **87 C7**
Basseterre **87 C7**
Bassein **41 J10**
Bastak **44 E3**
Bastar **40 H3**
Basti **40 D4**
Bastia **13 E8**
Bastogne **14 C3**
Bata **56 D1**
Bataan □ **36 B2**
Batabanó, G. de **86 B3**
Batac **36 A2**
Batagai **31 C11**
Batamay **31 C10**
Batang **34 C4**
Batangafo **55 G2**
Batangas **36 B2**
Batanta **37 E4**
Batdambang **38 B2**
Batemans B. **63 C5**
Batemans Bay **63 C5**
Bath **11 F5**
Bathurst *Australia* **63 B4**
Bathurst *Canada* **71 E7**
Bathurst, C. **68 A7**
Bathurst I. **70 B3**
Bathurst Harb. **62 D4**
Bathurst Inlet **68 B9**
Batlow **63 C4**
Batman **46 C5**
Batna **52 A7**
Baton Rouge **81 D8**
Batouri **56 D2**
Battambang =
Batdambang **38 B2**
Battipáglia **21 D5**
Battle Creek **76 C3**
Batu **49 E2**
Batu, Kepulauan **39 E1**
Batu Is. = Batu, Kepulauan
39 E1
Batu Pahat **39 D2**
Batuata **37 F2**
Baturaja **39 E2**
Baturité **92 C6**
Bau **39 D4**
Baubau **37 F2**
Baucau **37 F3**
Bauchi **53 F7**
Bauer, C. **62 B1**
Baukau = Baucau **37 F3**
Bauld, C. **71 D8**
Bauru **93 G4**
Bautzen **15 C8**
Bavaria = Bayern □ **15 D6**

Bawdwin **41 F11**
Bawean **39 F4**
Bawku **53 F5**
Bay City **76 C4**
Bay View **64 C7**
Bayamo **86 B4**
Bayan Har Shan **34 C4**
Bayan Hot = Alxa Zuoqi
35 C5
Bayanaūyl **29 D8**
Bayanhongor **35 B5**
Bayázeh **44 C3**
Baybay **36 B2**
Baydhabo = Baidoa **49 G3**
Bayern □ **15 D6**
Bayeux **12 B3**
Bayındır **23 E6**
Baykal, Oz. **30 D8**
Baykit **30 C7**
Bayombong **36 A2**
Bayovar **91 E2**
Bayqongyr **29 E7**
Bayram-Ali = Baýramaly
29 F7
Baýramaly **29 F7**
Bayramiç **23 E6**
Bayreuth **15 D6**
Bayrūt **46 D3**
Baytown **81 E6**
Baza **19 D4**
Bazaruto, I. do **59 C7**
Beachport **62 C2**
Beagle, Canal **95 G3**
Beardmore Glacier **96 C14**
Béarn **12 E3**
Beauce, Plaine de la
12 B4
Beaudesert **63 A5**
Beaufort **38 C5**
Beaufort Sea **66 B6**
Beaufort West **58 E4**
Beaumont **81 D6**
Beaune **13 C6**
Beauvais **12 B5**
Beaver → **69 C9**
Beawar **42 F9**
Bečej **22 B3**
Béchar **52 B5**
Bedford **11 E6**
Beenleigh **63 A5**
Be'er Sheva **47 E3**
Beersheba = Be'er Sheva
47 E3
Befale **56 D4**
Bega **63 C4**
Behbehān **47 E7**
Behshahr **44 B3**
Bei Jiang → **35 D6**
Bei'an **35 B7**
Beihai **35 D5**
Beijing **35 C6**
Beilpajah **63 B3**
Beinn na Faoghla =
Benbecula **10 C3**
Beira **59 B6**
Beirut = Bayrūt **46 D3**
Beitbridge **59 C6**
Beja *Portugal* **18 C2**

Béja *Tunisia* **54 A1**
Bejaïa **52 A7**
Béjar **18 B3**
Bejestān **44 C4**
Békéscsaba **16 E5**
Bela *India* **40 E4**
Bela *Pakistan* **42 F5**
Bela Crkva **22 B3**
Bela Vista *Brazil* **94 A5**
Bela Vista *Mozam.* **59 D6**
Belarus ■ **24 C2**
Belau = Palau ■ **36 C4**
Belawan **39 D1**
Belaya Tserkov = Bila
Tserkva **17 D10**
Belcher Chan. **70 B4**
Belcher Is. **71 D6**
Beled Weyne = Belet Uen
49 G4
Belém **92 C4**
Belet Uen **49 G4**
Belev **24 C4**
Belfast **11 D4**
Belfort **13 C7**
Belgaum **43 M9**
Belgium ■ **14 C3**
Belgorod **24 C4**
Belgorod-Dnestrovskiy =
Bilhorod-Dnistrovskyy
25 D3
Belgrade = Beograd **22 B3**
Beli Drim → **22 C3**
Belinyu **39 E3**
Beliton Is. = Belitung
39 E3
Belitung **39 E3**
Belize ■ **85 D7**
Belize City **85 D7**
Belkovskiy, Ostrov **30 B11**
Bell Bay **62 D4**
Bell Peninsula **70 C5**
Bell Ville **94 C4**
Bella Unión **94 C5**
Bella Vista **94 B5**
Bellary **43 M10**
Bellata **63 A4**
Belle-Île **12 C2**
Belle Isle **71 D8**
Belle Isle, Str. of **71 D8**
Belleville *Canada* **71 E6**
Belleville *U.S.A.* **75 F10**
Bellin = Kangirsuk **70 D7**
Bellingen **63 B5**
Bellingham **72 B2**
Bellingshausen Sea **96 A2**
Bellinzona **13 C8**
Belluno **20 A4**
Belmonte **93 F6**
Belmopan **85 D7**
Belo Horizonte **93 F5**
Belo-Tsiribihina **59 B8**
Beloit **75 D10**
Belokorovichi **17 C9**
Belomorsk **28 C4**
Belonia **41 F8**
Belorussia = Belarus ■
24 C2
Belovo **29 D9**
Beloye, Ozero **24 A4**
Beloye More **8 B13**

Belozersk **24 A4**
Beltana **62 B2**
Belterra **92 C3**
Beltsy = Bălţi **17 E8**
Belukha **29 E9**
Beluran **38 C5**
Belyy, Ostrov **28 B8**
Belyy Yar **29 D9**
Bemidji **75 B7**
Ben Lomond *N.S.W.,
Australia* **63 B5**
Ben Lomond *Tas.,
Australia* **62 D4**
Ben Nevis **10 C4**
Bena **53 F7**
Bena-Dibele **56 E4**
Benalla **63 C4**
Benares = Varanasi **40 E4**
Benavente **18 A3**
Benbecula **10 C3**
Benbonyathe Hill **62 B2**
Bend **72 D3**
Bender Beila **49 F5**
Bendery = Tighina **17 E9**
Bendigo **63 C3**
Benevento **20 D5**
Bengal, Bay of **41 J7**
Bengalūru = Bangalore
43 N10
Bengbu **35 C6**
Benghazi = Banghāzī
54 B3
Bengkalis **39 D2**
Bengkulu **39 E2**
Bengkulu □ **39 E2**
Benguela **58 A2**
Beni **57 D5**
Beni → **91 F5**
Beni Mellal **52 B4**
Beni Suef **54 C5**
Benidorm **19 C5**
Benin ■ **53 G6**
Benin, Bight of **53 H6**
Benin City **53 G7**
Benjamin Constant **90 D4**
Benoni **59 D5**
Bent **44 E4**
Benteng **37 F2**
Benton Harbor **76 C2**
Benue → **53 G7**
Benxi **35 B7**
Beo **36 D3**
Beograd **22 B3**
Beppu **33 G2**
Berat **23 D2**
Berau, Teluk **37 E4**
Berber **55 E5**
Berbera **49 E4**
Berbérati **56 D3**
Berbice → **90 B7**
Berdichev = Berdychiv
17 D9
Berdsk **29 D9**
Berdyansk **25 D4**
Berdychiv **17 D9**
Berebere **37 D3**
Bereda **49 E5**
Berehove **17 D6**
Berekum **53 G5**

Berestechko 17 C7
Bereza = Byaroza 17 B7
Berezhany 17 D7
Berezina = Byarezina →
  17 B10
BereZniki 28 D6
Berezovo 28 C7
Berga 19 A6
Bergama 23 E6
Bérgamo 13 D8
Bergen 8 C7
Bergerac 12 D4
Berhala, Selat 39 E2
Berhampore =
  Baharampur 40 E7
Berhampur = Brahmapur
  40 H5
Bering Sea 69 C1
Bering Strait 69 B3
Berja 19 D4
Berkeley 72 H2
Berkner I. 96 B4
Berlin 15 B7
Bermejo → Formosa,
  Argentina 94 B5
Bermejo → San Juan,
  Argentina 94 C3
Bermejo, Paso =
  Uspallata, P. de 94 C3
Bermuda ⊘ 67 F13
Bern 14 E4
Bernburg 15 C6
Berne = Bern 14 E4
Bernina, Piz 13 C8
Beroun 16 D2
Berri 62 B3
Berry Australia 63 B5
Berry France 12 C5
Bershad 17 D9
Bertoua 56 D2
Berwick-upon-Tweed
  10 D6
Besalampy 59 B8
Besançon 13 C7
Besar 39 E5
Bessarabia 17 E9
Bessarabka =
  Basarabeasca 17 E9
Bessemer 82 C4
Betanzos 18 A1
Bétaré Oya 56 C2
Bethel 69 B3
Bethlehem S. Africa 59 D5
Bethlehem U.S.A. 77 D8
Béthune 13 A5
Betong 39 D5
Betroka 59 C9
Bettiah 40 D5
Betul 43 J10
Beverley 11 E6
Beverly Hills 78 E3
Beynou 29 E6
Beypazarı 25 E3
Beyşehir Gölü 46 C2
Bezhitsa 24 C3
Béziers 13 E5
Bezwada = Vijayawada
  40 J3
Bhachau 43 H7
Bhadrakh 40 G6

Bhadravati 43 N9
Bhagalpur 40 E6
Bhakra Dam 42 D10
Bhamo 41 E11
Bhandara 43 J11
Bhanrer Ra. 43 H11
Bharat = India ■ 43 J10
Bharatpur 42 F10
Bhatpara 41 F7
Bhaunagar = Bhavnagar
  43 J8
Bhavnagar 43 J8
Bhawanipatna 40 H4
Bhilai = Bhilainagar-Durg
  40 G3
Bhilainagar-Durg 40 G3
Bhilsa = Vidisha 43 H10
Bhilwara 43 G9
Bhima → 43 L10
Bhind 42 F11
Bhiwandi 43 K8
Bhiwani 42 E10
Bhola 41 F8
Bhopal 43 H10
Bhubaneshwar 40 G5
Bhuj 43 H6
Bhumiphol Dam =
  Phumiphon, Khuan
  38 A1
Bhusawal 43 J9
Bhutan ■ 41 D8
Biafra, B. of = Bonny,
  Bight of 56 D1
Biak 37 E5
Biała Podlaska 17 B6
Białogard 16 A2
Białystok 17 B6
Biaro 37 D3
Biarritz 12 E3
Bibai 32 B2
Biberach 14 D5
Bida 53 G7
Bidar 43 L10
Biddeford 77 C10
Bié, Planalto de 58 A3
Bielefeld 14 B5
Biella 13 D8
Bielsk Podlaski 17 B6
Bielsko-Biała 16 D4
Bien Hoa 38 B3
Bienville, L. 71 D6
Big Horn Mts. = Bighorn
  Mts. 73 D10
Big Spring 80 C3
Big Trout L. 71 D5
Biğa 23 D6
Bigadiç 23 E7
Biggar 69 C9
Biggenden 63 A5
Bighorn → 73 C10
Bighorn Mts. 73 D10
Bihać 20 B5
Bihar 40 E5
Bihar □ 40 E5
Bihor, Munţii 17 E6
Bijagós, Arquipélago dos
  53 F2
Bijapur Chhattisgarh, India
  40 H3
Bijapur Karnataka, India
  43 L9

Bíjär 46 D6
Bijeljina 20 B7
Bijnor 42 E11
Bikaner 42 E8
Bikini Atoll 64 H11
Bila Tserkva 17 D10
Bilara 42 F8
Bilaspur 40 F4
Bilbao 19 A4
Bilbo = Bilbao 19 A4
Bilecik 25 E3
Bilhorod-Dnistrovskyy
  25 D3
Bilir 31 C11
Billings 73 D9
Billiton Is. = Belitung
  39 E3
Bilma 55 E1
Biloxi 81 D9
Biltine 55 F3
Bima 37 F1
Bina-Etawah 43 G11
Binalbagan 36 B2
Binalong 63 B4
Bīnālūd, Kūh-e 44 B4
Binatang = Bintangau
  39 D4
Binda 63 A4
Bindle 63 A4
Bindura 59 B6
Bingara N.S.W., Australia
  63 A5
Bingara Queens., Australia
  63 A3
Binghamton 77 C8
Bingöl 46 C5
Binh Dinh = An Nhon
  38 B3
Binh Son 38 A3
Binjai 39 D1
Binnaway 63 B4
Binongko 37 F2
Bintan 39 D2
Bintangau 39 D4
Bintulu 39 D4
Bintuni 37 E4
Binzert = Bizerte 54 A1
Bioko 53 H7
Bir 43 K9
Bir Atrun 55 E4
Bîr Mogreïn 52 C3
Birāk 54 C1
Birchip 62 C3
Birecik 46 C4
Bireuen 38 C1
Birlik 29 E8
Birmingham U.K. 11 E6
Birmingham U.S.A. 82 C4
Birmitrapur 40 F5
Birni Nkonni 53 F7
Birnin Kebbi 53 F6
Birr 11 E3
Birrie → 63 A4
Birsk 29 D6
Bîr Atrun 55 E4
Birur 43 N9
Bisa 37 E3
Biscay, B. of 12 D2
Biscoe Bay 96 B17
Biscoe Is. 96 A3

Bishkek 29 E8
Biskra 52 B7
Bislig 36 C3
Bismarck 74 B4
Bismarck Arch. 64 K9
Bissagos = Bijagós,
  Arquipélago dos 53 F2
Bissau 53 F2
Bistriţa 17 E7
Bistriţa → 17 E8
Bitlis 46 C5
Bitola 22 D3
Bitolj = Bitola 22 D3
Bitterfontein 58 E3
Bitterroot Range 73 D6
Biu 55 F1
Biwa-Ko 33 F5
Biysk 29 D9
Bizerte 54 A1
Bjelovar 20 B6
Björneborg = Pori 8 C10
Black Forest =
  Schwarzwald 14 D5
Black Hills 74 D3
Black Sea 25 E3
Black Volta → 53 G5
Blackball 65 E4
Blackburn 11 E5
Blackpool 11 E5
Blackwater → 11 E2
Blagodarnoye =
  Blagodarnyy 25 D5
Blagodarnyy 25 D5
Blagoevgrad 22 C4
Blagoveshchensk 31 D10
Blanc, Mont 13 D7
Blanca, B. 95 D4
Blanca Peak 79 B10
Blanche, C. 62 B1
Blanche, L. 62 A2
Blanes 19 B7
Blantyre 59 B6
Blayney 63 B4
Blednaya, Gora 28 B7
Blenheim 65 D5
Blida 52 A6
Bligh Sound 65 F2
Blodgett Iceberg Tongue
  96 A13
Bloemfontein 59 D5
Bloemhof 59 D5
Blois 12 C4
Bloomington Ill., U.S.A.
  75 E10
Bloomington Ind., U.S.A.
  76 E2
Blue Mts. 72 D4
Blue Nile = Nîl el Azraq →
  55 E5
Blue Ridge 83 A7
Bluefields 86 D3
Bluff 65 G3
Blumenau 94 B7
Bo 53 G3
Bo Hai 35 C6
Boa Vista 90 C6
Boatman 63 A4
Bobadah 63 B4
Bobbili 40 H4
Bobo-Dioulasso 53 F5

Bóbr ⇢ 16 B2
Bobraomby, Tanjon' i 59 A9
Bobruysk = Babruysk 17 B9
Boby, Pic 59 C9
Bôca do Acre 91 E5
Boca Raton 83 F7
Bocaranga 55 G2
Bochum 14 C4
Bodaybo 30 D9
Boden 8 B10
Bodensee 13 C8
Bodhan 43 K10
Bodø 8 B8
Bodrog ⇢ 16 D5
Bodrum 23 F6
Boende 56 E4
Bogalusa 81 D9
Bogan Gate 63 B4
Boggabilla 63 A5
Boggabri 63 B5
Bogo 36 B2
Bogong, Mt. 63 C4
Bogor 39 F3
Bogotá 90 C4
Bogotol 29 D9
Bogra 41 E7
Bohemian Forest = Böhmerwald 15 D7
Böhmerwald 15 D7
Bohol □ 36 C2
Bohol 37 E5
Bohol Sea 36 C2
Boise 72 E5
Boise City 80 A2
Bojador, C. 52 C3
Bojana ⇢ 22 D2
Bojnürd 44 B4
Bokhara ⇢ 63 A4
Bokoro 55 F2
Bolan Pass 42 E5
Bolbec 12 B4
Bole 34 B3
Bolekhiv 17 D6
Bolesławiec 16 C2
Bolgrad = Bolhrad 17 F9
Bolhrad 17 F9
Bolivia ■ 91 G6
Bollon 63 A4
Bolobo 56 E3
Bologna 20 B3
Bologoye 24 B3
Bolsena, L. di 20 C3
Bolsheche 29 D8
Bolshevik, Ostrov 30 B8
Bolshoy Atlym 28 C7
Bolshoy Begichev, Ostrov 30 B9
Bolshoy Kavkas = Caucasus Mountains 25 E5
Bolshoy Lyakhovskiy, Ostrov 31 B12
Bolton 11 E5
Bolu 23 E7
Bolvadin 46 C2
Bolzano 20 A3
Bom Jesus da Lapa 93 E5
Boma 56 F2
Bombala 63 C4
Bombay = Mumbai 43 K8

Bomboma 56 D3
Bomu ⇢ 56 D4
Bon, C. 21 F3
Bonaire 87 D6
Bonang 63 C4
Bonavista 71 E8
Bondo 56 D4
Bondoukou 53 G5
Bone, Teluk 37 E2
Bonerate 37 F2
Bonerate, Kepulauan 37 F2
Bong Son = Hoai Nhon 38 B3
Bongor 55 F2
Bonifacio 13 F8
Bonin Is. = Ogasawara Gunto 27 F16
Bonn 14 C4
Bonney, L. 62 C3
Bonny, Bight of 56 D1
Bonoi 37 E5
Bontang 39 D5
Bonthain 37 F1
Bonthe 53 G3
Bontoc 36 A2
Boolaboolka L. 62 B3
Booligal 63 B3
Boonah 63 A5
Boorindie 63 B4
Boorowa 63 B4
Boosaaso = Bosaso 49 E4
Boothia, Gulf of 70 B5
Boothia Pen. 68 A10
Booué 56 E2
Bor Serbia 22 B4
Bôr Sudan 55 G5
Bora 90 D7
Borda, C. 62 C2
Bordeaux 12 D3
Borden I. 70 B2
Borden Pen. 70 B5
Bordertown 62 C3
Bordj Fly Ste. Marie 52 C5
Bordj-in-Eker 52 D7
Bordj Omar Driss 52 C7
Borger 80 B3
Borhoyn Tal 35 B6
Borisoglebsk 24 C5
Borisov = Barysaw 17 A9
Borja 90 D3
Borkou 55 E2
Borkum 14 B4
Borley, C. 96 A9
Borneo 39 D4
Bornholm 9 D9
Borongan 36 B3
Borovichi 24 B3
Borşa 17 E7
Borüjerd 46 D7
Boryslav 17 D6
Bosa 21 D2
Bosanska Gradiška 20 B6
Bosaso 49 E4
Boshrūyeh 44 C4
Bosna ⇢ 20 B7
Bosna i Hercegovina = Bosnia-Herzegovina ■ 20 B6

Bosnia-Herzegovina ■ 20 B6
Bosnik 37 E5
Bosobolo 56 D3
Bosporus = İstanbul Boğazı 22 D7
Bossangoa 55 G2
Bosso 55 F1
Bosten Hu 34 B3
Boston U.K. 11 E6
Boston U.S.A. 77 C10
Bothnia, G. of 8 C10
Bothwell 62 D4
Botletle ⇢ 58 C4
Botoşani 17 E8
Botswana ■ 58 C4
Botucatu 93 G4
Bouaké 53 G4
Bouar 56 C3
Bouârfa 52 B5
Bouca 55 G2
Bougainville I. 64 K10
Bougie = Bejaïa 52 A7
Bougouni 53 F4
Boulder 74 E2
Boulder Dam = Hoover Dam 78 B5
Boulogne-sur-Mer 12 A4
Bouna 53 G5
Boundiali 53 G4
Bourbonnais 13 C5
Bourem 53 E5
Bourg-en-Bresse 13 C6
Bourg-St-Maurice 13 D7
Bourgas = Burgas 22 C6
Bourges 12 C5
Bourgogne □ 13 C6
Bourke 63 B4
Bournemouth 11 F6
Bowen Mts. 63 C4
Bowman I. 96 A12
Bowmans 62 B2
Bowral 63 B5
Bowraville 63 B5
Boyne ⇢ 11 E3
Boyoma, Chutes 57 D5
Boz Dağları 23 E7
Bozburun 23 F7
Bozcaada 23 E6
Bozdoğan 23 F7
Bozeman 73 D8
Bozoum 55 G2
Bra 13 D7
Brač 20 C6
Bracciano, L. di 20 C4
Bräcke 8 C9
Bradenton 83 F6
Bradford 11 E6
Braga 18 B1
Bragança Brazil 92 C4
Bragança Portugal 18 B2
Brahestad = Raahe 8 C10
Brahmanbaria 41 F8
Brahmani ⇢ 40 G6
Brahmapur 40 H5
Brahmaputra ⇢ 41 F7
Braidwood 63 C4
Brăila 17 F8
Branco ⇢ 90 D6

Brandenburg = Neubrandenburg 15 B7
Brandenburg 15 B7
Brandenburg □ 15 B7
Brandon 69 D10
Braniewo 16 A4
Bransfield Str. 96 A4
Brantford 76 C5
Brasil = Brazil ■ 93 E4
Brasiléia 91 F5
Brasília 93 F4
Braşov 17 F7
Brassey, Banjaran 38 D5
Bratislava 16 D3
Bratsk 30 D8
Braunau 15 D7
Braunschweig 14 B6
Bravo del Norte, Rio = Grande, Rio ⇢ 84 B5
Brawley 78 D5
Bray 11 E3
Bray, Pays de 12 B4
Brazil ■ 93 E4
Brazos ⇢ 81 E6
Brazzaville 56 E3
Brčko 20 B7
Breaksea Sd. 65 F2
Bream B. 64 A6
Bream Hd. 64 A6
Brecon 11 F5
Breda 14 C3
Bredasdorp 58 E4
Bregenz 14 E5
Breiðafjörður 8 B1
Brejo 92 C5
Bremen 14 B5
Bremerhaven 14 B5
Bremerton 72 C2
Brennerpass 15 E6
Bréscia 13 D9
Breslau = Wrocław 16 C3
Bressanone 20 A3
Brest Belarus 17 B6
Brest France 12 B1
Brest-Litovsk = Brest 17 B6
Bretagne □ 12 B2
Brett, C. 64 A6
Brewarrina 63 A4
Bria 55 G3
Briançon 13 D7
Bribie I. 63 A5
Bridgeport 77 D9
Bridgetown 87 D8
Bridgewater 71 E7
Bridgewater, C. 62 C3
Bridlington 11 D6
Bridport 62 D4
Brigham City 73 F7
Bright 63 C4
Brighton Australia 62 C2
Brighton U.K. 11 F6
Brindisi 21 D6
Brisbane 63 A5
Brisbane ⇢ 63 B5
Bristol U.K. 11 F5
Bristol U.S.A. 83 A6
Bristol B. 69 C3
Bristol Channel 11 F4
British Indian Ocean Terr. = Chagos Arch. ☑ 26 J9

British Isles 11 D4
British Virgin Is. ☑ 87 C7
Brittany = Bretagne □
   12 B2
Brive-la-Gaillarde 12 D4
Brixen = Bressanone
   20 A3
Brlik = Birlik 29 E8
Brno 16 D3
Brock I. 70 B2
Brocken 14 C6
Brodeur Pen. 70 B5
Brodnica 16 B4
Brody 17 C7
Broken Hill 62 B3
Bronte Park 62 D4
Brooloo 63 A5
Broome 60 D3
Broughton Island =
   Qikiqtarjuaq 70 C7
Brown, Pt. 62 B1
Brownsville 81 G5
Brownwood 80 D4
Bruay-la-Buissière 13 A5
Bruce, Mt. 60 E2
Bruck an der Mur 15 E8
Bruges = Brugge 14 C2
Brugge 14 C2
Brumado 93 E5
Brunei = Bandar Seri
   Begawan 38 D5
Brunei ■ 38 D5
Brunner, L. 65 E4
Brunswick =
   Braunschweig 14 B6
Brunswick 83 D7
Brunswick, Pen. de 95 G2
Brussel 14 C3
Brussels = Brussel 14 C3
Bruthen 63 C4
Bruxelles = Brussel 14 C3
Bryan 81 D5
Bryan, Mt. 62 B2
Bryansk 24 C2
Bu Craa 52 C3
Buapinang 37 E2
Buayan 36 C3
Bucak 46 C2
Bucaramanga 90 B4
Buchach 17 D7
Buchan 10 C5
Buckleboo 62 B2
Budalin 41 F10
Budapest 16 E4
Budd Coast 96 A12
Bude 11 F4
Budennovsk 25 E5
Budgewoi 63 B5
Budjala 56 D3
Buenaventura 90 C3
Buenos Aires 94 C5
Buenos Aires, L. 95 F2
Buffalo 77 C6
Bug = Buh → 25 D3
Bug → 16 B5
Buga 90 C3

Bugel, Tanjung 39 F4
Bugsuk I. 38 C5
Bugun Shara 35 B5
Buguruslan 29 D6
Buh → 25 D3
Buir Nur 35 B6
Bujumbura 57 E5
Bukavu 57 E5
Bukhara = Bukhoro 29 F7
Bukhoro 29 F7
Bukittinggi 39 E2
Bukoba 57 E6
Bula 37 E4
Bulahdelah 63 B5
Bulan 36 B2
Bulandshahr 42 E10
Buldan 23 E7
Bulgan 35 B5
Bulgaria ■ 22 C5
Bulgroo 63 A3
Bulloo → 63 A3
Bulloo Downs 62 A3
Bulloo L. 62 A3
Bulls 64 D6
Bulsar = Valsad 43 J8
Bulukumba 37 F2
Bulun 30 B10
Bumba 56 D4
Bumhpa Bum 41 D11
Bunbury 60 G2
Buncrana 11 D3
Bundaberg 63 A5
Bundi 43 G9
Bundoran 11 D2
Bungo-Suidō 33 G3
Bunia 57 D6
Bunji 42 B9
Buntok 39 E4
Bunyu 39 D5
Buol 37 D2
Buon Ma Thuot 38 B3
Buorkhaya, Mys 31 B11
Buqayq 47 F7
Bûr Acaba 49 G3
Bûr Safâga 54 C5
Bûr Saʿîd 54 B5
Bûr Sûdân 55 E6
Burao 49 F4
Buraydah 47 F5
Buraymī, Al Wāhāt al
   44 E3
Burdur 46 C2
Burdwan = Barddhaman
   40 F6
Burgas 22 C6
Burgos 18 A4
Burgundy = Bourgogne □
   13 C6
Burhaniye 23 E6
Burhanpur 43 J10
Burias I. 36 B2
Buriram 38 A2
Burkina Faso ■ 53 F5
Burlington Iowa, U.S.A.
   75 E9
Burlington N.C., U.S.A.
   83 A8

Burlington Vt., U.S.A.
   77 B9
Burlyu-Tyube 29 E8
Burma ■ 41 G11
Burnie 62 D4
Burnley 11 E5
Burnside → 68 B9
Burqān 47 E6
Burqin 34 B3
Burra 62 B2
Burren Junction 63 B4
Burrendong Dam 63 B4
Burrinjuck Res. 63 C4
Burruyacú 94 B4
Bursa 23 D7
Buru 37 E3
Burundi ■ 57 E6
Burutu 53 G7
Bury St. Edmunds 11 E7
Busan 35 C7
Büshehr 44 D2
Büshehr □ 44 D2
Bushire = Büshehr 44 D2
Businga 56 D4
Busto Arsízio 13 D8
Busu Djanoa 56 D4
Busuanga I. 36 B1
Buta 57 D5
Butare 57 E5
Butaritari 64 J12
Butembo 57 D5
Butha Qi 35 B7
Buton 37 E2
Butte 73 C7
Butterworth = Gcuwa
   59 E5
Butterworth 38 C2
Butuan 36 C3
Butung = Buton 37 E2
Buturlinovka 24 C5
Buur Hakaba = Bur Acaba
   49 G3
Buxoro = Bukhoro 29 F7
Buxtehude 14 B5
Buy 24 B5
Buyant-Uhaa 35 B6
Büyük Menderes → 23 F6
Büyükçekmece 22 D7
Buzău 17 F8
Buzău → 17 F8
Buzen 33 G2
Buzi → 59 B6
Buzuluk 29 D6
Byarezina → 17 B10
Byaroza 17 B7
Bydgoszcz 16 B3
Byelorussia = Belarus ■
   24 C2
Bykhaw 17 B10
Bykhov = Bykhaw 17 B10
Bylot I. 70 B6
Byrock 63 B4
Byron Bay 63 A5
Byrranga, Gory 30 B8
Byrranga Mts. = Byrranga,
   Gory 30 B8
Bytom 16 C4
Bytów 16 A3

C

Ca Mau 38 C3
Caála 58 A3
Cabanatuan 36 A2
Cabedelo 92 D7
Cabimas 90 A4
Cabinda 56 F2
Cabinda □ 56 F2
Cabinet Mts. 73 C6
Cabo Blanco 95 F3
Cabo Frio 93 G5
Cabo Pantoja 90 D3
Cabo Verde = Cape Verde
   Is. ■ 50 E1
Cabonga, Réservoir 71 E6
Caboolture 63 A5
Cabora Bassa Dam =
   Cahora Bassa, Reprêsa
   de 59 B6
Cabot Str. 71 E8
Cabra 18 D3
Cabrera 19 C7
Cabriel → 19 C5
Čačak 22 C3
Cáceres Brazil 91 G7
Cáceres Spain 18 C2
Cachimbo, Serra do 93 D2
Cachoeira 93 E6
Cachoeira do Sul 94 C6
Cachoeira de Itapemirim
   93 G5
Cacólo 56 G3
Caconda 58 A3
Cadibarrawirracanna, L.
   62 A2
Cadiz Phil. 36 B2
Cádiz Spain 18 D2
Cádiz, G. de 18 D2
Cadney Park 62 A1
Caen 12 B3
Caetité 93 E5
Cagayan de Oro 36 C2
Cágliari 21 E2
Cágliari, G. di 21 E2
Caguas 87 C6
Cahora Bassa, Reprêsa de
   59 B6
Cahors 12 D4
Cahul 17 F9
Caicara 90 B5
Caicó 92 D6
Caird Coast 96 B5
Cairns 61 D8
Cairo = El Qâhira 54 B5
Cairo 81 A9
Cajamarca 91 E3
Cajàzeiras 92 D6
Calabar 53 H7
Calábria □ 21 E6
Calafate 95 G2
Calahorra 19 A5
Calais 12 A4
Calama Brazil 91 E6
Calama Chile 94 A3
Calamar 90 A4
Calamian Group 36 B1
Calamocha 19 B5
Calang 38 D1
Calapan 36 B2

Călăraşi **22 B6**
Calatayud **19 B5**
Calauag **36 B2**
Calavite, C. **36 B2**
Calbayog **36 B2**
Calca **91 F4**
Calcutta = Kolkata **41 F7**
Caldas da Rainha **18 C1**
Caldera **94 B2**
Caldwell **72 E5**
Caledon → **59 E5**
Calgary **69 C8**
Cali **90 C3**
Calicut **43 P9**
California □ **78 B3**
California, G. de **84 B2**
Calingasta **94 C3**
Callabonna, L. **62 A3**
Callao **91 F3**
Caloundra **63 A5**
Caltagirone **21 F5**
Caltanissetta **21 F5**
Calulo **56 G2**
Calvi **13 E8**
Calvià **19 C7**
Calvinia **58 E3**
Camabatela **56 F3**
Camacupa **58 A3**
Camagüey **86 B4**
Camaná **91 G4**
Camargue **13 E6**
Camarones **95 E3**
Cambay = Khambhat
    43 H8
Cambay, G. of =
    Khambhat, G. of **43 J8**
Cambodia ■ **38 B3**
Cambrai **13 A5**
Cambrian Mts. **11 E5**
Cambridge *N.Z.* **64 B6**
Cambridge *U.K.* **11 E7**
Cambridge *U.S.A.* **77 C10**
Cambridge Bay =
    Ikaluktutiak **68 B9**
Cambundi-Catembo
    56 G3
Camden *Ark., U.S.A.*
    81 C7
Camden *N.J., U.S.A.*
    77 E8
Cameroon ■ **56 C2**
Cameroun, Mt. **53 H7**
Cametá **92 C4**
Caminha **18 B1**
Camira Creek **63 A5**
Camocim **92 C5**
Campana, I. **95 F1**
Campána □ **21 D5**
Campbell Town **62 D4**
Campbellton **71 E7**
Campbelltown **63 B5**
Campbeltown **10 F3**
Campeche **85 D6**
Campeche, Golfo de
    85 D6
Camperdown **62 C3**
Câmpina **17 F6**
Campina Grande **92 D6**
Campinas **94 A7**
Campo Grande **93 G3**

Campo Maior **92 C5**
Campobasso **20 D5**
Campos **93 G5**
Campos Belos **93 E4**
Câmpulung **17 F7**
Camrose **69 C8**
Çan **23 D6**
Can Tho **38 B3**
Canada ■ **68 C8**
Cañada de Gómez **94 C4**
Çanakkale **23 D6**
Çanakkale Boğazı **23 D6**
Cananea **84 A2**
Cananéia **93 F6**
Canarias, Is. **52 C2**
Canary Is. = Canarias, Is.
    52 C2
Canaveral, C. **83 G5**
Canavieiras **93 F6**
Canberra **63 C4**
Candelo **63 C4**
Candia = Iraklio **23 G5**
Canea = Chania **23 G5**
Canelones **94 C5**
Cañete *Chile* **94 D2**
Cañete *Peru* **91 F3**
Cangas de Narcea **18 A2**
Canguaretama **92 D6**
Canguçu **94 C6**
Caniapiscau → **70 D7**
Caniapiscau, L. **71 D7**
Canicattì **21 F4**
Canipaan **38 C5**
Çankırı **25 E3**
Cann River **63 C4**
Cannanore **43 P9**
Cannes **13 E7**
Canoas **94 B6**
Canora **69 C9**
Canowindra **63 B4**
Cantabria □ **18 A4**
Cantabrian Mts. =
    Cantábrica, Cordillera
    18 A3
Cantábrica, Cordillera
    18 A3
Cantal, Plomb du **13 D5**
Canterbury **11 F7**
Canterbury Bight **65 F4**
Canterbury Plains **65 E4**
Canton = Guangzhou
    35 D6
Canton **76 D5**
Canudos **91 E7**
Canutama **91 E6**
Cap-Haïtien **87 C5**
Capanaparo → **90 B5**
Cape Barren I. **62 D4**
Cape Breton I. **71 E7**
Cape Coast **53 G5**
Cape Dorset **70 C6**
Cape Dyer **70 C7**
Cape Girardeau **81 C7**
Cape Lisburne = Wevok
    69 B3
Cape Town **58 E3**
Cape Verde Is. ■ **50 E1**
Cape York Peninsula
    61 C7
Capela **93 E6**
Capim → **92 C4**

Capraia **13 E8**
Capri **21 D5**
Caprivi Strip **58 B4**
Captain's Flat **63 C4**
Caquetá → **90 D5**
Caracal **22 B5**
Caracas **90 A5**
Caracol **93 D5**
Caradoc **62 B3**
Carajás, Serra dos **92 D3**
Caransebeş **17 F6**
Caratasca, L. **86 C3**
Caratinga **93 F5**
Caraúbas **92 D6**
Caravaca de la Cruz
    19 C5
Caravelas **93 F6**
Caraveli **91 G4**
Carballo **18 A1**
Carbonara, C. **21 E2**
Carbondale **81 A9**
Carbonear **71 E8**
Carbónia **21 E2**
Carcassonne **12 E5**
Carcross **68 B6**
Cardamon Hills **43 Q10**
Cárdenas **86 B3**
Cardiff **11 F5**
Cardigan B. **11 E4**
Cardston **69 D8**
Carei **17 E6**
Carhué **94 D4**
Caria **23 F7**
Cariacica **93 G5**
Caribbean Sea **86 D5**
Cariboo Mts. **69 C7**
Carinda **63 B4**
Carinhanha **93 E5**
Carinthia = Kärnten □
    15 E7
Caripito **90 A6**
Carlisle **11 D5**
Carlow **11 E3**
Carlsbad **80 C1**
Carmacks **68 B6**
Carmarthen **11 F4**
Carmaux **12 D5**
Carmen **90 B3**
Carmen de Patagones
    95 E4
Carmona **18 D3**
Carnac **12 C2**
Carnarvon *Australia* **60 E1**
Carnarvon *S. Africa* **58 E4**
Carnegie, L. **60 F3**
Carnot **56 D3**
Carnot, C. **62 B2**
Carolina **92 D4**
Caroline I. **65 K15**
Caroline Is. **64 J10**
Caroní → **90 B6**
Caronie = Nébrodi, Monti
    21 F5
Caroona **63 B5**
Carpathians **16 D5**
Carpaţii Meridionali **17 F7**
Carpentaria, G. of **60 C6**
Carpentras **13 D6**
Carpi **20 B3**
Carpolac = Morea **62 C3**

Carrara **13 D9**
Carrauntoohill **11 E2**
Carrick-on-Suir **11 E3**
Carrieton **62 B2**
Carrizal Bajo **94 B2**
Carson City **72 G4**
Cartagena *Colombia*
    90 A3
Cartagena *Spain* **19 D5**
Cartago *Colombia* **90 C3**
Cartago *Costa Rica* **86 E3**
Carterton **65 D6**
Carthage **81 A6**
Caruaru **92 D6**
Carúpano **90 A6**
Carvoeiro **90 D6**
Carvoeiro, C. **18 C1**
Casablanca **52 B4**
Cascade Ra. **72 C3**
Cascais **18 C1**
Cascavel **94 A6**
Cáscina **20 C3**
Caserta **20 D5**
Caseyr, Raas = Asir, Ras
    49 E5
Casiguran **36 A2**
Casilda **94 C4**
Casino **63 A5**
Casiquiare → **90 C5**
Casma **91 E3**
Caspe **19 B5**
Casper **73 E10**
Caspian Sea **29 E6**
Castellammare di Stábia
    21 D5
Castelló de la Plana **19 C5**
Castelo Branco **18 C2**
Castelsarrasin **12 D4**
Castelvetrano **21 F4**
Casterton **62 C3**
Castilla-La Mancha □
    18 C4
Castilla y Leon □ **18 A3**
Castlebar **11 E2**
Castleblaney **11 D3**
Castlemaine **63 C3**
Castlereagh → **63 B4**
Castres **12 E5**
Castries **87 D7**
Castro **95 E2**
Castro Alves **93 E6**
Castuera **18 C3**
Cat I. **86 B4**
Catalão **93 F4**
Çatalca **22 D7**
Catalonia = Cataluña □
    19 B6
Cataluña □ **19 B6**
Catamarca **94 B3**
Catanduanes □ **36 B2**
Catanduva **93 G4**
Catánia **21 F5**
Catanzaro **21 E6**
Catarman **36 B2**
Cateel **36 B5**
Catoche, C. **85 C7**
Catrimani **90 C6**
Catskill Mts. **77 C8**
Cauca → **90 B4**

Caucaia 92 C6
Caucasus Mountains 25 E5
Caungula 56 F3
Cauquenes 94 D2
Caura → 90 B6
Cauvery → 43 P11
Cavan 11 D3
Cavendish 62 C3
Caviana, I. 92 B3
Cavite 36 B2
Cawndilla L. 62 B3
Cawnpore = Kanpur 40 D3
Caxias 92 C5
Caxias do Sul 94 B6
Cayambe 90 C3
Cayenne 92 A3
Cayman Is. ☑ 86 C3
Cazombo 58 A4
Ceanannus Mor 11 E3
Ceará = Fortaleza 92 C6
Ceará □ 92 D6
Ceará Mirim 92 D6
Cebollar 94 B3
Cebu 36 B2
Cecil Plains 63 A5
Cedar L. 69 C10
Cedar Rapids 75 E9
Cedro 92 D6
Ceduna 62 B1
Ceerigaabo = Erigavo 49 E4
Cefalù 21 E5
Cegléd 16 E4
Celaya 84 C4
Celebes = Sulawesi 37 E2
Celebes Sea 37 D2
Celje 20 A5
Celle 14 B6
Celtic Sea 11 F2
Central, Cordillera 90 C3
Central African Rep. ■ 56 C4
Central Makran Range 42 F4
Cephalonia = Kefalonia 23 E3
Ceram = Seram 37 E3
Ceram Sea = Seram Sea 37 E3
Ceres 94 B4
Cerignola 20 D5
Cerigo = Kythira 23 F4
Çerkeş 46 B2
Çerkezköy 22 D6
Cervera 19 B6
Cesena 20 B4
Česká Rep. = Czech Rep. ■ 16 D2
České Budějovice 16 D2
Českomoravská Vrchovina 16 D2
Çeşme 23 E6
Cessnock 63 B5
Cetinje 22 C2
Cetraro 21 E5
Ceuta 18 E3
Cévennes 13 D5

Ceylon = Sri Lanka ■ 43 R12
Chachapoyas 91 E3
Chachran 42 E7
Chad ■ 55 E2
Chad, L. = Tchad, L. 55 F1
Chadileuvú → 94 D3
Chadyr-Lunga = Ciadâr-Lunga 17 E9
Chagai Hills = Chāh Gay Hills 42 E3
Chagos Arch. ☑ 26 J9
Chāh Bahar 45 E5
Chāh Gay Hills 42 E3
Chahār Borjak 42 D3
Chaibasa 40 F5
Chakhānsūr 42 D3
Chakradharpur 40 F5
Chakwal 42 C8
Chala 91 G4
Chalcis = Halkida 23 E4
Chalhuanca 91 F4
Chalisgaon 43 J9
Chalky Inlet 65 G2
Challapata 91 G5
Chalon-sur-Saône 13 C6
Châlons-en-Champagne 13 B6
Chaman 42 D5
Chamba 42 C10
Chambal → 42 F11
Chambéry 13 D6
Chamical 94 C3
Chamonix-Mont Blanc 13 D7
Champagne 13 B6
Champaign 76 E1
Champlain, L. 77 B9
Chañaral 94 B2
Chandigarh 42 D10
Chandler 62 A1
Chandmani 34 B4
Chandpur 41 F8
Chandrapur 43 K11
Ch'ang Chiang = Chang Jiang → 35 C7
Chang Jiang → 35 C7
Changanacheri 43 Q10
Changane → 59 C6
Changchiak'ou = Zhangjiakou 35 B6
Ch'angchou = Changzhou 35 C6
Changchun 35 B7
Changde 35 D6
Changhai = Shanghai 35 C7
Changhua 35 D7
Changsha 35 D6
Changzhi 35 C6
Changzhou 35 C6
Chania 23 G5
Chanion, Kolpos 23 G4
Channapatna 43 N10
Channel Is. 11 G5
Channel-Port aux Basques 71 E8
Chantada 18 A2
Chanthaburi 38 B2

Chantrey Inlet 68 B10
Chanute 81 A6
Chao Phraya → 38 B2
Chaozhou 35 D6
Chapala, L. de 84 C4
Chapayevsk 24 C6
Chapleau 71 E5
Chapra = Chhapra 40 E5
Chara 31 D9
Charagua 91 G6
Charaña 91 G5
Chardara 29 E7
Chardzhou = Türkmenabat 29 F7
Charente → 12 D3
Chari → 55 F1
Chārīkār 42 B6
Chärjew = Türkmenabat 29 F7
Charleroi 14 C3
Charles, C. 77 F8
Charleston *S.C.*, *U.S.A.* 83 C8
Charleston *W. Va.*, *U.S.A.* 76 F5
Charlesville 56 F4
Charleville 63 A4
Charleville-Mézières 13 B6
Charlotte 83 B7
Charlotte Amalie 87 C6
Charlottesville 77 E6
Charlottetown 71 E7
Charlton 62 C3
Charlton I. 71 D6
Charolles 13 C6
Charters Towers 61 E8
Chartres 12 B4
Chascomús 94 D5
Châteaubriant 12 C3
Châteaulin 12 B1
Châteauroux 12 C4
Châtellerault 12 C4
Chatham = Chatham-Kent 71 E5
Chatham = Miramichi 71 E7
Chatham 11 F7
Chatham-Kent 71 E5
Chatrapur 40 H5
Châttagām = Chittagong 41 F8
Chattahoochee → 82 D5
Chattanooga 82 C4
Chaukan Pass 41 D11
Chaumont 13 B6
Chaves *Brazil* 92 C4
Chaves *Portugal* 18 B2
Cheb 16 C1
Cheboksary 24 B6
Chech, Erg 52 D5
Chechenia = Chechnia □ 25 E6
Checheno-Ingush Republic = Chechenia □ 25 E6
Chechnya = Chechenia □ 25 E6
Cheduba I. 41 H9
Cheepie 63 A4
Chegga 52 C4
Chegutu 59 B5

Chehalis 72 C2
Cheju-do = Jeju-do 35 C7
Chekiang = Zhejiang □ 35 D7
Cheleken = Hazar 29 F6
Chelford 95 D3
Chelkar = Shalqar 29 E6
Chelkar Tengiz, Solonchak 29 E7
Chelm 17 C6
Chełmno 16 B4
Chelmsford 11 F7
Cheltenham 11 F5
Chelyabinsk 29 D7
Chelyuskin, C. = Chelyuskin, Mys 30 B8
Chelyuskin, Mys 30 B8
Chemba 59 B6
Chemnitz 15 C7
Chenab → 42 D7
Chengchou = Zhengzhou 35 C6
Chengde 35 B6
Chengdu 35 C5
Chengjiang 34 D5
Ch'engtu = Chengdu 35 C5
Chennai 43 N12
Chenzhou 35 D6
Cheo Reo 38 B3
Cheom Ksan 38 B2
Cheongju 35 C7
Chepén 91 E3
Chepes 94 C3
Cher → 12 C4
Cherbourg 12 B3
Cherdyn 28 C6
Cherepanovo 29 D9
Cherepovets 24 B4
Chergui, Chott ech 52 B6
Cherikov = Cherykaw 17 B10
Cherkasy 24 D3
Cherlak 29 D8
Chernaya 30 B6
Chernigov = Chernihiv 24 C3
Chernihiv 24 C3
Chernivtsi 17 D7
Chernobyl = Chornobyl 17 C10
Chernovtsy = Chernivtsi 17 D7
Cherrapunji 41 E8
Cherven 17 B9
Chervonohrad 17 C7
Cherykaw 17 B10
Chesapeake 77 F7
Chesapeake B. 77 F7
Cheshskaya Guba 28 C5
Chester *U.K.* 11 E5
Chester *U.S.A.* 77 E8
Chesterfield 11 E6
Chesterfield, Îs. 64 L10
Chesterfield Inlet 68 B10
Chesterton Ra. 63 A4
Chetumal 85 D7
Cheviot Hills 10 D5
Chew Bahir 55 H6
Cheyenne 74 E2

Cheyenne → **74 C4**
Chhapra **40 E5**
Chhatarpur **43 G11**
Chhindwara **43 H11**
Chi → **38 A2**
Chiai **35 D7**
Chiávari **13 D8**
Chiavenna **13 C8**
Chiba **33 F7**
Chibemba **58 B2**
Chibia **58 B2**
Chibougamau **71 E6**
Chicacole = Srikakulam **40 H4**
Chicago **76 D2**
Chichagof I. **69 C6**
Chichester **11 F6**
Ch'ich'iaherh = Qiqihar **35 B7**
Chickasha **80 B5**
Chiclana de la Frontera **18 D2**
Chiclayo **91 E3**
Chico **72 G3**
Chico → *Chubut, Argentina* **95 E3**
Chico → *Santa Cruz, Argentina* **95 F3**
Chicoutimi **71 E6**
Chidambaram **43 P11**
Chidley, C. **70 C7**
Chiemsee **15 E7**
Chiese → **13 D9**
Chieti **20 C5**
Chiguana **91 H5**
Chihli, G. of = Bo Hai **35 C6**
Chihuahua **84 B3**
Chiili = Shīeli **29 E7**
Chik Bollapur **43 N10**
Chikmagalur **43 N9**
Chilapa **84 D5**
Chilas **42 B9**
Childers **63 A5**
Chile ■ **94 D2**
Chile **91 E3**
Chilete **91 E3**
Chililabombwe **59 A5**
Chilin = Jilin **35 B7**
Chilka L. **40 H5**
Chillán **94 D2**
Chiloé, I. de **95 E2**
Chilpancingo **84 D5**
Chilung **35 D7**
Chilwa, L. **59 B7**
Chimbay **29 E6**
Chimborazo **90 D3**
Chimbote **91 E3**
Chimkent = Shymkent **29 E7**
Chimoio **59 B6**
Chin □ **41 F9**
China ■ **35 D5**
Chinan = Jinan **35 C6**
Chinandega **85 E7**
Chincha Alta **91 F3**
Chinchilla **63 A5**
Chinchou = Jinzhou **35 B7**
Chinde **59 B7**
Chindwin → **41 G10**

Chingola **59 A5**
Ch'ingtao = Qingdao **35 C7**
Chinguetti **52 D3**
Chinhoyi **59 B6**
Chiniot **42 D8**
Chinnampo = Namp'o **35 C7**
Chinon **12 C4**
Chióggia **20 B4**
Chíos = Hios **23 E6**
Chipata **59 A6**
Chiquián **91 F3**
Chiquinquira **90 B4**
Chirchiq **29 E7**
Chiredzi **59 C6**
Chirmiri **40 F4**
Chisapani Garhi **40 D5**
Chisasibi **71 D6**
Chisimaio **49 H3**
Chişinău **17 E9**
Chistopol **24 B7**
Chita **30 D9**
Chitral **42 B7**
Chitré **86 E3**
Chittagong **41 F8**
Chittagong □ **41 E8**
Chittaurgarh **43 G9**
Chittoor **43 N11**
Chitungwiza **59 B6**
Chiusi **20 C3**
Chivasso **13 D7**
Chivilcoy **94 B4**
Chkalov = Orenburg **29 D6**
Choele Choel **95 D3**
Chojnice **16 B3**
Cholet **12 C3**
Choluteca **85 E7**
Choma **59 B5**
Chomolungma = Everest, Mt. **40 C6**
Chomutov **16 C1**
Chon Buri **38 B2**
Chone **90 D3**
Ch'öngjin **35 B7**
Chongqing **35 D5**
Chongui **30 F**
Chonos, Arch. de los **95 F2**
Chop **17 D6**
Chora Sfakion **23 G5**
Chornobyl **17 C10**
Chortkiv **17 D7**
Chorzów **16 C4**
Chos-Malal **94 D2**
Choszczno **16 B2**
Chotila **43 H7**
Choybalsan **35 B6**
Christchurch **65 E5**
Christmas I. = Kiritimati **65 J15**
Chū = Shū **29 E8**
Ch'uanchou = Quanzhou **35 D6**
Chula Vista **78 D4**
Chulucanas **90 E2**

Chulym → **29 D9**
Chumbicha **94 B3**
Chumphon **38 B1**
Chuna → **30 D7**
Chuncheon **35 C7**
Chungking = Chongqing **35 D5**
Chunya **57 F6**
Chuquibamba **91 G4**
Chuquicamata **94 A3**
Chur **13 C8**
Churachandpur **41 E9**
Churchill **68 C10**
Churchill → *Man., Canada* **68 C10**
Churchill → *Nfld. & L., Canada* **71 D7**
Churchill, C. **68 C10**
Churchill Falls **71 D7**
Churchill L. **69 C9**
Churu **42 E9**
Chushal **42 C11**
Chusovoy **28 D6**
Chuuk = Truk **64 J10**
Chuvash Republic = Chuvashia □ **24 B6**
Chuvashia □ **24 B6**
Ciadâr-Lunga **17 E9**
Cicero **76 E2**
Ciechanów **16 B5**
Ciego de Ávila **86 B4**
Ciénaga **90 A4**
Cienfuegos **86 B3**
Cieza **19 C5**
Cijara, Embalse de **18 C3**
Cilician Gates P. **46 C3**
Cill Chainnigh = Kilkenny **11 E3**
Cimişlia **17 E9**
Cimone, Mte. **20 B3**
Cinca → **19 B6**
Cincar **20 C7**
Cincinnati **76 E3**
Çine **23 F2**
Cinto, Mte. **13 E8**
Circle **69 B5**
Cirebon **39 F3**
Citlaltépetl = Orizaba, Pico de **84 D5**
Città del Vaticano = Vatican City ■ **20 D4**
Città di Castello **20 C4**
Ciudad Bolívar **90 B6**
Ciudad de México **84 D5**
Ciudad del Carmen **85 D6**
Ciudad Delicias = Delicias **84 B3**
Ciudad Guayana **90 B6**
Ciudad Juárez **84 A3**
Ciudad Madero **84 C5**
Ciudad Mante **84 C5**
Ciudad Obregón **84 B3**
Ciudad Real **18 C4**
Ciudad Rodrigo **18 B2**
Ciudad Victoria **84 C5**
Civitanova Marche **20 C4**
Civitavécchia **20 C3**
Cizre **46 C5**
Clare **62 B2**
Clarence → *Australia* **63 A5**

Clarence → *N.Z.* **65 E5**
Clarence, I. **95 G2**
Clarence I. **96 A4**
Clarie Coast **96 A13**
Clarke I. **62 D4**
Clarksdale **81 B8**
Clarksville **82 A4**
Claveria **36 A2**
Clear, C. **11 F2**
Clearwater **83 F6**
Clearwater Mts. **73 C6**
Clermont-Ferrand **13 D5**
Cleveland *Australia* **63 A5**
Cleveland *U.S.A.* **76 D5**
Clifden **65 G2**
Clifton **63 A5**
Clifton Hills **62 A2**
Clinton *N.Z.* **65 G3**
Clinton *U.S.A.* **75 E9**
Clinton Colden L. **68 B9**
Clones **11 D3**
Clonmel **11 E3**
Clovis **80 B2**
Cluj-Napoca **17 E6**
Clunes **62 C3**
Clutha → **65 G3**
Clyde **65 F3**
Clyde → **10 D4**
Clyde, Firth of **10 D4**
Clyde River **70 B7**
Coari **90 D6**
Coast Mts. **68 C7**
Coast Ranges **72 F2**
Coats I. **70 C5**
Coats Land **96 B5**
Coatzacoalcos **85 D6**
Cobar **63 B4**
Cóbh **11 F2**
Cobham **62 B3**
Cobija **91 F5**
Cobram **63 C4**
Coburg **15 C6**
Cocanada = Kakinada **40 J4**
Cochabamba **91 G5**
Cochin **43 Q10**
Cochin China = Nam-Phan **38 B3**
Cochrane **71 E5**
Cochrane, L. **95 F2**
Cockburn **62 B3**
Cockburn, Canal **95 G2**
Coco → **86 D3**
Cocobeach **56 D1**
Cod, C. **77 C10**
Codajás **90 D6**
Codó **92 C5**
Coeur d'Alene **72 C5**
Coffeyville **81 A6**
Coffin B. **62 B2**
Coffin Bay Peninsula **62 B2**
Coffs Harbour **63 B5**
Cognac **12 D3**
Cohuna **63 C3**
Coiba, I. de **86 E3**
Coig → **95 G3**
Coihaique **95 F2**
Coimbatore **43 P10**
Coimbra *Brazil* **91 G7**

Coimbra *Portugal* 18 B1
Coín 18 D3
Cojímies 90 C3
Colac 62 C3
Colatina 93 F5
Colbeck, C. 96 B17
Colbinabbin 63 C3
Colchester 11 F7
Colebrook 62 D4
Coleman 69 D8
Coleraine *Australia* 62 C3
Coleraine *U.K.* 11 D3
Coleridge, L. 65 E4
Colesberg 59 E5
Colhué Huapi, L. 95 F3
Colima 84 D4
Colinas 93 D5
Coll 10 C3
Collaguasi 91 H5
Collarenebri 63 A4
Collina, Passo di 20 B3
Collingwood 64 D5
Colmar 13 B7
Colo → 63 B5
Cologne = Köln 14 C4
Colomb-Béchar = Béchar
52 B5
Colombia ■ 90 C4
Colombo 43 R11
Colón *Cuba* 86 B3
Colón *Panama* 85 F9
Colonia del Sacramento
94 C5
Colonia Dora 94 B4
Colonsay 10 E3
Colorado □ 79 A10
Colorado → *Argentina*
95 D4
Colorado → *N. Amer.*
78 E5
Colorado Plateau 79 B7
Colorado Springs 74 F2
Columbia *Mo., U.S.A.*
75 F8
Columbia *S.C., U.S.A.*
83 B7
Columbia *Tenn., U.S.A.*
82 B4
Columbia → 72 C1
Columbia, C. 70 A7
Columbia, District of □
77 E7
Columbia Basin 72 C4
Columbretes, Is. 19 C6
Columbus *Ga., U.S.A.*
82 C5
Columbus *Miss., U.S.A.*
82 C3
Columbus *Ohio, U.S.A.*
76 E4
Colville → 69 A4
Colville, C. 64 B6
Colwyn Bay 11 E5
Comácchio 20 B4
Comallo 95 E2
Comilla 41 F8
Comino, C. 21 D2
Committee B. 70 C5
Commonwealth B. 96 A14
Commoron Cr. → 63 A5

Communism Pk. = imeni
Ismail Samani, Pik
29 F8
Como 13 D8
Como, Lago di 13 D8
Comodoro Rivadavia
95 F3
Comorin, C. =
Kanyakumari 43 Q10
Comoros ■ 51 H8
Compiègne 13 B5
Compton Downs 63 B4
Comrat 17 E9
Conakry 53 G3
Conara 62 D4
Concarneau 12 C2
Conceição da Barra 93 F6
Concepción *Bolivia* 91 G6
Concepción *Chile* 94 D2
Concepción *Paraguay*
94 A5
Concepción, L. 91 G6
Concepción del Oro 84 C4
Concepción del Uruguay
94 C5
Conchos → 84 B3
Concord *N.C., U.S.A.*
83 B7
Concord *N.H., U.S.A.*
77 C10
Concordia *Argentina*
94 C5
Concórdia *Brazil* 90 D5
Condamine 63 A5
Condeúba 93 E5
Condobolin 63 B4
Conegliano 20 B4
Confuso → 94 B5
Congo (Brazzaville) =
Congo ■ 56 E3
Congo (Kinshasa) =
Congo, Dem. Rep. of
the ■ 56 E4
Congo ■ 56 E3
Congo → 56 F2
Congo, Dem. Rep. of
the ■ 56 E4
Conjeeveram =
Kanchipuram 43 N11
Conlea 63 B3
Conn, L. 11 D2
Connacht □ 11 E2
Connecticut □ 77 D9
Connecticut → 77 D9
Connemara 11 E2
Conran, C. 63 C4
Conselheiro Lafaiete
93 G5
Constance = Konstanz
14 E5
Constance, L. = Bodensee
13 C8
Constanţa 22 B7
Constantine 52 A7
Constitución 94 D2
Contai 40 G6
Contamana 91 E4
Contas → 93 E6
Conway, L. 62 A2
Coober Pedy 62 A1

Cooch Behar = Koch Bihar
41 D7
Cook, B. 95 H2
Cook, Mt. = Aoraki Mount
Cook 65 E4
Cook Inlet 69 C4
Cook Is. 65 L14
Cook Strait 65 D6
Cooktown 61 D8
Coolabah 63 B4
Cooladdi 63 A4
Coolah 63 B4
Coolamon 63 B4
Coolangatta 63 A5
Cooma 63 C4
Coonabarabran 63 B4
Coonamble 63 B4
Coondapoor 43 N9
Coongoola 63 A4
Cooninnie, L. 62 A2
Cooper Cr. → *N. Terr.,*
Australia 60 C5
Cooper Cr. → *S. Austral.,*
Australia 62 A2
Coorong, The 62 C2
Cooroy 63 A5
Cootamundra 63 B4
Cooyar 63 A5
Copenhagen = København
9 D8
Copiapó 94 B2
Copiapó → 94 B2
Coppermine = Kugluktuk
68 B8
Coppermine → 68 B8
Coquimbo 94 C2
Corabia 22 C5
Coracora 91 G4
Coral Harbour 70 C5
Coral Sea 64 L10
Corato 21 D6
Corby 11 E6
Corcaigh = Cork 11 F2
Corcubión 18 A1
Córdoba *Argentina* 94 C4
Córdoba *Spain* 18 D3
Córdoba, Sierra de 94 C4
Cordova 69 B5
Corfu = Kerkyra 23 E2
Coria 18 C2
Corigliano Cálabro 21 E6
Corinna 62 D4
Corinth = Korinthos 23 F4
Corinth, G. of =
Korinthiakos Kolpos
23 E4
Corinto 93 F5
Cork 11 F2
Çorlu 22 D6
Corner Brook 71 E8
Corneşti 17 E9
Cornwall 71 E6
Cornwall I. 70 B4
Cornwallis I. 70 B4
Corny Pt. 62 B2
Coro 90 A5
Coroatá 92 C5
Corocoro 91 G5
Coroico 91 G5

Coromandel 64 B6
Corona 62 B3
Coronation Gulf 68 B8
Coronation I. 96 A4
Coronel 94 D2
Coronel Dorrego 94 D4
Coronel Suárez 94 D4
Corowa 63 C4
Corpus Christi 80 F5
Corrib, L. 11 E2
Corrientes 94 B5
Corrientes → 90 D4
Corrientes, C. *Colombia*
90 B3
Corrientes, C. *Mexico*
84 C3
Corriverton 90 B7
Corse □ 13 E8
Corse, C. 13 E8
Corsica = Corse □ 13 E8
Corsicana 81 E5
Corte 13 E8
Cortés, Mar de =
California, G. de 84 B2
Çorum 25 E3
Corumbá 91 G7
Corunna = A Coruña
18 A1
Corvallis 72 D2
Cosenza 21 E6
Costa Blanca 19 C5
Costa Brava 19 B7
Costa del Sol 18 D3
Costa Dorada 19 B6
Costa Rica ■ 86 E3
Cotabato 36 C2
Cotagaita 91 H5
Côte d'Azur 13 E7
Côte-d'Ivoire = Ivory
Coast ■ 53 G4
Cotentin 12 B3
Cotonou 53 G6
Cotopaxi 90 D3
Cotswold Hills 11 F5
Cottbus 15 C8
Couedic, C. du 62 C2
Coulman I. 96 B15
Council Bluffs 75 E7
Courantuyne → 90 B7
Courtrai = Kortrijk 14 C2
Coventry 11 E6
Covilhã 18 B2
Covington 76 E3
Cowal, L. 63 B4
Cowangie 62 C3
Cowarie 62 A2
Cowell 62 B2
Cowra 63 B4
Coxim 93 F3
Cox's Bazar 41 G8
Cozumel, Isla 85 C7
Craboon 63 B4
Cracow = Kraków 16 C4
Cracow 63 A5
Cradock 59 E5
Craigavon 11 D3
Crailsheim 14 D6
Craiova 22 B4
Cranbrook *Australia* 62 D4
Cranbrook *Canada* 69 D8

Crateús 92 D5
Crato 92 D6
Crawley 11 F6
Crazy Mts. 73 C8
Crema 13 D8
Cremona 13 D9
Cres 20 B5
Crete = Kriti 23 G5
Créteil 12 B5
Creus, C. de 19 A7
Creuse → 12 C4
Crewe 11 E5
Criciúma 94 B7
Crimean Pen. = Krymskyy
 Pivostriv 25 D3
Crişul Negru → 16 E5
Crna → 22 D3
Crna Gora =
 Montenegro ■ 22 C2
Crna Gora 22 C2
Crna Reka = Crna →
 22 D3
Croatia ■ 20 B6
Crocker, Banjaran 38 C5
Croker, C. 60 C5
Cromer 11 E7
Cromwell 65 F3
Cronulla 63 B5
Crookwell 63 B4
Cross Sound 69 C6
Crotone 21 E6
Crows Nest 63 A5
Crowsnest Pass 69 D8
Cruz Alta 94 B6
Cruz del Eje 94 C4
Cruzeiro do Sul 91 E4
Crystal Brook 62 B2
Csongrád 16 E5
Cuamba 59 A7
Cuando → 58 B4
Cuando = Kwango →
 56 E3
Cuanza → 56 F2
Cuba ■ 86 B4
Cubango → 58 B4
Cúcuta 90 B4
Cuddalore 43 P11
Cuddapah 43 M11
Cuenca Ecuador 90 D3
Cuenca Spain 19 B4
Cuenca, Serranía de
 19 C5
Cuernavaca 84 D5
Cuevas del Almanzora
 19 D5
Cuevo 91 H6
Cuiabá 93 F2
Cuiabá → 93 F2
Cuito → 58 B4
Culcairn 63 C4
Culgoa → 63 A4
Culiacán 84 C3
Culion 36 B2
Cullarin Ra. 63 B4
Cullera 19 C5
Culuene → 93 E3
Culverden 65 E5
Cumaná 90 A6
Cumberland 77 E6
Cumberland Pen. 70 C7
Cumberland Plateau
 76 F3
Cumberland Sd. 70 C7
Cumborah 63 A4
Cumbum 43 M11
Cummins 62 B2
Cumnock 63 B4
Cunene → 58 B2
Cúneo 13 D7
Cunnamulla 63 A4
Cupica, G. de 90 B3
Curaçay → 90 D4
Curiapo 90 B6
Curicó 94 C2
Currabubula 63 B5
Currais Novos 92 D6
Curralinho 92 C4
Currie 62 C3
Curtea de Argeş 17 F7
Curtis Group 62 C4
Curuápanema → 92 C2
Curuçá 92 C4
Curup 39 E2
Cururupu 92 C5
Curuzú Cuatiá 94 B5
Cusco = Cuzco 91 F4
Cuttaburra → 63 A3
Cuttack 40 G5
Cuvier I. 64 B6
Cuxhaven 14 B5
Cuyo 36 B2
Cuzco Bolivia 91 H5
Cuzco Peru 91 F4
Cwmbran 11 F5
Cyclades 23 F5
Cygnet 62 D4
Cyprus ■ 46 D3
Cyrenaica 54 C3
Czech Rep. ■ 16 D2
Częstochowa 16 C4

D

Da Hinggan Ling 35 B7
Da Lat 38 B3
Da Nang 38 A3
Da Qaidam 34 C4
Daba Shan 35 C5
Dabo = Pasirkuning 39 E2
Dabola 53 F3
Dabra 43 G11
Dacca = Dhaka 41 F8
Dacca = Dhaka □ 41 E8
Dachau 15 D6
Dadanawa 90 C7
Dadra & Nagar Haveli □
 43 J8
Dadu 42 F5
Daegu 35 C7
Daejeon 35 C7
Daet 36 B2
Dagana 53 E2
Dagestan □ 25 E6
Daghestan Republic =
 Dagestan □ 25 E6
Dagö = Hiiumaa 24 B1
Dagupan 36 A2
Dahlak Kebir 49 D3
Dahod 43 H9
Daiō-Misaki 33 F5
Daisetsu-Zan 32 B8
Dakar 53 F2
Dakhla 52 D2
Dakhla, El Wâhât el-
 54 C4
Dakhovskaya 25 E5
Đakovica 22 C3
Dalälven → 9 C9
Dalaman → 23 F7
Dalandzadgad 35 B5
Dalap-Uliga-Darrit =
 Majuro 64 J12
Dälbandīn 42 E4
Dalby 63 A5
Dali 34 D5
Dalian 35 C7
Daliang Shan 34 D5
Dallarnil 63 A5
Dallas 81 C5
Dalmacija 20 C6
Dalmatia = Dalmacija
 20 C6
Dalnegorsk 32 A4
Daloa 53 G4
Dalton 82 B5
Dalton Iceberg Tongue
 96 A13
Daly Waters 60 D5
Daman 43 J8
Damanhûr 54 B5
Damar 37 F3
Damaraland 58 C3
Damascus = Dimashq
 46 D4
Damāvand 44 C3
Damāvand, Qolleh-ye
 44 C3
Damba 56 F3
Dâmbovita → 22 B6
Dāmghān 44 B3
Damiel 18 C4
Damietta = Dumyât 54 B5
Damoh 43 H11
Dampier 60 E2
Dampier, Selat 37 E4
Danbury 77 D9
Dandeldhura 40 C3
Dandeli 43 M9
Dandenong 63 C4
Dandong 35 B7
Danger Is. = Pukapuka
 65 L14
Dangla Shan = Tanggula
 Shan 34 C4
Danilov 24 B5
Danilov 24 B5
Dankhar Gompa 42 C11
Danmark = Denmark ■
 9 D7
Dannemora 9 F11
Dannevirke 64 D7
Danube = Dunărea →
 17 F9
Danville 83 A4
Danzig = Gdańsk 16 A4
Dao = Tobias Fornier
 36 B2
Dar el Beida = Casablanca
 52 B4
Dar es Salaam 57 F7
Dārāb 44 D3
Daraj 54 B1
Darband 42 B8
Darbhanga 40 D5
Dardanelles = Çanakkale
 Boğazı 23 D6
Dârfûr 55 F3
Dargai 42 B7
Darganata 29 E7
Dargaville 64 A5
Darica 22 D7
Darién, G. del 90 B3
Darjeeling = Darjiling
 40 D7
Darjiling 40 D7
Darling → 62 B3
Darling Downs 63 A5
Darling Ra. 60 G2
Darlington 11 D6
Darłowo 16 A3
Darmstadt 14 D5
Darnah 54 B3
Darnley, C. 96 A10
Darnley B. 68 B7
Dart, C. 96 B18
Dartmoor 11 F5
Dartmouth 71 E7
Dartmouth Res. 63 A4
Darvaza 29 E6
Darvel, Teluk = Lahad
 Datu, Telok 36 D1
Darwha 43 J10
Darwin 60 C5
Daryoi Amu =
 Amudarya → 29 E6
Dās 44 E3
Dashen, Ras 57 B7
Dashoguz 29 E6
Dasht → 42 G2
Datça 23 F6
Datia 43 G11
Datong 35 B6
Datu, Tanjung 39 D3
Datu Piang 36 C2
Datuk, Tanjong = Datu,
 Tanjung 39 D3
Daugava → 24 B1
Daugavpils 24 B2
Daulpur 42 F10
Dauphin 69 C9
Dauphiné 13 D6
Davangere 43 M9
Davao 36 C3
Davao G. 36 C3
Dävar Panäh = Sarävän
 45 E5
Davenport 75 E9
David 86 E3
David Gorodok = Davyd
 Haradok 17 B8
Davis Sea 96 A11
Davis Str. 6 C14
Davos 13 C8
Davyd Haradok 17 B8
Dawei = Tavoy 38 B1
Dawna Ra. 41 J12
Dawson 68 B6
Dawson, I. 95 G2
Dax 12 E3

Daxian 35 C5
Daxue Shan 34 C5
Daylesford 62 C3
Dayr az Zawr 46 D5
Dayton 76 E3
Daytona Beach 83 E7
De Aar 58 E4
Deakin 60 G4
Deal I. 62 C3
Deán Funes 94 C4
Death Valley 78 B4
Debar 22 D3
Debre Markos 55 F6
Debrecen 16 E5
Decatur Ala., U.S.A. 82 B4
Decatur Ill., U.S.A. 75 F10
Deccan 43 L11
Děčín 16 C2
Dedéagach =
   Alexandroupoli 22 D5
Dee → 10 C5
Deepwater 63 A5
Deer Lake 71 C8
Deggendorf 15 D7
Deh Bīd 44 D3
Dehi Titan 42 C2
Dehibat 54 B1
Dehkareqan 46 C6
Dehra Dun 42 D11
Dej 17 E6
Dekese 56 E4
Delano 78 C3
Delaware □ 77 E8
Delegate 63 C4
Delgo 55 D5
Delhi 42 E10
Delice → 25 F3
Delicias 84 B3
Déline 68 B3
Delmenhorst 14 B5
Deloraine 62 D4
Delungra 63 A5
Delvinë 23 E3
Demanda, Sierra de la
   18 A4
Demavend = Damāvand,
   Qolleh-ye 44 C3
Dembidolo 55 G5
Demini → 90 D6
Demirci 23 E7
Demirköy 22 D6
Dempo 39 E2
Den Bosch =
   's-Hertogenbosch
   14 C3
Den Haag =
   's-Gravenhage 14 B3
Den Helder 14 B3
Denali = McKinley, Mt.
   69 B4
Denau 29 F7
Dendang 39 E3
Denia 19 C6
Denial B. 62 B1
Deniliquin 63 C3
Denizli 25 G4
Denman Glacier 96 A11
Denmark ■ 9 D7

Denmark Str. 66 C17
Denpasar 39 F5
Denton 80 C5
D'Entrecasteaux Is. 61 B9
Denver 74 F2
Deoghar 40 E6
Deolali 43 K8
Deoria 40 D4
Deosai Mts. 42 B9
Dera Ghazi Khan 42 D7
Dera Ismail Khan 42 D7
Derbent 25 E6
Derby Australia 60 D3
Derby U.K. 11 E6
Derg, L. 11 E2
Dergaon 41 D9
Derry = Londonderry
   11 D3
Des Moines 75 E8
Des Moines → 75 E9
Desaguadero → 91 G5
Dese 49 E2
Desna → 17 C10
Desolación, I. 95 G2
Despeñaperros, Paso
   18 C4
Dessau 15 C7
Dessye = Dese 49 E2
D'Estrees B. 62 C2
Detmold 14 C5
Detroit 76 C4
Deva 17 F6
Devakottai 43 Q11
Deventer 14 B4
Devon I. 70 B5
Devonport Australia 62 D4
Devonport N.Z. 64 B6
Dewas 43 H10
Deyhūk 44 C4
Deyyer 44 E2
Dezfūl 47 D7
Dezhneva, Mys 31 C16
Dhaka 41 E8
Dhaka □ 41 E8
Dhamtari 40 G3
Dhanbad 40 F6
Dhangarhi 40 C3
Dhankuta 40 D6
Dhar 43 H9
Dharmapuri 43 N11
Dhaulagiri 40 C4
Dhenkanal 40 G5
Dhodhekánisos =
   Dodecanese 23 F6
Dhrol 43 H7
Dhubaibah 44 F3
Dhuburi 41 D7
Dhule 43 J9
Dhut → 49 E5
Diafarabé 53 F5
Diamantina 93 F5
Diamantina → 62 A2
Diamantino 93 E2

Diamond Harbour 40 F7
Dibaya-Lubue 56 E3
Dibbi 49 G3
Dibrugarh 41 D10
Didiéni 53 F4
Diefenbaker, L. 69 C9
Diego Suarez =
   Antsiranana 59 A9
Dieppe 12 B4
Digby 71 E7
Dighinala 41 F9
Digne-les-Bains 13 D7
Digos 36 C3
Digul → 37 F5
Dihang = Brahmaputra →
   41 F7
Dijlah, Nahr → 47 E6
Dijon 13 C6
Dikimdya 31 D10
Dikson 28 B9
Dikti Oros 23 G5
Dili 37 F3
Dilli = Delhi 42 E10
Dillingham 69 C4
Dilolo 56 G4
Dilston 62 D4
Dimashq 46 D4
Dimbaza 59 E5
Dimboola 62 C3
Dîmbovița = Dâmbovița →
   22 B6
Dimitrovgrad Bulgaria
   22 C5
Dimitrovgrad Russia 24 C6
Dimitrovo = Pernik 22 C4
Dinagat 36 B3
Dinajpur 41 E7
Dinan 12 B2
Dinant 14 C3
Dinar 46 C2
Dīnār, Kūh-e 44 D2
Dinara Planina 20 B6
Dinard 12 B2
Dinaric Alps = Dinara
   Planina 20 B6
Dindigul 43 P11
Dingle 11 E1
Dingwall 10 C4
Dinosaur △ 73 F9
Dipolog 36 C2
Dir 42 B7
Dire Dawa 49 F3
Dirfis Oros 23 E4
Dirranbandi 63 A4
Disa 43 G8
Disappointment, L. 60 E3
Disaster B. 63 C4
Discovery B. 62 C3
Disteghil Sar 42 A9
District of Columbia □
   77 E7
Distrito Federal □ 93 F4
Diu 43 J7
Divinópolis 93 G5
Divnoye 25 D5
Diyarbakır 46 C5
Diz Chah 44 C3
Djakarta = Jakarta 39 F3
Djambala 56 E2
Djanet 52 D7
Djawa = Jawa 39 F3

Djelfa 52 B6
Djerba, Î. de 54 B1
Djerid, Chott 52 B7
Djibouti 49 E3
Djibouti ■ 49 E3
Djolu 56 D4
Djoum 56 D2
Djourab, Erg du 55 E2
Dmitriya Lapteva, Proliv
   31 B12
Dnepr = Dnipro → 25 D3
Dneprodzerzhinsk =
   Dniprodzerzhynsk
   25 D3
Dnepropetrovsk =
   Dnipropetrovsk 25 D4
Dnestr = Dnister →
   17 E10
Dnieper = Dnipro →
   25 D3
Dniester = Dnister →
   17 E10
Dnipro → 25 D3
Dniprodzerzhynsk 25 D3
Dnipropetrovsk 25 D4
Dnister → 17 E10
Dnistrovskyy Lyman
   17 E10
Dnyapro = Dnipro →
   25 D3
Doba 55 G2
Doberai, Jazirah 37 E4
Dobo 37 F4
Doboj 20 B7
Dobrich 22 C6
Dobruja 22 B7
Dobrush 17 B10
Dodecanese 23 F6
Dodecanisa = Dodecanese
   23 F6
Dodge City 80 A3
Dodoma 57 F7
Doha = Ad Dawḩah 44 E2
Dohazari 41 F9
Doi 37 D3
Dois Irmãos, Sa. 93 D5
Dolak, Pulau 37 F5
Dolbeau-Mistassini 71 E6
Dole 13 C6
Dolomites = Dolomiti
   20 A3
Dolomiti 20 A3
Dolores 94 D5
Dolphin, C. 95 G5
Dolphin and Union Str.
   68 B8
Dombarovskiy 29 D6
Dominica ■ 87 C7
Dominican Rep. ■ 87 C5
Domodóssola 13 C8
Domville, Mt. 63 A5
Don → Russia 25 D4
Don → U.K. 10 C5
Don Benito 18 C3
Donald 62 C3
Donau = Dunărea →
   17 F9
Donauwörth 14 D6
Doncaster 11 E6
Dondo, Teluk 37 D2

Donegal 11 D2
Donets → 25 D5
Donetsk 25 D4
Donggala 37 E1
Dongola 55 E5
Dongting Hu 35 D6
Donington 11 E5
Donnelly's Crossing 64 A5
Donostia = Donostia-San
  Sebastián 19 A5
Donostia-San Sebastián
  19 A5
Dora Báltea → 13 D8
Dorchester, C. 70 C6
Dordogne → 12 D3
Dordrecht 14 C3
Dori 53 F5
Dornbirn 14 E5
Doro, Kavo 23 E5
Dorohoi 17 E8
Döröö Nuur 34 B4
Dorrigo 63 B5
Dortmund 14 C4
Dos Bahías, C. 95 E3
Dos Hermanas 18 D3
Dosso 53 F6
Dothan 82 D5
Douai 13 A5
Douala 53 H7
Douarnenez 12 B1
Double Island Pt. 63 A5
Doubs → 13 C6
Doubtful Sd. 65 F2
Doubtless B. 64 A5
Douglas I. of Man 11 D4
Douglas U.S.A. 79 E8
Dourados 94 A6
Douro → 18 B1
Dover Australia 62 D4
Dover U.K. 11 F7
Dover, Str. of 11 F7
Dovrefjell 8 C7
Dowlat Yār 45 C6
Dowlatābād 44 D4
Drăgăşani 22 B5
Dragichyn 17 B7
Dragoman, Prokhod
  22 C4
Draguignan 13 E7
Drake 63 A5
Drakensberg 59 E5
Drama 22 D5
Drammen 9 D8
Drau = Drava → 20 B7
Drava → 20 B7
Dresden 15 C7
Dreux 12 B4
Drin → 22 C2
Drina → 20 B7
Drobeta-Turnu Severin
  22 B4
Drochia 17 D8
Drogheda 11 E3
Drogichin = Dragichyn
  17 B7
Drogobych = Drohobych
  17 D6
Drohobych 17 D6
Droichead Atha =
  Drogheda 11 E3

Dromedary, C. 63 C5
Dronning Maud Land
  96 B7
Druk Yul = Bhutan ■
  41 D8
Drumheller 69 C8
Drummond Pt. 62 B2
Drut → 17 B10
Drygalski I. 96 A11
Dubā 47 F3
Dubai = Dubayy 44 E3
Dūbāsari 17 E9
Dūbāsari Vdkhr. 17 E9
Dubawnt → 68 B9
Dubawnt L. 68 B9
Dubayy 44 E3
Dubbo 63 B4
Dublin Ireland 11 E3
Dublin U.S.A. 83 C6
Dubno 17 C7
Dubois 81 D8
Dubossary = Dūbāsari
  17 E9
Dubossary Vdkhr. =
  Dūbāsari Vdkhr. 17 E9
Dubovka 24 D5
Dubréka 53 G3
Dubrovitsa = Dubrovytsya
  17 C8
Dubrovnik 20 C7
Dubrovytsya 17 C8
Dudhi 40 E4
Dudinka 30 C6
Dūghī Kalā 42 C3
Dugi Otok 20 B5
Duisburg 14 C4
Dujiangyan 34 C5
Dukhān 44 E2
Duki 42 D6
Dulce → 94 C4
Dulit, Banjaran 39 D4
Duluth 75 B8
Dum Duma 41 D10
Dumaguete 36 C2
Dumai 39 D2
Dumaran 36 B1
Dumfries 11 D5
Dumyât 54 B5
Dún Dealgan = Dundalk
  11 D3
Dún Laoghaire 11 E3
Duna = Dunărea → 17 F9
Dunaj = Dunărea → 17 F9
Dunakeszi 16 E4
Dunărea → 17 F9
Dunaújváros 16 E4
Dunav = Dunărea →
  17 F9
Dunback 65 F4
Dunbar 10 D5
Duncan 80 B5
Dundalk 11 D3
Dundas 64 D2
Dundee 10 C5
Dundoo 63 A3
Dunedin 65 F4
Dunfermline 10 C5
Dungarvan 11 E3
Dungog 63 B5
Dungu 57 D5
Dunhuang 34 B4

Dunkerque 12 A5
Dunkirk = Dunkerque
  12 A5
Dúnleary = Dún Laoghaire
  11 E3
Dunolly 62 C3
Dunstan Mts. 65 F3
Durance → 13 E6
Durango Mexico 84 C4
Durango Spain 19 A4
Durazno 94 C5
Durazzo = Durrës 22 D2
Durban 59 D6
Düren 14 C4
Durg = Bhilainagar-Durg
  40 G3
Durgapur 40 F6
Durham U.K. 11 D6
Durham U.S.A. 83 B8
Durham Downs 63 A4
Durmitor 22 C2
Durrës 22 D2
Dursunbey 23 E7
D'Urville, Tanjung 37 E5
D'Urville I. 65 D5
Dushak 29 F7
Dushanbe 29 F7
Dusky Sd. 65 F2
Düsseldorf 14 C4
Dutch Harbor 69 C3
Duyun 35 D5
Dvina, Severnaya →
  28 C5
Dvinsk = Daugavpils
  24 B2
Dwarka 43 H6
Dyatlovo = Dzyatlava
  17 B7
Dyer, C. 70 C7
Dyer Plateau 96 B3
Dyersburg 81 A9
Dymer 17 C10
Dynevor Downs 63 A3
Dzerzhinsk 24 B5
Dzhambul = Taraz 29 E8
Dzhankoy 25 D3
Dzhardzhan 30 C10
Dzhezkazgan =
  Zhezqazghan 29 E7
Dzhizak = Jizzakh 29 E7
Działdowo 16 B5
Dzierżoniów 16 C3
Dzungaria = Junggar Pendi
  34 B3
Dzungarian Basin =
  Junggar Pendi 34 B3
Dzungarian Gate = Alataw
  Shankou 34 B3
Dzüünmod 35 B5
Dzyarzhynsk 17 B8
Dzyatlava 17 B7

E

Earnslaw, Mt. 65 F3
East Bengal 41 E7
East Beskids = Vychodné
  Beskydy 17 D5
East C. = Dezhneva, Mys
  31 C16

East C. 64 B8
East China Sea 35 C7
East Falkland 95 G5
East Kilbride 10 D4
East London 59 E5
East Main = Eastmain
  71 D6
East Orange 77 D8
East St. Louis 75 F9
East Sea = Japan, Sea of
  32 D4
East Timor ■ 37 F3
East Toorale 63 B4
Eastbourne N.Z. 65 D6
Eastbourne U.K. 11 F7
Eastern Ghats 43 N11
Eastmain 71 D6
Eastmain → 71 D6
Eau Claire 75 C9
Eau Claire, L. à l' 71 D6
Eberswalde-Finow 15 B7
Ebetsu 32 B7
Ebolowa 56 D2
Ebro → 19 B6
Eceabat 23 D6
Ech Chéliff 52 A6
Echo Bay 68 B8
Echuca 63 C3
Ecija 18 D3
Eclipse Sd. 70 B6
Ecuador ■ 90 D3
Ed Dar el Beida =
  Casablanca 52 B4
Ed Debba 55 E5
Ed Dueim 55 F5
Eddystone Pt. 62 D4
Édéa 53 H8
Eden 63 C4
Eder → 14 C5
Edessa 23 D4
Édhessa = Edessa 23 D4
Edievale 65 F3
Edinburg 80 F4
Edinburgh 10 D5
Edineţ 17 D8
Edirne 22 D6
Edithburgh 62 C2
Edmonton 69 C8
Edmundston 71 E7
Edremit 23 E6
Edremit Körfezi 23 E6
Edson 69 C8
Edward → 62 C3
Edward, L. 57 E5
Edward VII Land 96 C17
Edwards Plateau 80 D3
Eesti = Estonia ■ 24 B2
Égadi, Ísole 21 F4
Eger = Cheb 16 C1
Eger 16 E5
Egio 23 E4
Eglinton I. 70 B2
Egmont, C. 64 C5
Egmont, Mt. = Taranaki,
  Mt. 64 C5
Egmont △ 64 C6
Eğridir 46 C2
Eğridir Gölü 46 C2
Egypt ■ 54 C5
Eibar 19 A4

Eidsvold 63 A5
Eifel 14 C4
Eigg 10 C3
Eil 49 F4
Eildon, L. 63 C4
Eindhoven 14 C3
Eire = Ireland ■ 11 E3
Eirunepé 91 E5
Eisenach 14 C6
Eisenerz 15 E8
Eivissa 19 C6
Ekaterinburg =
   Yekaterinburg 29 D7
Eketahuna 64 D6
Ekibastuz 29 D8
El Aaiún 52 C3
El 'Alamein 54 B4
El Asnam = Ech Chéliff
   52 A6
El Bayadh 52 B6
El Centro 78 D5
El Cerro 91 G6
El Cuy 95 D3
El Dere 49 G4
El Diviso 90 C3
El Djouf 53 D4
El Dorado Ark., U.S.A.
   81 C7
El Dorado Kans., U.S.A.
   80 A5
El Dorado Venezuela
   90 B6
El Escorial 18 B3
El Faiyûm 54 C5
El Fâsher 55 F4
El Ferrol = Ferrol 18 A1
El Fuerte 84 B3
El Gal 49 E5
El Geneina = Al Junaynah
   55 F3
El Gîza 54 C5
El Homeur 52 C6
El Iskandarîya 54 B4
El Jadida 52 B4
El Khârga 54 C5
El Khartûm 55 E5
El Lucero 84 B3
El Maestrazgo 19 B5
El Mahalla el Kubra 54 B5
El Mansûra 54 B5
El Minyâ 54 C5
El Obeid 55 F5
El Odaiya 55 F4
El Oued 52 B7
El Paso 79 E9
El Prat de Llobregat 19 B7
El Puerto de Santa María
   18 D2
El Qâhira 54 B5
El Reno 80 B5
El Salvador ■ 85 E7
El Suweis 54 C5
El Tigre 90 B6
El Turbio 95 G2
El Uqsur 54 C5
El Vigía 90 B4
El Wak 57 D8
El Wuz 55 E5
Elat 47 E3
Elâzığ 46 C4

Elba 20 C3
Elbasan 22 D3
Elbe → 14 B5
Elbert, Mt. 79 A9
Elbeuf 12 B4
Elbing = Elbląg 16 A4
Elbląg 16 A4
Elbrus 25 E5
Elburz Mts. = Alborz,
   Reshteh-ye Kühhä-ye
   44 B3
Elche 19 C5
Elda 19 C5
Elde → 15 B6
Eldoret 57 D7
Elefantes → 59 C6
Elektrostal 24 B4
Elephant I. 96 A4
Eleuthera 86 A4
Elgin U.K. 10 C5
Elgin U.S.A. 76 C1
Elgon, Mt. 57 D6
Eliase 37 F4
Elista 25 D5
Elizabeth Australia 62 B2
Elizabeth U.S.A. 77 D8
Elizabeth City 85 A8
Elizabethton 83 A6
Elk 16 B6
Elkhart 76 D3
Elkhovo 22 C6
Elko 72 F6
Ellas = Greece ■ 23 E4
Ellef Ringnes I. 70 B3
Ellery, Mt. 63 C4
Ellesmere I. 70 B3
Ellesmere, L. 65 G5
Ellesmere I. 70 B6
Ellice Is. = Tuvalu ■
   64 K12
Elliot Lake 71 E5
Elliston 62 B1
Ellore = Eluru 40 J3
Ellsworth Land 96 B2
Ellsworth Mts. 96 B2
Elmore 63 C4
Elmshorn 14 B5
Eltham 64 C6
Eluru 40 J3
Elvas 18 C2
Elx = Elche 19 C5
Ely 11 E7
eMalahleni 59 D5
Emämrüd 44 B3
Embarcación 94 A4
Embetsu 32 A7
Embi 29 E6
Embi → 29 E6
Embrun 13 D7
Emden 14 B4
Emet 23 E4
Emi Koussi 55 E2
Emine, Nos 22 C6
Emissi, Tarso 54 D2
Emmen 14 B4
Empalme 84 B2
Empangeni 59 D6
Empedrado 94 B5
Empty Quarter = Rub' al
   Khälï 48 D4
Ems → 14 B4

En Nahud 55 F4
Enare = Inarijärvi 8 B11
Enarotali 37 E5
Encanto, C. 36 A2
Encarnación 94 B5
Encounter B. 62 C2
Ende 37 F2
Enderby Land 96 A9
Enewetak Atoll 64 H11
Enez 23 D6
Engaño, C. 36 A2
Engaru 32 A8
Engels 24 C6
Enggano 39 F2
England □ 11 E6
Englewood 74 F2
English Bazar = Ingraj
   Bazar 40 E7
English Channel 11 F5
Enid 80 B5
Enna 21 F5
Ennedi 55 E3
Enngonia 63 A4
Ennis 11 E2
Enniskillen 11 D3
Enns → 15 D8
Enschede 14 B4
Ensenada 84 A1
Entebbe 57 D6
Entre Ríos □ 94 C5
Entroncamento 18 C1
Enugu 53 G7
Eólie, Ís. 21 E5
Épernay 13 B5
Ephesus 23 F6
Épinal 13 B7
Equatorial Guinea ■
   56 D1
Er Rachidia 52 B5
Er Rahad 55 F5
Er Rif 52 A5
Eräwadï Myit =
   Irrawaddy → 41 K10
Eräwadï Myitwanya =
   Irrawaddy, Mouths of
   the 41 K10
Erbil = Arbïl 46 C5
Erciyaş Daği 46 C3
Érd 16 E4
Erdek 23 D6
Erebus, Mt. 96 B15
Erechim 94 B6
Ereğli Konya, Turkey
   46 C3
Ereğli Zonguldak, Turkey
   25 E3
Eresma → 18 B3
Erfurt 15 C6
Ergani 46 C4
Érice 21 E4
Erie 77 C5
Erie, L. 76 C5
Erigavo 49 E4
Erimanthos 23 F3
Erimo-misaki 32 C8
Eritrea ■ 49 E2
Erlangen 15 D6
Ermenek 46 C3
Erne, Lower L. 11 D3
Erode 43 P10

Eromanga 63 A3
Erramala Hills 43 M11
Ertis = Irtysh → 28 C7
Erzgebirge 15 C7
Erzincan 25 F4
Erzurum 25 F5
Es Sahrâ' Esh Sharqîya
   54 C5
Es Sînâ' 54 C5
Esan-Misaki 32 C7
Esashi Hokkaidö, Japan
   32 A8
Esashi Hokkaidö, Japan
   32 C7
Esbjerg 9 D7
Esbo = Espoo 9 C10
Esch-sur-Alzette 13 B6
Escuinapa de Hidalgo
   84 C3
Esenguly 29 F6
Eşfahän 44 C2
Esh Sham = Dimashq
   46 D4
Esil = Ishim → 29 D8
Esker 71 D7
Eskilstuna 9 D9
Eskimo Point = Arviat
   68 B10
Ekişehir 25 F3
Esla → 18 B2
Eslämäbäd-e Gharb 46 D6
Eşme 23 E7
Esmeraldas 90 C3
España = Spain ■ 18 C4
Esperance 60 G3
Espichel, C. 18 C1
Espinazo, Sierra del =
   Espinhaço, Serra do
   93 F5
Espinhaço, Serra do 93 F5
Espírito Santo □ 93 G5
Espíritu Santo 64 L11
Espoo 9 C10
Esquel 95 E2
Esquina 94 C5
Essaouira 52 B4
Essen 14 C4
Essequibo → 90 B7
Esslingen 14 D5
Estados, I. de Los 95 G4
Estância 93 E6
Estevan 69 D9
Estonia ■ 24 B2
Estrela, Serra da 18 B2
Estremoz 18 C2
Estrondo, Serra do 92 D4
Esztergom 16 E4
Etadunna 62 A2
Étampes 12 B5
Etawah 42 F11
eThekwini = Durban 59 D6
Ethiopia ■ 49 F2
Ethiopian Highlands 49 F2
Etna 21 F5
Etosha Pan 58 B3
Euboea = Evia 23 E5
Eucumbene, L. 63 C4
Eufaula 82 E5
Eugene 72 E2
Eugowra 63 B4

Eulo 63 A4
Euphrates = Furāt, Nahr
al → 47 E6
Eureka Canada 70 B5
Eureka U.S.A. 72 F1
Euroa 63 C4
Europa, Île 59 C8
Europa, Picos de 18 A3
Europa, Pt. 18 D3
Evans Head 63 A5
Evanston 76 C2
Evansville 76 F2
Everard, L. 62 B1
Everest, Mt. 40 C6
Everett 72 C2
Everglades △ 83 G7
Evia 23 E5
Évora 18 C2
Évreux 12 B4
Evros → 22 D6
Évry 12 B5
Évvoia = Evia 23 E5
Ewo 56 E2
Exaltación 91 F5
Exeter 11 F4
Exmoor 11 F5
Exmouth 11 F5
Extremadura □ 18 C2
Eyasi, L. 57 E6
Eyre (North), L. 62 A2
Eyre (South), L. 62 A2
Eyre, L. 60 F6
Eyre Mts. 65 F3
Eyre Pen. 62 B2
Ezine 23 E6

F

F.Y.R.O.M. =
Macedonia ■ 22 D3
Fabriano 20 C4
Fada 55 E3
Fada-n-Gourma 53 F6
Faddeyevskiy, Ostrov
31 B12
Faenza 20 B3
Færoe Is. = Føroyar ☑
6 C4
Fǎgǎras 17 F7
Fagnano, L. 95 G3
Fahraj 45 E4
Fahūd 44 F4
Fair Isle 10 B6
Fairbanks 69 B5
Fairfield Ala., U.S.A. 82 C4
Fairfield Calif., U.S.A.
72 G2
Fairlie 65 F4
Fairweather, Mt. 69 C6
Faisalabad 42 D8
Faizabad 40 D4
Fakfak 37 E4
Falaise 12 B3
Falam 41 F9
Falconara Maríttima 20 C4
Falcone, C. de 20 D2
Faleshty = Fǎlesti 17 E8
Fǎlesti 17 E8
Falkland Is. ☑ 95 G5
Falkland Sd. 95 G5

Fall River 77 D10
Falmouth 11 F4
Fǎlticeni 17 E8
Falun 9 C9
Famagusta 46 D3
Fano 20 C4
Fao = Al Fāw 47 E7
Faradje 57 D5
Farafangana 59 C9
Farāh 42 C3
Farāh □ 42 C3
Faranah 53 F3
Farasān, Jazā'ir 49 D3
Farasan Is. = Farasān,
Jazā'ir 49 D3
Fareham 11 F6
Farewell, C. 64 D5
Farghona 29 E8
Farīmān 45 C4
Farina 62 B2
Faro Brazil 92 C2
Faro Portugal 18 D2
Farrāshband 44 D3
Farrukhabad-cum-
Fatehgarh 42 F11
Fārs □ 44 D3
Farsala 23 E4
Fartak, Râs 47 E3
Fǎryāb □ 45 B6
Fasā 44 D3
Fasano 21 D6
Fastiv 17 C9
Fastov = Fastiv 17 C9
Fatagar, Tanjung 37 E4
Fatehgarh 42 F11
Fatehpur Raj., India 42 F9
Fatehpur Ut. P., India
40 E3
Favara 21 F4
Favignana 21 F4
Faxaflói 8 C1
Faya-Largeau 55 E2
Fayd 47 F5
Fayette Ark., U.S.A.
81 A6
Fayetteville N.C., U.S.A.
83 B8
Fazilka 42 D9
Fdérik 52 D3
Feather → 72 G3
Featherston 65 D6
Fécamp 12 B4
Feilding 64 D6
Feira de Santana 93 E6
Feldkirch 14 E5
Felipe Carrillo Puerto
85 D7
Felixstowe 11 F7
Fenoarivo Atsinanana
59 B9
Fenyang 35 C6
Feodosiya 25 D4
Ferdows 45 C4
Ferfer 49 F4
Fergana = Farghona 29 E8
Fermo 20 C4
Fermont 71 D7
Fernando de Noronha
92 C7

Fernando Póo = Bioko
53 H7
Ferozepore = Firozpur
42 D9
Ferrara 20 B3
Ferreñafe 91 E3
Ferret, C. 12 D3
Ferrol 18 A1
Fès 52 B5
Fetesti 22 B6
Fetlar 10 A6
Fez = Fès 52 B5
Fezzan 54 C2
Fianarantsoa 59 C9
Fier 23 D2
Figeac 12 D5
Figueira da Foz 18 B1
Figueres 19 A7
Figuig 52 B5
Fiji ■ 64 L12
Filiatra 23 F3
Filyos Çayı → 46 B3
Fingoè 59 A6
Finike 46 C2
Finisterre, C. = Fisterra, C.
18 A1
Finland ■ 8 C11
Finland, G. of 9 D11
Finlay → 68 C7
Finley 63 C4
Finniss, C. 62 B1
Fiora → 20 C3
Fiordland △ 65 F2
Firat = Furāt, Nahr al →
47 E6
Firenze 20 C3
Firozabad 42 F11
Firozpur 42 D9
Fīrūzābād 44 D3
Fīrūzkūh 44 C3
Fish → 58 D3
Fishguard 11 E4
Fisterra, C. 18 A1
Fitz Roy 95 F3
Fizi 57 E5
Flagstaff 79 C7
Flåm 8 C7
Flaming Gorge Res. 73 F9
Flamingo, Teluk 37 F5
Flanders = Flandre 14 C2
Flandre 14 C2
Flathead L. 73 C7
Flattery, C. 72 B1
Flensburg 14 A5
Flers 12 B3
Flesko, Tanjung 37 D2
Flin Flon 69 C9
Flinders → 61 D7
Flinders I. 62 C4
Flinders Ranges 62 B2
Flint 76 C4
Flint I. 65 L15
Flinton 63 A4
Florence = Firenze 20 C3
Florence Ala., U.S.A.
82 B4
Florence S.C., U.S.A.
83 B8

Florence, L. 62 A2
Flores 37 F2
Flores Sea 37 F2
Floresti 17 E9
Floriano 92 D5
Florianópolis 94 B7
Florida 94 C5
Florida □ 83 F6
Florida, Straits of 86 B3
Florina 23 D3
Florø 8 C7
Fluk 37 E3
Flushing = Vlissingen
14 C2
Fly → 61 B7
Flying Fish, C. 96 B1
Foça 23 E6
Focsani 17 F8
Fóggia 20 D5
Föhr 14 A5
Foix 12 E4
Folda 8 B8
Foligno 20 C4
Folkestone 11 F7
Fond du Lac 75 D10
Fondi 20 D4
Fongafale 64 K12
Fonsagrada = A
Fonsagrada 18 A2
Fonseca, G. de 85 E7
Fontainebleau 13 B5
Fonte Boa 90 D5
Fontenay-le-Comte 12 C3
Foochow = Fuzhou 35 D6
Forbes 63 B4
Fords Bridge 63 A4
Forestier Pen. 62 D4
Forfar 10 C5
Forlì 20 B4
Formentera 19 C6
Formentor, C. de 19 C7
Former Yugoslav Republic
of Macedonia =
Macedonia ■ 22 D3
Fórmia 20 D4
Formosa = Taiwan ■
35 D7
Formosa 94 B5
Formosa, Serra 93 E3
Formosa B. = Ungwana B.
57 E8
Føroyar ☑ 6 C4
Forsayth 61 D7
Forst 15 C8
Fort Albany 71 D5
Fort Collins 74 E2
Fort Dauphin = Taolanaro
59 D9
Fort-de-France 87 D7
Fort Dodge 75 D7
Fort Franklin = Déline
68 B7
Fort George = Chisasibi
71 D6
Fort Good Hope 68 B7
Fort Lauderdale 83 F7
Fort Liard 68 B7
Fort Macleod 69 D8
Fort McPherson 68 B6

Fort Myers 83 F7
Fort Norman = Tulita
68 B7
Fort Peck L. 73 C10
Fort Pierce 83 F7
Fort Providence 68 B8
Fort Resolution 68 B8
Fort Rupert =
Waskaganish 71 D6
Fort Scott 81 A6
Fort Shevchenko 29 E6
Fort Simpson 68 B7
Fort Smith *Canada* 68 B8
Fort Smith *U.S.A.* 81 B6
Fort Walton Beach 82 D4
Fort Wayne 76 D3
Fort William 10 C4
Fort Worth 80 C5
Fort Yukon 69 B5
Fortaleza 92 C6
Forür 44 E3
Foshan 35 D6
Fossano 13 D7
Fougères 12 B3
Foula 10 A5
Fourni 23 F6
Fouta Djallon 53 F3
Foveaux Str. 65 G3
Foxe Basin 70 C6
Foxe Chan. 70 C5
Foxe Pen. 70 C6
Foxton 64 D6
Foz do Iguaçu 94 B6
Franca 93 G4
Francavilla Fontana 21 D6
France ■ 13 C5
Frances 62 C3
Franceville 56 E2
Francistown 59 C5
Franche-Comté □ 13 C6
Francisco 63 C4
Frankston 63 C4
Frantsa Iosifa, Zemlya
28 A6
Franz Josef Land =
Frantsa Iosifa, Zemlya
28 A6
Fraser → 69 D7
Fraser I. 63 A5
Fraserburgh 10 C5
Fray Bentos 94 C5
Fredericksburg 77 F7
Fredericton 71 E7
Frederikshavn 9 D8
Fredrikstad 9 D8
Free State □ 59 D5
Freeport *Bahamas* 86 A4
Freeport *U.S.A.* 75 D10
Freetown 53 G3
Fregenal de la Sierra
18 C2

Freiburg 14 E4
Freire 95 D2
Freising 15 D6
Freistadt 15 D8
Fréjus 13 E7
Fremont 78 B2
French Guiana ☑ 92 B3
French Polynesia ☑
65 M16
Fresco → 92 D3
Freshfield, C. 96 A14
Fresnillo 84 C4
Fresno 78 B3
Freycinet Pen. 62 D4
Fria, C. 58 B2
Frías 94 B3
Friedrichshafen 14 E5
Frobisher B. 70 C7
Frobisher Bay = Iqaluit
70 C7
Frome → 62 A2
Frome, L. 62 B2
Frosinone 20 D4
Frunze = Bishkek 29 E8
Frutal 93 F4
Frýdek-Místek 16 D4
Fuchou = Fuzhou 35 D6
Fuchū 33 F3
Fuengirola 18 D3
Fuentes de Oñoro 18 B2
Fuerte → 84 B3
Fuerte Olimpo 91 H7
Fuerteventura 52 C3
Fuhai 34 B3
Fuji 33 F6
Fuji-San 33 F6
Fujian □ 35 D6
Fujiyama, Mt. = Fuji-San
33 F6
Fukien = Fujian □ 35 D6
Fukuchiyama 33 F4
Fukue-Shima 33 G1
Fukui 33 E5
Fukuoka 33 G2
Fukushima 33 E7
Fukuyama 33 F3
Fulda 14 C5
Fulda → 14 C5
Funabashi 33 F7
Funchal 52 B2
Fundación 90 A4
Fundão 18 B2
Fundy, B. of 71 E7
Funtua 53 F7
Furāt, Nahr al → 47 E6
Furneaux Group 62 D4
Fürstenwalde 15 B8
Fürth 14 D6
Furukawa 33 E7
Fury and Hecla Str. 70 C5
Fusagasuga 90 C4
Fushun 35 B7
Fuxin 35 B7
Fuyuan 35 B8
Fuzhou 35 D6
Fyn 9 D8

G

Gabela 56 G2
Gabès 54 B1
Gabès, G. de 54 B1
Gabon ■ 56 E2
Gaborone 59 C5
Gabrovo 22 C5
Gachsārān 44 D2
Gadag 43 M9
Gadarwara 43 H11
Gadhada 43 J7
Gadsden 82 B4
Gadwal 43 L10
Gafsa 52 B7
Gagnoa 53 G4
Gagnon 71 D7
Gaillimh = Galway 11 E2
Gainesville *Fla., U.S.A.*
83 E6
Gainesville *Ga., U.S.A.*
83 B6
Gainesville *Tex., U.S.A.*
80 C5
Gairdner, L. 62 B2
Galashiels 10 D5
Galați 17 F9
Galatina 21 D7
Galcaio 49 F4
Galdhøpiggen 8 C7
Galela 37 D3
Galesburg 75 E9
Galich 24 B5
Galicia □ 18 A2
Galilee, Sea of = Yam
Kinneret 46 D3
Gállego → 19 B5
Gallegos → 95 G3
Gallinas, Pta. 90 A4
Gallipoli = Gelibolu 23 D6
Gallipoli 21 D6
Gällivare 8 B10
Galloway, Mull of 11 D4
Galveston 81 E6
Gálvez 94 C4
Galway 11 E2
Galway B. 11 E2
Gambia ■ 53 F2
Gambia → 53 F2
Gambier, Îs. 65 M17
Gambier Is. 62 C2
Gamboma 56 E3
Gan Jiang → 35 D6
Ganäveh 44 D2
Gäncä 25 E6
Gand = Gent 14 C2
Ganda 58 A2
Gandak → 40 E5
Gandava 42 E5
Gander 71 E8
Gandhi Sagar 43 G9
Gandía 19 C5
Ganedidalem = Gani
37 E3
Ganga → 41 F8
Ganganagar 42 E8
Gangaw 41 F10
Gangdisê Shan 40 B3
Ganges = Ganga → 41 F8
Gangneung 35 C7

Gangtok 41 D7
Gani 37 E3
Gansu □ 34 C5
Ganta 53 G4
Gantheaume, C. 62 C2
Gantsevichi = Hantsavichy
17 B8
Ganyem = Genyem 37 E6
Ganzhou 35 D6
Gaoua 53 F5
Gaoual 53 F3
Gaoxiong = Kaohsiung
35 D7
Gap 13 D7
Gar 34 C2
Garabogazköl Aylagy
29 E6
Garagum 29 F6
Garanhuns 92 D6
Garda, L. di 20 B4
Garden City 80 A3
Gardēz 42 C6
Gardo 49 F4
Gargano, Mte. 20 D5
Garigliano → 20 D4
Garland 73 F7
Garm 29 F8
Garmisch-Partenkirchen
14 E6
Garmsär 44 C3
Garoe 49 F4
Garonne → 12 D3
Garoowe = Garoe 49 F4
Garoua 55 G1
Garrison Res. =
Sakakawea, L. 74 B4
Garry, L. 68 B9
Garvie Mts. 65 F3
Garwa = Garoua 55 G1
Garzê 34 C5
Garzón 90 C3
Gasan Kuli = Esenguly
29 F6
Gascogne 12 E4
Gascogne, G. de 12 D2
Gascony = Gascogne
12 E4
Gaspé 71 E7
Gaspé, C. 71 E7
Gaspé Pen. = Gaspésie,
Pén. de la 71 E7
Gaspésie, Pén. de la
71 E7
Gasteiz = Vitoria-Gasteiz
19 A4
Gastonia 83 B7
Gastre 95 E3
Gata, C. de 19 D4
Gata, Sierra de 18 B2
Gateshead 11 D6
Gauhati = Guwahati 41 D8
Gäväter 45 E5
Gavdos 23 G5
Gävle 9 C9
Gawilgarh Hills 43 J10
Gawler 62 B2
Gaxun Nur 34 B5
Gaya *India* 40 E5
Gaya *Niger* 53 F6

Gayndah **63 A5**
Gaysin = Haysyn **17 D9**
Gayvoron = Hayvoron **17 D9**
Gaza **47 E3**
Gaza Strip ■ **47 E3**
Gaziantep **64 C4**
Gazimağosa = Famagusta **46 D3**
Gazli **29 E7**
Gcuwa **59 E5**
Gdańsk **16 A4**
Gdańska, Zatoka **16 A4**
Gdov **24 B2**
Gdynia **16 A4**
Gebe **37 D3**
Gebze **22 D7**
Gedaref **55 F6**
Gediz → **23 E6**
Gedser **9 E8**
Geelong **63 C3**
Geesthacht **14 B6**
Geidam **55 F1**
Gejiu **34 D5**
Gela **21 F5**
Gelibolu **23 D6**
Gelsenkirchen **14 C4**
Gemena **56 D3**
Gemerek **46 C4**
Gemlik **23 D7**
General Acha **94 D4**
General Alvear *B. Aires, Argentina* **94 D5**
General Alvear *Mendoza, Argentina* **94 D4**
General Belgrano **94 D5**
General Juan Madariaga **94 D5**
General La Madrid **94 D4**
General MacArthur **36 B3**
General Pico **94 D4**
General Pinedo **94 B4**
General Santos **36 C3**
General Villegas **94 D4**
Geneva = Genève **14 E4**
Geneva, L. = Léman, L. **13 C7**
Genève **14 E4**
Genil → **18 D3**
Gennargentu, Mti. del **21 D2**
Genoa = Génova **13 D8**
Genoa **63 C4**
Génova **13 D8**
Génova, G. di **20 C2**
Gent **14 C2**
Genyem **37 E6**
Georga, Zemlya **28 A5**
George **58 E4**
George → **70 D7**
George, L. *N.S.W., Australia* **63 B4**
George, L. *S. Austral., Australia* **62 C3**
George River = Kangiqsualujjuaq **70 D7**
George Sound **65 F2**
George Town *Cayman Is.* **86 C3**
George Town *Malaysia* **38 C2**

George V Land **96 A14**
George VI Sound **96 B3**
Georgetown = Janjanbureh **53 F3**
Georgetown **90 B7**
Georgia □ **83 C6**
Georgia ■ **25 E5**
Georgian B. **71 E5**
Georgiyevsk **25 E5**
Gera **15 C7**
Geral de Goiás, Serra **93 E4**
Geraldton **60 F1**
Gerede **46 B3**
Gereshk **42 D4**
Germany ■ **14 C6**
Germiston **59 D5**
Gernika-Lumo **19 A4**
Gerona = Girona **19 B7**
Geser **37 E4**
Getafe **18 B4**
Gettysburg **77 E7**
Getxo **19 A4**
Getz Ice Shelf **96 B18**
Ghaghara → **40 E5**
Ghana ■ **53 G5**
Ghanzi **58 C4**
Ghardaïa **52 B6**
Gharyān **54 B1**
Ghat **54 D1**
Ghats, Eastern **43 N11**
Ghats, Western **43 N9**
Ghawdex = Gozo **21 F5**
Ghayl **47 G6**
Ghazal, Bahr el → *Chad* **55 F2**
Ghazâl, Bahr el → *Sudan* **55 G5**
Ghaziabad **42 E10**
Ghazipur **40 E4**
Ghaznī **42 C6**
Ghaznī □ **42 C6**
Ghent = Gent **14 C2**
Gheorghe Gheorghiu-Dej = Oneşti **17 E8**
Ghowr □ **42 C4**
Ghugus **43 K11**
Ghūrīān **42 B2**
Gia Lai = Plei Ku **38 B3**
Gian **36 C3**
Gianitsa **23 D4**
Giarabub = Al Jaghbūb **54 C3**
Giarre **21 F5**
Gibeon **58 D3**
Gibraltar ☑ **18 D3**
Gibraltar, Str. of **18 E3**
Gibson Desert **60 E4**
Giebnegáisi = Kebnekaise **8 B9**
Giessen **14 C5**
Gifu **33 F5**
Gíglio **20 C3**
Gijón **18 A3**
Gila → **78 D5**
Gīlān □ **46 C7**
Gilbert Is. **64 J12**
Gilgandra **63 B4**
Gilgit **42 B9**
Gilles, L. **62 B2**

Gilmore **63 C4**
Gin Gin **63 A5**
Ginir **49 F3**
Giona, Oros **23 E4**
Giresun **25 E4**
Girga **54 C5**
Giridih **40 E6**
Girne = Kyrenia **46 D3**
Giron = Kiruna **8 B10**
Girona **19 B7**
Gironde → **12 D3**
Girvan **10 D4**
Gisborne **64 C8**
Gisenyi **57 E5**
Gitega **57 E5**
Githio **23 F4**
Giuba → **49 G3**
Giurgiu **22 C5**
Giza = El Gîza **54 C5**
Gizab **42 C4**
Gizycko **16 A5**
Gjirokastër **23 D3**
Gjoa Haven **68 B10**
Glace Bay **71 E8**
Gladstone *Queens., Australia* **61 E9**
Gladstone *S. Austral., Australia* **62 B2**
Glåma = Glomma → **9 C8**
Glasgow **10 D4**
Glazov **28 D6**
Gleiwitz = Gliwice **16 C4**
Glen Canyon △ **79 B7**
Glen Innes **63 A5**
Glendale **78 D7**
Glenelg → **62 C3**
Glenmorgan **63 A4**
Glenorchy **62 D4**
Glenreagh **63 B5**
Glenrothes **10 C5**
Glens Falls **77 C9**
Gliwice **16 C4**
Głogów **16 C3**
Glomma → **9 C8**
Glorieuses, Îs. **59 A9**
Gloucester *Australia* **63 B5**
Gloucester *U.K.* **11 F5**
Glusk **17 B9**
Gmünd **15 D8**
Gmunden **15 E7**
Gniezno **16 B3**
Goa **43 M8**
Goa □ **43 M8**
Goalen Hd. **63 C5**
Goalpara **41 D8**
Goba **49 F2**
Gobabis **58 C3**
Gobi **35 B6**
Godavari → **40 J4**
Godavari Pt. **40 J4**
Godhra **43 H8**
Gods → **69 C10**
Gods L. **69 C10**
Godthåb = Nuuk **66 C14**
Goeie Hoop, Kaap die = Good Hope, C. of **58 E3**
Gogra = Ghaghara → **40 E5**
Goiânia **93 F4**
Goiás **93 F3**

Goiás □ **93 E4**
Goio-Erê **94 A6**
Gojra **42 D8**
Gökçeada **23 D5**
Gökova Körfezi **23 F6**
Gokteik **41 F11**
Gold Coast **63 A5**
Golden B. **64 D5**
Golden Gate **72 H2**
Goldsboro **83 B9**
Goleniów **16 B2**
Golfo Aranci **20 D2**
Golspie **10 C5**
Goma **57 E5**
Gomel = Homyel **17 B10**
Gomera **52 C2**
Gómez Palacio **84 B4**
Gomogomo **37 F4**
Gomoh **40 F6**
Gompa = Ganta **53 G4**
Gonābād **44 C4**
Gonaïves **87 C5**
Gonbad-e Kāvūs **44 B3**
Gonda **40 D3**
Gonder **55 F6**
Gönen **23 D6**
Gonghe **34 C5**
Gongolgon **63 B4**
Good Hope, C. of **58 E3**
Goodooga **63 A4**
Goolgowi **63 B4**
Goombalie **63 A4**
Goondiwindi **63 A5**
Gooray **63 A5**
Gop **43 H6**
Göppingen **14 D5**
Gorakhpur **40 D4**
Goražde **20 C7**
Gordon → **62 D4**
Gore *Australia* **63 A5**
Gore *Ethiopia* **55 G6**
Gore *N.Z.* **65 G3**
Gorgān **44 B3**
Gorgona, I. **90 C3**
Gorízia **20 B4**
Gorkiy = Nizhniy Novgorod **24 B5**
Gorkovskoye Vdkhr. **24 B5**
Görlitz **15 C8**
Gorlovka = Horlivka **25 D4**
Gorna Dzhumayo = Blagoevgrad **22 C4**
Gorna Oryakhovitsa **22 C5**
Gorno-Altay □ **29 D9**
Gorno-Altaysk **29 D9**
Gorno Slinkino = Gornopravdinsk **29 C8**
Gornopravdinsk **29 C8**
Gornyy **32 A3**
Gorodenka = Horodenka **17 D7**
Gorodok = Horodok **17 D6**
Gorokhov = Horokhiv **17 C7**
Gorontalo **37 D2**
Gorzów Wielkopolski **16 B2**
Gosford **63 B5**
Goshogawara **32 C7**

Goslar 14 C6
Gospič 20 B5
Göta kanal 9 D9
Göteborg 9 D8
Gotha 14 C6
Gothenburg = Göteborg
9 D8
Gotland 9 D9
Gotō-Rettō 33 G1
Göttingen 14 C5
Gottwaldov = Zlín 16 D3
Gouda 14 B3
Gouin, Rés. 71 E6
Goulburn 63 B4
Gouro 55 E2
Governador Valadares
93 F5
Goya 94 B5
Goyder Lagoon 62 A2
Goyllarisquisga 91 F3
Goz Beïda 55 F3
Gozo 21 F5
Graaff-Reinet 58 E4
Gračac 20 B5
Gracias a Dios, C. 86 D3
Grado 18 A2
Gradule 63 A4
Grafton 63 A5
Graham Bell, Ostrov =
Greem-Bell, Ostrov
28 A7
Graham Land 96 A3
Grahamstown 59 E5
Grajaú 92 D4
Grajaú → 92 C5
Grampian Highlands =
Grampian Mts. 10 C4
Grampian Mts. 10 C4
Grampians, The 62 C3
Gran Canaria 52 C2
Gran Chaco 94 B4
Gran Paradiso 13 D7
Gran Sasso d'Itália 20 C4
Granada Nic. 85 E7
Granada Spain 18 D4
Granby 71 E6
Grand Bahama I. 86 A4
Grand Bassam 53 G5
Grand Canyon 79 B6
Grand Cayman 86 C3
Grand Coulee Dam 72 C4
Grand Falls 71 E7
Grand Falls-Windsor
71 E8
Grand Forks 74 E5
Grand Island 74 E5
Grand Rapids Canada
69 C10
Grand Rapids U.S.A.
76 C3
Grand St-Bernard, Col du
13 D7
Grand Teton 73 E8
Grande → Bolivia 91 G6
Grande → Bahia, Brazil
93 E5
Grande → Minas Gerais,
Brazil 93 G3
Grande, B. 95 G3
Grande, Rio → 84 B5

Grande Baleine, R. de
la → 71 D6
Granite City 75 F9
Granity 65 D4
Granja 92 C5
Granollers 19 B7
Grantham 11 E6
Granville 12 B3
Grasse 13 E7
Grassmere 62 B3
Graulhet 12 E4
's-Gravenhage 14 B3
Gravesend 63 A5
Graz 15 E8
Great Abaco I. = Abaco I.
86 A4
Great Australian Bight
60 G4
Great Barrier I. 64 B6
Great Barrier Reef 61 D8
Great Basin 72 G5
Great Bear → 68 B7
Great Bear L. 68 B7
Great Belt = Store Bælt
9 D8
Great Divide, The = Great
Dividing Ra. 61 E8
Great Dividing Ra. 61 E8
Great Falls 73 C8
Great Inagua I. 86 B5
Great Indian Desert = Thar
Desert 42 F7
Great Karoo 58 E4
Great Khingan Mts. = Da
Hinggan Ling 35 B7
Great Lake 62 D4
Great Ouse → 11 E7
Great Ruaha → 57 F7
Great Saint Bernard
Pass = Grand St-
Bernard, Col di 13 D7
Great Salt Desert = Kavīr,
Dasht-e 44 C3
Great Salt L. 73 F7
Great Salt Lake Desert
73 F7
Great Sandy Desert 60 E3
Great Sangi = Sangihe,
Pulau 37 D3
Great Slave L. 68 B8
Great Smoky Mts. △
83 B6
Great Victoria Desert
60 F4
Great Wall 35 C5
Great Yarmouth 11 E7
Great Zab = Zāb al
Kabīr → 46 C5
Greater Antilles 86 C5
Greater Sudbury =
Sudbury 71 E5
Greater Sunda Is. 39 F4
Gredos, Sierra de 18 B3
Greece ■ 23 E4
Greeley 74 E2
Greely Fd. 70 A5
Greem-Bell, Ostrov 28 A7
Green → 79 A8
Green Bay 76 B2
Green C. 63 C5

Greenland ⊠ 66 C9
Greenock 10 D4
Greensboro 83 A8
Greenville Ala., U.S.A.
82 D4
Greenville Miss., U.S.A.
81 C8
Greenville N.C., U.S.A.
83 B9
Greenville S.C., U.S.A.
83 B6
Greenwood Miss., U.S.A.
81 C8
Greenwood S.C., U.S.A.
83 B6
Gregory, L. 62 A2
Greifswald 15 A7
Greiz 15 C7
Gremikha 28 C4
Grenada ■ 87 D7
Grenfell 63 B4
Grenoble 13 D6
Grey → 65 E4
Grey Ra. 63 A3
Greymouth 65 E4
Greytown 65 D6
Griffin 83 C5
Griffith 63 B4
Grimari 55 G3
Grimaylov = Hrymayliv
17 D8
Grimsby 11 E6
Gris-Nez, C. 12 A4
Grise Fiord 70 B5
Grodno = Hrodna 17 B6
Grodzyanka = Hrodzyanka
17 B9
Grójec 16 C5
Groningen 14 B4
Grootfontein 58 B3
Grosser Arber 15 D7
Grosseto 20 C3
Grossglockner 15 E7
Groznyy 25 E6
Grudziądz 16 B4
Gryazi 24 C4
Gryazovets 28 D5
Gua 40 F5
Guadalajara Mexico 84 C4
Guadalajara Spain 18 B4
Guadalcanal 64 K11
Guadalete → 18 D2
Guadalquivir → 18 D2
Guadalupe =
Guadeloupe ☑ 87 C7
Guadalupe, Sierra de
18 C3
Guadarrama, Sierra de
18 B4
Guadeloupe ☑ 87 C7
Guadiana → 18 D2
Guadix 18 D4
Guafo, Boca del 95 E2
Guaíra 94 A6
Guaitecas, Is. 95 E2
Guajará-Mirim 91 F5
Guajira, Pen. de la 90 A4
Gualeguaychú 94 C5
Guam ☑ 64 H9
Guamúchil 84 B3

Guanahani = San Salvador
I. 86 B5
Guanajuato 84 C4
Guandacol 94 B3
Guane 86 B3
Guangdong □ 35 D6
Guangxi Zhuangzu
Zizhiqu □ 35 D5
Guangzhou 35 D6
Guanipa → 90 B6
Guantánamo 86 B4
Guantánamo B. 86 B5
Guaporé → 91 F5
Guaqui 91 G5
Guarapuava 94 B6
Guarda 18 B2
Guardafui, C. = Asir, Ras
49 E5
Guasdualito 90 B4
Guatemala 85 E6
Guatemala ■ 85 D6
Guaviare → 90 C5
Guaxupé 93 G4
Guayaquil 90 D3
Guayaquil, G. de 90 D2
Guaymas 84 B2
Guddu Barrage 42 E6
Gudur 43 M11
Guecho = Getxo 19 A4
Guelph 76 C5
Guéret 12 C4
Guernica = Gernika-Lumo
19 A4
Guernsey 11 G5
Guidónia-Montecélio
20 C4
Guiji 59 C6
Guildford 11 F6
Guilin 35 D6
Guimarães 18 B1
Guimaras □ 36 B2
Guinea ■ 53 F3
Guinea, Gulf of 51 F3
Guinea-Bissau ■ 53 F3
Guingamp 12 B2
Güiria 90 A6
Guiuan 36 B3
Guiyang 35 D5
Guizhou □ 35 D5
Gujarat □ 43 H7
Gujranwala 42 C9
Gujrat 42 C9
Gulbarga 43 L10
Gulf, The = Persian Gulf
44 E2
Gulgong 63 B4
Güllük 23 F6
Gülshat 29 E8
Gulu 57 D6
Gümüşhane 46 B4
Gumzai 37 F4
Guna 43 G10
Gunnedah 63 B5
Gunningbar Cr. → 63 B4
Gunsan 35 C7
Guntakal 43 M10
Guntur 40 J3
Gunungapi 37 F3
Gunungsitoli 39 D1
Gunza 56 G2

Gupis 42 A8
Gürchän 46 D7
Gurdaspur 42 C9
Gurkha 40 C5
Gurley 63 A4
Gurupá 92 C3
Gurupá, I. Grande de 92 C3
Gurupi → 92 C4
Guryev = Atyraū 29 E6
Gusau 53 F7
Güstrow 15 B7
Gütersloh 14 C5
Guthrie 80 B5
Guwahati 41 D8
Guyana ■ 90 B7
Guyane française = French Guiana ⊘ 92 B3
Guyenne 12 D4
Guyra 63 B5
Güzelyurt = Morphou 46 D3
Gwa 41 J10
Gwabegar 63 B4
Gwädar 42 G3
Gwalior 42 F11
Gwanda 59 C5
Gwangju 35 C7
Gwanju = Gwangju 35 C7
Gweru 59 B5
Gwydir → 63 A4
Gyandzha = Gäncä 25 E6
Gyaring Hu 34 C4
Gydanskiy Poluostrov 28 B3
Gympie 63 A5
Gyöngyös 16 E4
Győr 16 E3
Gyula 16 E5
Gyumri 25 E5
Gyzylarbat = Serdar 29 F6

H

Haarlem 14 B3
Haast → 65 E3
Haboro 32 A7
Hachijō-Jima 33 G6
Hachinohe 32 C7
Hadarba, Ras 54 D6
Hadd, Ra's al 45 F4
Hadejia 53 F7
Haden 63 A5
Hadera 46 D3
Hadhramaut = Hadramawt 49 D4
Hadramawt 49 D4
Haeju 35 C7
Haerhpin = Harbin 35 B7
Hafar al Bāṭin 47 E6
Hafizabad 42 C8
Haflong 41 E9
Haft Gel 47 E7
Hagen 14 C4
Hagerstown 77 E7
Hagi 33 F2
Hagondange 13 B7
Hague, C. de la 12 B3
Hague, The = 's-Gravenhage 14 B3

Haguenau 13 B7
Haidarābād = Hyderabad 43 L11
Haifa = Ḥefa 46 D3
Haikou 35 D6
Ḥā'il 47 F5
Hailar 35 B6
Hailun 35 B7
Hailuoto 8 B10
Hainan □ 35 E5
Haiphong 35 D5
Haiti ■ 87 C5
Haiya 55 E6
Hajdúböszörmény 16 E5
Haji Ibrahim 46 C6
Hajnówka 17 B6
Hakodate 32 C7
Hala 42 G6
Ḥalab 46 C4
Ḥalabjah 46 D6
Halaib 54 D6
Halberstadt 15 C6
Halcombe 64 D6
Halcon 36 B2
Halden 9 D8
Haldia 40 F7
Haldwani 42 E11
Halfmoon Bay 65 G3
Halifax Canada 71 E7
Halifax U.K. 11 E6
Ḥalīl → 44 E4
Halkida 23 E4
Hall Beach = Sanirajak 70 C5
Hall Pen. 70 C7
Ḥallāniyat, Jazā'ir al 49 D6
Halle 15 C6
Hallett 62 B2
Halmahera 37 D3
Halmstad 9 D8
Hälsingborg = Helsingborg 9 D8
Ḥālūl 44 E3
Hamada 33 F3
Hamadān 46 D7
Hamadān □ 46 D7
Ḥamāh 46 D4
Hamamatsu 33 F5
Hamar 8 C8
Hamburg 14 B5
Hämeenlinna 8 C10
Hameln 14 B5
Hamersley Ra. 60 E2
Hamhŭng 35 C7
Hami 34 B4
Hamilton Australia 62 C3
Hamilton Canada 71 E6
Hamilton N.Z. 64 B6
Hamilton U.K. 10 D4
Hamilton → 62 A2
Hamley Bridge 62 B2
Hamlin = Hameln 14 B5
Hamm 14 C4
Hammerfest 8 A10
Hammond 76 D2
Hampden 65 F4
Hampton 77 F7
Han Pijesak 20 B7
Hanamaki 32 D7
Hanau 14 C5

Hancock 75 C7
Handan 35 C6
Hangayn Nuruu 34 B4
Hangchou = Hangzhou 35 C7
Hangzhou 35 C7
Hangzhou Wan 35 C7
Hania = Chania 23 G5
Ḥanīsh 49 E3
Hankö 9 D10
Hanle 42 C11
Hanmer Springs 65 E5
Hanna 69 C8
Hannibal 75 F9
Hannover 14 B5
Hanoi 35 D5
Hanover = Hannover 14 B5
Hansi 42 E9
Hanson, L. 62 B2
Hantsavichy 17 B8
Hanzhong 35 C5
Haora 40 F7
Haparanda 8 B10
Happy Valley-Goose Bay 71 D7
Hapur 42 E10
Ḥaql 47 E3
Har 37 F4
Har Hu 34 C4
Har Us Nuur 34 B4
Haraḍ 47 F7
Haraisan Plateau = Huraysān 47 G6
Haranomachi 33 E7
Harare 59 B6
Haraz 55 F2
Harbin 35 B7
Hardangerfjorden 8 C7
Hardwar = Haridwar 42 E11
Hardy, Pen. 95 H3
Harer 49 F3
Hargeisa 49 F3
Hari → 39 E2
Haridwar 42 E11
Haringhata → 41 G7
Ḥarīrūd 45 C5
Harīrūd → 42 A2
Harlingen 80 F5
Harlow 11 F7
Harney Basin 72 E4
Härnösand 8 C9
Harricana → 71 D6
Harris 10 C3
Harris, L. 62 B2
Harrisburg 77 D7
Harrison, C. 70 D8
Harrogate 11 D6
Hart, L. 62 B2
Hartford 77 D9
Hartlepool 11 D6
Harvey 76 D2
Harwich 11 F7
Haryana □ 42 E10
Haryn → 17 B8
Harz 14 C6
Hasa 47 F7
Haskovo = Khaskovo 22 D5

Hassi Messaoud 52 B7
Hastings N.Z. 64 C7
Hastings U.K. 11 F7
Hastings U.S.A. 74 E5
Hastings Ra. 63 B5
Hatay 46 C4
Hatfield P.O. 62 B3
Hatgal 34 A5
Hathras 42 F11
Hatia 41 F8
Hattah 62 B3
Hatteras, C. 83 B10
Hattiesburg 81 D9
Hatvan 16 E4
Hau Bon = Cheo Reo 38 B3
Haugesund 9 D7
Hauraki G. 64 B6
Haut Atlas 52 B4
Hautah, Waḥât al 47 G6
Havana = La Habana 86 B3
Havant 11 F6
Havel → 15 B7
Havelock 65 D5
Haverfordwest 11 F4
Havlíčkův Brod 16 D2
Havre 73 B9
Havre-St.-Pierre 71 D7
Havza 46 B3
Hawai'i □ 78 H12
Hawaiian Is. 78 H12
Hawea, L. 65 F3
Hawera 64 C6
Hawick 10 D5
Hawke B. 64 C7
Hawker 62 B2
Hawkwood 63 A5
Hay 63 B3
Hay River 68 B8
Haya = Tehoru 37 E3
Hayastan = Armenia ■ 25 E5
Hayes → 69 C10
Hayrabolu 22 D6
Haysyn 17 D9
Hayvoron 17 D9
Hazar 29 F6
Hazärän, Küh-e 44 D4
Hazaribag 40 F5
Healesville 63 C4
Hearst 71 E5
Hebei □ 35 C6
Hebel 63 A4
Hebron = Al Khalīl 47 E3
Hebron 70 D7
Hechi 35 D5
Hechuan 35 C5
Heerlen 13 A6
Ḥefa 46 D3
Hefei 35 C6
Hegang 35 B8
Heidelberg 14 D5
Heihe 35 A7
Heilbronn 14 D5
Heilongjiang □ 35 B7
Heilunkiang = Heilongjiang □ 35 B7
Heimaey 8 C1
Heinze Kyun 41 K11

Hejaz = Ḥijāz 47 F4
Hekımhan 46 C4
Hekou 34 D5
Helena *Ark., U.S.A.* 81 B8
Helena *Mont., U.S.A.* 73 C7
Helensville 64 B6
Helgoland 14 A4
Heligoland = Helgoland 14 A4
Heligoland B. = Deutsche Bucht 14 A5
Hellas = Greece ■ 23 E4
Hellespont = Çanakkale Boğazı 23 D6
Hellín 19 C5
Helmand □ 42 D3
Helmand → 42 D2
Helmand, Hamun 45 D5
Helmsdale 10 B5
Helsingborg 9 D8
Helsingfors = Helsinki 9 C11
Helsinki 9 C11
Helwân 54 C5
Hemel Hempstead 11 F6
Henan □ 35 C6
Henares → 18 B4
Henashi-Misaki 32 C6
Henderson 83 A8
Hendon 63 A5
Hengyang 35 D6
Henrietta Maria, C. 71 D5
Hentiyn Nuruu 35 B5
Henty 63 C4
Henzada 41 J10
Heraklion = Iraklio 23 G5
Herät 42 B3
Herät □ 42 B3
Herceg-Novi 22 C2
Hereford 11 E5
Herford 14 B5
Hermidale 63 B4
Hermite, I. 95 H3
Hermon, Mt. = Shaykh, J. ash 46 D3
Hermosillo 84 B2
Hernád → 16 E5
Heroica Nogales = Nogales 84 A2
Herrick 62 D4
's-Hertogenbosch 14 C3
Hesse = Hessen □ 14 C5
Hessen □ 14 C5
Hexham 11 D5
Heywood 62 C3
Hialeah 83 G7
Hibbing 75 B8
Hibbs B. 62 D4
Hickory 83 B7
Hicks, Pt. 63 C4
Hidalgo del Parral 84 B3
Higashiajima-San 33 E7
Higashiōsaka 33 F4
High Point 83 B8
High River 69 C8
High Tatra = Tatry 16 D4
High Wycombe 11 F6
Hiiumaa 24 B1
Ḥijārah, Ṣaḥrā' al 47 E6

Ḥijāz 47 F4
Hijo = Tagum 36 C3
Hikurangi *Gisborne, N.Z.* 64 C7
Hikurangi *Northland, N.Z.* 64 A6
Hildesheim 14 B5
Hillston 63 B4
Hilo 78 J13
Hilversum 14 B3
Himachal Pradesh □ 42 D10
Himalaya 40 C5
Himatnagar 43 H8
Himeji 33 F4
Himi 33 E5
Ḥimş 46 D4
Hindmarsh, L. 62 C3
Hindu Bagh 42 D5
Hindu Kush 42 B7
Hindupur 43 N10
Hinganghat 43 J11
Hingoli 43 K10
Hinna = Imi 49 F3
Hinojosa del Duque 18 C3
Hinthada = Henzada 41 J10
Hios 23 E6
Hirakud Dam 40 G4
Hiroo 32 C8
Hirosaki 32 C7
Hiroshima 33 F3
Hisar 42 E7
Hispaniola 87 C5
Hitachi 33 E7
Hjälmaren 9 D9
Hkakabo Razi 41 C11
Hlyboka 17 D7
Ho Chi Minh City = Thanh Pho Ho Chi Minh 38 B3
Hoai Nhon 38 B3
Hoare B. 70 C7
Hobart 62 D4
Hobbs Coast 96 B18
Hodaka-Dake 33 E5
Hodeida = Al Ḥudaydah 49 E3
Hodgson 69 C10
Hódmezővásárhely 16 E5
Hodna, Chott el 52 A6
Hodonín 16 D3
Hoek van Holland 14 B3
Hof 15 C6
Hofsjökull 8 C2
Hōfu 33 F2
Hogan Group 62 C4
Hoggar = Ahaggar 52 D7
Hoh Xil Shan 34 C3
Hoher Rhön = Rhön 14 C5
Hohhot 35 B6
Hoi An 38 A3
Hokianga Harbour 64 A5
Hokitika 65 E4
Hokkaidō □ 32 B8
Holbrook 63 C4
Holguín 86 B4
Hollywood 83 G7
Holman 68 A8
Holstebro 9 D7
Holyhead 11 E4

Homalin 41 E10
Hombori 53 E5
Home B. 70 C7
Homer 69 C4
Homs = Ḥimş 46 D4
Homyel 17 B10
Hon Chong 38 B2
Honan = Henan □ 35 C6
Honbetsu 32 B8
Honduras ■ 85 E7
Honduras, G. de 85 D7
Hønefoss 9 C8
Honfleur 12 B4
Hong Kong □ 35 D6
Hongjiang 35 D5
Hongshui He → 35 D5
Hongze Hu 35 C6
Honiara 64 K10
Honjō 32 D7
Honolulu 78 H12
Honshū 33 F9
Hood, Mt. 72 D3
Hooghly = Hugli → 40 G7
Hook of Holland = Hoek van Holland 14 B3
Hoorn 14 B3
Hoover Dam 78 B5
Hope, L. 62 A2
Hopedale 70 D7
Hopei = Hebei □ 35 C6
Hopetoun 62 C3
Hopetown 58 D4
Hoquiam 72 C2
Horlick Mts. 96 C1
Horlivka 25 D4
Hormoz 44 E3
Hormoz, Jaz.-ye 44 E4
Hormozgān □ 44 E3
Hormuz, Str. of 44 E4
Horn 15 D8
Horn, Cape = Hornos, C. de 95 H3
Hornavan 8 B9
Hornos, C. de 95 H3
Horodenka 17 D7
Horodok *Khmelnytskyy, Ukraine* 17 D8
Horodok *Lviv, Ukraine* 17 D6
Horokhiv 17 C7
Horqin Youyi Qianqi 35 B7
Horqueta 94 A4
Horsham 62 C3
Horton → 68 B7
Hose, Gunung-Gunung 39 D4
Hoshangabad 43 H10
Hoshiarpur 42 D9
Hospet 43 M10
Hoste, I. 95 H3
Hot Springs 81 B7
Hotan 34 C2
Hotazel 58 D4
Houhora Heads 64 A5
Houlton 77 A12
Houma 81 E8
Houston 81 E6
Hovd □ 34 B4
Hövsgöl Nuur 34 A5
Howard 63 A5

Howe, C. 63 C5
Howitt, L. 62 A2
Howrah = Haora 40 F7
Höxter 14 C5
Hoy 10 B5
Høyanger 8 C7
Hoyerswerda 15 C8
Hpa-an = Pa-an 41 J11
Hpunan Pass 41 D11
Hradec Králové 16 C2
Hrodna 17 B6
Hrodzyanka 17 B9
Hrvatska = Croatia ■ 20 B6
Hrymayliv 17 D8
Hsenwi 41 F11
Hsiamen = Xiamen 35 D6
Hsian = Xi'an 35 C5
Hsinhailien = Lianyungang 35 C6
Hsüchou = Xuzhou 35 C6
Hua Hin 38 B1
Huacho 91 F3
Huai He → 35 C6
Huainan 35 C6
Huallaga → 90 E3
Huambo 58 A3
Huancabamba 91 E3
Huancane 91 G5
Huancavelica 91 F3
Huancayo 91 F3
Huang Hai = Yellow Sea 35 C7
Huang He → 35 C6
Huangliu 35 E5
Huangshan 35 D6
Huangshi 35 C6
Huánuco 91 E3
Huaraz 91 E3
Huarmey 91 F3
Huascarán, Nevado 91 E3
Huasco 94 B2
Huatabampo 84 B3
Hubei □ 35 C6
Hubli 43 M9
Huddersfield 11 E6
Hudiksvall 8 C9
Hudson → 77 D8
Hudson Bay 70 C5
Hudson Mts. 96 B2
Hudson Str. 70 C7
Hue 38 A3
Huelva 18 D2
Huesca 19 A5
Hughenden 61 E7
Hugli → 40 G7
Huila, Nevado del 90 C3
Huinca Renancó 94 C4
Huize 34 D5
Hukawng Valley 41 D11
Hulan 35 B7
Ḥulayfā' 47 F5
Hull = Kingston upon Hull 11 E6
Hull 71 E6
Hulun Nur 35 B6
Humahuaca 94 A3
Humaitá 91 E6
Humber → 11 E6
Humboldt 69 C9

Humboldt → 72 F4
Hume, I. 63 C4
Hün 54 C2
Húnaflói 8 B1
Hunan ■ 16 E4
Hunedoara 17 F6
Hungary ■ 16 E4
Hungerford 63 A3
Húngnam 35 C7
Hunsrück 14 D4
Hunter I. 62 D3
Hunter Ra. 63 B5
Hunterville 64 C6
Huntington 76 E4
Huntington Beach 78 D3
Huntly N.Z. 64 B6
Huntly U.K. 10 C5
Huntsville Canada 71 E6
Huntsville U.S.A. 82 B4
Huonville 62 D4
Hupeh = Hubei □ 35 C6
Hurayšán 47 G6
Huron, L. 76 B4
Hurunui → 65 E5
Húsavík 8 B2
Huși 17 E9
Hutchinson 80 A5
Hutton, Mt. 63 A4
Hvar 20 C6
Hwang Ho = Huang He → 35 C6
Hwange 59 B5
Hyargas Nuur 34 B4
Hyderabad India 43 L11
Hyderabad Pakistan 42 G6
Hydra 23 F4
Hyères 13 E7
Hyères, Îs. d' 13 E7
Hyūga 33 G2

I

I-n-Gall 53 E7
Iaco → 91 E5
Ialomița → 22 B6
Iași 17 E8
Iba 36 A2
Ibadan 53 G6
Ibagué 90 C3
Ibar → 22 C3
Ibarra 90 C3
Ibiá 93 F4
Ibiapaba, Sa. da 92 C5
Ibicaraí 93 E6
Ibiza = Eivissa 19 C6
Ibonma 37 E4
Ibotirama 93 E5
Ibu 37 D3
Ibusuki 33 H2
Ica 91 F3
Içá → 90 D5
Içana 90 C5
İçel 46 C3
Iceland ■ 8 B2
Ich'ang = Yichang 35 C6
Ichchapuram 40 H5
Ichihara 33 F7
Ichilo → 91 G6
Ichinomiya 33 F5
Ichinoseki 32 D7
Idaho □ 73 D7

Idaho Falls 73 E7
Idar-Oberstein 14 D4
Idensalmi = Iisalmi 8 C11
Idfû 54 D5
Ídhra = Hydra 23 F4
Idi 38 C1
Idi, Oros = Psiloritis, Oros 23 G5
Idiofa 56 E3
Idlib 46 D4
Idlip 46 D4
Ierapetra 23 G5
Iesi 20 C4
Ife 53 G6
Iforas, Adrar des 52 E6
Igarapava 93 G4
Igarka 28 C9
Iglésias 21 E2
Igloolik 70 C5
Igluligaarjuk = Chesterfield Inlet 68 B10
Iglulik = Igloolik 70 C5
İğneada Burnu 22 D7
Igoumenitsa 23 E3
Iguaçu → 94 B6
Iguaçu, Cat. del 94 B6
Iguaçu Falls = Iguaçu, Cat. del 94 B6
Iguala 84 D5
Igualada 19 B6
Iguassu = Iguaçu → 94 B6
Iguatu 92 D6
Iharana 59 A10
Ihosy 59 C9
Iida 33 F5
Iisalmi 8 C11
Ijebu-Ode 53 G6
IJsselmeer 14 B3
Ikaluktutiak 68 B9
Ikaria 23 F6
Ikeda 33 F3
Ikela 56 E4
Iki 33 G1
Ikopa → 59 B9
Ikparjuk = Arctic Bay 70 B5
Ilagan 36 A2
Īlām 46 D6
Ilawa 16 B4
Ile → 29 E8
Île-de-France □ 12 B5
Ilebo 56 E4
Ilesha 53 G6
Ilhéus 93 E6
Ili = Ile → 29 E8
Iligan 36 C2
Illampu = Ancohuma, Nevado 91 G5
Illana B. 36 C2
Illapel 94 C2
Iller → 14 D5
Illimani, Nevado 91 G5
Ilmen, Ozero 24 B3
Ilo 91 G4
Iloilo 36 B2
Ilorin 53 G6
Ilwaki 37 F3
Imabari 33 F3
Imandra, Ozero 28 C4

Imari 33 G1
Imatra 8 C11
imeni 26 Bakinskikh Komissarov = Neftçala 46 C7
imeni Ismail Samani, Pik 29 F8
Imeri, Serra 90 C5
Imi 49 F3
Ímola 20 B3
Imperatriz 92 D4
Impéria 13 E8
Imperial Dam 78 D5
Impfondo 56 D3
Imphal 41 E9
İmroz = Gökçeada 23 D5
Imuruan B. 36 B1
In Salah 52 C6
Ina 33 F5
Inangahua 65 D4
Inanwatan 37 E4
Iñapari 91 F5
Inari 8 B11
Inarijärvi 8 B11
Inca 19 C7
İnce Burun 25 E3
Incheon 35 C7
İncirliova 23 F6
Incomáti → 59 D6
Indalsälven → 8 C9
Indaw 41 E11
Independence Kans., U.S.A. 81 A6
Independence Mo., U.S.A. 75 F7
India ■ 43 J10
Indian → 83 F7
Indiana □ 76 D3
Indianapolis 76 E2
Indigirka → 31 B12
Indonesia ■ 39 E4
Indore 43 H9
Indravati → 40 H3
Indre □ 12 C4
Indre → 12 C4
Indus → 43 G5
İnebolu 25 E3
Inglewood Queens., Australia 63 A5
Inglewood Vic., Australia 62 C3
Inglewood N.Z. 64 C6
Ingolstadt 15 D6
Ingraj Bazar 40 E7
Ingrid Christensen Coast 96 A10
Ingulec = Inhulec 25 D3
Inhambane 59 C7
Inharrime 59 C7
Inhulec 25 D3
Ining = Yining 29 E9
Inírida → 90 C5
Injune 63 A4
Inland Kaikoura Ra. 65 D5
Inland Sea = Setonaikai 33 F3
Inle L. 41 G11
Inn → 15 D7
Innamincka 62 A3
Inner Hebrides 10 C3

Inner Mongolia = Nei Monggol Zizhiqu □ 35 B6
Innsbruck 15 E6
Inongo 56 E3
Inoucdjouac = Inukjuak 70 D6
Inowrocław 16 B4
Insein 41 J11
International Falls 75 A8
Inukjuak 70 D6
Inútil, B. 95 G2
Inuvik 68 B6
Invercargill 65 G3
Inverell 63 A5
Invergordon 10 C4
Inverness 10 C4
Inverurie 10 C5
Investigator Group 62 B1
Investigator Str. 62 C2
Inya 29 D9
Inza 24 C6
Ioannina 23 E3
Ioio = Piloritis? ...
Ionian Is. = Ionioi Nisoi 23 E3
Ionian Sea 21 F6
Ionioi Nisoi 23 E3
Ios 23 F5
Iowa □ 75 D8
Iowa City 75 E9
Ipameri 93 F4
Ipatinga 93 F5
Ipiales 90 C3
Ipin = Yibin 35 D5
Ipixuna 91 E4
Ipoh 38 D2
Ippy 55 G3
Ipsala 22 D6
Ipswich Australia 63 A5
Ipswich U.K. 11 E7
Ipu 92 C5
Iqaluit 70 C7
Iquique 91 H4
Iquitos 90 D4
Iracoubo 92 A3
Iráklio 23 G5
Iráklion = Iraklio 23 G5
Iran ■ 44 C3
Iran, Pegunungan 39 D4
Iran Ra. = Iran, Pegunungan 39 D4
Īrānshahr 45 E5
Irapuato 84 C4
Iraq ■ 46 D5
Ireland ■ 11 E3
Irian Jaya = Papua □ 37 E5
Iringa 57 F7
Iriri → 92 C3
Irish Republic ■ 11 E3
Irish Sea 11 E4
Irkineyeva 30 D7
Irkutsk 30 D8
Irō-Zaki 33 F6
Iron Baron 62 B2
Iron Gate = Portile de Fier 22 B4
Iron Knob 62 B2
Ironwood 75 B9
Irpin 17 C10

Irrara Cr. → 63 A4
Irrawaddy □ 41 J10
Irrawaddy → 41 K10
Irrawaddy, Mouths of the 41 K10
Irtysh → 28 C7
Irún 19 A5
Irunea = Pamplona 19 A5
Irvine 10 D4
Irymple 62 B3
Isabela 36 C2
Ísafjörður 8 B1
Isahaya 33 G2
Isar → 15 D7
Íschia 21 D4
Ise-Wan 33 F5
Isère → 13 D6
Isérnia 20 D5
Isfahan = Eşfahān 44 C2
Ishikari-Gawa → 32 B7
Ishikari-Wan 32 B7
Ishim → 29 D8
Ishinomaki 32 D7
Ishkuman 42 A8
Isil Kul 29 D8
Isiro 57 D5
İskenderun 46 C4
Iskür → 22 C5
Islamabad 42 C8
Island = Iceland ■ 8 B2
Island L. 69 C10
Island Lagoon 62 B2
Islands, B. of 64 A6
Islay 10 D3
Isle → 12 D3
Isle of Wight □ 11 F6
Ismail = Izmayil 17 F9
Ismâ'ilîya 47 E3
Ísparta 46 C2
Íspica 21 F5
Israel ■ 46 E3
Issoire 13 D5
Issyk-Kul, Ozero = Ysyk-Köl 29 E8
İstanbul 22 D7
İstanbul Boğazı 22 D7
Istiea 23 E4
Istra 20 B4
Istres 13 E6
Istria = Istra 20 B4
Itaberaba 93 E5
Itabira 93 F5
Itabuna 93 E6
Itaipú, Reprêsa de 94 B6
Itaituba 92 C2
Itajaí 94 B7
Italy ■ 20 C4
Itapecuru-Mirim 92 C5
Itaperuna 93 G5
Itapicuru → Bahia, Brazil 93 E6
Itapicuru → Maranhão, Brazil 92 C5
Itapipoca 92 C6
Itaquí 94 B5
Ithaca = Ithaki 23 E3
Itháki 23 E3
Itō 33 F6
Itonamas → 91 F6
Ituiutaba 93 F4

Itumbiara 93 F4
Iturbe 94 A3
Itzehoe 14 B5
Ivanava 17 B7
Ivanhoe 63 B3
Ivano-Frankivsk 17 D7
Ivanovo = Ivanava 17 B7
Ivanovo 24 B5
Ivatsevichy 17 B7
Ivrea 13 D7
Ivujivik 70 C6
Iwahig 38 C5
Iwaizumi 32 D7
Iwaki 33 E7
Iwakuni 33 F3
Iwamizawa 32 B7
Iwanai 32 B7
Iwata 33 F5
Iwate-Gawa → 32 D7
Iwo 53 G6
Ixiamas 91 F5
Izhevsk 28 D6
Izmayil 17 F9
İzmir 23 E6
İzmit = Kocaeli 25 E2
İznik Gölü 23 D7
Izu-Shotō 33 F7
Izumi-Sano 33 F4
Izumo 33 F3
Izyaslav 17 C8

J

Jabalpur 43 H11
Jablah 46 D4
Jablanica 22 D3
Jablonec nad Nisou 16 C2
Jaboatão 92 D6
Jaca 19 A5
Jacareí 94 A7
Jackson Australia 63 A4
Jackson Mich., U.S.A. 76 C3
Jackson Miss., U.S.A. 81 C8
Jackson Tenn., U.S.A. 82 B3
Jackson B. 65 E3
Jacksons 65 E4
Jacksonville Fla., U.S.A. 83 D7
Jacksonville Ill., U.S.A. 75 F9
Jacksonville N.C., U.S.A. 83 B9
Jacmel 87 C5
Jacobabad 42 E6
Jacobina 93 E5
Jacundá → 92 C3
Jade Mt. = Yü Shan 35 D7
Jaén Peru 91 E3
Jaén Spain 18 D4
Jaffa = Tel Aviv-Yafo 46 D3
Jaffa, C. 62 C2
Jaffna 43 Q12
Jagadhri 42 D10
Jagdalpur 40 H3
Jagodina 22 B3

Jagraon 42 D9
Jagtial 43 K11
Jaguariaíva 94 A7
Jaguaribe → 92 C6
Jahrom 44 D3
Jailolo 37 D3
Jailolo, Selat 37 D3
Jaipur 42 F9
Jakarta 39 F3
Jalālābād 42 B7
Jalapa Enríquez = Xalapa 84 D5
Jalas, Jabal al 47 F4
Jalgaon Maharashtra, India 43 J10
Jalgaon Maharashtra, India 43 J9
Jalna 43 K9
Jalón → 19 B5
Jalpaiguri 41 D7
Jaluit I. 64 J11
Jamaica ■ 86 C4
Jamalpur Bangla. 41 E7
Jamalpur India 40 E6
Jamanxim → 92 C2
Jambe 37 E4
Jambi 39 E2
Jambi □ 39 E2
Jambongan, Pulau 38 C5
James → 74 D6
James B. 71 D5
James Ross I. 96 A4
Jamestown Australia 62 B2
Jamestown N. Dak., U.S.A. 74 B5
Jamestown N.Y., U.S.A. 77 C6
Jamkhandi 43 L9
Jammu 42 C9
Jammu & Kashmir □ 42 B10
Jamnagar 43 H7
Jamshedpur 40 F6
Jand 42 C8
Jandaq 44 C3
Jandowae 63 A5
Janesville 75 D10
Janjanbureh 53 F3
Januária 93 F5
Jaora 43 H9
Japan ■ 33 F5
Japan, Sea of 32 D4
Japen = Yapen 37 E5
Japurá → 90 D5
Jaqué 90 B3
Jarama → 18 B4
Jarvis I. 65 K15
Jäsk 44 E4
Jasper 82 C4
Jászberény 16 E4
Jataí 93 F3
Játiva = Xátiva 19 C5
Jaú 93 G4
Jauja 91 F3
Jaunpur 40 E4
Java = Jawa 39 F3
Java Sea 39 E3
Jawa 39 F3
Jaya, Puncak 37 E5

Jayanti 41 D7
Jayapura 37 E6
Jayawijaya, Pegunungan 37 E5
Jaynagar 40 D6
Jebel, Bahr el → 55 G5
Jedburgh 10 D5
Jedda = Jiddah 47 G4
Jędrzejów 16 C5
Jefferson City 75 F8
Jega 53 F6
Jeju-do 35 C7
Jelenia Góra 16 C2
Jelgava 24 B1
Jena 15 C6
Jeonju 35 C7
Jeparit 62 C3
Jequié 93 E5
Jequitinhonha 93 F5
Jequitinhonha → 93 F6
Jérémie 86 C5
Jerez de la Frontera 18 D2
Jerez de los Caballeros 18 C2
Jerid, Chott el = Djerid, Chott 52 B7
Jerilderie 63 C4
Jersey 11 G5
Jersey City 77 D8
Jerusalem 47 E3
Jervis B. 63 C4
Jesi = Iesi 20 C4
Jessore 41 F7
Jeypore 40 H4
Jhal Jhao 42 F4
Jhalawar 43 G10
Jhang Maghiana 42 D8
Jhansi 43 G11
Jharsuguda 40 G5
Jhelum 42 C8
Jhelum → 42 D8
Jhunjhunu 42 E9
Jiamusi 35 B8
Ji'an 35 D6
Jiangmen 35 D6
Jiangsu □ 35 C6
Jiangxi □ 35 D6
Jiao Xian = Jiaozhou 35 C7
Jiaozhou 35 C7
Jiaxing 35 C7
Jiayi = Chiai 35 D7
Jibuti = Djibouti ■ 49 E3
Jiddah 47 G4
Jido 41 C10
Jihlava 16 D2
Jihlava → 16 D3
Jijiga 49 F3
Jilin 35 B7
Jilong = Chilung 35 D7
Jima 55 G6
Jiménez 84 B4
Jinan 35 C6
Jindabyne 63 C4
Jindřichův Hradec 16 D2
Jingdezhen 35 D6
Jinggu 34 D5
Jinhua 35 D6
Jining
  Nei Monggol Zizhiqu, China 35 B6

Jining Shandong, China 35 C6
Jinja 57 D6
Jinnah Barrage 42 C7
Jinzhou 35 B7
Jiparaná → 91 E6
Jipijapa 90 D2
Jiu → 22 C4
Jiujiang 35 D6
Jiuquan 34 C4
Jixi 35 B8
Jizzakh 29 E7
Joaçaba 94 B6
João Pessoa 92 D7
Joaquín V. González 94 B4
Jodhpur 42 F8
Joensuu 8 C11
Jogjakarta = Yogyakarta 39 F4
Johannesburg 59 D5
Johnson City 83 A6
Johnston Falls = Mambilima Falls 57 G5
Johnstown 77 D6
Johor Bahru 39 D2
Joinville 94 B7
Joinville I. 96 A4
Joliet 76 D1
Joliette 71 E6
Jolo 36 C2
Jome 37 E3
Jones Sound 70 B5
Jonesboro 81 B8
Jönköping 9 D8
Jonquière 71 E6
Joplin 81 A6
Jordan ■ 47 E4
Jorhat 41 D10
Jorong 39 E4
Jos 53 G7
Jotunheimen 8 C7
Jowzjān □ 45 B6
Juan de Fuca, Str. of. 72 B1
Juan Fernández, Arch. de 89 G3
Juárez 94 D5
Juàzeiro 93 D5
Juàzeiro do Norte 92 D6
Juba = Giuba → 49 G3
Jubbulpore = Jabalpur 43 H11
Juby, C. 52 C3
Júcar = Xúquer → 19 C5
Juchitán de Zaragoza 85 D5
Jugoslavia = Serbia ■ 22 B3
Juiz de Fora 93 G5
Juli 91 G5
Juliaca 91 G4
Jullundur 42 D9
Jumilla 19 C5
Jumla 40 C4
Jumna → = Yamuna → 40 E3
Junagadh 43 J7
Jundiaí 94 A7
Juneau 69 C6

Junee 63 B4
Junggar Pendi 34 B3
Junín 94 C4
Junín de los Andes 95 D2
Jūniyah 46 D3
Jur, Nahr el → 55 G4
Jura = Jura, Mts. du 13 C7
Jura 10 D4
Jura = Schwäbische Alb 14 D5
Jura, Mts. du 13 C7
Juruá → 90 D5
Juruena → 91 E7
Juruti 92 C2
Justo Daract 94 C3
Jutland = Jylland 9 D7
Juventud, I. de la 86 B3
Jwaneng 58 C4
Jylland 9 D7
Jyväskylä 8 C11

K

K2 42 B10
Kaapstad = Cape Town 58 E3
Kabaena 37 F2
Kabala 53 G3
Kabale 57 E6
Kabalo 57 F5
Kabanjahe 39 D1
Kabarai 37 E4
Kabardino-Balkar Republic = Kabardino-Balkaria □ 25 E5
Kabardino-Balkaria □ 25 E5
Kabarega Falls = Murchison Falls 57 D6
Kabasalan 36 C2
Kabīr Kūh 47 D6
Kabompo → 58 A4
Kabongo 57 F5
Kabūd Gonbad 44 B4
Kābul 42 B6
Kābul □ 42 B6
Kābul → 42 C8
Kaburuang 37 D3
Kabwe 59 A5
Kachchh, Gulf of 43 H6
Kachchh, Rann of 43 G6
Kachin □ 41 D11
Kachiry 29 D8
Kaçkar 25 E5
Kadan Kyun 38 B1
Kadina 62 B2
Kadiyevka = Stakhanov 25 D4
Kadoma 59 B5
Kâdugli 55 F4
Kaduna 53 F7
Kaédi 53 E3
Kaesŏng 35 C7
Kāf 47 E4
Kafan = Kapan 25 F6
Kafanchan 53 G7
Kafue → 59 B5
Kaga Bandoro 55 G2
Kagan 29 F7

Kağızman 46 B5
Kagoshima 33 H2
Kagul = Cahul 17 F9
Kahayan → 39 E4
Kahnūj 44 E4
Kaho'olawe 78 H12
Kahramanmaraş 46 C4
Kahurangi △ 65 D5
Kai, Kepulauan 37 F4
Kai Besar 37 F4
Kai Is. = Kai, Kepulauan 37 F4
Kai Kecil 37 F4
Kaiapoi 65 E5
Kaieteur Falls 90 B7
Kaifeng 35 C6
Kaikohe 64 A5
Kaikoura 65 E5
Kaimana 37 E4
Kaimanawa Mts. 64 C6
Kainji Res. 53 F6
Kaipara Harbour 64 B6
Kaironi 37 E4
Kairouan 54 A1
Kaiserslautern 14 D4
Kaitaia 64 A5
Kaitangata 65 G3
Kajaani 8 C11
Kajabbi 61 D6
Kajana = Kajaani 8 C11
Kajo Kaji 55 H5
Kakamega 57 D6
Kakanui Mts. 65 F4
Kakhovka 25 D3
Kakhovske Vdskh. 25 D3
Kakinada 40 J4
Kalaallit Nunaat = Greenland ☒ 66 C9
Kalabagh 42 C7
Kalabahi 37 F2
Kalach 24 C5
Kaladan → 41 G9
Kalahari 58 C4
Kalakan 31 D9
K'alak'unlun Shank'ou = Karakoram Pass 42 B10
Kalamata 23 F4
Kalamazoo 76 C3
Kalan 46 C4
Kalao 37 F2
Kalaotoa 37 F2
Kalat 42 E5
Kalce 20 B5
Kale 23 F7
Kalegauk Kyun 41 K11
Kalemie 57 F5
Kalewa 41 F10
Kalgoorlie-Boulder 60 G3
Kaliakra, Nos 22 C7
Kalianda 39 F3
Kalibo 36 B2
Kalima 57 E5
Kalimantan 39 E4
Kalimantan Barat □ 39 D4
Kalimantan Selatan □ 39 E5
Kalimantan Tengah □ 39 E4
Kalimantan Timur □ 39 D5
Kálimnos 23 F6
Kaliningrad 24 C1

Kalinkavichy 17 B9
Kalinkovichi = Kalinkavichy 17 B9
Kalispell 73 B6
Kalisz 16 C4
Kallsjön 8 C8
Kalmar 9 D9
Kalmyk Republic = Kalmykia □ 25 D6
Kalmykia □ 25 D6
Kalocsa 16 E4
Kaluga 24 C4
Kalush 17 D7
Kalutara 43 R11
Kama → 29 D6
Kamaishi 32 D7
Kamarān 49 D3
Kamchatka, Poluostrov 31 D13
Kamchatka Pen. = Kamchatka, Poluostrov 31 D13
Kamchiya → 22 C6
Kamen 29 D9
Kamen-Rybolov 32 A3
Kamenjak, Rt 20 B4
Kamenka Bugskaya = Kamyanka-Buzka 17 C7
Kamensk Uralskiy 29 D7
Kamin-Kashyrskyy 17 C7
Kamina 57 F5
Kamloops 69 C7
Kampala 57 D6
Kampar → 39 D2
Kampen 14 B3
Kampong Chhnang 38 B2
Kampong Saom 38 B2
Kampot 38 B2
Kampuchea = Cambodia ■ 38 B3
Kampungbaru = Tolitoli 37 D2
Kamrau, Teluk 37 E4
Kamui-Misaki 32 B7
Kamyanets-Podilskyy 17 D8
Kamyanka-Buzka 17 C7
Kamyshin 24 C6
Kanaaupscow 71 D6
Kanagi 32 C7
Kananga 56 F4
Kanash 24 B6
Kanastraíon, Ákra = Paliouri, Akra 23 E4
Kanazawa 33 E5
Kanchanaburi 38 B1
Kanchenjunga 40 D7
Kanchipuram 43 N11
Kandahār 42 D4
Kandahār □ 42 D4
Kandalaksha 8 B12
Kandalu 42 E3
Kandangan 39 E5
Kandi 53 F6
Kandla 43 H7
Kandos 63 B4
Kandy 43 R12
Kangaroo I. 62 C2
Kangāvar 46 D7
Kangean, Kepulauan 39 F5

Kangean Is. = Kangean, Kepulauan **39 F5**
Kangiqliniq = Rankin Inlet **68 B10**
Kangiqsualujjuaq **70 D7**
Kangiqsujuaq **70 C6**
Kangiqtugaapik = Clyde River **70 B7**
Kangirsuk **70 D7**
Kangto **41 D9**
Kaniapiscau = Caniapiscau → **70 D7**
Kaniapiscau, L. = Caniapiscau, L. **71 D7**
Kanin, Poluostrov **28 C5**
Kanin Nos, Mys **28 C5**
Kanin Pen. = Kanin, Poluostrov **28 C5**
Kaniva **62 C3**
Kankakee **76 D2**
Kankan **53 F4**
Kankendy = Xankändi **25 F6**
Kanker **40 G3**
Kannapolis **83 B7**
Kannauj **42 F11**
Kannod **43 H10**
Kano **53 F7**
Kanowit **39 D4**
Kanoya **33 J4**
Kanpetlet **41 G9**
Kanpur **40 D3**
Kansas □ **74 F5**
Kansas City *Kans., U.S.A.* **75 F7**
Kansas City *Mo., U.S.A.* **75 F7**
Kansk **30 D7**
Kansu = Gansu □ **34 C5**
Kanyakumari **43 Q10**
Kanye **59 C5**
Kaohsiung **35 D7**
Kaolack **53 F2**
Kapan **25 F6**
Kapanga **56 F4**
Kapchagai = Qapshaghay **29 E8**
Kapela = Velika Kapela **20 B5**
Kapfenberg **15 E8**
Kapiri Mposhi **59 A5**
Käpisä □ **45 C7**
Kapit **39 D4**
Kapiti I. **65 D6**
Kapoeta **55 H5**
Kaposvár **16 E3**
Kaptai L. **41 F9**
Kapuas → **39 E3**
Kapuas Hulu, Pegunungan **39 D4**
Kapuas Hulu Ra. = Kapuas Hulu, Pegunungan **39 D4**
Kapunda **62 B2**
Kapuni **64 C6**
Kaputar, Mt. **63 B5**
Kara **28 C7**
Kara Bogaz Gol, Zaliv = Garabogazköl Aylagy **29 E6**

Kara Kalpak Republic = Qoraqalpoghistan □ **29 E6**
Kara Kum = Garagum **29 F6**
Kara Sea **28 B8**
Karabiğa **23 D6**
Karabük **46 B3**
Karaburun **23 E6**
Karabutak = Qarabutaq **29 E7**
Karacabey **23 D7**
Karacasu **23 F7**
Karachi **43 G5**
Karad **43 L9**
Karaganda = Qaraghandy **29 E8**
Karagayly = Qaraghayly **29 E8**
Karaikal **43 P11**
Karaikkudi **43 P11**
Karakalpakstan = Qoraqalpoghistan □ **29 E6**
Karakas **29 E9**
Karakelong **36 D3**
Karakitang **37 D3**
Karakol **29 E8**
Karakoram Pass **42 B10**
Karakoram Ra. **42 B10**
Karalon **30 D9**
Karaman **46 C3**
Karamay **34 B3**
Karambu **39 E5**
Karamea Bight **65 D4**
Karasburg **58 D3**
Karasino **28 C9**
Karasuk **29 D8**
Karatau, Khrebet = Qarataü **29 E7**
Karatsu **33 G2**
Karawanken **20 A5**
Karazhal = Qarazhal **29 E8**
Karbalā' **47 D6**
Karcag **16 E5**
Karditsa **23 E3**
Karelia □ **8 C12**
Karelian Republic = Karelia □ **8 C12**
Karg‌nrüd **46 C7**
Kargasok **29 D9**
Kargat **29 D9**
Kargil **42 B10**
Kariba, L. **59 B5**
Kariba Dam **59 B5**
Kariba Gorge **59 B5**
Karimata, Kepulauan **39 E3**
Karimata, Selat **39 E3**
Karimata Is. = Karimata, Kepulauan **39 E3**
Karimnagar **43 K11**
Karimunjawa, Kepulauan **39 F4**
Karin **49 E4**
Karkaralinsk = Qarqaraly **29 E8**
Karkinitska Zatoka **25 D3**
Karkinitskiy Zaliv = Karkinitska Zatoka **25 D3**

Karkük = Kirkük **46 D6**
Karlovac **20 B5**
Karlovo **22 C5**
Karlovy Vary **16 C1**
Karlsbad = Karlovy Vary **16 C1**
Karlskrona **9 D9**
Karlsruhe **14 D5**
Karlstad **9 D8**
Karnal **42 E10**
Karnali → **40 C3**
Karnaphuli Res. = Kaptai L. **41 F9**
Karnataka □ **43 N10**
Kärnten □ **15 E7**
Karonga **57 F6**
Karoonda **62 C2**
Karora **55 E6**
Karpathos **23 G6**
Kars **25 E5**
Karsakpay **29 E7**
Karshi = Qarshi **29 F7**
Karsun **24 C6**
Karufa **37 E4**
Karungu **57 E6**
Karviná **16 D4**
Karwar **43 M9**
Kasai → **56 E3**
Kasama **57 G6**
Kasandra Kolpos **23 D4**
Kasaragod **43 N9**
Kasba L. **68 B9**
Kasempa **59 A5**
Kasenga **57 G5**
Käshän **44 C2**
Kashgar = Kashi **34 C2**
Kashi **34 C2**
Kashk-e Kohneh **42 B3**
Käshmar **44 C4**
Kashun Noerh = Gaxun Nur **34 B5**
Kasimov **24 C5**
Kasiruta **37 E3**
Kasongo **57 E5**
Kasongo Lunda **56 F3**
Kasos **37 E4**
Kassalâ **55 E6**
Kassel **14 C5**
Kastamonu **25 E3**
Kasur **42 D9**
Katanga □ **57 F4**
Katangi **43 J11**
Katerini **23 D4**
Katha **41 E11**
Kathiawar **43 H7**
Kathmandu = Katmandu **40 D5**
Katihar **40 E6**
Katima Mulilo **58 B4**
Katingan = Mendawai → **39 E4**
Katiola **53 G4**
Katmandu **40 D5**
Katoomba **63 B5**
Katowice **16 C4**
Katsina **53 F7**
Kattegat **9 D8**
Kaua'i **78 G11**
Kaunas **24 C1**
Kavala **22 D5**

Kavalerovo **32 A4**
Kavīr, Dasht-e **44 C3**
Kaw **92 B3**
Kawagoe **33 F6**
Kawaguchi **33 F6**
Kawardha **40 G3**
Kawasaki **33 F6**
Kawasi **37 E3**
Kawawachikamach **71 D7**
Kawerau **64 C7**
Kawhia **64 C6**
Kawhia Harbour **64 C6**
Kawio, Kepulauan **36 D3**
Kawnro **41 F12**
Kawthoolei = Kayin □ **41 H11**
Kawthule = Kayin □ **41 H11**
Kaya **53 F5**
Kayah □ **41 H11**
Kayan → **39 D5**
Kayeli **37 E3**
Kayes **53 F3**
Kayin □ **41 H11**
Kayoa **37 D3**
Kayrunnera **62 B3**
Kayseri **46 C3**
Kazachye **31 B11**
Kazakhstan ■ **29 E7**
Kazan **24 B6**
Kazanlŭk **22 C5**
Kazatin = Kozyatyn **17 D9**
Käzerün **44 D2**
Kazym → **28 C7**
Kea **23 F5**
Kebnekaise **8 B9**
Kebri Dehar **49 F3**
Kecskemét **16 E4**
Kediri **39 F4**
Keelung = Chilung **35 D7**
Keetmanshoop **58 D3**
Kefalonia **23 E3**
Kefamenanu **37 F2**
Keffi **53 G7**
Keflavík **8 C1**
Keighley **11 E6**
Keimoes **58 D4**
Keith **62 C3**
Kekri **42 G9**
Kël **30 C10**
Kelang = Klang **39 D2**
Kells = Ceanannus Mor **11 E3**
Kelowna **69 D8**
Kelso **65 F3**
Keluang = Kluang **39 D2**
Kem **28 C4**
Kema **37 D3**
Kemah **46 C4**
Kemerovo **29 D9**
Kemi **8 B10**
Kemi älv = Kemijoki → **8 B10**
Kemi träsk = Kemijärvi **8 B11**
Kemijärvi **8 B11**
Kemijoki → **8 B10**
Kemp Land **96 A9**
Kempsey **63 B5**
Kempten **14 E6**

Kendal 39 F4
Kendall 63 B5
Kendari 37 E2
Kendawangan 39 E4
Kendrapara 40 G6
Kenema 53 G3
Keng Tawng 41 G12
Keng Tung 41 G12
Kenitra 52 B4
Kennedy, Mt. 41 F9
Kennewick 72 C4
Kenogami → 71 D5
Kenosha 76 C2
Kent Group 62 C4
Kent Pen. 68 B9
Kentaū 29 E7
Kentucky □ 76 F3
Kentville 71 D7
Kenya ■ 57 D7
Kenya, Mt. 57 E7
Kepi 37 F5
Kerala □ 43 P10
Kerang 62 C3
Kerch 25 D4
Kericho 57 E7
Kerinci 39 E2
Kerki = Atamyrat 29 F7
Kerkyra 23 E2
Kermadec Is. 64 M13
Kermadec Trench 65 N13
Kermān 44 D4
Kermān □ 44 D4
Kermānshāh 46 D6
Kerrobert 69 C9
Kerulen → 35 B6
Kerzaz 52 C5
Keşan 22 D6
Kesennuma 32 D7
Kestenga 28 C4
Ket → 29 D9
Ketapang 39 E4
Ketchikan 69 C6
Kętrzyn 16 A4
Key West 86 B3
Khabarovo 28 C7
Khabarovsk 31 E11
Khābūr → 46 D5
Khairpur 42 F6
Khakassia □ 30 D6
Khalkhāl 46 C7
Khalkís = Halkida 23 E4
Khalmer Yu 28 C7
Khalturin 24 B6
Khalūf 49 D9
Khambhat 43 H8
Khambhat, G. of 43 J8
Khamir 49 D9
Khānābād 45 B7
Khānaqīn 46 D6
Khandwa 43 J10
Khanewal 42 D7
Khaniá = Chania 23 G5
Khanka, L. 32 A3
Khankendy = Xankändi 25 F6
Khanty-Mansiysk 29 C7
Khapcheranga 30 E9
Kharagpur 40 F6
Kharan Kalat 42 E4
Kharānaq 44 C3

Kharda 43 K9
Kharg = Khārk, Jazīreh-ye 47 E7
Khârga, El Wâhât-el 54 C5
Khargon 43 J9
Khārk, Jazīreh-ye 47 E7
Kharkiv 24 D4
Kharkov = Kharkiv 24 D4
Kharovsk 24 B5
Kharta 22 D7
Khartoum = El Khartûm 55 E5
Khasan 32 B2
Khāsh 42 E2
Khaskovo 22 D5
Khatanga 30 B8
Khatanga → 30 B8
Khaybar, Ḥarrat 47 F5
Khed Brahma 43 G8
Khemmarat 38 A3
Khenchela 52 A7
Kherson 25 D3
Kheta → 30 B8
Khilok 30 D9
Khíos = Hios 23 E6
Khiuma = Hiiumaa 24 B1
Khiva 29 E7
Khīyāv 46 C6
Khmelnik 17 D8
Khmelnitskiy = Khmelnytskyy 17 D8
Khmelnytskyy 17 D8
Khmer Rep. = Cambodia ■ 38 B3
Khodoriv 17 D7
Khodzent = Khüjand 29 E7
Khojak Pass 42 D5
Kholm Afghan. 45 B6
Kholm Russia 24 B3
Khomeyn 44 C2
Khon Kaen 38 A2
Khorat = Nakhon Ratchasima 38 B2
Khorramābād 46 D7
Khorrāmshahr 47 E7
Khotyn 17 D8
Khouribga 52 B4
Khowst 42 C6
Khoyniki 17 C9
Khu Khan 38 B2
Khudzhand = Khüjand 29 E7
Khūgīānī 42 D4
Khüjand 29 E7
Khulna 41 F7
Khulna □ 41 F7
Khūr 44 C4
Khurayş 47 F7
Khush 42 C3
Khushab 42 C8
Khuzdar 42 F5
Khvor 44 C3
Khvormūj 44 D2
Khvoy 46 C6
Khyber Pass 42 B7
Kiama 63 B5
Kiamba 36 C2

Kiangsi = Jiangxi □ 35 D6
Kiangsu = Jiangsu □ 35 C6
Kibombo 57 E5
Kibrıs = Cyprus ■ 46 D3
Kibwezi 57 E7
Kicking Horse Pass 69 C8
Kidal 53 E6
Kidnappers, C. 64 C7
Kiel 14 A6
Kiel Canal = Nord-Ostsee-Kanal 14 A5
Kielce 16 C5
Kieler Bucht 14 A6
Kiev = Kyyiv 17 C10
Kiffa 53 E3
Kifrī 46 D6
Kigali 57 E6
Kigoma-Ujiji 57 E5
Kihee 62 A3
Kii-Sanchi 33 F5
Kikinda 22 B3
Kikládhes = Cyclades 23 F5
Kikwit 56 E3
Kilcoy 63 A5
Kilimanjaro 57 E7
Kilis 46 C4
Kiliya 17 F9
Kilkenny 11 E3
Kilkis 23 D4
Killarney Australia 63 A5
Killarney Ireland 11 E2
Killeen 80 D5
Killini 23 F4
Kilmarnock 10 D4
Kilmore 63 C3
Kilosa 57 F7
Kilrush 11 E2
Kilwa Kivinje 57 F7
Kimaam 37 F5
Kimba 62 B2
Kimberley Australia 60 D4
Kimberley S. Africa 58 D4
Kimmirut 70 C7
Kimry 24 B4
Kinabalu, Gunung 38 C5
Kindia 53 F3
Kindu 57 E5
Kineshma 24 B5
King George B. 95 G4
King George I. 96 A4
King George Is. 71 D5
King I. = Kadan Kyun 38 B1
King I. 62 C3
King William I. 68 B10
Kingait = Cape Dorset 70 C6
Kingaok = Bathurst Inlet 68 B9
Kingaroy 63 A5
Kingoonya 62 B2
Kings Canyon △ 78 B3
King's Lynn 11 E7
Kingscote 62 C2
Kingsport 83 A6
Kingston Canada 71 E6
Kingston Jamaica 86 C4
Kingston N.Z. 65 F3

Kingston South East 62 C2
Kingston upon Hull 11 E6
Kingstown 87 D7
Kingsville 80 F5
Kınık 23 E6
Kinkala 56 E2
Kinleith 64 C6
Kinsale 11 F2
Kinsha = Chang Jiang → 35 C7
Kinshasa 56 E3
Kinston 83 B9
Kiparissia 23 F3
Kiparissiakos Kolpos 23 F3
Kipushi 59 A5
Kirghizia = Kyrgyzstan ■ 29 E8
Kiribati ■ 64 K12
Kırıkkale 25 F3
Kirillov 24 B4
Kirin = Jilin 35 B7
Kirinyaga = Kenya, Mt. 57 E7
Kiritimati 65 J15
Kirkcaldy 10 C5
Kirkcudbright 11 D4
Kirkee 43 K8
Kirkland Lake 71 E5
Kırklareli 22 D6
Kirkük 46 D6
Kirkwall 10 B5
Kirov 28 D5
Kirovabad = Gäncä 25 E6
Kirovograd = Kirovohrad 25 D3
Kirovohrad 25 D3
Kirovsk = Babadayhan 29 F7
Kirovskiy 32 A3
Kirsanov 24 C5
Kırşehir 25 F3
Kirthar Range 42 F5
Kiruna 8 B10
Kiryū 33 E6
Kisangani 57 D5
Kisar 37 F3
Kiselevsk 29 D9
Kishanganj 40 D7
Kishangarh 42 F7
Kishb, Ḥarrat al 47 G5
Kishinev = Chişinău 17 E9
Kishtwar 42 C9
Kisii 57 E6
Kiskőrös 16 E4
Kiskunfélegyháza 16 E4
Kiskunhalas 16 E4
Kislovodsk 25 E5
Kismayu = Chisimaio 49 H3
Kiso-Gawa → 33 F5
Kissidougou 53 G3
Kisumu 57 E6
Kita 53 F4
Kitaibaraki 33 E7
Kitakyūshū 33 G2
Kitale 57 D7
Kitami 32 B8
Kitchener 71 E5

Kitega = Gitega 57 E5
Kithira = Kythira 23 F4
Kithnos 23 E5
Kitikmeot □ 68 B9
Kittakittaooloo, L. 62 A2
Kitui 57 E7
Kitwe 59 A5
Kivertsi 17 C7
Kivu, L. 57 E5
Kiyev = Kyyiv 17 C10
Kiyevskoye Vdkhr. =
  Kyyivske Vdskh. 17 C10
Kızıl Irmak → 25 E4
Kizlyar 25 E6
Kizyl-Arvat = Serdar 29 F6
Kladno 16 C2
Klagenfurt 15 E8
Klaipėda 24 B1
Klamath Falls 72 E3
Klamath Mts. 72 F2
Klang 39 D2
Klarälven → 9 C8
Klatovy 16 D1
Klerksdorp 59 D5
Kletsk = Klyetsk 17 B8
Kłodzko 16 C3
Klondike 68 B6
Klouto 53 G4
Kluane L. 68 B6
Kluang 39 D2
Kluczbork 16 C4
Klyetsk 17 B8
Knossos 23 G5
Knox Coast 96 A12
Knoxville 83 B6
Koartac = Quaqtaq 70 C7
Koba 37 F4
Kobarid 20 A4
Köbe 33 F4
København 9 D8
Koblenz 14 C4
Kobroor 37 F4
Kobryn 17 B7
Kocaeli 25 E2
Kočani 22 D4
Koch Bihar 41 D7
Kochi = Cochin 43 Q10
Kōchi 33 G3
Kochiu = Gejiu 34 D5
Kodiak 69 C4
Kodiak I. 69 C4
Kofiau 37 E3
Koforidua 53 G5
Kōfu 33 F6
Kogan 63 A5
Kohat 42 C7
Kohima 41 E10
Kohkīlūyeh va Būyer
  Aḥmadī □ 44 D2
Kohler Ra. 96 B1
Kokand = Qŭqon 29 E8
Kokas 37 E4
Kokchetav = Kökshetaū
  29 D7
Koko Kyunzu 41 K9
Kokomo 76 D2
Kökshetaū 29 D7
Koksoak → 70 D7
Kokstad 59 E5
Kola 37 F4

Kola Pen. = Kolskiy
  Poluostrov 8 B13
Kolaka 37 E2
Kolar 43 N11
Kolar Gold Fields 43 N11
Kolayat 42 F8
Kolepom = Dolak, Pulau
  37 F5
Kolguyev, Ostrov 28 C5
Kolhapur 43 L9
Kolín 16 C2
Kolkata 41 F7
Kollam = Quilon 43 Q10
Köln 14 C4
Kolo 16 B4
Kołobrzeg 16 A2
Kolomna 24 B4
Kolomyya 17 D7
Kolonodale 37 E2
Kolosib 41 E9
Kolpashevo 29 D9
Kolpino 24 B3
Kolskiy Poluostrov 8 B13
Kolwezi 57 G5
Kolyma → 31 C13
Komatsu 33 E5
Komi □ 28 C6
Kommunarsk = Alchevsk
  25 D4
Kommunizma, Pik = imeni
  Ismail Samani, Pik
  29 F8
Komodo 37 F1
Komoran, Pulau 37 F5
Komotini 22 D5
Kompong Cham 38 B3
Kompong Chhnang =
  Kampong Chhnang
  38 B2
Kompong Som =
  Kampong Saom 38 B2
Komrat = Comrat 17 E9
Komsomolets, Ostrov
  30 A7
Kon Tum 38 B3
Konar = 42 B7
Konch 42 G11
Kondoa 57 E7
Kondoz 45 B7
Kondoz □ 45 B7
Köneürgench 29 E6
Kong 53 G5
Kong, Koh 38 B2
Konglu 41 D11
Kongolo 57 F5
Konin 16 B4
Konjic 20 C6
Konosha 28 C5
Konotop 24 C3
Konqi He → 34 B4
Końskie 16 C5
Konstanz 14 E5
Kontagora 53 F7
Konya 46 C3
Konya Ovası 46 C3
Kooloonong 62 B3
Koonibba 62 B1
Koorawatha 63 B4
Kootenay L. 69 D8
Kopaonik 22 C3

Koper 20 B4
Kopi 62 B2
Koprivnica 20 A6
Kopychyntsi 17 D7
Korab 22 D3
Korçë 23 D3
Korčula 20 C6
Kordestan = Kurdistan
  46 D5
Kordestān □ 46 D6
Kordofân 55 F4
Korea, North ■ 35 C7
Korea, South ■ 35 C7
Korea Bay 35 C7
Korea Strait 35 C7
Korets 17 C8
Korhogo 53 G4
Korinthiakos Kolpos 23 E4
Korinthos 23 F4
Kōriyama 33 E7
Korneshty = Corneşti
  17 E9
Koro 53 G4
Korogwe 57 F7
Koror = Melekeok 36 C4
Körös → 16 E5
Korosten 17 C9
Korostyshev 17 C9
Kortrijk 14 C2
Kos 23 F6
Kościan 16 B3
Kosciuszko, Mt. 63 C4
Kosha 54 D5
K'oshih = Kashi 34 C2
Koshiki-Rettō 33 H1
Košice 16 D5
Kosovo ■ 22 C3
Kosovska Mitrovica 22 C3
Kôstî 55 F5
Kostopil 17 C8
Kostroma 24 B5
Kostrzyn 16 B2
Koszalin 16 A3
Kota 43 G9
Kota Belud 38 C5
Kota Bharu 38 C2
Kota Kinabalu 38 C5
Kota Kubu Bharu 39 D2
Kota Tinggi 39 D2
Kotaagung 39 F2
Kotabaru 39 E5
Kotabumi 39 E2
Kotamobagu 37 D2
Kotelnich 24 B6
Kotelnyy, Ostrov 31 B11
Kotka 9 C11
Kotlas 28 C5
Kotor 22 C2
Kotovsk 17 E9
Kotri 42 G6
Kotturu 43 M10
Kotuy → 30 B8
Kotzebue 69 B3
Koudougou 53 F5
Kouilou → 56 E2
Koula Moutou 56 E2
Koulen = Kulen 38 B2
Koumra 55 G2
Kounradskiy 29 E8
Kousséri 55 F1

Kouvola 8 C11
Kovel 17 C7
Kovrov 24 B5
Koyampattur =
  Coimbatore 43 P10
Köyceğiz 23 F7
Kozan 46 C3
Kozani 23 D3
Kozhikode = Calicut 43 P9
Kozyatyn 17 D9
Kra, Isthmus of = Kra, Kho
  Khot 38 B1
Kra, Kho Khot 38 B1
Kracheh 38 B3
Kragujevac 22 B3
Krajina 20 B6
Krakatau = Rakata, Pulau
  39 F3
Krakatoa = Rakata, Pulau
  39 F3
Kraków 16 C4
Kraljevo 22 C3
Kramatorsk 25 D4
Kranj 20 A5
Kraśnik 16 C6
Krasnoarmeysk 29 D5
Krasnodar 25 D4
Krasnoperekopsk 25 D3
Krasnoselkup 28 C9
Krasnoturinsk 28 D7
Krasnoyarsk 30 D7
Krasnyy Luch 25 D4
Krasnyy Yar 25 D6
Krefeld 14 C4
Kremen 20 B5
Kremenchuk 24 D3
Kremenchuksk Vdskh.
  24 D3
Kremenets 17 C7
Krems 15 D8
Kribi 56 D1
Krichev = Krychaw 17 B10
Krishna → 40 K3
Krishnanagar 41 F7
Kristiansand 9 D7
Kristiansund 8 C7
Kriti 23 G5
Krivoy Rog = Kryvyy Rih
  25 D3
Krk 20 B5
Kronprins Olav Kyst 96 A9
Kronshtad 24 B2
Kroonstad 59 D5
Kropotkin Irkutsk, Russia
  30 D9
Kropotkin Krasnodar,
  Russia 25 D5
Krotoszyn 16 C3
Krung Thep = Bangkok
  38 B2
Krupki 17 A9
Kruševac 22 C3
Krychaw 17 B10
Krymskiy Poluostrov =
  Krymskyy Pivostriv
  25 D3
Krymskyy Pivostriv 25 D3
Kryvyy Rih 25 D3

Ksar el Kebir **52 B4**
Ksar es Souk = Er
  Rachidia **52 B5**
Kuala Lipis **39 D2**
Kuala Lumpur **39 D2**
Kuala Sepetang **38 D2**
Kuala Terengganu **38 C2**
Kualajelai **39 E4**
Kualakapuas **39 E4**
Kualakurun **39 E4**
Kualapembuang **39 E4**
Kualasimpang **39 D1**
Kuandang **37 D2**
Kuangchou = Guangzhou
  35 D6
Kuantan **39 D2**
Kuba = Quba **25 E6**
Kuban ➤ **25 D4**
Kuching **39 D4**
Kucing = Kuching **39 D4**
Kuda **43 H7**
Kudat **38 C5**
Kudymkar **28 D6**
Kueiyang = Guiyang
  35 D5
Kufra Oasis = Al Kufrah
  54 D3
Kufstein **15 E7**
Kugaaruk = Pelly Bay
  70 C5
Kugluktuk **68 B8**
Küh-e 'Alijūq **44 D2**
Küh-e Sorkh **44 C4**
Kühak **42 F3**
Kühhā-ye-Bashākerd
  45 E4
Kühpāyeh **44 C3**
Kuito **58 A3**
Kuji **32 C7**
Kukës **22 C3**
Kula **23 E7**
Kulasekarappattinam
  43 Q11
Kulen **38 B2**
Külob **29 F7**
Kulsary **29 E6**
Kulunda **29 D8**
Kulwin **62 C3**
Kulyab = Külob **29 F7**
Kum Tekei **29 E8**
Kumagaya **33 E6**
Kumai **39 E4**
Kumamba, Kepulauan
  37 E5
Kumamoto **33 G2**
Kumanovo **22 C3**
Kumara **65 E4**
Kumasi **53 G5**
Kumba **53 H7**
Kumbakonam **43 P11**
Kumbarilla **63 A5**
Kumon Bum **41 D11**
Kunama **63 C4**
Kungala **63 A5**
Kungrad = Qŭngirot
  29 E6
Kungur **29 D6**
Kunlong **41 F12**
Kunlun Shan **34 C3**
Kunming **34 D5**

Kunya-Urgench =
  Köneürgench **29 E6**
Kuopio **8 C11**
Kupa ➤ **20 B6**
Kuqa **34 B3**
Kür ➤ **25 E6**
Kura = Kür ➤ **25 E6**
Kurdistan **46 D5**
Kürdzhali **22 D5**
Kure **33 F3**
Kurgaldzhinskiy **29 D8**
Kurgan **29 D7**
Kuria Maria Is. =
  Hallāniyat, Jazā'ir al
  49 D6
Kurigram **41 E7**
Kuril Is. = Kurilskiye
  Ostrova **31 E12**
Kurilskiye Ostrova **31 E12**
Kurnool **43 L11**
Kurow **65 F4**
Kurri Kurri **63 B5**
Kursk **24 C4**
Kuruktag **34 B3**
Kuruman **58 D4**
Kurume **33 G2**
Kus Gölü **23 D6**
Kuşadası **23 F6**
Kushimoto **33 G4**
Kushiro **32 B9**
Kushtia **41 F7**
Kuskokwim B. **69 C3**
Kustanay = Qostanay
  29 D7
Kütahya **25 F3**
Kutaisi **25 E5**
Kutaraja = Banda Aceh
  38 C1
Kutch, Gulf of = Kachchh,
  Gulf of **43 H6**
Kutch, Rann of = Kachchh,
  Rann of **43 G6**
Kutno **16 B4**
Kutu **56 E3**
Kutum **55 F3**
Kuujjuaq **70 D7**
Kuujjuarapik **71 D6**
Kuusamo **8 B11**
Kuwait = Al Kuwayt **47 E7**
Kuwait ■ **47 E6**
Kuybyshev = Samara
  24 C7
Kuybyshev **29 D8**
Kuybyshevskoye Vdkhr.
  24 B6
Kuyumba **30 C7**
Kuzey Anadolu Dağları
  25 E4
Kuznetsk **24 C6**
Kvarner **20 B5**
Kvarnerič **20 B5**
Kwajalein **64 J11**
Kwakoegron **92 A2**
KwaMashu **59 D5**
Kwando ➤ **58 B4**
Kwangchow = Guangzhou
  35 D6
Kwango ➤ **56 E3**
Kwangsi-Chuang =
  Guangxi Zhuangzu
  Zizhiqu □ **35 D5**

Kwangtung =
  Guangdong □ **35 D6**
Kwatisore **37 E4**
KwaZulu Natal □ **59 D6**
Kweichow = Guizhou □
  35 D5
Kwekwe **59 B5**
Kwidzyn **16 B4**
Kwoka **37 E4**
Kyabra Cr. ➤ **63 A3**
Kyabram **63 C4**
Kyancutta **62 B2**
Kyaukpadaung **41 G10**
Kyaukpyu **41 H9**
Kyaukse **41 G11**
Kyneton **63 C3**
Kyō-ga-Saki **33 F4**
Kyoga, L. **57 D6**
Kyogle **63 A5**
Kyonpyaw **41 J10**
Kyōto **33 F4**
Kypros = Cyprus ■ **46 D3**
Kyrenia **46 D3**
Kyrgyzstan ■ **29 E8**
Kyrtylakh **31 C10**
Kystatyam **30 C10**
Kythira **23 F4**
Kyunhla **41 F10**
Kyūshū **33 G2**
Kyustendil **22 C4**
Kyusyur **30 B10**
Kyyiv **17 C10**
Kyyivske Vdskh. **17 C10**
Kyzyl Kum **29 E7**
Kyzyl-Kyya **29 E8**
Kyzyl-Orda = Qyzylorda
  29 E7

L

La Alcarria **19 B4**
La Asunción **90 A6**
La Banda **94 B3**
La Carlota **94 C4**
La Ceiba **85 D7**
La Cocha **94 B3**
La Coruña = A Coruña
  18 A1
La Crosse **75 D9**
La Estrada = A Estrada
  18 A1
La Grande ➤ **71 D6**
La Grange **82 C3**
La Guaira **90 A5**
La Habana **86 B3**
La Línea de la Concepción
  18 D3
La Mancha **19 C4**
La Palma **52 C2**
La Palma del Condado
  18 D2
La Paragua **90 B6**
La Paz Entre Ríos,
  Argentina **94 C5**
La Paz San Luis, Argentina
  94 C3
La Paz Bolivia **91 G5**
La Paz Mexico **84 C2**
La Pedrera **90 D5**
La Plata **94 D5**

La Quiaca **94 A3**
La Rioja **94 B3**
La Rioja □ **19 A4**
La Robla **18 A3**
La Roche-sur-Yon **12 C3**
La Rochelle **12 C3**
La Roda **19 C4**
La Romana **87 C6**
La Serena **94 B2**
La Seu d'Urgell **19 A6**
La Seyne-sur-Mer **13 E6**
La Spézia **13 D8**
La Tortuga **87 D6**
La Tuque **71 E6**
La Unión **95 E2**
La Urbana **90 B5**
La Vall d'Uixó **19 C5**
La Vega **87 C5**
Laas Caanood = Las Anod
  49 F4
Labe = Elbe ➤ **14 B5**
Labé **53 F3**
Laboulaye **94 C4**
Labrador **71 D7**
Labrador City **71 D7**
Labrador Sea **70 D8**
Lábrea **91 E6**
Labuan **38 C5**
Labuan, Pulau **38 C5**
Labuha **37 E3**
Labuhanbajo **37 F2**
Labuk, Teluk **38 C5**
Labyrinth, L. **62 B2**
Labytnangi **28 C7**
Lac La Biche **69 C8**
Lac la Martre = Wha Ti
  68 B8
Lacanau **12 D3**
Laccadive Is. =
  Lakshadweep Is. **26 G9**
Lacepede B. **62 C2**
Lachlan ➤ **63 B3**
Lacombe **69 C8**
Ladakh Ra. **42 B10**
Lādīz **45 D5**
Ladoga, L. = Ladozhskoye
  Ozero **8 C12**
Ladozhskoye Ozero **8 C12**
Ladysmith **59 D5**
Lae **61 B8**
Lafayette **81 D7**
Lafia **53 G7**
Laghmān □ **45 C7**
Laghouat **52 B6**
Lagonoy G. **36 B2**
Lagos Nigeria **53 G6**
Lagos Portugal **18 D1**
Laguna **94 B7**
Lagunas **90 E3**
Lahad Datu **36 C1**
Lahad Datu, Telok **36 D1**
Lahat **39 E2**
Lahewa **39 D1**
Lāhījān **46 C7**
Lahn ➤ **14 C4**
Lahore **42 D9**
Lahti **8 C11**
Lahtis = Lahti **8 C11**
Laï **55 G2**
Laidley **63 A5**

Laila = Layla **47 G6**
Lairg **10 B4**
Laizhou **35 C6**
Lajes **94 B6**
Lake Cargelligo **63 B4**
Lake Charles **81 D7**
Lake City **83 D6**
Lake Harbour = Kimmirut **70 C7**
Lake Worth **83 F7**
Lakeland **83 E7**
Lakes Entrance **63 C4**
Lakewood **76 D5**
Lakhnau = Lucknow **40 D3**
Lakonikos Kolpos **23 F4**
Lakor **37 F3**
Lakota **53 G4**
Lakshadweep Is. **26 G9**
Lalaghat **41 E9**
L'Albufera **19 C5**
Lalín **18 A1**
Lalitapur **40 D5**
Lamaing **41 K11**
Lamas **91 E3**
Lambaréné **56 E2**
Lambert Glacier **96 B10**
Lamego **18 B2**
Lameroo **62 C3**
Lamia **23 E4**
Lamon B. **36 B2**
Lampa **91 G4**
Lampedusa **21 G4**
Lampione **21 G4**
Lampung □ **39 F2**
Lamu **57 E8**
Lāna'i **78 H12**
Lanak La **42 B11**
Lanak'o Shank'ou = Lanak La **42 B11**
Lancaster *U.K.* **11 D5**
Lancaster *U.S.A.* **77 D7**
Lancaster Sd. **70 B5**
Lanchow = Lanzhou **35 C5**
Lanciano **20 C5**
Landeck **14 E6**
Landes **12 D3**
Landi Kotal **42 B7**
Land's End **11 F4**
Landshut **15 D7**
La'nga Co **40 B3**
Langjökull **8 C2**
Langkawi, Pulau **38 C1**
Langkon **36 B5**
Langreo **18 A3**
Langres **13 C6**
Langres, Plateau de **13 C6**
Langsa **38 D1**
Languedoc **13 E5**
Lannion **12 B2**
Lansdowne **63 B5**
Lansing **75 D4**
Lanusei **21 E2**
Lanzarote **52 C3**
Lanzhou **35 C5**
Laoag **36 A2**
Laoang **36 B3**
Laohekou **35 C6**
Laon **13 B5**

Laos ■ **38 A3**
Laparan **36 C1**
Lapland = Lappland **8 B10**
Lappland **8 B10**
Lapseki **23 D6**
Laptev Sea **30 B10**
L'Áquila **20 C4**
Lär **44 E3**
Laramie **74 E2**
Larantuka **37 F2**
Larap **36 B2**
Larat **37 F4**
Lariang **37 E1**
Larisa **23 E4**
Larnaca **46 D3**
Larne **11 D4**
Larrimah **60 D5**
Larsen Ice Shelf **96 A3**
Larvik **9 D8**
Laryak **29 C8**
Las Anod **49 F4**
Las Cruces **79 D9**
Las Flores **94 D5**
Las Lajas **94 D2**
Las Lomitas **94 A4**
Las Palmas **52 C2**
Las Plumas **95 E3**
Las Varillas **94 C4**
Las Vegas **78 B5**
Lash-e Joveyn **42 D2**
Lashio **41 F11**
Lassen Pk. **72 F3**
Lastoursville **56 E2**
Lastovo **20 C6**
Latacunga **90 D3**
Latakia = Al Lādhiqīyah **46 D3**
Latina **20 D4**
Latium = Lazio □ **20 C4**
Latrobe **62 D4**
Latvia ■ **24 B1**
Lauchhammer **15 C7**
Launceston **62 D4**
Laurel **81 D9**
Lauria **21 D5**
Lausanne **14 E4**
Laut **38 D3**
Laut Kecil, Kepulauan **39 E5**
Laval **12 B3**
Lavrio **23 F5**
Lawas **38 D5**
Lawele **37 F2**
Lawng Pit **41 E11**
Lawrence *N.Z.* **65 F3**
Lawrence *U.S.A.* **75 F7**
Lawton **80 B4**
Layla **47 G6**
Lazio □ **20 C4**
Lazo **32 B3**
Le Creusot **13 C6**
Le Havre **12 B4**
Le Mans **12 C4**
Le Mont-St-Michel **12 B3**
Le Puy-en-Velay **13 D5**
Le Touquet-Paris-Plage **12 A4**
Le Tréport **12 A4**
Le Verdon-sur-Mer **12 D3**

Leamington Spa = Royal Leamington Spa **11 E6**
Leavenworth **75 F7**
Lebak **36 C2**
Lebanon ■ **46 D3**
Lębork **16 A3**
Lebrija **18 D2**
Lebu **94 D2**
Lecce **21 D7**
Lecco **13 D8**
Lech ➤ **14 D6**
Łęczyca **16 B4**
Leeds **11 E6**
Leer **14 B4**
Leeton **63 B4**
Leeuwarden **14 B3**
Leeuwin, C. **60 G2**
Leeward Is. **87 C7**
Lefkada **23 E3**
Leganés **18 B4**
Legazpi **36 B2**
Leghorn = Livorno **20 C3**
Legionowo **16 B5**
Legnago **20 B3**
Legnica **16 C3**
Legume **63 A5**
Leh **42 B10**
Leicester **11 E6**
Leiden **14 B3**
Leie ➤ **14 C2**
Leine ➤ **14 B5**
Leinster □ **11 E3**
Leipzig **15 C7**
Leiria **18 C1**
Leitrim **11 D2**
Leizhou Bandao **35 D6**
Leleque **95 E2**
Léman, L. **13 C7**
Lemhi Ra. **73 D7**
Lena ➤ **30 B10**
Leninogorsk **29 D9**
Leninsk **25 D6**
Leninsk-Kuznetskiy **29 D9**
Lenmalu **37 E4**
Lens **13 A5**
Lentini **21 F5**
Leoben **15 E8**
Leodhas = Lewis **10 B3**
León *Mexico* **84 C4**
León *Nic.* **85 E7**
León *Spain* **18 A3**
León, Montes de **18 A2**
Leongatha **63 C4**
Leova **17 E9**
Lepel = Lyepyel **24 C2**
Lepikha **31 C10**
Lérida = Lleida **19 B6**
Lerwick **10 A6**
Les Cayes **86 C5**
Les Sables-d'Olonne **12 C3**
Lesbos **23 E6**
Leskovac **22 C3**
Lesotho ■ **59 D5**
Lesosibirsk **32 A3**
Lesozavodsk **32 A3**
Lesser Antilles **87 D7**
Lesser Sunda Is. **37 F2**
Lésvos = Lesbos **23 E6**
Leszno **16 C3**
Lethbridge **69 D8**

Leti, Kepulauan **37 F3**
Leti Is. = Leti, Kepulauan **37 F3**
Leticia **90 D4**
Letpadan **41 J10**
Letpan **41 H10**
Letterkenny **11 D3**
Leuser, G. **39 D1**
Leuven **14 C3**
Levanger **8 C8**
Levin **64 D6**
Lévis **71 E6**
Levka Oros **23 G5**
Levkás = Lefkada **23 E3**
Levkôsia = Nicosia **46 D3**
Levskigrad = Karlovo **22 C5**
Lewis **10 B3**
Lewisporte **71 E8**
Lewiston *Idaho, U.S.A.* **72 C5**
Lewiston *Maine, U.S.A.* **77 B10**
Lexington *Ky., U.S.A.* **76 E3**
Lexington *N.C., U.S.A.* **83 B7**
Leyte □ **36 B2**
Lezhë **22 D2**
Lhasa **34 D4**
Lhazê **34 D3**
Lhokkruet **38 D1**
Lhokseumawe **38 C1**
L'Hospitalet de Llobregat **19 B7**
Liancourt Rocks **33 E2**
Lianga **36 C3**
Lianyungang **35 C6**
Liaoning □ **35 B7**
Liaoyuan **35 B7**
Liard ➤ **68 B7**
Libau = Liepāja **24 B1**
Libenge **56 D3**
Liberal **80 A3**
Liberec **16 C2**
Liberia ■ **53 G4**
Lībīya, Sahrâ' **54 C4**
Lobobo, Tanjung **37 E3**
Libourne **12 D3**
Libreville **56 D1**
Libya ■ **54 C2**
Libyan Desert = Lībīya, Sahrâ' **54 C4**
Licantén **94 D2**
Licata **21 F4**
Lichinga **59 A7**
Lida **17 B7**
Liechtenstein ■ **14 E5**
Liège **14 C3**
Liegnitz = Legnica **16 C3**
Lienyünchiangshih = Lianyungang **35 C6**
Lienz **15 E7**
Liepāja **24 B1**
Lietuva = Lithuania ■ **24 B1**
Liffey ➤ **11 E3**
Lifford **11 D3**
Lightning Ridge **63 A4**
Liguria □ **13 D8**

Ligurian Sea 20 C2
Lijiang 34 D5
Likasi 57 G5
Lille 13 A5
Lillehammer 8 C8
Lilongwe 59 A6
Liloy 36 C2
Lim → 20 C7
Lima Indonesia 37 E3
Lima Peru 91 F3
Lima U.S.A. 76 D3
Lima → 18 B1
Limassol 46 D3
Limay Mahuida 94 D3
Limbang 38 D5
Limbe 53 H7
Limbri 63 B5
Limburg 14 C5
Limeira 93 G4
Limerick 11 E2
Limfjorden 9 D7
Limia = Lima → 18 B1
Limnos 23 E5
Limoges 12 D4
Limón 86 E3
Limousin □ 12 D4
Limoux 12 E5
Limpopo → 59 D6
Limuru 57 E7
Linares Chile 94 D2
Linares Mexico 84 C5
Linares Spain 18 C4
Lincoln Argentina 94 C4
Lincoln N.Z. 65 E4
Lincoln U.K. 11 E6
Lincoln U.S.A. 75 E6
Linden 90 B7
Lindesnes 9 D7
Lindi 57 F7
Lindos 23 F7
Lingayen 36 A2
Lingayen G. 36 A2
Lingen 14 B4
Lingga 39 E2
Lingga, Kepulauan 39 E2
Lingga Arch. = Lingga,
  Kepulauan 39 E2
Linguère 53 E2
Linhai 35 D7
Linhares 93 F5
Linköping 9 D9
Linosa 21 G4
Lins 93 G4
Linville 63 A5
Linz 15 D8
Lion, G. du 13 E6
Lions, G. of = Lion, G. du
  13 E6
Lipa 36 B2
Lípari 21 E5
Lipari, Is. = Eólie, Ís. 21 E5
Lipcani 17 D8
Lipetsk 24 C4
Lipkany = Lipcani 17 D8
Lipovets 17 D9
Lippe → 14 C4
Liptrap, C. 63 C4
Lira 57 D6
Liria = Lliria 19 C5

Lisala 56 D4
Lisboa 18 C1
Lisbon = Lisboa 18 C1
Lisburn 11 D3
Lisichansk = Lysychansk
  25 D4
Lisieux 12 B4
Liski 24 C4
Lismore 63 A5
Liston 63 A5
Listowel 11 E2
Litani → Lebanon 46 D3
Litani → S. Amer. 30 E
Lithgow 63 B5
Lithino, Akra 23 G5
Lithuania ■ 24 B1
Litoměřice 16 C2
Little Barrier I. 64 B6
Little Khingan Mts. = Xiao
  Hinggan Ling 35 B7
Little Laut Is. = Laut Kecil,
  Kepulauan 39 E5
Little Missouri → 74 B3
Little River 65 E5
Little Rock 81 B7
Little Zab = Zāb aş
  Şaghīr → 46 C5
Liukang Tenggaja =
  Sabalana, Kepulauan
  37 F1
Liuwa Plain 58 A4
Liuzhou 35 D5
Livadia 23 E4
Liverpool Canada 71 E7
Liverpool U.K. 11 E5
Liverpool Plains 63 B5
Liverpool Ra. 63 B5
Livingstone 59 B5
Livny 24 C4
Livorno 20 C3
Ljubljana 20 A5
Llancanelo, Salina 94 D3
Llanelli 11 F4
Llanes 18 A3
Llano Estacado 80 C3
Llanos 90 C4
Lleida 19 B6
Lliria 19 C5
Llobregat → 19 B7
Lloret de Mar 19 B7
Llucmajor 19 C7
Llullaillaco, Volcán 94 A3
Loa → 94 A2
Lobatse 59 D5
Lobería 94 D5
Lobito 58 A2
Locarno 13 C8
Loch Garman = Wexford
  11 E3
Loches 12 C4
Lock 62 B2
Lodhran 42 E7
Lodi Italy 13 D8
Lodi U.S.A. 72 G3
Lodja 56 E4
Lodwar 57 D7
Łódź 16 C4
Lofoten 8 B9
Logan 73 F8

Logan, Mt. 68 B5
Logone → 55 F2
Logroño 19 A4
Lohardaga 40 F5
Loi-kaw 41 H11
Loir → 12 C3
Loire → 12 C2
Loja Ecuador 90 D3
Loja Spain 18 D3
Loji = Kawasi 37 E3
Lokitaung 57 D7
Lokkan tekojärvi 8 B11
Lokoja 53 G7
Lom 22 C4
Lomami → 56 D4
Lomblen 37 F2
Lombok 39 F5
Lomela 56 E4
Lomela → 56 E4
Lomond, L. 10 C4
Lompobatang 37 F1
Londa 43 M9
London Canada 71 E5
London U.K. 11 F6
Londonderry C. 60 C4
Londonderry 11 D3
Londonderry, I. 95 H2
Londrina 94 A6
Long Beach 78 D3
Long I. Bahamas 86 B4
Long I. U.S.A. 77 D9
Long Xuyen 38 B3
Longford Australia 62 D4
Longford Ireland 11 E3
Longiram 39 E5
Longnawan 39 D4
Longreach 61 E7
Longview Tex., U.S.A.
  81 C6
Longview Wash., U.S.A.
  72 C2
Lons-le-Saunier 13 C6
Lop Nor = Lop Nur 34 B4
Lop Nur 34 B4
Lopez, C. 56 E1
Lora → 42 D4
Lora, Hāmūn-i- 42 E4
Lora Cr. → 62 A2
Lora del Río 18 D3
Lorain 76 D4
Loralai 42 D6
Lorca 19 D5
Lord Howe I. 64 N10
Lord Howe Rise 64 N11
Lorestān □ 46 D6
Loreto 92 D4
Lorient 12 C2
Lorne 62 C3
Lorraine □ 13 B7
Los Alamos 79 C9
Los Andes 94 C2
Los Angeles Chile 94 D2
Los Angeles U.S.A. 78 C3
Los Blancos 94 A4

Los Hermanos Is. 90 A6
Los Mochis 84 B3
Los Roques Is. 90 A5
Los Testigos, Is. 90 A6
Los Vilos 94 C2
Lošinj 20 B5
Lot → 12 D4
Lota 94 D2
Loubomo 56 E2
Louga 53 E2
Lougheed I. 70 B3
Louis Trichardt 59 C5
Louis XIV, Pte. 71 D6
Louisiade Arch. 61 C9
Louisiana □ 81 D8
Louisville 76 E3
Loulé 18 D1
Lourdes 12 E3
Louth Australia 63 B4
Louth U.K. 11 E6
Louvain = Leuven 14 C3
Lovech 22 C5
Lowell 77 C10
Lower California = Baja
  California 84 A1
Lower Hutt 65 D6
Lower Saxony =
  Niedersachsen □ 14 B5
Lower Tunguska =
  Tunguska, Nizhnyaya →
  30 C6
Lowestoft 11 E7
Lowgar □ 45 C7
Łowicz 16 B4
Loxton 62 B3
Loyalty Is. = Loyauté, Îs.
  64 M11
Loyang = Luoyang 35 C6
Loyauté, Îs. 64 M11
Loyev = Loyew 17 C10
Loyew 17 C10
Luachimo 56 F4
Lualaba → 57 D5
Luan Chau 38 B4
Luanda 56 F2
Luangwa → 59 A6
Luanshya 59 A5
Luapula → 57 F5
Luarca 18 A2
Luau 56 G4
Lubang Is. 36 B2
Lubango 58 A2
Lubbock 80 C3
Lübeck 15 B6
Lubero = Luofu 57 E5
Lubin 16 C3
Lublin 17 C6
Lubnān = Lebanon ■
  46 D3
Lubuk Antu 39 D4
Lubuklinggau 39 E2
Lubuksikaping 39 D2
Lubumbashi 59 A5
Lubutu 57 E5
Lucca 20 C3
Lucena Phil. 36 B2
Lucena Spain 18 D3
Lucerne = Luzern 13 C8
Luckenwalde 15 B7
Lucknow 40 D3
Lüda = Dalian 35 C7

Lüderitz 58 D3
Ludhiana 42 D9
Ludwigsburg 14 D5
Ludwigshafen 14 D5
Lufira → 57 F5
Lufkin 81 D6
Luga 24 B2
Lugano 13 C8
Lugansk = Luhansk 25 D4
Lugh Ganana 49 G3
Lugo *Italy* 20 B3
Lugo *Spain* 18 A2
Lugoj 17 F5
Lugovoy = Qulan 29 E8
Luhansk 25 D4
Luichow Pen. = Leizhou
   Bandao 35 D6
Luimneach = Limerick
   11 E2
Luís Correia 92 C5
Luitpold Coast 96 B5
Luiza 56 F4
Lukanga Swamp 59 A5
Lukenie → 56 E3
Łuków 17 C6
Luleå 8 B10
Luleälven → 8 B10
Lüleburgaz 22 D6
Lulonga → 56 D3
Lulua → 56 D3
Lumbala N'guimbo 58 A4
Lumsden 65 F3
Lumut, Tanjung 39 E3
Lund 9 D8
Lundazi 59 A6
Lundu 39 D3
Lüneburg 14 B6
Lüneburg Heath =
   Lüneburger Heide 14 B6
Lüneburger Heide 14 B6
Lunéville 13 B7
Lunglei 41 F9
Luni 42 G8
Luni → 43 G7
Luninets = Luninyets
   17 B8
Luninyets 17 B8
Luofu 57 E5
Luoyang 35 C6
Lurgan 11 D3
Lusaka 59 B5
Lusambo 56 E4
Lushnjë 23 D2
Luta = Dalian 35 C7
Lutherstadt Wittenberg
   15 C7
Luton 11 F6
Łutselk'e 68 B8
Lutsk 17 C7
Lützow Holmbukta 96 A8
Luuq = Lugh Ganana
   49 G3
Luwuk 37 E2
Luxembourg 13 B7
Luxembourg ■ 14 D4
Luxor = El Uqsur 54 C5
Luza 24 A6
Luzern 13 C8
Luzhou 35 D5
Luziânia 93 F4

Luzon 36 A2
Lviv 17 D7
Lvov = Lviv 17 D7
Lyakhavichy 17 B8
Lyakhovskiye, Ostrova
   31 B12
Lydenburg 59 D6
Lydia 23 E7
Lyell 65 D5
Lyepyel 24 C2
Lynchburg 77 F6
Lynd Ra. 63 A4
Lyndhurst 62 B2
Lynn Lake 69 C9
Lyon 13 D6
Lyonnais 13 D6
Lyons = Lyon 13 D6
Lys = Leie → 14 C2
Lysychansk 25 D4
Lyttelton 65 E5
Lyubertsy 24 B4
Lyuboml 17 C7

M

Ma'alah 47 F6
Ma'ān 47 E3
Ma'anshan 35 C6
Ma'arrat an Nu'mān 46 D4
Maas → 14 C3
Maastricht 13 A6
McAllen 80 F4
Macao = Macau 35 D6
Macapá 92 B3
Macau *Brazil* 92 D6
Macau *China* 35 D6
Maceió 93 D6
Macerata 20 C4
Macfarlane, L. 62 B2
Macgillycuddy's Reeks
   11 F2
McGregor Ra. 62 A3
Mach 42 E5
Machado = Jiparaná →
   91 E6
Machakos 57 E7
Machala 90 D3
Machilipatnam 40 J3
Machiques 90 A4
Machupicchu 91 F4
Macintyre → 63 A5
Mackay 61 E8
Mackay, L. 60 E4
Mackenzie → 68 B6
Mackenzie City = Linden
   90 B7
Mackenzie King I. 70 B2
Mackenzie Mts. 68 B6
McKinley, Mt. 69 B4
McKinney 81 C5
Macksville 63 B5

Maclean 63 A5
Maclear 59 E5
Macleay → 63 B5
McMurdo Sd. 96 B15
Mâcon *France* 13 C6
Macon *U.S.A.* 83 C6
McPherson Ra. 63 A5
Macquarie Harbour 62 D4
MacRobertson Land
   96 B10
Macumba → 62 A2
Madadeni 59 D6
Madagascar ■ 59 C9
Madā'in Sālih 47 F4
Madama 54 D1
Madaripur 41 F8
Madauk 41 J11
Madaya 41 F11
Maddalena 20 D2
Madeira 52 B2
Madeira → 90 D7
Madeleine, Îs. de la 71 E7
Madha 43 L9
Madhya Pradesh □
   43 H10
Madikeri 43 N9
Madimba 56 E3
Madingou 56 E2
Madison 75 D10
Madiun 39 F4
Madras = Chennai 43 N12
Madras = Tamil Nadu □
   43 P10
Madre, L. 80 F5
Madre, Sierra 36 A2
Madre de Dios → 91 F5
Madre de Dios, I. 95 G1
Madre Occidental, Sierra
   84 B3
Madrid 18 B4
Madurai 43 Q11
Madurantakam 43 N11
Mae Sot 38 A1
Maebashi 33 E6
Maevatanana 59 B9
Mafeteng 59 D5
Maffra 63 C4
Mafia I. 57 F7
Mafra *Brazil* 94 B7
Mafra *Portugal* 18 C1
Magadan 31 D13
Magallanes, Estrecho de
   95 G2
Magangué 90 B4
Magdalen Is. = Madeleine,
   Îs. de la 71 E7
Magdalena *Argentina*
   94 D5
Magdalena *Bolivia* 91 F6
Magdalena → 90 A4
Magdeburg 15 B6
Magelang 39 F4
Magellan's Str. =
   Magallanes, Estrecho de
   95 G2
Maggiore, Lago 13 D8
Magnetic Pole (North)
   70 A2
Magnetic Pole (South)
   96 A13

Magnitogorsk 29 D6
Magoša = Famagusta
   46 D3
Maguarinho, C. 92 C4
Mağusa = Famagusta
   46 D3
Magwe 41 G10
Magyarország =
   Hungary ■ 16 E4
Mahābād 46 C6
Mahabo 59 C8
Mahajanga 59 B9
Mahakam → 39 E5
Mahalapye 59 C5
Maḥallāt 44 C2
Mahanadi → 40 G6
Maharashtra □ 43 J9
Mahbubnagar 43 L10
Mahdia 54 A1
Mahenge 57 F7
Maheno 65 F4
Mahesana 43 H8
Mahia Pen. 64 C7
Mahilyow 17 B10
Mahinerangi, L. 65 F3
Mahón = Maó 19 C8
Mai-Ndombe, L. 56 E3
Maicurú → 92 C3
Maidstone 11 F7
Maiduguri 55 F1
Maijdi 41 F8
Maikala Ra. 40 G3
Main → 14 D5
Maine 12 C3
Maingkwan 41 D11
Mainit, L. 36 C3
Mainland *Orkney, U.K.*
   10 B5
Mainland *Shet., U.K.*
   10 A6
Mainz 14 C5
Maipú 94 D5
Maiquetía 90 A5
Mairabari 41 D9
Maitland *N.S.W., Australia*
   63 B5
Maitland *S. Austral.,*
   Australia 62 B2
Maizuru 33 F4
Majene 37 E1
Majorca = Mallorca 19 C7
Majuro 64 J12
Makale 37 E1
Makale 37 E1
Makarikari = Makgadikgadi
   Salt Pans 59 C5
Makasar = Ujung Pandang
   37 F1
Makasar, Selat 37 E1
Makasar, Str. of =
   Makasar, Selat 37 E1
Makat = Maqat 29 E6
Makedonija =
   Macedonia ■ 22 D3
Makeyevka = Makiyivka
   25 D4
Makgadikgadi Salt Pans
   59 C5
Makhachkala 25 E6
Makhado = Louis Trichardt
   59 C5

Makhfar al Buşayyah 47 E6
Makian 37 D3
Makīnsk 29 D8
Makiyivka 25 D4
Makkah 47 G4
Makó 16 E5
Makokou 56 D2
Makrai 43 H10
Makran 45 E5
Makran Coast Range 42 G4
Maksimkin Yar 29 D9
Mākū 46 C6
Makurazaki 33 H2
Makurdi 53 G7
Malabar Coast 43 P9
Malacca, Straits of 38 D1
Maladzyechna 17 A8
Málaga 18 D3
Malagasy Rep. = Madagascar ■ 59 C9
Malakâl 55 G5
Malakand 42 B7
Malang 39 F4
Malanje 56 F3
Mälaren 9 D9
Malargüe 94 D3
Malaryta 17 C7
Malatya 46 C4
Malawi ■ 59 A6
Malawi, L. 59 A6
Malay Pen. 38 C2
Malaybalay 36 C3
Malāyer 46 D7
Malaysia ■ 38 D4
Malazgirt 25 F5
Malbooma 62 B1
Malbork 16 A4
Malden I. 65 K15
Maldives ■ 26 H9
Maldonado 94 C6
Maleas, Akra 23 F4
Malegaon 43 J9
Malema 59 A7
Malha 55 E4
Mali ■ 53 E5
Mali → 41 E11
Maliku 37 E2
Malili 37 E2
Malin Hd. 10 D3
Malindi 57 E8
Malines = Mechelen 14 C3
Malino 37 D2
Malita 36 C3
Malkara 23 D6
Mallacoota Inlet 63 C4
Mallaig 10 C4
Mallawi 54 C5
Mallorca 19 C7
Mallow 11 E2
Malmö 9 D8
Malolos 36 B2
Malpelo, I. de 90 C2
Malta ■ 21 G5
Maltahöhe 58 C3
Maluku 37 E3
Maluku □ 37 E3
Maluku Sea = Molucca Sea 37 E2

Malvan 43 L8
Malvinas, Is. = Falkland Is. ☑ 95 G5
Malyn 17 C9
Malyy Lyakhovskiy, Ostrov 31 B12
Mamahatun 46 C5
Mamanguape 92 D6
Mamasa 37 E1
Mamberamo → 37 E5
Mambilima Falls 57 G5
Mamburao 36 B2
Mamoré → 91 F5
Mamou 53 F3
Mamuju 37 E1
Man 53 G4
Man, I. of 11 D4
Man Na 41 F11
Manaar, G. of = Mannar, G. of 43 Q11
Manacapuru 90 D6
Manacor 19 C7
Manado 37 D2
Managua 85 E7
Manakara 59 C9
Manama = Al Manāmah 44 E2
Mananjary 59 C9
Manaos = Manaus 90 D7
Manapouri 65 F2
Manapouri, L. 65 F2
Manas 34 B3
Manas → 41 D8
Manasir 44 E2
Manaung 41 H9
Manaus 90 D7
Manchester U.K. 11 E5
Manchester U.S.A. 77 C10
Mand → 44 D3
Mandal 9 D7
Mandala, Puncak 37 E6
Mandalay 41 F11
Mandale = Mandalay 41 F11
Mandalī 46 D6
Mandar, Teluk 37 E1
Mandaue 36 B2
Mandi 42 D10
Mandimba 59 A7
Mandioli 37 E3
Mandla 40 F3
Mandritsara 59 B9
Mandsaur 43 G9
Mandvi 43 H6
Mandya 43 N10
Manfalût 54 C5
Manfredónia 20 D5
Mangalia 22 C7
Mangalore 43 N9
Mangaweka 64 C6
Manggar 39 E3
Manggawitu 37 E4
Mangghystaū Tübegi 29 E6
Mangkalihat, Tanjung 37 D1
Mangla Dam 42 C8
Mangnai 34 C4
Mango 53 F6
Mangoche 59 A7

Mangoky → 59 C8
Mangole 37 E3
Mangonui 64 A5
Mangueira, L. da 94 C6
Mangyshlak, Poluostrov = Mangghystaū Tübegi 29 E6
Manica 59 B6
Manicoré 91 E6
Manicouagan → 71 E7
Manicouagan, Rés. 71 D7
Manīfah 47 F7
Manihiki 65 L14
Manila 36 B2
Manila B. 36 B2
Manilla 63 B5
Manipur □ 41 E9
Manipur → 41 F10
Manisa 23 E6
Manitoba □ 69 C10
Manitoba, L. 69 C10
Manitoulin I. 71 E5
Manitowoc 76 B2
Manizales 90 B3
Manjhand 42 G6
Manjra → 43 K10
Manmad 43 J9
Manna 39 E2
Mannahill 62 B3
Mannar 43 Q11
Mannar, G. of 43 Q11
Mannar I. 43 Q11
Mannheim 14 D5
Mannum 62 B2
Manokwari 37 E4
Manono 57 F5
Manosque 13 E6
Manresa 19 B6
Mansa 57 G5
Mansel I. 70 C5
Mansfield Australia 63 C4
Mansfield U.K. 11 E6
Mansfield U.S.A. 76 D4
Manta 90 D2
Mantalingajan, Mt. 38 C5
Mantes-la-Jolie 12 B4
Manthani 43 K11
Mántova 20 B3
Mantua = Mántova 20 B3
Manu 91 F4
Manuel Alves → 93 E4
Manui 37 E2
Manukau 64 B6
Manych-Gudilo, Ozero 25 D5
Manzai 42 C7
Manzanares 18 C4
Manzanillo Cuba 86 B4
Manzanillo Mexico 84 D4
Manzhouli 35 B6
Mao Chad 55 F1
Maó Spain 19 C8
Maoke, Pegunungan 37 E5
Maoming 35 D6
Mapam Yumco 40 B3
Mapia, Kepulauan 37 D4
Mapuera → 90 D7
Maputo 59 D6
Maqat 29 E6

Maqnā 47 E3
Maquan He = Brahmaputra → 41 F7
Maquela do Zombo 56 F3
Maquinchao 95 E3
Mar Chiquita, L. 94 C4
Mar del Plata 94 D5
Mar Menor 19 D5
Maraã 90 D5
Marabá 92 D4
Maracá, I. de 92 B3
Maracaibo 90 A4
Maracaibo, L. de 90 B4
Maracay 90 A5
Maradi 53 F7
Marāgheh 46 C6
Marāh 47 F6
Marajó, I. de 92 C4
Marand 46 C6
Maranguape 92 C6
Maranhão = São Luís 92 C5
Maranhão □ 92 D4
Maranoa → 63 A4
Marañón → 90 D4
Marão 59 C6
Maraş = Kahramanmaraş 46 C4
Maratua 37 D1
Marbella 18 D3
Marburg 14 C5
Marche 12 C4
Marchena 18 D3
Mardan 42 B8
Mardin 46 C5
Marek = Stanke Dimitrov 22 C4
Margarita, I. de 90 A6
Margaritovo 32 B4
Margate 11 F7
Marghilon 29 E8
Mārgow, Dasht-e 42 D3
Mari El □ 24 B6
Mari El Republic = Mari El □ 24 B6
Maria I. 62 D4
Maria van Diemen, C. 64 A5
Mariana Trench 64 H9
Maribor 20 A5
Marie Byrd Land 96 B18
Mariecourt = Kangiqsujuaq 70 C6
Mariental 58 C3
Mariinsk 29 D9
Marília 93 G3
Marín 18 A1
Marinduque 36 B2
Maringá 94 A6
Marion 81 A9
Mariscal Estigarribia 91 H6
Maritime Alps = Maritimes, Alpes 13 D7
Maritimes, Alpes 13 D7
Maritsa = Évros → 22 D6
Mariupol 25 D4
Marīvān 46 D6
Marka = Merca 49 G3
Markham, Mt. 96 C15

Marks 24 C6
Marla 62 A1
Marmagao 43 M8
Marmara 23 D6
Marmara, Sea of =
  Marmara Denizi 22 D7
Marmara Denizi 22 D7
Marmaris 23 F7
Marmolada, Mte. 20 A3
Marne → 13 B5
Maroantsetra 59 B9
Marondera 59 B6
Maroni → 92 A3
Maroochydore 63 A5
Maroona 62 C3
Maroua 55 F1
Marovoay 59 B9
Marquesas Is. =
  Marquises, Îs. 65 K17
Marquises, Îs. 65 K17
Marrakech 52 B4
Marrawah 62 D3
Marree 62 A2
Marrowie Cr. → 63 B4
Marrupa 59 A7
Marsá Matrûh 54 B4
Marsabit 57 D7
Marsala 21 F4
Marsden 63 B4
Marseille 13 E6
Marseilles = Marseille
  13 E6
Marshall 81 C6
Marshall Is. ■ 64 J12
Marshalltown 75 D8
Martaban 41 J11
Martaban, G. of 41 J11
Martapura Kalimantan,
  Indonesia 39 E4
Martapura Sumatera,
  Indonesia 39 E2
Martigues 13 E6
Martinborough 65 D6
Martinique ☑ 87 D7
Martinsville 83 A8
Marton 64 D6
Martos 18 D4
Marudi 39 D4
Maruf 42 D5
Marugame 33 F3
Marwar 42 G8
Mary 29 F7
Maryborough = Port
  Laoise 11 E3
Maryborough Queens.,
  Australia 63 A5
Maryborough Vic.,
  Australia 62 C3
Maryland ☐ 77 E7
Marystown 71 E8
Maryvale 63 A5
Marzūq 54 C1
Marzūq, Idehān 54 D1
Masaka 57 E6
Masalembo, Kepulauan
  39 F4
Masalima, Kepulauan
  39 F5
Masamba 37 E2
Masan 35 C7

Masandam, Ra's 44 E4
Masasi 57 G7
Masaya 85 E7
Mascara 52 A6
Masela 37 F3
Maseru 59 D5
Mashābih 47 F4
Mashhad 44 B4
Māshkel, Hāmūn-i- 42 E3
Mashki Chāh 42 E3
Mashonaland 59 B6
Masindi 57 D6
Masjed Soleyman 47 E7
Mask, L. 11 E2
Maskin 44 F4
Masoala, Tanjon' i 59 B10
Masohi = Amahai 37 E3
Mason City 75 D8
Masqat 45 F4
Massa 13 D9
Massachusetts ☐ 77 C9
Massakory 55 F2
Massangena 59 C6
Massena 77 B8
Massénya 55 F2
Massif Central 13 D5
Massinga 59 C7
Masson I. 96 A11
Mastanli = Momchilgrad
  22 D5
Masterton 65 D6
Mastuj 42 A8
Masty 17 B7
Masuda 33 F2
Masvingo 59 C6
Mata-au = Clutha →
  65 G3
Matabeleland 59 B5
Matad 35 B6
Matadi 56 F2
Matagalpa 85 E7
Matagami 71 E6
Matagami, L. 71 E6
Matak 39 D3
Matam 53 E3
Matamoros Coahuila,
  Mexico 84 B4
Matamoros Tamaulipas,
  Mexico 84 B5
Ma'ţan as Sarra 54 D3
Matanzas 86 B3
Matapan, C. = Tenaro,
  Ákra 23 F4
Mataram 39 F5
Matarani 91 G4
Mataró 19 B7
Mataura 65 G3
Matehuala 84 C4
Matera 21 D6
Mathraki 21 E7
Mathura 42 F10
Mati 36 C3
Matiri Ra. 65 D5
Mato Grosso ☐ 93 E3
Mato Grosso, Planalto do
  93 F3
Mato Grosso do Sul ☐
  93 F3

Matochkin Shar 28 B6
Matosinhos 18 B1
Maţruḩ 45 F4
Matsue 33 F3
Matsumae 32 C7
Matsumoto 33 E6
Matsusaka 33 F5
Matsuyama 33 G3
Mattagami → 71 D5
Mattancheri 43 Q10
Matthews Ridge 90 B6
Matucana 91 F3
Matún = Khowst 42 C6
Maturín 90 B6
Mau Ranipur 43 G11
Maubeuge 13 A5
Maude 63 B3
Maudin Sun 41 K10
Maués 90 D7
Mauganj 40 E3
Maui 78 H12
Maulamyaing = Moulmein
  41 J11
Maumere 37 F2
Maun 58 B4
Maungmagan Kyunzu
  41 K11
Mauritania ■ 53 E3
Mauritius ■ 51 H9
Mawk Mai 41 G11
Mawlaik 41 F10
Mawlamyine = Moulmein
  41 J11
Mawson Coast 96 A10
Mayaguana 87 B5
Mayagüez 87 C6
Maydena 62 D4
Mayenne → 12 C3
Maykop 25 E5
Mayo 90 D4
Mayo L. 68 B6
Mayon Volcano 36 B2
Mayor I. 64 B7
Mayotte ☑ 59 A9
Mayu 37 D3
Mazabuka 59 B5
Mazagán = El Jadida
  52 B4
Mazagão 92 C3
Mazán 90 D4
Māzandarān ☐ 44 B3
Mazar-e Sharīf 45 B6
Mazara del Vallo 21 F4
Mazarrón 19 D5
Mazaruni → 90 B7
Mazatlán 84 C3
Māzhān 44 C4
Mazīnān 44 B4
Mazoe → 59 B6
Mazurian Lakes =
  Mazurski, Pojezierze
  16 B5
Mazurski, Pojezierze
  16 B5
Mazyr 17 C9
Mbabane 59 D6
Mbaïki 56 D3
Mbala 57 F6
Mbale 57 D6
Mbalmayo 56 D2
Mbandaka 56 D3

Mbanza Congo 56 F2
Mbanza Ngungu 56 F2
Mbarara 57 E6
Mbeya 57 F6
Mbini = Río Muni ☐ 56 D2
Mbour 53 F2
Mbuji-Mayi 56 F4
Mdantsane 59 E5
Mead, L. 78 B5
Mearim → 92 C5
Meaux 13 B5
Mecca = Makkah 47 G4
Mechelen 14 C3
Mecheria 52 B5
Mecklenburg 15 B6
Mecklenburger Bucht
  15 A6
Medan 39 D1
Medanosa, Pta. 95 F3
Médéa 52 A6
Medellín 90 B3
Medford 72 E2
Medgidia 22 B7
Medicine Bow Mts.
  73 F10
Medicine Hat 69 C8
Medina = Al Madīnah
  47 F4
Medina del Campo 18 B3
Medina Sidonia 18 D3
Medinipur 40 F6
Mediterranean Sea 50 C5
Médoc 12 D3
Medveditsa → 24 D5
Medvezhyegorsk 28 C4
Meekatharra 60 F2
Meerut 42 E10
Megara 23 F4
Meghalaya ☐ 41 E8
Meighen I. 70 B4
Meiktila 41 G10
Meissen 15 C7
Meizhou 35 D6
Mejillones 94 A1
Mekhtar 42 D6
Meknès 52 B4
Mekong → 38 C3
Mekongga 37 E2
Mekvari = Kür → 25 E6
Melagiri Hills 43 N10
Melaka 39 D2
Melalap 38 C5
Melanesia 64 K10
Melbourne Australia 63 C3
Melbourne U.S.A. 83 E7
Melekeok 36 C4
Mélèzes → 70 D6
Melfort 69 C9
Melilla 19 E4
Melitopol 25 D4
Melk 15 D8
Melo 94 C6
Melolo 37 F2
Melrose 63 B4
Melun 13 B5
Melville 69 C9
Melville I. Australia 60 C5
Melville I. Canada 70 B2
Melville Pen. 70 C5
Memboro 37 F1

Memel = Klaipėda **24 B1**
Memmingen **14 E6**
Mempawah **39 D3**
Memphis *Tenn., U.S.A.*
 82 B3
Memphis *Tex., U.S.A.*
 80 B3
Ménaka **53 E6**
Menan = Chao Phraya →
 38 B2
Mendawai → **39 E4**
Mende **13 D5**
Mendocino, C. **72 F1**
Mendoza **94 C3**
Mene Grande **90 B4**
Menemen **23 E6**
Menggala **39 E3**
Mengzi **34 D5**
Menindee **62 B3**
Menindee L. **62 B3**
Meningie **62 C2**
Menominee **76 B2**
Menongue **58 A3**
Menorca **19 C7**
Mentawai, Kepulauan
 39 E1
Menton **13 E7**
Meppel **14 B4**
Meran = Merano **20 A3**
Merano **20 A3**
Merauke **37 F6**
Merbein **62 B3**
Merca **49 G3**
Merced **78 B2**
Mercedes *B. Aires,*
 Argentina **94 C5**
Mercedes *Corrientes,*
 Argentina **94 B5**
Mercedes *San Luis,*
 Argentina **94 C3**
Mercedes *Uruguay* **94 C5**
Mercer **64 B6**
Mercy, C. **70 C7**
Meredith, C. **95 G4**
Mergui Arch. = Myeik
 Kyunzu **38 B1**
Mérida *Mexico* **85 C7**
Mérida *Spain* **18 C2**
Mérida *Venezuela* **90 B4**
Meridian **82 C3**
Merirumã **92 B3**
Merriwa **63 B5**
Merseburg **15 C6**
Mersin = İçel **46 C3**
Mersing **39 D2**
Merthyr Tydfil **11 F5**
Mértola **18 D2**
Meru **57 D7**
Mesa **79 D7**
Meshed = Mashhad **44 B4**
Mesologi **23 E3**
Mesopotamia = Al Jazirah
 46 D5
Messina = Musina **59 C6**
Messina **21 E5**
Messina, Str. di **21 E5**
Messini **23 F4**
Messiniakos Kolpos **23 F4**
Mesta → **22 D5**
Meta → **90 B5**

Meta Incognita Pen. **70 C7**
Metairie **81 E8**
Metán **94 B4**
Methven **65 E4**
Metlakatla **69 C6**
Mettur Dam **43 P10**
Metz **13 B7**
Meulaboh **39 D1**
Meureudu **38 C1**
Meuse → **13 A6**
Mexiana, I. **92 C4**
Mexicali **84 A1**
México **84 D5**
Mexico ■ **84 C4**
México, Ciudad de **84 D5**
Mexico, G. of **85 B7**
Meymaneh **42 B4**
Mezen **28 C5**
Mezen → **28 C5**
Mézenc, Mt. **13 D6**
Mezőkövesd **16 E5**
Mezőtúr **16 E5**
Mhow **43 H9**
Miami **83 G7**
Miami Beach **83 G7**
Mīāndowāb **46 C6**
Miandrivazo **59 B9**
Mīāneh **46 C6**
Mianwali **42 C7**
Miass **29 D7**
Michigan □ **76 C3**
Michigan, L. **76 C2**
Michurin **22 C6**
Michurinsk **24 C5**
Micronesia **64 H11**
Micronesia, Federated
 States of ■ **64 J10**
Middelburg **58 E5**
Middlesbrough **11 D6**
Midi, Canal du → **12 E4**
Midland **80 D3**
Midyat **46 C5**
Midzŏr **22 C4**
Międzychód **16 B2**
Międzyrzec Podlaski
 17 C6
Mielec **16 C5**
Mieres **18 A3**
Mikhaylovgrad = Montana
 22 C4
Mikines **23 F4**
Mikonos = Mykonos **23 F5**
Milagro **90 D3**
Milan = Milano **13 D8**
Milang **62 B2**
Milano **13 D8**
Milâs **23 F6**
Milazzo **21 E5**
Mildura **62 B3**
Miles **63 A5**
Miletus **23 F6**
Milford Haven **11 F4**
Milford Sd. **65 F2**
Milford Sound **65 F2**
Milh, Bahr al = Razāzah,
 Buḥayrat ar **47 D5**
Mill I. **96 A12**
Millau **13 D5**
Millennium I. = Caroline I.
 65 K15

Millicent **62 C3**
Millinocket **77 B11**
Millmerran **63 A5**
Milne Inlet **70 B5**
Milos **23 F5**
Milparinka **62 A3**
Milton **65 G3**
Milton Keynes **11 E6**
Milwaukee **76 C2**
Min Jiang → *Fujian, China*
 35 D6
Min Jiang → *Sichuan,*
 China **35 D5**
Mīnā Su'ud **47 E7**
Mīnā'al Aḥmadī **47 E7**
Mīnāb **44 E4**
Minamata **33 G2**
Minas **94 C5**
Minas Gerais □ **93 F4**
Minbu **41 G10**
Minden **14 B5**
Mindiptana **37 F6**
Mindoro **36 B2**
Mindoro Str. **36 B2**
Mingäçevir Su Anbarı
 25 E6
Mingechaurskoye Vdkhr. =
 Mingäçevir Su Anbarı
 25 E6
Mingin **41 F10**
Mingteke Daban = Mintaka
 Pass **42 A9**
Minho = Miño → **18 B1**
Minho **18 B1**
Minna **53 G7**
Minneapolis **75 C8**
Minnesota □ **75 B7**
Minnipa **62 B2**
Miño → **18 B1**
Minorca = Menorca **19 C7**
Minot **74 A4**
Minsk **24 C3**
Mińsk Mazowiecki **16 B5**
Mintaka Pass **42 A9**
Minto, L. **70 D6**
Minutang **41 C11**
Mira **20 B4**
Mirabello, Kolpos **23 G5**
Miraj **43 L9**
Miram Shah **42 C7**
Miramichi **71 E7**
Miranda **93 G2**
Miranda de Ebro **19 A4**
Miranda do Douro **18 B2**
Miri **38 D4**
Mirim, L. **94 C6**
Mirpur Khas **42 G6**
Mirzapur **40 E4**
Mirzapur-cum-Vindhyachal
 = Mirzapur **40 E4**
Mish'āb, Ra's al **47 E7**
Mishan **35 B8**
Misool **37 E4**
Miṣr = Egypt ■ **54 C5**
Miṣrātah **54 B2**

Misriç **46 C5**
Missinaibi → **71 D5**
Mississippi □ **81 C9**
Mississippi → **81 E9**
Mississippi River Delta
 81 E9
Missoula **73 C7**
Missouri □ **75 F8**
Missouri → **75 F9**
Mistassini, L. **71 D6**
Misurata = Miṣrātah **54 B2**
Mitchell *Australia* **63 A4**
Mitchell *U.S.A.* **74 D5**
Mitchell → **61 D7**
Mitilini **23 E6**
Mito **33 E7**
Mitrovica = Kosovska
 Mitrovica **22 C3**
Mittagong **63 B5**
Mittimatalik = Pond Inlet
 70 B6
Mitú **90 C4**
Mitumba, Mts. **57 F5**
Mitwaba **57 F5**
Miyake-Jima **33 F6**
Miyako **32 D7**
Miyakonojō **33 H2**
Miyazaki **33 H2**
Miyet, Bahr el = Dead Sea
 47 E3
Mizal **47 G6**
Mizdah **54 B1**
Mizoram □ **41 F9**
Mjøsa **8 C8**
Mladá Boleslav **16 C2**
Mlange = Mulanje **59 B7**
Mława **16 B5**
Mljet **20 C6**
Mmabatho **59 D5**
Mo i Rana **8 B8**
Moa **37 F3**
Moalie Park **62 A3**
Mobaye **56 D4**
Mobayi **56 D4**
Mobile **82 D2**
Moçambique =
 Mozambique ■ **59 B8**
Moçambique **59 B8**
Mochudi **59 C5**
Mocimboa da Praia **57 G8**
Mocoa **90 C3**
Mocuba **59 B7**
Modane **13 D7**
Módena **20 B3**
Modesto **78 B2**
Módica **21 F5**
Modimolle **59 C5**
Moe **63 C4**
Moengo **92 A3**
Mogadishu = Muqdisho
 49 G4
Mogador = Essaouira
 52 B4
Mogami-Gawa → **32 D7**
Mogaung **41 E11**
Mogi das Cruzes **94 A7**
Mogilev = Mahilyow
 17 B10
Mogilev-Podolskiy =
 Mohyliv-Podilskyy
 17 D8

Mogok 41 F11
Mohács 16 F4
Moḥammadābād 44 B4
Mohyliv-Podilskyy 17 D8
Moisie → 71 D7
Mojave Desert 78 C4
Mokai 64 C6
Mokau 64 C6
Mokokchung 41 D10
Mokopane 59 C5
Mokra Gora 22 C3
Molchanovo 29 D9
Moldavia = Moldova ■
   17 E9
Molde 8 C7
Moldova ■ 17 E9
Moldoveanu, Vf. 17 F7
Molepolole 59 C5
Molfetta 20 D6
Moline 75 E9
Mollendo 91 G4
Molodechno =
   Maladzyechna 17 A8
Moloka'i 78 H12
Molong 63 B4
Molopo → 58 D4
Molu 37 F4
Molucca Sea 37 E2
Moluccas = Maluku 37 E3
Moma 59 B7
Mombasa 57 E7
Mombetsu 32 B12
Momchilgrad 22 D5
Mompós 90 B4
Mon → 41 G10
Mona, Canal de la = Mona
   Passage 87 C6
Mona Passage 87 C6
Monaco ■ 13 E7
Monahans 80 D2
Monastir = Bitola 22 D3
Moncayo, Sierra del 19 B5
Mönchengladbach 14 C4
Monchique 18 D1
Monclova 84 B4
Moncton 71 E7
Mondego → 18 B1
Mondeodo 37 E2
Mondoví 13 D7
Monforte de Lemos 18 A2
Mong Hsu 41 G12
Mong Kung 41 G11
Mong Nai 41 G11
Mong Pawk 41 F12
Mong Ton 41 G12
Mong Wa 41 G13
Mong Yai 41 F12
Mongalla 55 G5
Monghyr = Munger 40 E6
Mongibello = Etna 21 F5
Mongo 55 F2
Mongolia ■ 35 B5
Mongu 58 B4
Monkoto 56 E4
Monópoli 21 D6
Monroe La., U.S.A. 81 D7
Monroe N.C., U.S.A.
   83 B7
Monrovia 53 G3
Mons 14 C2

Monse 37 E2
Mont-de-Marsan 12 E3
Mont-Laurier 71 E6
Mont-St-Michel, Le 12 B3
Montalbán 19 B5
Montana 22 C4
Montana □ 73 C9
Montargis 13 C5
Montauban 12 D4
Montbéliard 13 C7
Montceau-les-Mines
   13 C6
Monte Alegre 92 C3
Monte Azul 93 F5
Monte-Carlo 13 E7
Monte Caseros 94 C5
Monte Comán 94 C3
Monte Santu, C. di 21 D2
Montecristo 20 C5
Montego Bay 86 C4
Montélimar 13 D6
Montemorelos 84 B5
Montenegro ■ 22 C2
Montepuez 59 A7
Monterey 78 B2
Montería 90 B3
Monterrey 84 B4
Montes Claros 93 F5
Montesilvano 20 C5
Montevideo 94 C5
Montgomery 82 C4
Montilla 18 D3
Montluçon 13 C5
Montmorillon 12 C4
Montoro 18 C3
Montpellier 13 E5
Montréal 71 E6
Montrose U.K. 10 C5
Montrose U.S.A. 79 A9
Montserrat ☑ 87 C7
Montsinéry 30 E
Monywa 41 F10
Monza 13 D8
Monze 59 B5
Monze, C. 43 G5
Monzón 19 B6
Moolawatana 62 A2
Moomin Cr. → 63 A4
Moonie 63 A5
Moonie → 63 A4
Moonta 62 B2
Moose Jaw 69 C9
Moosomin 69 C9
Moosonee 71 D5
Mopti 53 F5
Moqor 42 C5
Moquegua 91 G4
Mora 8 C8
Moradabad 42 E11
Morafenobe 59 B8
Moramanga 59 B9
Moratuwa 43 R11
Morava → Serbia 22 B3
Morava → Slovak Rep.
   16 D3
Moravian Hts. =
   Českomoravská
   Vrchovina 16 D2
Morawhanna 90 B7
Moray Firth 10 C5

Morden 69 D10
Mordovian Republic =
   Mordvinia □ 24 C5
Mordvinia □ 24 C5
Morea 62 C3
Moree 63 A4
Morelia 84 D4
Morella 19 B5
Morena, Sierra 18 C3
Moreton I. 63 A5
Morgan City 81 E8
Morioka 32 D7
Morlaix 12 B2
Morne Constant 30 C
Mornington 63 C4
Mornington, I. 95 F1
Moro G. 36 C2
Morocco ■ 52 B4
Morogoro 57 F7
Morombe 59 C8
Morón 86 B4
Mörön → 35 B6
Morón de la Frontera
   18 D3
Morondava 59 C8
Morotai 37 D3
Moroto 57 D6
Morphou 46 D3
Morrinhos 93 F4
Morrinsville 64 B6
Morristown 83 A6
Morshansk 24 C5
Morteros 94 C4
Mortlake 62 C3
Morundah 63 B4
Moruya 63 C5
Morvan 13 C6
Morven 63 A4
Morwell 63 C4
Moscos Is. 41 L11
Moscow = Moskva 24 B4
Moscow 72 C5
Mosel → 13 A7
Moselle = Mosel → 13 A7
Mosgiel 65 F4
Moshi 57 E7
Mosjøen 8 B8
Moskva 24 B4
Mosonmagyaróvár 16 E3
Mosquera 90 C2
Moss Vale 63 B5
Mossburn 65 F3
Mosselbaai 58 E4
Mossendjo 56 E2
Mossgiel 63 B3
Mossoró 92 D6
Most 16 C1
Mostaganem 52 A6
Mostar 20 C6
Mostardas 94 C6
Mostiska = Mostyska
   17 D6
Mosty = Masty 17 B7
Mostyska 17 D6
Mosul = Al Mawşil 46 C5
Motihari 40 D5
Motril 18 D4
Motueka 65 D5
Motueka → 65 D5
Moudros 23 E5

Mouila 56 E2
Moulamein 63 C3
Moulins 13 C5
Moulmein 41 J11
Moundou 55 G2
Mount Aspiring △ 65 F3
Mount Barker 62 C2
Mount Cook 65 E4
Mount Eba 62 B2
Mount Gambier 62 C3
Mount Hope N.S.W.,
   Australia 63 B4
Mount Hope S. Austral.,
   Australia 62 B2
Mount Howitt 62 A3
Mount Isa 61 E6
Mount Lofty Ranges
   62 B2
Mount Margaret 63 A3
Mount Maunganui 64 B7
Mount Perry 63 A5
Moura Brazil 90 D6
Moura Portugal 18 C2
Mourdi, Dépression du
   55 E3
Moussoro 55 F2
Moutong 37 D2
Moyale 49 G2
Moyen Atlas 52 B4
Moyo 39 F5
Moyyero → 30 C8
Moyynty 29 E8
Mozambique =
   Moçambique 59 B8
Mozambique ■ 59 B7
Mozambique Chan. 51 H8
Mozdok 25 E5
Mozyr = Mazyr 17 C9
Mpanda 57 F6
Mpika 59 A6
Mpwapwa 57 F7
Mthatha 59 E5
Mu Us Shamo 35 C5
Muar 39 D2
Muarabungo 39 E2
Muaraenim 39 E2
Muarajuloi 39 E4
Muarakaman 39 E5
Muaratebo 39 E2
Muaratembesi 39 E2
Muaratewe 39 E4
Mubarraz = Al Mubarraz
   47 F7
Mubi 55 F1
Muckadilla 63 A4
Mucuri 93 F6
Mudanjiang 35 B7
Mudanya 23 D7
Mudgee 63 B4
Mufulira 59 A5
Mugi 33 G4
Muğla 23 F7
Mugu 40 C4
Muhammad Qol 54 D6
Mühlhausen 14 C6
Mühlig Hofmann fjell
   96 B7
Mujnak = Muynak 29 E6
Mukacheve 17 D6
Mukachevo = Mukacheve
   17 D6

Mukah **39 D4**
Mukden = Shenyang **35 B7**
Mukomuko **39 E2**
Muktsar **42 D9**
Mukur = Moqor **42 C5**
Mula **19 C5**
Mulanje **59 B7**
Mulchén **94 D2**
Mulde → **15 C7**
Mulgathing **62 B1**
Mulhacén **18 D4**
Mulhouse **13 C7**
Mull **10 C4**
Mullengudgery **63 B4**
Muller, Pegunungan **39 D4**
Mullingar **11 E3**
Mullumbimby **63 A5**
Multan **42 D7**
Mumbai **43 K8**
Muna **37 F2**
München **15 D6**
Munchen-Gladbach = Mönchengladbach **14 C4**
Muncie **76 D3**
Münden **14 C5**
Mundo Novo **93 E5**
Mungallala **63 A4**
Mungallala Cr. → **63 A4**
Mungbere **57 D5**
Munger **40 E6**
Munich = München **15 D6**
Muñoz Gamero, Pen. **95 G2**
Münster **14 C4**
Munster □ **11 E2**
Muntok **39 E3**
Muqdisho **49 G4**
Murallón, Cerro **95 F2**
Murang'a **57 E7**
Murashi **24 B6**
Muratlı **22 D6**
Murchison → **60 F1**
Murchison, Mt. **96 B15**
Murchison Falls **57 D6**
Murcia **19 D5**
Murcia □ **19 D5**
Mureş → **22 A3**
Mureşul = Mureş → **22 A3**
Murfreesboro **82 B4**
Murgab **29 F8**
Murghob = Murgab **29 F8**
Murgon **63 A5**
Müritz **15 B7**
Murmansk **8 B12**
Murom **24 B5**
Muroran **32 B7**
Muroto **33 G4**
Muroto-Misaki **33 G4**
Murray → **62 C2**
Murray Bridge **62 C2**
Murrumbidgee → **62 B3**
Murrumburrah **63 B4**
Murrurundi **63 B5**
Murtoa **62 C3**
Murwara **40 F3**
Murwillumbah **63 A5**
Mürzzuschlag **15 E8**
Muş **46 C5**

Mûsa, Gebel **47 E3**
Musa Khel **42 D6**
Mûsa Qal'eh **42 C4**
Musala *Bulgaria* **22 C4**
Musala *Indonesia* **39 D1**
Muscat = Masqat **45 F4**
Muscatine **75 E9**
Musgrave Ranges **60 F5**
Mushie **56 E3**
Musi → **39 E2**
Musina **59 C6**
Muskogee **81 B6**
Musoma **57 E6**
Mussoorie **42 D11**
Mustafakemalpaşa **23 D7**
Mustang **40 C4**
Musters, L. **95 F3**
Muswellbrook **63 B5**
Mût *Egypt* **54 C4**
Mut *Turkey* **46 C3**
Mutare **59 B6**
Muting **37 F6**
Mutoray **30 C8**
Mutsu **32 C7**
Mutsu-Wan **32 C7**
Muynak **29 E6**
Muzaffarabad **42 B8**
Muzaffargarh **42 D7**
Muzaffarnagar **42 E10**
Muzaffarpur **40 D5**
Muzhi **28 C8**
Muztag **34 C3**
Mvuma **59 B6**
Mwanza *Dem. Rep. of the Congo* **57 F5**
Mwanza *Tanzania* **57 E6**
Mweka **56 E4**
Mweru, L. **57 F5**
Mwinilunga **58 A4**
My Tho **38 B3**
Myanaung **41 H10**
Myanmar = Burma ■ **41 G11**
Myaungmya **41 J10**
Mycenæ = Mikines **23 F4**
Myeik Kyunzu **38 B1**
Myingyan **41 G10**
Myitkyina **41 E11**
Mykolayiv **25 D3**
Mykonos **23 F5**
Mymensingh **41 E8**
Mýrdalsjökull **8 C2**
Mysia **23 E6**
Mysore = Karnataka □ **43 N10**
Mysore **43 N10**
Myszków **16 C4**
Mytishchi **24 B4**

N

Na Hearadh = Harris **10 C3**
Naab → **15 D7**
Nababeep **58 D3**
Naberezhnyye Chelny **29 D6**
Nabeul **54 A1**
Nabire **37 E5**
Näblus = Nābulus **46 D3**

Nābulus **46 D3**
Nacala **59 A8**
Nachingwea **57 G7**
Nacogdoches **81 D6**
Nacozari de García **84 A3**
Nadiad **43 H8**
Nadüshan **44 C3**
Nadvira **17 D7**
Nadvornaya = Nadvirna **17 D7**
Nadym **28 C8**
Nadym → **28 C8**
Nafpaktos **23 E3**
Nafplio **23 F4**
Nafud ad Dahy **47 G6**
Nafud Desert = An Nafūd **47 E5**
Naga **36 B2**
Nagaland □ **41 E10**
Nagano **33 E6**
Nagaoka **33 E6**
Nagappattinam **43 P11**
Nagar Parkar **43 G7**
Nagasaki **33 G1**
Nagaur **42 F8**
Nagercoil **43 Q10**
Nagîneh **44 C4**
Nagoya **33 F5**
Nagpur **43 J11**
Nagykanizsa **16 E3**
Nagykőrös **16 E4**
Naha **33 D7**
Nahāvand **46 D7**
Nā'ifah **48 D5**
Nain *Canada* **70 D7**
Nā'īn *Iran* **44 C3**
Nairn **10 C5**
Nairobi **57 E7**
Najaf = An Najaf **47 D6**
Najafābād **44 C2**
Najd **47 F5**
Najibabad **42 E11**
Nakamura **33 G3**
Nakashibetsu **32 B9**
Nakhichevan = Naxçıvan **25 F6**
Nakhichevan Rep. = Naxçıvan □ **25 F6**
Nakhodka **31 E14**
Nakhon Phanom **38 A2**
Nakhon Ratchasima **38 B2**
Nakhon Sawan **38 A2**
Nakhon Si Thammarat **38 C2**
Nakina **71 D5**
Nakuru **57 E7**
Nal → **42 G4**
Nalchik **25 E5**
Nalgonda **43 L11**
Nallamalai Hills **43 M11**
Nam Co **34 C4**
Nam-Phan **38 B3**
Namak, Daryācheh-ye **44 C3**
Namak, Kavir-e **44 C4**
Namaland **58 D3**
Namangan **29 E8**
Namapa **59 A7**
Namber **37 E4**
Nambour **63 A5**

Nambucca Heads **63 B5**
Namib Desert **58 C2**
Namibe **58 B2**
Namibia ■ **58 C3**
Namibwoestyn = Namib Desert **58 C2**
Namlea **37 E3**
Namoi → **63 B4**
Nampa **72 E5**
Nampo **35 C7**
Nampō-Shotō **33 H7**
Nampula **59 B7**
Namrole **37 E3**
Namse Shankou **40 C4**
Namtu **41 F11**
Namur **14 C3**
Nan-ch'ang = Nanchang **35 D6**
Nanaimo **69 D7**
Nanango **63 A5**
Nanao **33 E5**
Nanchang **35 D6**
Nanching = Nanjing **35 C6**
Nanchong **35 C5**
Nancy **13 B7**
Nanda Devi **42 D11**
Nanded **43 K10**
Nandewar Ra. **63 B5**
Nandurbar **43 J9**
Nandyal **43 M11**
Nanga-Eboko **56 D2**
Nanga Parbat **42 B9**
Nangapinoh **39 E4**
Nangarhār □ **42 B7**
Nangatayap **39 E4**
Nanjing **35 C6**
Nanking = Nanjing **35 C6**
Nanning **35 D5**
Nanping **35 D6**
Nansei-Shotō = Ryūkyū-rettō **35 D7**
Nansen Sd. **70 A4**
Nantes **12 C3**
Nantucket I. **77 D10**
Nanuque **93 F5**
Nanusa, Kepulauan **36 D3**
Nanyang **35 C6**
Nanyuki **57 D7**
Nao, C. de la **19 C6**
Napa **72 G2**
Napier **64 C7**
Naples = Nápoli **21 D5**
Naples **83 F7**
Napo → **90 D4**
Nápoli **21 D5**
Nappa Merrie **62 A3**
Nara **53 E4**
Naracoorte **62 C3**
Naradhan **63 B4**
Narasapur **40 J3**
Narathiwat **38 C2**
Narayanganj **41 F8**
Narayanpet **43 L10**
Narbonne **13 E5**
Nardò **21 D7**
Narew → **16 B5**
Narin **42 A6**
Narmada → **43 J8**
Narodnaya **28 C6**
Narooma **63 C5**
Narrabri **63 B4**

Narran → 63 A4
Narrandera 63 B4
Narromine 63 B4
Narsimhapur 43 H11
Naruto 33 F4
Narva 24 B2
Narvik 8 B9
Naryan-Mar 28 C6
Naryilco 62 A3
Narym 29 D9
Narymskoye 29 E9
Naryn 29 E8
Naseby 65 F4
Naser, Buheirat en 54 D5
Nashville 82 A4
Nasik 43 K8
Nasirabad 42 F9
Nassarawa 53 G7
Nassau 86 A4
Nassau, B. 95 H3
Nasser, L. = Naser,
   Buheirat en 54 D5
Natal Brazil 92 D6
Natal Indonesia 39 D1
Naţanz 44 C2
Natashquan 71 D7
Natashquan → 71 D7
Natchez 81 D8
Nathalia 63 C4
Nathdwara 43 G9
Natitingou 53 F6
Natkyizin 41 K11
Natron, L. 57 E7
Natuna Besar, Kepulauan
   39 D3
Natuna Is. = Natuna Besar,
   Kepulauan 39 D3
Natuna Selatan,
   Kepulauan 39 D3
Naturaliste, C. 62 D4
Naujaat = Repulse Bay
   70 C5
Naumburg 15 C6
Nauru ■ 64 K11
Naushahra = Nowshera
   42 B8
Nauta 90 D4
Nautanwa 40 D4
Navahrudak 17 B7
Navalmoral de la Mata
   18 C3
Navarino, I. 95 H3
Navarra □ 19 A5
Năvodari 22 B7
Navoi = Nawoiy 29 E7
Navojoa 84 B3
Navsari 43 J8
Nawabshah 42 F6
Nawakot 40 D5
Nawalgarh 42 F9
Nawāsif, Ḩarrat 47 G5
Nawoiy 29 E7
Naxçıvan 25 F6
Naxçıvan □ 25 F6
Naxos 23 F5
Nāy Band 44 E3
Naypyidaw 41 H11
Nayoro 32 A8
Nazas → 84 B4
Nazili 23 F7
Ndalatando 56 F2

Ndélé 55 G3
Ndjamena 55 F1
Ndola 59 A5
Neagh, Lough 11 D3
Neales → 62 A2
Near Is. 69 C1
Neath 11 F5
Nebine Cr. → 63 A4
Nebitdag = Balkanabat
   29 F6
Nebraska □ 74 E5
Nébrodi, Monti 21 F5
Neckar → 14 D5
Necochea 94 D5
Nederland =
   Netherlands ■ 14 B3
Neemuch = Nimach 43 G9
Neepawa 69 C10
Negapatam =
   Nagappattinam 43 P11
Negele 49 F2
Negombo 43 R11
Negotin 22 B4
Negrais, C. = Maudin Sun
   41 K10
Negro → Argentina 95 E4
Negro → Brazil 90 D6
Negro → Uruguay 94 C5
Negros 36 C2
Nei Monggol Zizhiqu □
   35 B6
Neijiang 35 D5
Neiva 90 C3
Nejd = Najd 47 F5
Nellore 43 M11
Nelson Canada 69 D8
Nelson N.Z. 65 D5
Nelson → 69 C10
Nelson, C. 62 C3
Nelson, Estrecho 95 G2
Nelson Lakes △ 65 D5
Néma 53 E4
Neman = Nemunas →
   24 B1
Nemuro 32 B9
Nemuro-Kaikyō 32 B9
Nenagh 11 E2
Nenjiang 35 B7
Nepal ■ 40 D5
Nepalganj 40 C3
Neretva → 20 C6
Ness, L. 10 C4
Nesterov 17 C6
Nesvizh = Nyasvizh 17 B8
Netherlands ■ 14 B3
Netherlands Antilles ☑
   87 D6
Nettilling L. 70 C6
Neubrandenburg 15 B7
Neumünster 14 A5
Neunkirchen 14 D4
Neuquén 94 D3
Neuquén → 94 D3
Neuruppin 15 B7
Neustrelitz 15 B7
Neva → 24 B3
Nevada □ 72 G5
Nevers 13 C5
Nevertire 63 B4

Nevinnomyssk 25 E5
Nevşehir 46 C3
New Amsterdam 90 B7
New Angledool 63 A4
New Bedford 77 D10
New Bern 83 B9
New Britain Papua N. G.
   64 K10
New Britain U.S.A. 77 D9
New Brunswick □ 71 E7
New Caledonia ☑ 64 M11
New Castile = Castilla-La
   Mancha □ 18 C4
New Delhi 42 E10
New England Ra. 63 B5
New Forest △ 11 F6
New Glasgow 71 E7
New Hampshire □ 77 C10
New Haven 77 D9
New Hebrides =
   Vanuatu ■ 64 L11
New Ireland 64 K10
New Jersey □ 77 E9
New Liskeard 71 E6
New London 77 D9
New Mexico □ 79 C9
New Norfolk 62 D4
New Orleans 81 E8
New Plymouth 64 C6
New Providence 86 A4
New Siberian Is. =
   Novosibirskiye Ostrova
   31 B12
New South Wales □
   63 B4
New York 77 D9
New York □ 77 C8
New Zealand ■ 64 D7
Newark 77 D8
Newburgh 77 D8
Newbury 11 F6
Newcastle 63 B5
Newcastle-upon-Tyne
   11 D6
Newfoundland &
   Labrador □ 71 D8
Newman 60 E2
Newport I. of W., U.K.
   11 F6
Newport Newport, U.K.
   11 F5
Newport U.S.A. 77 D10
Newport News 77 F7
Newquay 11 F4
Newry 11 D3
Newton Boyd 63 A5

Nhill 62 C3
Niagara Falls Canada
   71 E6
Niagara Falls U.S.A. 77 C6
Niah 39 D4
Niamey 53 F6
Nias 39 D1
Nicaragua ■ 85 E7
Nicaragua, L. de 85 E7
Nicastro 21 E6
Nice 13 E7
Nichinan 33 H2
Nicobar Is. 27 D11
Nicosia 46 D3
Nicoya, Pen. de 85 F7
Niedersachsen □ 14 B5
Niemen = Nemunas →
   24 B1
Nienburg 14 B5
Nieuw Amsterdam 92 A2
Nieuw Nickerie 92 A2
Niğde 46 C3
Niger ■ 53 E7
Niger → 53 G7
Nigeria ■ 53 G7
Nightcaps 65 F3
Nihon = Japan ■ 33 F5
Nii-Jima 33 F6
Niigata 33 E6
Ni'ihau 78 H10
Niitsu 33 E6
Nijmegen 14 C3
Nikiniki 37 F2
Nikolayev = Mykolayiv
   25 D3
Nikolayevsk 24 C6
Nikopol 25 D3
Nikshahr 45 E5
Nikšić 22 C2
Nîl, Nahr en → 54 B5
Nîl el Abyad → 55 E5
Nîl el Azraq → 55 E5
Nile = Nîl, Nahr en →
   54 B5
Nimach 43 G9
Nîmes 13 E6
Nimfaíon, Ákra = Pines,
   Akra 23 D5
Nimmitabel 63 C4
Nîmrūz □ 45 D5
Ninawá 46 C5
Nindigully 63 A4
Nineveh = Nînawâ 46 C5
Ningbo 35 D7
Ningpo = Ningbo 35 D7
Ningsia Hui A.R. = Ningxia
   Huizu Zizhiqu □ 35 C5
Ningxia Huizu Zizhiqu □
   35 C5
Niobrara → 74 D5
Nioro du Sahel 53 E4
Niort 12 C3
Nipawin 69 C9
Nipigon, L. 71 E5
Nipissing, L. 71 E6
Nippon = Japan ■ 33 F5
Niquelândia 93 E4
Nirmal 43 K11
Nirmali 40 D6
Niš 22 C3

Niṣāb *Si. Arabia* **47 E6**
Niṣāb *Yemen* **49 E4**
Nistru = Dnister ➤ **17 E10**
Niṭā' **47 F7**
Niterói **93 G5**
Niue **65 L14**
Niut **39 D4**
Nivernais **13 C5**
Nizamabad **43 K11**
Nizamghat **41 C10**
Nizhnevartovsk **29 C8**
Nizhneyansk **31 B11**
Nizhniy Novgorod **24 B5**
Nizhniy Tagil **29 D6**
Nizhyn **24 C3**
Nkhata Bay **57 G6**
Nkhotakota **59 A6**
Nkongsamba **53 H7**
Nmai ➤ **41 E11**
Noakhali = Maijdi **41 F8**
Nobeoka **33 G2**
Nocera Inferiore **21 D5**
Nockatunga **62 A3**
Nogales *Mexico* **84 A2**
Nogales *U.S.A.* **79 E7**
Nōgata **33 G2**
Noginsk **30 C7**
Noires, Mts. **12 B2**
Noirmoutier, Î. de **12 C2**
Nojima-Zaki **33 F6**
Nok Kundi **42 E3**
Nokhtuysk **30 C9**
Nola **56 B3**
Nome **69 B3**
Nong Khai **38 A2**
Noondoo **63 A4**
Noranda = Rouyn-Noranda **71 E6**
Nord-Ostsee-Kanal **14 A5**
Norderney **14 B4**
Norderstedt **14 B5**
Nordfriesische Inseln **14 A5**
Nordhausen **14 C6**
Nordkapp **8 A11**
Nordrhein-Westfalen □ **14 C4**
Nordvik **30 B9**
Norfolk **77 F7**
Norfolk I. **64 M11**
Norge = Norway ■ **8 C8**
Norilsk **30 C6**
Norley **63 A3**
Norman **80 B5**
Norman Wells **68 B7**
Normandie **12 B4**
Normandy = Normandie **12 B4**
Normanton **61 D7**
Norquinco **95 E2**
Norrköping **9 D9**
Norrland **8 C9**
Norseman **60 G4**
North, C. **71 E7**
North Battleford **69 C9**
North Bay **71 E6**
North Bend **72 E1**
North C. **64 A5**
North Cape = Nordkapp **8 A11**

North Carolina □ **83 B7**
North Channel **11 D4**
North Dakota □ **74 B4**
North East Frontier Agency = Arunachal Pradesh □ **41 C10**
North Frisian Is. = Nordfriesische Inseln **14 A5**
North I. **64 B5**
North Korea ■ **35 C7**
North Lakhimpur **41 D10**
North Magnetic Pole **70 A2**
North Minch **10 B4**
North Ossetia □ **25 E5**
North Pagai, I. = Pagai Utara, Pulau **39 E2**
North Platte **74 E4**
North Platte ➤ **74 E4**
North Rhine Westphalia = Nordrhein-Westfalen □ **14 C4**
North Saskatchewan ➤ **69 C8**
North Sea **10 D8**
North Taranaki Bight **64 C6**
North Thompson ➤ **69 C7**
North Uist **10 C3**
North West C. **60 E1**
North West Frontier □ **42 B8**
North West Highlands **10 C4**
North West River **71 D7**
Northampton **11 E6**
Northern Circars **43 M4**
Northern Ireland □ **11 D3**
Northern Marianas ✪ **64 H9**
Northern Sporades **23 E4**
Northern Territory □ **60 D5**
Northland □ **64 A5**
Northumberland, C. **62 C3**
Northumberland Str. **71 E7**
Northwest Territories □ **68 B9**
Norton Sd. **69 B3**
Norway ■ **8 C8**
Norway House **69 C10**
Norwegian B. **70 B5**
Norwegian Sea **6 B5**
Norwich **11 E7**
Noshiro **32 C7**
Nosok **28 B9**
Noṣratābād **45 D4**
Nossob ➤ **58 D4**
Nosy Barren **59 B8**
Nosy Bé **59 A9**
Nosy Boraha **59 B9**
Nosy Varika **59 C9**
Noteć ➤ **16 B2**
Notre Dame B. **71 E8**
Notre-Dame-de-Koartac = Quaqtaq **70 C7**
Notre-Dame-d'Ivugivic = Ivujivik **70 C6**

Nottaway ➤ **71 D6**
Nottingham **11 E6**
Nottingham I. **70 C6**
Nouâdhibou **52 D2**
Nouâdhibou, Râs **52 D2**
Nouakchott **53 E2**
Nouméa **64 M11**
Nouveau Comptoir = Wemindji **71 D6**
Nouvelle-Calédonie = New Caledonia ✪ **64 M11**
Nova Casa Nova **93 D5**
Nova Friburgo **93 G5**
Nova Iguaçu **93 G5**
Nova Iorque **92 D5**
Nova Lima **93 F5**
Nova Scotia □ **71 E7**
Nova Venécia **93 F5**
Nova Zagora **22 C5**
Novara **13 D8**
Novaya Ladoga **24 A3**
Novaya Lyalya **29 D7**
Novaya Zemlya **28 B6**
Novgorod **24 B3**
Novgorod-Severskiy = Novhorod-Siverskiy **24 C3**
Novhorod-Siverskyy **24 C3**
Novi Lígure **13 D8**
Novi Pazar **22 C3**
Novi Sad **22 B2**
Novo Mesto **20 B5**
Novo Remanso **93 D5**
Novoaltaysk **29 D9**
Novocherkassk **25 D5**
Novogrudok = Navahrudak **17 B7**
Novohrad-Volynskyy **17 C8**
Novokachalinsk **32 A3**
Novokuybyshevsk **24 C6**
Novokuznetsk **29 D9**
Novomoskovsk **24 C4**
Novorossiysk **25 E4**
Novorybnoye **30 B9**
Novoselytsya **17 D8**
Novoshakhtinsk **25 D4**
Novosibirsk **29 D9**
Novosibirskiye Ostrova **31 B12**
Novotroitsk **29 D6**
Novouzensk **24 C6**
Novovolynsk **17 C7**
Novska **20 B6**
Novyy Port **28 C8**
Nowa Sól **16 C2**
Nowgong **41 D9**
Nowra **63 B5**
Nowy Targ **16 D5**
Nowy Tomyśl **16 B3**
Noyon **13 B5**
Nsanje **59 B7**
Nubian Desert = Nûbîya, Es Sahrâ en **54 D5**
Nûbîya, Es Sahrâ en **54 D5**
Nuboai **37 E5**
Nueltin L. **68 B10**

Nueva Rosita **84 B4**
Nuéve de Julio **94 D4**
Nuevitas **86 B4**
Nuevo, G. **95 E4**
Nuevo Laredo **84 B5**
Nugget Pt. **65 G3**
Nuhaka **64 C7**
Nukey Bluff **62 B2**
Nukuʻalofa **65 M13**
Nukus **29 E6**
Nullarbor Plain **60 G4**
Numalla, L. **63 A3**
Numan **55 G1**
Numazu **33 F6**
Numfoor **37 E4**
Numurkah **63 C4**
Nunavut □ **70 C5**
Nuneaton **11 E6**
Nunivak I. **69 B3**
Nunkun **42 C10**
Núoro **21 D2**
Nuremberg = Nürnberg **15 D6**
Nuriootpa **62 B2**
Nürnberg **15 D6**
Nurran, L. = Terewah, L. **63 A4**
Nusa Tenggara Barat □ **39 F5**
Nusa Tenggara Timur □ **37 F2**
Nushki **42 E5**
Nuuk **66 C14**
Nuwakot **40 C4**
Nuweveldberge **58 E4**
Nuyts Arch. **62 B1**
Nyahururu **57 D7**
Nyaingêntanglha Shan **34 C4**
Nyâlâ **55 F3**
Nyasa, L. = Malawi, L. **59 A6**
Nyasvizh **17 B8**
Nyda **28 C8**
Nyíregyháza **17 E5**
Nylstroom = Modimolle **59 C5**
Nymagee **63 B4**
Nyngan **63 B4**
Nyoman = Nemunas ➤ **24 B1**
Nysa **16 C3**
Nysa ➤ **16 B2**
Nyslott = Savonlinna **8 C11**
Nystad = Uusikaupunki **9 C10**
Nyurba **30 C9**
Nzega **57 E6**
Nzérékoré **53 G4**
Nzeto **56 F2**

O

Ō-Shima **33 F6**
Oahe, L. **74 C4**
Oʻahu **78 H12**
Oak Ridge **83 A5**
Oakey **63 A5**
Oakland **78 B1**

Oamaru 65 F4
Oates Land 96 A15
Oaxaca 84 D5
Ob → 28 C7
Oba 71 E5
Oban 10 C4
Obbia 49 F4
Oberhausen 14 C4
Oberon 63 B4
Obi, Kepulauan 37 E3
Óbidos 92 C2
Obihiro 32 B8
Obilatu 37 E3
Obo 57 C5
Oborzerskaya = Obozerskiy
  28 C5
Obozerskiy 28 C5
Obskaya Guba 28 C8
Obuasi 53 G5
Ocala 83 E6
Ocaña 18 C4
Occidental, Cordillera
  90 C3
Ocean I. = Banaba 64 K11
Oceanside 78 D4
Ocnița 17 D8
Ôda 33 F3
Odate 32 C7
Odawara 33 F6
Ödemiş 23 E7
Odense 9 D8
Oder → 15 B8
Odesa 25 D3
Odessa = Odesa 25 D3
Odessa 80 D2
Odienné 53 G4
Odintsovo 24 B4
Odra = Oder → 15 B8
Odzi 59 B6
Oeiras 92 D5
Offa 53 G6
Offenbach 14 C5
Offenburg 14 D4
Oga 32 D6
Oga-Hantō 32 D6
Ōgaki 33 F5
Ogasawara Gunto 27 F16
Ogbomosho 53 G6
Ogden 73 F7
Ogdensburg 77 B8
Oglio → 20 B3
Ogooué = 56 E1
Ogowe = Ogooué →
  56 E1
Ohai 65 F2
Ohakune 64 C6
Ohanet 52 C7
Ohata 32 C7
Ohau, L. 65 F3
Ohio □ 76 D4
Ohio → 76 F1
Ohře → 16 C2
Ohrid 22 D3
Ohridsko Jezero 23 D3
Oise → 12 B5
Ōita 33 G2
Oiticica 92 D5
Ojos del Salado, Cerro
  94 B3

Oka → 28 D5
Okaba 37 F5
Okahandja 58 C3
Okanogan → 72 B4
Okara 42 D8
Okavango Delta 58 B4
Okavango Swamp =
  Okavango Delta 58 B4
Okayama 33 F3
Okazaki 33 F5
Okeechobee, L. 83 F7
Okefenokee Swamp
  83 D6
Okhotsk, Sea of 31 D12
Oki-Shotō 33 E3
Okinawa-Jima 35 D7
Oklahoma □ 80 B5
Oklahoma City 80 B5
Okmulgee 81 B6
Oknitsa = Ocnița 17 D8
Oksibil 37 E6
Oktabrsk = Oktyabrsk
  29 E6
Oktyabrsk 29 E6
Oktyabrskiy = Aktsyabrski
  17 B9
Oktyabrskoy Revolyutsii,
  Ostrov 30 B7
Oktyabrskoye 28 C7
Okuru 65 E3
Okushiri-Tō 32 B6
Öland 9 D9
Olary 62 B3
Olavarría 94 D4
Oława 16 C3
Ólbia 20 D2
Old Castile = Castilla y
  Leon □ 18 A3
Old Crow 68 B6
Oldenburg 14 B5
Oldham 11 E5
Olekma → 31 C10
Olekminsk 31 C10
Oleksandriya 17 C8
Olenek 30 C9
Olenek → 30 B10
Oléron, Î. d' 12 D3
Oleśnica 16 C3
Olevsk 17 C8
Olhão 18 D2
Olifants = Elefantes →
  59 C6
Olivenza 18 C2
Ollagüe 91 H5
Olomouc 16 D3
Olongapo 36 B2
Olot 19 A7
Olsztyn 16 B5
Olt → 22 C5
Oltenița 22 B6
Olympos Oros 23 D4
Olympia Greece 23 F3
Olympia U.S.A. 72 C2
Olympic Mts. 72 C2
Olympus, Mt. = Olympos
  Oros 23 D4
Olympus, Mt. = Uludağ
  23 D7

Om → 29 D8
Ōmagari 32 D7
Omagh 11 D3
Omaha 75 E7
Oman ■ 48 C6
Oman, G. of 45 E4
Omaruru 58 C3
Omate 91 G4
Omboué 56 E1
Ombrone → 20 C3
Omdurmân 55 E5
Ometepec 84 D5
Omo → 55 G6
Omsk 29 D8
Ōmu 32 A8
Omul, Vf. 17 F7
Omuramba Omatako →
  58 B4
Ōmuta 33 G2
Onang 37 E1
Onda 19 C5
Ondangwa 58 B3
Öndörhaan 35 B6
Onega 28 C4
Onega, L. = Onezhskoye
  Ozero 8 C13
Oneşti 17 E8
Onezhskoye Ozero 8 C13
Ongarue 64 C6
Onilahy → 59 C8
Onitsha 53 G7
Ontario □ 71 E5
Ontario, L. 77 C7
Oodnadatta 62 A2
Oostende 14 C2
Ootacamund =
  Udagamandalam
  43 P10
Opala 56 E4
Opava 16 D3
Opole 16 C3
Oporto = Porto 18 B1
Opotiki 64 C7
Opua 64 A6
Opunake 64 C5
Opunohu, B. d' 30 H
Oradea 17 E6
Öræfajökull 8 C2
Orai 42 G11
Oral = Zhayyq → 29 E6
Oral 24 C7
Oran 52 A5
Orange Australia 63 B4
Orange France 13 D6
Orange U.S.A. 81 D7
Orange → 58 D3
Orange, C. 92 B3
Orange Free State = Free
  State □ 59 D5
Orangeburg 83 D7
Oranienburg 15 B7
Oranje = Orange → 58 D3
Orapa 59 C5
Oras 36 B3
Orbetello 20 C3
Orbost 63 C4
Orchila, I. 90 A5
Ordos = Mu Us Shamo
  35 C5

Ordu 46 B4
Ore Mts. = Erzgebirge
  15 C7
Örebro 9 D9
Oregon □ 72 E3
Orekhovo-Zuyevo 24 B4
Orel 24 C4
Ören 23 F6
Orenburg 29 D6
Orense = Ourense 18 A2
Orepuki 65 G2
Orfanos Kolpos 23 D5
Orgaz 18 C4
Orgeyev = Orhei 17 E9
Orhaneli 23 E7
Orhangazi 23 D7
Orhei 17 E9
Orhon Gol → 35 A5
Orient 62 A3
Oriental, Cordillera 90 B4
Orihuela 19 C5
Orinoco → 90 B6
Orissa □ 40 G5
Oristano 21 E2
Oristano, G. di 21 E2
Orizaba 84 D5
Orizaba, Pico de 84 D5
Orkney Is. 10 B5
Orlando 83 E7
Orléanais 12 C5
Orléans 12 C4
Ormara 42 G4
Ormoc 36 B2
Ormond 64 C7
Örnsköldsvik 8 C9
Orocué 90 C4
Orol Dengizi = Aral Sea
  29 E6
Oroquieta 36 C2
Orosháza 16 E5
Ororoso 62 B2
Orsha 24 C3
Orsk 29 D6
Orşova 22 B4
Ortaca 23 F7
Ortegal, C. 18 A2
Orthez 12 E3
Ortigueira 18 A2
Ortles 13 C9
Ortón → 91 F5
Orümiyeh 46 C6
Orümiyeh, Daryācheh-ye
  46 C6
Oruro 91 G5
Oruzgān □ 42 C5
Orvieto 20 C4
Oryakhovo 22 C4
Ōsaka 33 F4
Ösel = Saaremaa 24 B1
Osh 29 E8
Oshakati 58 B3
Oshawa 71 E6
Oshkosh 74 E3
Oshmyany = Ashmyany
  17 A7
Oshogbo 53 G6
Oshwe 56 E3
Osijek 20 B7
Osipovichi = Asipovichy
  17 B9

Osizweni 59 **D6**
Oskarshamn 9 **D9**
Öskemen 29 **E9**
Oslo 9 **D8**
Oslofjorden 9 **D8**
Osmanabad 43 **K10**
Osmaniye 46 **C4**
Osnabrück 14 **B5**
Osorno 95 **E2**
Ossa, Mt. 62 **D4**
Ossa, Oros 23 **E4**
Ostend = Oostende 14 **C2**
Oster 17 **C10**
Österdalälven 8 **C8**
Österreich = Austria ■
15 **E8**
Östersund 8 **C8**
Ostfriesische Inseln 14 **B4**
Ostrava 16 **D4**
Ostróda 16 **B4**
Ostroh 17 **C8**
Ostrołęka 16 **B5**
Ostrów Mazowiecka
16 **B5**
Ostrów Wielkopolski
16 **C3**
Ostrowiec-Świętokrzyski
16 **C5**
Ostuni 21 **D6**
Osuna 18 **A3**
Oswego 77 **C7**
Otago □ 65 **F3**
Otago Harbour 65 **F4**
Otaki 64 **D6**
Otaru 32 **B7**
Otaru-Wan = Ishikari-Wan
32 **B7**
Otavalo 90 **C3**
Otjiwarongo 58 **C3**
Otoineppu 32 **A8**
Otorohanga 64 **C6**
Otranto 21 **D7**
Otranto, C. d' 21 **D7**
Otranto, Str. of 21 **D7**
Ōtsu 33 **F4**
Ottawa = Outaouais ➜
71 **E6**
Ottawa 71 **E6**
Ottawa Is. 70 **D5**
Ottumwa 75 **E8**
Oturkpo 53 **G7**
Otway, B. 95 **G2**
Otway, C. 62 **C3**
Otwock 16 **B5**
Ouachita Mts. 81 **B6**
Ouadda 55 **G3**
Ouagadougou 53 **F5**
Ouahran = Oran 52 **A5**
Ouallene 52 **D6**
Ouanda Djallé 55 **G3**
Ouaqui 30 **E**
Ouargla 52 **B7**
Ouarzazate 52 **B4**
Oubangi ➜ 56 **E3**
Oudtshoorn 58 **E4**
Ouessant, Î. d' 12 **B1**
Ouesso 56 **D3**
Ouest, Pte. de l' 30 **A**
Ouezzane 52 **B4**
Oujda 52 **B5**

Oulu 8 **B11**
Oulujärvi 8 **C11**
Oulujoki ➜ 8 **B11**
Oum Chalouba 55 **E3**
Oum Hadjer 55 **F2**
Ounianga Sérir 55 **E3**
Ourense 18 **A2**
Ouricuri 92 **D5**
Ouro Prêto 93 **G5**
Ouse 62 **D4**
Outaouais ➜ 71 **E6**
Outer Hebrides 10 **C3**
Outjo 58 **C3**
Ouyen 62 **C3**
Ovalle 94 **C2**
Ovamboland 58 **B3**
Ovambo = Ovamboland
58 **B3**
Owase 33 **F5**
Owbeh 42 **B3**
Owen Sound 71 **E5**
Owen Stanley Ra. 61 **B8**
Owo 53 **G7**
Owyhee ➜ 72 **E5**
Oxford N.Z. 65 **E5**
Oxford U.K. 11 **F6**
Oxnard 78 **C3**
Oxus = Amudarya ➜
29 **E6**
Oya 39 **D4**
Oyama 33 **E6**
Oyem 56 **D2**
Oyo 53 **G6**
Ozamiz 36 **C2**
Ozark Plateau 81 **A8**
Ózd 16 **D5**

P

Pa-an 41 **J11**
Paarl 58 **E3**
Pab Hills 42 **F5**
Pabianice 16 **C4**
Pabna 41 **E7**
Pacaja ➜ 92 **C3**
Pacaraima, Sa. 90 **C6**
Pacasmayo 91 **E3**
Pachpadra 42 **G8**
Pachuca 84 **C5**
Padaido, Kepulauan 37 **E5**
Padang 39 **E2**
Padangpanjang 39 **E2**
Padangsidempuan 39 **D1**
Paderborn 14 **C5**
Padloping Island 70 **C7**
Pádova 20 **B3**
Padua = Pádova 20 **B3**
Paducah 76 **F1**
Paeroa 64 **B6**
Pag 20 **B5**
Pagadian 36 **C2**
Pagai Selatan, Pulau
39 **E2**
Pagai Utara, Pulau 39 **E2**
Pagalu = Annobón 51 **G4**
Pagastikos Kolpos 23 **E4**
Pagatan 39 **E5**

Pahiatua 64 **D6**
Päijänne 8 **C11**
Painan 39 **E2**
Paint Hills = Wemindji
71 **D6**
Painted Desert 79 **C7**
País Vasco □ 19 **A4**
Paisley 10 **D4**
Paita 90 **E2**
Pajares, Puerto de 18 **A3**
Pakistan ■ 42 **E7**
Pakokku 41 **G10**
Paktīā □ 42 **C6**
Pakxe 38 **A3**
Pala 55 **G2**
Palagruža 20 **C6**
Palam 43 **K10**
Palampur 42 **C10**
Palana 62 **C4**
Palanan 36 **A2**
Palanan Pt. 36 **A2**
Palangkaraya 39 **E4**
Palani Hills 43 **P10**
Palanpur 43 **G8**
Palapye 59 **C5**
Palatka 83 **D7**
Palau ■ 36 **C4**
Palawan 38 **C5**
Palayankottai 43 **Q10**
Paleleh 37 **D2**
Palembang 39 **E2**
Palencia 18 **A3**
Palermo 21 **E4**
Palestine 81 **D6**
Paletwa 41 **G9**
Palghat 43 **P10**
Pali 42 **G8**
Palikir 64 **J10**
Paliouri, Akra 23 **E4**
Palitana 43 **J7**
Palk Bay 43 **Q11**
Palk Strait 43 **Q11**
Pallanza = Verbánia 13 **D8**
Palm Springs 78 **D4**
Palma, B. de 19 **C7**
Palma de Mallorca 19 **C7**
Palmares 92 **D6**
Palmas, C. 53 **H4**
Palmas, G. di 21 **E2**
Palmeira dos Índios 93 **D6**
Palmer 69 **B5**
Palmer Arch. 96 **A3**
Palmer Land 96 **B3**
Palmerston 65 **F4**
Palmerston North 64 **D6**
Palmi 21 **E5**
Palmira 90 **C3**
Palmyra = Tudmur 46 **D4**
Palopo 37 **E2**
Palos, C. de 19 **D5**
Palu Indonesia 37 **E1**
Palu Turkey 46 **C5**
Pamiers 12 **E4**
Pamir 29 **F8**
Pamlico Sd. 83 **B10**
Pampa 80 **A4**
Pampanua 37 **E2**
Pampas Argentina 94 **D4**
Pampas Peru 91 **F4**
Pamplona Colombia
90 **B4**

Pamplona Spain 19 **A5**
Panaji 43 **M8**
Panamá 85 **F9**
Panamá ■ 86 **E4**
Panamá, G. de 86 **E4**
Panama Canal 86 **E4**
Panama City 82 **D5**
Panão 91 **E3**
Panay 36 **B2**
Panay G. 36 **B2**
Pančevo 22 **B3**
Pandan 36 **B2**
Pandharpur 43 **L9**
Pando, L. = Hope, L.
62 **A2**
Panevėžys 24 **B1**
Pang-Long 41 **F12**
Pang-Yang 41 **F12**
Pangani 57 **F7**
Pangfou = Bengbu 35 **C6**
Pangkajene 37 **E1**
Pangkalanbrandan 39 **D1**
Pangkalanbuun 39 **E4**
Pangkalpinang 39 **E3**
Pangnirtung 70 **C7**
Pangutaran Group 36 **C2**
Panjgur 42 **F4**
Panjim = Panaji 43 **M8**
Panjnad Barrage 42 **E7**
Pannirtuuq = Pangnirtung
70 **C7**
Panorama 94 **A6**
Pantar 37 **F2**
Pante Macassar 37 **F2**
Pante Makasar = Pante
Macassar 37 **F2**
Pantelleria 21 **F3**
Paoting = Baoding 35 **C6**
Paot'ou = Baotou 35 **B6**
Paoua 55 **G2**
Pápa 16 **E3**
Papakura 64 **B6**
Papantla 84 **C5**
Papar 38 **C5**
Paparoa △ 65 **E4**
Papeete 65 **L16**
Papua □ 37 **E5**
Papua New Guinea ■
64 **K9**
Papudo 94 **C2**
Papun 41 **H11**
Pará = Belém 92 **C4**
Pará □ 92 **C3**
Paracatu 93 **F4**
Paracel Is. 38 **A4**
Parachilna 62 **B2**
Paradip 40 **G6**
Parado 37 **F1**
Paraguá ➜ 90 **B6**
Paraguaçu ➜ 93 **E6**
Paraguaná, Pen. de 90 **A4**
Paraguay ■ 94 **A5**
Paraguay ➜ 94 **B5**
Paraíba = João Pessoa
92 **D7**
Paraíba □ 92 **D6**
Parakou 53 **G6**
Paramaribo 92 **A2**
Paraná Argentina 94 **C4**

Paraná *Brazil* 93 E4
Paraná ☐ 94 A6
Paraná ➤ 94 C5
Paranaguá 94 B7
Paranaíba 93 F3
Paranaíba ➤ 93 G3
Paranapanema ➤ 94 A6
Paranas 36 B3
Parang *Maguindanao, Phil.* 36 C2
Parang *Sulu, Phil.* 36 C2
Parângul Mare, Vf. 17 F6
Paratinga 93 E5
Parattah 62 D4
Parbhani 43 K10
Parchim 15 B6
Pardo ➤ *Bahia, Brazil* 93 F6
Pardo ➤ *Mato Grosso, Brazil* 93 G3
Pardubice 16 C2
Parecis, Serra dos 91 F7
Parepare 37 E1
Parga 23 E3
Pariaguán 90 B6
Parigi 37 E2
Parika 90 B7
Parima, Serra 90 C6
Parinari 90 D4
Parintins 92 C2
Pariparit Kyun 41 K9
Paris *France* 12 B5
Paris *U.S.A.* 81 C6
Park Range 73 G10
Parkersburg 76 E5
Parkes 63 B4
Parla 18 B4
Parma 13 D9
Parnaguá 93 E5
Parnaíba 92 C5
Parnaíba ➤ 92 C5
Parnassos 23 E4
Pärnu 24 B1
Paroo ➤ 63 B3
Paros 23 F5
Parral 94 D2
Parry Is. 70 B3
Parry Sound 71 E6
Partinico 21 E4
Paru ➤ 92 C3
Parván ☐ 42 B6
Parvatipuram 40 H4
Pas, The 69 C9
Pasadena *Calif., U.S.A.* 78 C3
Pasadena *Tex., U.S.A.* 81 E6
Pascagoula 81 D9
Paşcani 17 E8
Pasco 72 C4
Pasco, Cerro de 91 F3
Pasirkuning 39 E2
Pašman 20 C5
Pasni 42 G3
Paso de Indios 95 E3
Passau 15 D7
Passero, C. 21 F5
Passo Fundo 94 B6
Passos 93 G4

Pastaza ➤ 90 D3
Pasto 90 C3
Patagonia 95 F3
Patan = Lalitapur 40 D5
Patan 43 H8
Patani 37 D3
Patchewollock 62 C3
Patea 64 C6
Paternò 21 F5
Paterson 77 D8
Pathankot 42 C9
Pathein = Bassein 41 J10
Patiala 42 D10
Patkai Bum 41 D10
Patmos 23 F6
Patna 40 E5
Patos, L. dos 94 C6
Patos de Minas 93 F4
Patquía 94 C3
Patra 23 E3
Patraikos Kolpos 23 E3
Patras = Patra 23 E3
Patrocínio 93 F4
Pattani 38 C2
Patuakhali 41 F8
Pau 12 E3
Pauk 41 G10
Paulistana 92 D5
Paulo Afonso 93 D6
Pavia 13 D8
Pavlodar 29 D8
Pavlograd = Pavlohrad 25 D4
Pavlohrad 25 D4
Pavlovo 24 B5
Pavlovsk 24 C5
Pawtucket 77 D10
Paxi 23 E3
Payakumbuh 39 E2
Payne Bay = Kangirsuk 70 D7
Payne, L. 70 D6
Paysandú 94 C5
Paz, B. de la 84 C2
Pazar 46 B5
Pazardzhik 22 C5
Peace ➤ 68 C8
Peak Hill 63 B4
Peake Cr. ➤ 62 A2
Peawanuck 71 D5
Pebane 59 B7
Pebas 90 D4
Peć 22 C3
Pechenga 28 C4
Pechenizhyn 17 D7
Pechora ➤ 28 C6
Pechorskaya Guba 28 C6
Pecos ➤ 80 E3
Pécs 16 E4
Pedder, L. 62 D4
Pedra Azul 93 F5
Pedreiras 92 C5
Pedro Afonso 93 D4
Pedro Juan Caballero 94 A5
Peebinga 62 B3
Peel ➤ *Australia* 63 B5
Peel ➤ *Canada* 68 B6
Peera Peera Poolanna L. 62 A2

Pegasus Bay 65 E5
Pegu 41 J11
Pegu Yoma 41 H10
Pehuajó 94 D4
Peine 14 B6
Peip'ing = Beijing 35 C6
Peipus, L. = Chudskoye, Ozero 24 B2
Peixe 93 E4
Pekalongan 39 F3
Pekanbaru 39 D2
Pekin 75 E10
Peking = Beijing 35 C6
Pelagie, Is. 21 G4
Pelaihari 39 E4
Peleaga, Vf. 17 F6
Peleng 37 E2
Peljesac 20 C6
Pelly ➤ 68 B6
Pelly Bay 70 C5
Peloponnese ☐ 23 F4
Peloro, C. 21 E5
Pelorus Sd. 65 D5
Pelotas 94 C6
Pelvoux, Massif du 13 D7
Pematangsiantar 39 D1
Pemba 59 A8
Pemba I. 57 F7
Pembroke *Canada* 71 E6
Pembroke *U.K.* 11 F4
Penang = Pinang 38 C2
Penápolis 94 A6
Peñarroya-Pueblonuevo 18 C3
Peñas, C. de 18 A3
Peñas, G. de 95 F2
Pench'i = Benxi 35 B7
Pend Oreille, L. 72 C5
Pendembu 53 G3
Pendleton 72 C4
Penedo 93 E6
Penguin 62 D4
Peniche 18 C1
Penida, Nusa 39 F5
Peninsular Malaysia ☐ 39 D2
Penmarch, Pte. de 12 C1
Pennines 11 D5
Pennsylvania ☐ 77 D7
Penny Str. 70 B4
Penola 62 C3
Penong 60 G5
Penrhyn 65 K15
Penrith 63 B5
Pensacola 82 D4
Pensacola Mts. 96 C4
Penshurst 62 C3
Penticton 69 D8
Pentland Firth 10 B5
Penza 24 C6
Penzance 11 F4
Peoria 75 E10
Perabumulih 39 E2
Perche, Collines du 12 B4
Perdido, Mte. 19 A6
Perdu, Mt. = Perdido, Mte. 19 A6
Pereira 90 C3
Perekerten 62 B3
Pereyaslav-Khmelnytskyy 24 C3

Pergamino 94 C4
Péribonka ➤ 71 E6
Perico 94 A3
Périgueux 12 D4
Perijá, Sierra de 90 B4
Perlas, Arch. de las 86 E4
Perm 29 D6
Pernambuco = Recife 92 D7
Pernatty Lagoon 62 B3
Pernik 22 C4
Perpendicular Pt. 63 B5
Perpignan 13 E5
Persepolis 44 D3
Pershotravensk 17 C8
Pervouralsk 29 D6
Pésaro 20 C4
Pescara 20 C5
Peshawar 42 B7
Peshkopi 22 D3
Pesqueira 92 D6
Petah Tiqwa 46 D3
Petauke 59 A6
Peter I. Øy 96 A2
Peterborough *Australia* 62 B2
Peterborough *Canada* 71 E6
Peterborough *U.K.* 11 E6
Peterhead 10 C6
Petersburg *Alaska, U.S.A.* 69 C6
Petersburg *Va., U.S.A.* 77 F7
Petit Barachois 30 A
Petitsikapau L. 71 D7
Petlad 43 H8
Peto 85 C7
Petone 65 D5
Petra Velikogo, Zaliv 32 B3
Petrich 22 D4
Petrikov = Pyetrikaw 17 B9
Petrolândia 93 D6
Petrolina 93 D5
Petropavl 29 D7
Petropavlovsk = Petropavl 29 D7
Petropavlovsk-Kamchatskiy 31 D13
Petrópolis 93 G5
Petroşani 17 F6
Petrovaradin 22 B2
Petrovsk 24 C5
Petrozavodsk 8 C12
Peureulak 38 D1
Pforzheim 14 D5
Phagwara 42 D9
Phalodi 42 F8
Phan Rang 38 B3
Phangan, Ko 38 C2
Phangnga 38 C1

Phatthalung 38 C2
Phetchabun 38 A2
Philadelphia 77 E8
Philippine Trench =
  Mindanao Trench 36 B3
Philippines ■ 36 B2
Philippopolis = Plovdiv
  22 C5
Phillip I. 63 C4
Phillott 63 A4
Phitsanulok 38 A2
Phnom Dangrek 38 B2
Phnom Penh 38 B2
Phnom Penh = Phnom
  Penh 38 B2
Phoenix 79 D6
Phra Nakhon Si Ayutthaya
  38 B2
Phuket 38 C1
Phumiphon, Khuan 38 A1
Piacenza 13 D8
Pialba 63 A5
Pian Cr. → 63 B4
Pianosa 20 C3
Piatra Neamţ 17 E8
Piauí □ 92 D5
Piave → 20 B4
Pibor Post 55 G5
Picardie □ 13 B5
Picardy = Picardie □
  13 B5
Pichilemu 94 C2
Pico Truncado 95 F3
Picton Australia 63 B5
Picton N.Z. 65 D6
Picún Leufú 95 D3
Piedmont = Piemonte □
  13 D7
Piedras, R. de las →
  91 F5
Piedras Negras 84 B4
Pielinen 8 C11
Piemonte □ 13 D7
Piet Retief 59 D6
Pietermaritzburg 59 D6
Pietersburg = Polokwane
  59 C5
Pietrosul, Vf. Maramureș,
  Romania 17 E7
Pietrosul, Vf. Suceava,
  Romania 17 E7
Pigüe 94 D4
Piła 16 B3
Pilar 94 B5
Pilcomayo → 94 B5
Pilibhit 42 E11
Pilica → 16 C5
Pilipinas = Philippines ■
  36 B2
Pilos 23 F3
Pimba 62 B2
Pimenta Bueno 91 F6
Pimentel 91 E3
Pinang 38 C2
Pinar del Río 86 B3
Pınarhisar 22 D6
Pińczów 16 C5
Pindos Oros 23 E3
Pindus Mts. = Pindos Oros
  23 E3
Pine Bluff 81 B7

Pine Point 68 B8
Pinega → 28 C5
Pinerolo 13 D7
Pines, Akra 23 D5
Ping → 38 A2
Pingdong 35 D7
Pingliang 35 C5
Pingxiang 35 D5
Pinhel 18 B2
Pini 39 D1
Pinios → 23 E4
Pinnaroo 62 C3
Pinrang 37 E1
Pinsk 17 B8
Pintados 91 H5
Pinyug 24 A6
Piombino 20 C3
Pioner, Ostrov 30 B7
Piopiotaki = Milford Sd.
  65 F2
Piorini, L. 90 D6
Piotrków Trybunalski
  16 C4
Pīp 45 E5
Piquiri → 94 A6
Piracicaba 94 A7
Piracuruca 92 C5
Piræus = Pireas 23 F4
Piraiévs = Pireas 23 F4
Pirané 94 B5
Pirapora 93 F5
Pireas 23 F4
Pirgos 23 F3
Pirin Planina 22 D4
Pírineos = Pyrénées 12 E4
Piripiri 92 C5
Pirmasens 14 D4
Pirot 22 C4
Piru 37 E3
Pisa 20 C3
Pisagua 91 G4
Pisciotta 21 D5
Pisco 91 F3
Písek 16 D2
Pishan 34 C2
Pising 37 F2
Pistóia 20 C3
Pisuerga → 18 B3
Pitarpunga L. 62 B3
Pitcairn I. 65 M17
Piteå 8 B10
Pitești 22 B5
Pithapuram 40 J4
Pittsburg 81 A6
Pittsburgh 77 D5
Pittsworth 63 A5
Piura 90 E2
Placentia 71 E8
Placentia B. 71 E8
Plainview 80 B3
Plaka, Akra 23 G6
Plakhino 28 C9
Plasencia 18 B2
Plastun 32 A5
Plata, Río de la → 94 C5
Plátani → 21 F4
Platte → 75 F7
Plauen 15 C7
Plei Ku 38 B3
Plenty, B. of 64 B7

Plevlja 22 C2
Płock 16 B4
Plöckenstein 15 D7
Ploiești 22 B6
Plovdiv 22 C5
Plumtree 59 C5
Plymouth 11 F4
Plzeň 16 D1
Po → 20 B4
Po Hai = Bo Hai 35 C6
Pobedy, Pik 29 E8
Pocatello 73 E7
Poços de Caldas 93 G4
Podgorica 22 C2
Podilska Vysochyna 17 D8
Podolsk 24 B4
Poh 37 E2
Pohnpei 64 J10
Poinsett, C. 96 A12
Pointe-à-Pitre 87 C7
Pointe-Noire 56 E2
Poitiers 12 C4
Poitou 12 C3
Pokaran 42 F7
Pokataroo 63 A4
Pola = Pula 20 B4
Polan 45 E5
Poland ■ 16 B5
Polatsk 24 B2
Polesye = Pripet Marshes
  17 B9
Police 16 B2
Poligiros 23 D4
Polillo Is. 36 B2
Pollachi 43 P10
Polnovat 28 C7
Polokwane 59 C5
Polonne 17 C8
Polonnoye = Polonne
  17 C8
Poltava 24 D3
Polunochnoye 28 C7
Polynesia 65 L15
Polynésie française =
  French Polynesia ☑
  65 M16
Pombal 18 C1
Poméria 20 D4
Pomorskie, Pojezierze
  16 B3
Ponape = Pohnpei 64 J10
Ponca City 80 A5
Ponce 87 C6
Pond Inlet 70 B6
Pondicherry = Puducherry
  43 P11
Ponferrada 18 A2
Ponnani 43 P9
Ponnyadaung 41 F10
Ponta Grossa 94 B6
Ponta Pora 94 A5
Pontarlier 13 C7
Pontchartrain, L. 81 D8
Ponte Nova 93 G5
Pontevedra 18 A1
Pontiac 76 C4
Pontianak 39 E3
Pontine Is. = Ponziane,
  Ísole 21 D4
Pontine Mts. = Kuzey
  Anadolu Dağları 25 E4

Pontivy 12 B2
Pontoise 12 B5
Ponziane, Ísole 21 D4
Poochera 62 B1
Poole 11 F6
Poona = Pune 43 K8
Poonamalee 43 N11
Poopelloe L. 63 B3
Poopó, L. de 91 G5
Popayán 90 C3
Popigay 30 B9
Popilah L. 62 B3
Popio L. 62 B3
Poplar Bluff 81 A8
Popocatépetl, Volcán
  84 D5
Popokabaka 56 F3
Porbandar 43 J6
Porcupine → 69 B5
Pordenone 20 B4
Pori 8 C10
Porkkala = Porkkala 9 G12
Porkkala 9 G12
Porlamar 90 A6
Poronaysk 31 E15
Poroshiri-Dake 32 B8
Porpoise B. 96 A13
Port Alberni 69 D7
Port Angeles 72 B2
Port Arthur Australia 62 D4
Port Arthur U.S.A. 81 E7
Port Augusta 62 B2
Port Augusta West 62 B2
Port Broughton 62 B2
Port Chalmers 65 F4
Port Darwin 95 G5
Port Davey 62 D4
Port Dickson 39 D2
Port Elizabeth 59 E5
Port Fairy 62 C3
Port-Gentil 56 E1
Port Harcourt 53 H7
Port Harrison = Inukjuak
  70 D6
Port Hawkesbury 71 E7
Port Hedland 60 E2
Port Hope Simpson 71 D8
Port Huron 76 C4
Port Kenny 62 B1
Port Lairge = Waterford
  11 E3
Port Laoise 11 E3
Port Lincoln 62 B2
Port Loko 53 G3
Port Louis 51 J9
Port MacDonnell 62 C3
Port Macquarie 63 B5
Port Moresby 61 B8
Port Nelson 69 C10
Port Nolloth 58 D3
Port Nouveau-Québec =
  Kangiqsualujjuaq 70 D7
Port of Spain 87 D7
Port Pegasus 65 G2
Port Phillip B. 63 C3
Port Pirie 62 B2
Port Safaga = Bûr Safâga
  54 C5
Port Said = Bûr Sa'îd
  54 B5

Port St. Johns =
  Umzimvubu 59 E5
Port Shepstone 59 E6
Port Stanley = Stanley
  95 G5
Port Sudan = Bûr Sûdân
  55 E6
Port Talbot 11 F5
Port-Vendres 13 E5
Port Vila 64 L11
Port Wakefield 62 B2
Porta Orientalis 22 B4
Portadown 11 D3
Portage la Prairie 69 D10
Portalegre 18 C2
Portbou 19 A7
Portile de Fier 22 B4
Portimão 18 D1
Portland N.S.W., Australia
  63 B4
Portland Vic., Australia
  62 C3
Portland Maine, U.S.A.
  77 C10
Portland Oreg., U.S.A.
  72 D2
Portland B. 62 C3
Porto 18 B1
Pôrto Alegre 94 C6
Pôrto de Móz 92 C3
Porto Empédocle 21 F4
Pôrto Esperança 91 G7
Pôrto Franco 92 D4
Pôrto Mendes 94 A6
Pôrto Murtinho 91 H7
Pôrto Nacional 93 E4
Porto-Novo 53 G6
Porto Santo, I. de 52 B2
Pôrto Seguro 93 F6
Porto Tórres 20 D2
Pôrto União 94 B6
Pôrto Válter 91 E4
Porto-Vecchio 13 F8
Pôrto Velho 91 E6
Portoferráio 20 C3
Portoscuso 21 E2
Portoviejo 90 D2
Portree 10 C3
Portsmouth U.K. 11 F6
Portsmouth U.S.A. 77 F7
Porttipahdan tekojärvi
  8 B11
Portugal ■ 18 C1
Porvenir 95 G2
Posadas 94 B5
Poso 37 E2
Posse 93 E4
Possession I. 96 B15
Poste-de-la-Baleine =
  Kuujjuarapik 71 D6
Postmasburg 58 D4
Postojna 20 B5
Potchefstroom 59 D5
Potenza 21 D5
Poteriteri, L. 65 G2
Potgietersrus = Mokopane
  59 C5
Poti 25 E5
Potomac → 77 E7
Potosí 91 G5

Pototan 36 B2
Potrerillos 94 B3
Potsdam 15 B7
Poughkeepsie 77 D9
Považská Bystrica 16 D4
Poverty B. 64 C8
Póvoa de Varzim 18 B1
Povungnituk = Puvirnituq
  70 C6
Powder → 74 B2
Powell, L. 79 B7
Poyang Hu 35 D6
Požarevac 22 B3
Poznań 16 B3
Pozo Almonte 91 H5
Pozoblanco 18 C3
Pozzuoli 21 D5
Prachuap Khiri Khan
  38 B1
Prado 93 F6
Prague = Praha 16 C2
Praha 16 C2
Prainha Amazonas, Brazil
  91 E6
Prainha Pará, Brazil 92 C3
Prairies 69 C9
Prapat 39 D1
Prata 93 F4
Prato 20 C3
Pravia 18 A2
Praya 39 F5
Preobrazheniye 32 B3
Preparis North Channel
  41 K9
Preparis South Channel
  41 K9
Přerov 16 D3
Preservation Inlet 65 G2
Presidencia Roque Saenz
  Peña 94 B4
Presidente Epitácio 93 G3
Presidente Prudente
  93 G3
Prespa, L. = Prespansko
  Jezero 23 D3
Prespansko Jezero 23 D3
Presque Isle 77 A11
Preston 11 E5
Pretoria 59 D5
Preveza 23 E3
Příbram 16 D2
Prichard 82 D3
Prieska 58 D4
Prilep 22 D3
Priluki = Pryluky 24 C3
Prime Seal I. 62 D4
Prince Albert 69 C9
Prince Albert Mts. 96 B15
Prince Albert Pen. 68 A8
Prince Albert Sd. 68 A8
Prince Alfred, C. 70 B1
Prince Charles I. 70 C6
Prince Charles Mts.
  96 B10
Prince Edward I. □ 71 E7
Prince of Wales I. 68 A10
Prince Patrick I. 70 B2
Principe da Beira 91 F6
Prins Harald Kyst 96 B8
Prinsesse Astrid Kyst
  96 B7

Prinsesse Ragnhild Kyst
  96 B8
Pripet = Prypyat →
  17 C10
Pripet Marshes 17 B9
Pripyat Marshes = Pripet
  Marshes 17 B9
Pripyats = Prypyat →
  17 C10
Priština 22 C3
Privas 13 D6
Privolzhskaya
  Vozvyshennost 24 C6
Prizren 22 C3
Proddatur 43 M11
Progreso 85 C7
Prokopyevsk 29 D9
Prokuplje 22 C3
Prome 41 H10
Propriá 93 E6
Prosna → 16 B3
Prostějov 16 D3
Proston 63 A5
Provence 13 E6
Providence 77 D10
Providencia, I. de 86 D3
Provins 13 B5
Provo 73 F8
Pruszków 16 B5
Prut → 17 F9
Pruzhany 17 B7
Prydz B. 96 A10
Pryluky 24 C3
Prypyat → 17 C10
Przhevalsk = Karakol
  29 E8
Psara 23 E5
Psiloritis, Oros 23 G5
Pskov 24 B2
Ptich = Ptsich → 17 B9
Ptsich → 17 B9
Puán 94 D4
Pucallpa 91 E4
Puducherry 43 P11
Pudukkottai 43 P11
Puebla 84 D5
Pueblo 74 F2
Puelches 94 D3
Puente Alto 94 C2
Puente-Genil 18 D3
Puerto Aisén 95 F2
Puerto Ayacucho 90 B5
Puerto Barrios 85 D7
Puerto Bermúdez 91 F4
Puerto Bolívar 90 D3
Puerto Cabello 90 A5
Puerto Cabezas 86 D3
Puerto Carreño 90 B5
Puerto Chicama 91 E3
Puerto Coig 95 G3
Puerto Cortés 85 D7
Puerto Cumarebo 90 A5
Puerto Deseado 95 F3
Puerto Heath 91 F5
Puerto La Cruz 90 A6
Puerto Leguízamo 90 D4
Puerto Lobos 95 E3
Puerto Madryn 95 E3
Puerto Maldonado 91 F5
Puerto Montt 95 E2

Puerto Natales 95 G2
Puerto Páez 90 B5
Puerto Pinasco 94 A5
Puerto Plata 87 C5
Puerto Princesa 36 C1
Puerto Rico ☑ 87 C6
Puerto Sastre 91 H7
Puerto Suárez 91 G7
Puerto Wilches 90 B4
Puertollano 18 C3
Pueyrredón, L. 95 F2
Pugachev 24 C6
Puget Sound 72 C2
Puigcerdà 19 A6
Pukaki, L. 65 F4
Pukapuka 65 L14
Pukekohe 64 B6
Pula 20 B4
Pulandian 35 C7
Puławy 16 C5
Pullman 72 C5
Pulog, Mt. 36 A2
Pułtusk 16 B5
Puná, I. 90 D2
Punakaiki 65 E4
Punakha Dzong 41 D7
Punata 91 G5
Punch 42 C7
Pune 43 K8
Punjab □ India 42 D9
Punjab □ Pakistan 42 D8
Puno 91 G4
Punta Alta 94 D4
Punta Arenas 95 G2
Punta de Díaz 94 B2
Puntabie 62 B1
Puntarenas 86 E3
Punto Fijo 90 A4
Puquio 91 F4
Pur → 28 C8
Puracé, Vol. 90 C3
Puralia = Puruliya 40 F6
Puri 40 H5
Purnia 40 E6
Purukcahu 39 E4
Puruliya 40 F6
Purus → 90 D6
Pusan = Busan 35 C7
Pushkino 24 C6
Putao 41 D11
Putaruru 64 C6
Puthein Myit → 41 K10
Putignano 21 D6
Puting, Tanjung 39 E4
Putorana, Gory 30 C7
Puttalam 43 Q11
Puttgarden 15 A6
Putumayo → 90 D5
Putussibau 39 D4
Puvirnituq 70 C6
Puy-de-Dôme 13 D5
Pwllheli 11 E4
Pyapon 41 J10
Pyasina → 30 B6
Pyatigorsk 25 E5
Pyè = Prome 41 H10
Pyetrikaw 17 B9
Pyinmana 41 H11
P'yŏngyang 35 C7
Pyrénées 12 E1
Pyu 41 H11

Q

Qä'emshahr 44 B3
Qahremānshahr =
Kermānshāh 46 D6
Qaidam Pendi 34 C4
Qal'at al Akhḍar 47 E4
Qalāt-i-Ghilzai 45 C6
Qal'eh Shaharak 42 B4
Qamani'tuaq = Baker Lake
68 B10
Qamruddin Karez 42 D6
Qandahār = Kandahār
42 D4
Qandahār = Kandahār □
42 D4
Qapshaghay 29 E8
Qarabutaq 29 E7
Qarachuk 46 C5
Qaraghandy 29 E8
Qaraghayly 29 E8
Qarataū Kazakhstan 29 E7
Qarataū Zhambyl,
Kazakhstan 29 E8
Qarazhal 29 E8
Qardho = Gardo 49 F4
Qarqan 34 C4
Qarqan He → 34 C3
Qarqaraly 29 E8
Qarshi 29 F7
Qasr-e Qand 45 E5
Qasr Farâfra 54 C4
Qatar ■ 44 E2
Qattâra, Munkhafed el
54 C4
Qattâra Depression =
Qattâra, Munkhafed el
54 C4
Qausiuittuq = Resolute
70 B4
Qāyen 44 C4
Qazaqstan =
Kazakhstan ■ 29 E7
Qazvīn 46 C7
Qena 54 C5
Qeshm 44 E4
Qikiqtarjuaq 70 C7
Qila Saifullāh 42 D6
Qilian Shan 34 C4
Qingdao 35 C7
Qinghai □ 34 C4
Qinghai Hu 34 C4
Qinhuangdao 35 C6
Qinzhou 35 D5
Qiqihar 35 B7
Qitai 34 B3
Qom 44 C2
Qomolangma Feng =
Everest, Mt. 40 C6
Qomsheh 44 C2
Qonduz = Kondoz 45 B7
Qonduz = Kondoz □
45 B7
Qoqon = Qŭqon 29 E8
Qoraqalpoghiston □
29 E6
Qostanay 29 D7
Quambatook 62 C3
Quambone 63 B4
Quan Long = Ca Mau
38 C3

Quang Ngai 38 A3
Quanzhou 35 D6
Quaqtaq 70 C7
Quartu Sant'Élena 21 E2
Quba 25 E6
Qūchān 44 B4
Queanbeyan 63 C4
Québec 71 E6
Québec □ 71 E6
Queen Alexandra Ra.
96 C15
Queen Charlotte Is. 68 C6
Queen Charlotte Sd.
69 C7
Queen Elizabeth Is. 66 B9
Queen Mary Land 96 B11
Queen Maud G. 68 B9
Queen Maud Land =
Dronning Maud Land
96 B7
Queen Maud Mts. 96 C16
Queenscliff 63 C3
Queensland □ 61 E7
Queenstown Australia
62 D4
Queenstown N.Z. 65 F3
Queenstown S. Africa
59 E5
Queimadas 93 E6
Quelimane 59 B7
Quelpart = Jeju-do 35 C7
Querétaro 84 C4
Quetta 42 D5
Quezon City 36 B2
Qui Nhon 38 B3
Quibaxe 56 F2
Quibdo 90 B3
Quiberon 12 C2
Quilán, C. 95 E2
Quillabamba 91 F4
Quillagua 91 H5
Quillota 94 C1
Quilon 43 Q10
Quilpie 63 A3
Quimili 94 B4
Quimper 12 B1
Quimperlé 12 C2
Quincy 75 F9
Quines 94 C3
Quintanar de la Orden
18 C4
Quinyambie 62 B3
Quipungo 58 A2
Quirindi 63 B5
Quissanga 59 A8
Quito 90 D3
Quixadá 92 C6
Qulan 29 E8
Qŭnghirot 29 E6
Quondong 62 B3
Quorn 62 B2
Qŭqon 29 E8
Quseir 54 C5
Quzhou 35 D6
Qyzylorda 29 E7

R

Raahe 8 C10
Raba 37 F1
Rába → 16 E3

Rabat Malta 21 G5
Rabat Morocco 52 B4
Rabaul 64 K10
Râbigh 47 G4
Râbniţa 17 E9
Race, C. 71 E8
Rach Gia 38 B3
Racine 76 C2
Rădăuţi 17 E8
Radekhiv 17 C7
Radekhov = Radekhiv
17 C7
Radom 16 C5
Radomsko 16 C4
Radomyshl 17 C9
Radstock, C. 62 B1
Rae 68 B8
Rae Bareli 40 D3
Rae Isthmus 70 C5
Raetihi 64 C6
Rafaela 94 C4
Rafḩā 47 E5
Rafsanjān 44 D4
Ragachov 17 B10
Ragama 43 R11
Raglan 64 B6
Ragusa 21 F5
Raha 37 E2
Rahaeng = Tak 38 A1
Rahimyar Khan 42 E7
Raichur 43 L10
Raigarh 40 G4
Railton 62 D4
Rainier, Mt. 72 C3
Raipur 40 G3
Ra'is 47 G4
Raj Nandgaon 40 G3
Raja, Ujung 39 D1
Raja Ampat, Kepulauan
37 E3
Rajahmundry 40 J3
Rajang → 39 D4
Rajapalaiyam 43 Q10
Rajasthan □ 42 F8
Rajasthan Canal = Indira
Gandhi Canal 42 F8
Rajgarh 43 G10
Rajkot 43 H7
Rajpipla 43 J8
Rajshahi 41 E7
Rakaia 65 E5
Rakaia → 65 E5
Rakan, Ra's 44 E2
Rakaposhi 42 A9
Rakata, Pulau 39 F3
Rakhiv 17 D7
Rakitnoye 32 A4
Rakiura △ 65 G2
Raleigh 83 B8
Ramanathapuram 43 Q11
Rame Hd. 63 C4
Ramechhap 40 D6
Ramelau 37 F3
Ramgarh Jharkhand, India
40 F5
Ramgarh Raj., India 42 F7
Ramnad =
Ramanathapuram
43 Q11
Râmnicu Sărat 17 F8

Râmnicu Vâlcea 17 F7
Rampur 42 E11
Rampur Hat 40 E6
Ramree I. 41 H9
Ramtek 43 J11
Ranaghat 41 F7
Ranau 38 C5
Rancagua 94 C2
Ranchi 40 F5
Randers 9 D8
Rangaunu B. 64 A5
Rangia 41 D8
Rangiora 65 E5
Rangitaiki → 64 B7
Rangitata → 65 E4
Rangitoto ke te tonga =
D'Urville I. 65 D5
Rangon → 41 J11
Rangoon 41 J11
Rangpur 41 E7
Ranibennur 43 M9
Raniganj 40 F6
Raniwara 43 G8
Rankin Inlet 68 B10
Rankins Springs 63 B4
Ranohira 59 C9
Ranong 38 C1
Ransiki 37 E4
Rantauprapat 39 D1
Rantemario 37 E1
Rapa 65 M16
Rapallo 13 D8
Räpch 45 E4
Raper, C. 70 C7
Rapid City 74 C3
Rarotonga 65 M14
Ra's al Khaymah 44 E4
Ra's Lānūf 54 B2
Rasht 46 C7
Rat Islands 69 C1
Ratangarh 42 E9
Rathenow 15 B7
Ratlam 43 H9
Ratnagiri 43 L8
Raukumara Ra. 64 C7
Rauma 8 C10
Raumo = Rauma 8 C10
Raurkela 40 F5
Rausu-Dake 32 A9
Rava-Ruska 17 C6
Rava Russkaya =
Rava-Ruska 17 C6
Rävar 44 D4
Ravenna 20 B4
Ravensburg 14 E5
Ravi → 42 D7
Rawalpindi 42 C8
Rawene 64 A5
Rawlins 73 F10
Rawson 95 E3
Ray, C. 71 E8
Rayadurg 43 M10
Rayagada 40 H4
Raz, Pte. du 12 B1
Razāzah, Buḩayrat ar
47 D5
Razazah, L. = Razāzah,
Buḩayrat ar 47 D5
Razdel'naya = Rozdilna
17 E10

Razgrad 22 C6
Razim, Lacul 22 B7
Ré, Î. de 12 C3
Reading *U.K.* 11 F6
Reading *U.S.A.* 77 D8
Realicó 94 D4
Rebi 37 F4
Rebiana 54 D3
Rebun-Tō 32 A7
Rechytsa 17 B10
Recife 92 D7
Reconquista 94 B5
Recreo 94 B3
Red → 81 D8
Red Cliffs 62 B3
Red Deer 69 C8
Red River of the North →
74 A6
Red Sea 48 C2
Red Tower Pass = Turnu
Roşu, P. 17 F7
Redcar 11 D6
Redcliffe 63 A5
Redding 72 F2
Redditch 11 E6
Redon 12 C2
Redondela 18 A1
Redondo City 78 B1
Ree, L. 11 E2
Reefton 65 E4
Regensburg 15 D7
Reggâne = Zaouiet
Reggâne 52 C6
Réggio di Calábria 21 E5
Réggio nell'Emília 20 B3
Reghin 17 E7
Regina 69 C9
Rehoboth 58 C3
Rehovot 46 E3
Reichenbach 15 C7
Reidsville 83 A8
Reigate 11 F6
Reims 13 B6
Reina Adelaida, Arch.
95 G2
Reindeer L. 69 C9
Reinga, C. 64 A5
Reinosa 18 A3
Remarkable, Mt. 62 B2
Remeshk 45 E4
Rendang 72 G4
Rengat 39 E2
Reni 17 F9
Renmark 62 B3
Rennes 12 B3
Reno 72 G4
Reno → 20 B4
Rentería 19 A5
Republican → 74 F6
Repulse Bay 70 C5
Requena *Peru* 90 E4
Requena *Spain* 19 C5
Reşadiye = Datça 23 F6
Resht = Rasht 46 C7
Resistencia 94 B5
Reşiţa 17 F5
Resolute 70 B4
Resolution I. *Canada*
70 C7
Resolution I. *N.Z.* 65 F2

Rethimno 23 G5
Réunion ☑ 51 J9
Reus 19 B6
Reutlingen 14 D5
Reval = Tallinn 24 B1
Revelstoke 69 C8
Revillagigedo, Is. de
84 D2
Rewa 40 E3
Rewari 42 E10
Rey Bouba 55 G1
Rey Malabo 53 H7
Reykjavík 8 C1
Reynosa 84 B5
Rhein → 14 C4
Rhein-Main-Donau-Kanal
15 D6
Rheine 14 B4
Rheinland-Pfalz □ 14 C4
Rhin = Rhein → 14 C4
Rhine = Rhein → 14 C4
Rhineland-Palatinate =
Rheinland-Pfalz □
14 C4
Rhode Island □ 77 D10
Rhodes 23 F7
Rhodope Mts. = Rhodopi
Planina 22 D5
Rhodopi Planina 22 D5
Rhön 14 C5
Rhondda 11 F5
Rhône → 13 E6
Rhum 10 C3
Riachão 92 D4
Riasi 42 C9
Riau □ 39 E2
Riau, Kepulauan 39 D2
Riau Arch. = Riau,
Kepulauan 39 D2
Ribadeo 18 A2
Ribeirão Prêto 93 G4
Riberalta 91 F5
Riccarton 65 E5
Richards Bay 59 D6
Richland 72 C4
Richmond *N.Z.* 65 D5
Richmond *Calif., U.S.A.*
72 H2
Richmond *Va., U.S.A.*
77 F7
Richmond Ra. 63 A5
Ridder = Leninogorsk
29 D9
Ried 15 D7
Riesa 15 C7
Rieti 20 C4
Rif = Er Rif 52 A5
Rīga 24 B1
Riga, G. of 24 B1
Rīgas Jūras Līcis = Riga,
G. of 24 B1
Rīgestān 42 D4
Rigolet 70 D8
Riiser-Larsen-halvøya
96 A8
Rijeka 20 B5
Rijhm, Wadi ar → 47 F5
Rímini 20 B4
Rinca 37 F1

Rinconada 94 A3
Rinjani 39 F5
Río Branco *Brazil* 91 E5
Rio Branco *Uruguay* 94 C6
Río Cuarto 94 C4
Rio de Janeiro 93 G5
Rio de Janeiro □ 93 G5
Río Gallegos 95 G3
Rio Grande *Argentina*
95 G3
Rio Grande *Brazil* 94 C6
Rio Grande → 84 B5
Rio Grande de
Santiago → 84 C3
Rio Grande do Norte □
92 D6
Rio Grande do Sul □
94 B6
Rio Largo 93 D6
Río Mulatos 91 G5
Río Muni □ 56 D2
Rio Negro 94 B7
Rio Verde 93 F3
Ríobamba 90 D3
Ríohacha 90 A4
Ríosucio *Caldas, Colombia*
90 B3
Ríosucio *Choco, Colombia*
90 B3
Rishiri-Tō 32 A7
Riva del Garda 20 B3
Rivadavia 94 B2
Rivera 94 C5
Riverside 78 D4
Riverton *Australia* 62 B2
Riverton *N.Z.* 65 G2
Riviera di Levante 13 D8
Riviera di Ponente 13 D8
Rivière-du-Loup 71 E7
Rivne 17 C8
Rívoli 13 D7
Rívoli B. 62 C3
Riyadh = Ar Riyāḑ 47 F6
Rize 25 E5
Rizzuto, C. 21 E6
Roanne 13 C6
Roanoke 77 F6
Robbins I. 62 D4
Robertson I. 96 A4
Robertstown 62 B2
Roberval 71 E6
Robinvale 62 B3
Roboré 91 G7
Robson, Mt. 69 C8
Roca, C. da 18 C1
Rocas, I. 92 C7
Rocha 94 C6
Rochefort 12 D3
Rochester *Minn., U.S.A.*
75 C8
Rochester *N.Y., U.S.A.*
77 C7
Rock, The 63 C4
Rock Hill 83 B7
Rock Island 75 E9
Rock Springs 73 F9
Rockefeller Plateau
96 C18
Rockford 75 D10

Rockhampton 61 E9
Rocky Mount 83 B9
Rocky Mts. 68 C7
Rod 42 E3
Rodez 13 D5
Ródhos = Rhodes 23 F7
Rodney, C. 64 B6
Roes Welcome Sd. 70 C5
Rogachev = Ragachow
17 B10
Rogagua, L. 91 F5
Rogatyn 17 D7
Rogoaguado, L. 91 F5
Rohri 42 F6
Rohtak 42 E10
Roi Et 38 A2
Rojo, C. 84 C5
Rokan → 39 D2
Rolândia 94 A6
Roma *Australia* 63 A4
Roma *Italy* 20 D4
Romaine → 71 D7
Roman 17 E8
Romang 37 F3
Romania ■ 22 B5
Romans-sur-Isère 13 D6
Romblon 36 B2
Rome = Roma 20 D4
Rome 82 B5
Romorantin-Lanthenay
12 C4
Roncador, Serra do 93 E3
Ronda 18 D3
Rondônia □ 91 F6
Rondonópolis 93 F3
Ronge, L. la 69 C9
Roniu, Mt. 30 H
Ronne Ice Shelf 96 B3
Roorkee 42 E10
Roosevelt → 91 E6
Roosevelt I. 96 B16
Roquetas de Mar 19 D4
Roraima □ 90 C6
Roraima, Mt. 90 B6
Rosa, Monte 13 D7
Rosario *Argentina* 94 C4
Rosário *Brazil* 92 C5
Rosario *Mexico* 84 C3
Rosario *Paraguay* 94 A5
Rosario de la Frontera
94 B3
Rosário do Sul 94 C6
Roscommon 11 E2
Roseau *Dominica* 87 C7
Roseau *U.S.A.* 75 A7
Rosebery 62 D4
Roseburg 72 E2
Rosenheim 15 E7
Roses, G. de 19 A7
Rosetown 69 C9
Roseville 72 G3
Rosewood 63 A5
Rosignano Maríttimo
20 C3
Rosignol 90 B7
Roşiori de Vede 22 B5
Roslavl 24 C3
Roslyn 63 B4
Ross *Australia* 62 D4
Ross *N.Z.* 65 E4

Ross I. 96 B15
Ross Ice Shelf 96 C16
Ross Sea 96 B15
Rossano 21 E6
Rossiya = Russia ■
  26 C10
Rosslare 11 E3
Rosso 53 E2
Rossosh 24 C4
Rostock 15 A7
Rostov Don, Russia 25 D4
Rostov Yaroslavl, Russia
  24 B4
Roswell 80 C1
Rotherham 11 E6
Roto 63 B4
Rotondo, Mte. 13 E8
Rotoroa, L. 65 D5
Rotorua 64 C7
Rotorua, L. 64 C7
Rotterdam 14 C3
Rottweil 14 D5
Rotuma 64 L12
Roubaix 13 A5
Rouen 12 B4
Round Mt. 63 B5
Rousse = Ruse 22 C5
Roussillon 13 E5
Rouyn-Noranda 71 E6
Rovaniemi 8 B11
Rovereto 20 B3
Rovigo 20 B3
Rovinj 20 B4
Rovno = Rivne 17 C8
Rovuma = Ruvuma →
  57 G8
Rowena 63 A4
Roxas 36 B2
Roxburgh 65 F3
Royal Leamington Spa
  11 E6
Royan 12 D3
Rozdilna 17 E10
Rozhyshche 17 C7
Rtishchevo 24 C5
Ruahine Ra. 64 C6
Ruapehu 64 C6
Ruapuke I. 65 G3
Rub' al Khālī 48 D4
Rubio 90 B4
Rubtsovsk 29 D9
Rudall 62 B2
Rudolfa, Ostrov 28 A6
Rufiji → 57 F7
Rufino 94 C4
Rugby 11 E6
Rügen 15 A7
Ruhr → 14 C4
Rukwa, L. 57 F6
Rum = Rhum 10 C3
Rumāḩ 47 F6
Rumania = Romania ■
  22 B5
Rumbêk 55 G4
Rumia 16 A4
Rumoi 32 B7
Runanga 65 E4
Runaway, C. 64 B7
Rundu 58 B3
Ruoqiang 34 C3

Rupa 41 D9
Rupat 39 D2
Rupert → 71 D6
Rupert House =
  Waskaganish 71 D6
Rurrenabaque 91 F5
Ruschuk = Ruse 22 C5
Ruse 22 C5
Russas 92 C6
Russellkonda 40 H5
Russia ■ 26 C10
Russkaya Polyana 29 D8
Rustavi 25 E6
Rustenburg 59 D5
Ruteng 37 F2
Ruvuma → 57 G8
Ruwenzori 57 E6
Rwanda ■ 57 E6
Ryazan 24 C4
Ryazhsk 24 C5
Rybache = Rybachye
  29 E9
Rybachye 29 E9
Rybinsk 24 B4
Rybinskoye Vdkhr. 24 B4
Rybnitsa = Rábniţa 17 E9
Rylstone 63 B4
Ryōtsu 32 D6
Rypin 16 B4
Ryukyu Is. = Ryūkyū-rettō
  35 D7
Ryūkyū-rettō 35 D7
Rzeszów 16 C5
Rzhev 16 C3

S

Sa Dec 38 B3
Sa'ādatābād 44 D3
Saale → 15 C6
Saalfeld 15 C6
Saar → 13 B7
Saarbrücken 14 D4
Saaremaa 24 B1
Šabac 22 B2
Sabadell 19 B7
Sabah □ 38 C5
Ṣabāḩ, Wadi → 47 G7
Sabalān, Kūhhā-ye 46 C6
Sabalana, Kepulauan
  37 F1
Sábanalarga 90 A4
Sabang 38 C1
Sabará 93 F5
Saberania 37 E5
Sabhā 54 C1
Sabinas 84 B4
Sabinas Hidalgo 84 B4
Sablayan 36 B2
Sable, C. Canada 71 E7
Sable, C. U.S.A. 86 A3
Sable I. 71 E8
Sabrina Coast 96 A12
Sabulubbek 39 E1
Sabzevār 44 B4
Sabzvārān 44 D4
Săcele 17 F7
Sachsen □ 15 C7
Sachsen-Anhalt □ 15 C7
Sacramento 72 G3

Sacramento → 72 G3
Sacramento Mts. 79 D10
Sadd el Aali 54 D5
Sado 32 E6
Sadon 41 E11
Safi 52 B4
Safid Kūh 42 B3
Saga 33 G2
Sagar 43 M9
Sagarmatha = Everest, Mt.
  40 C7
Sagil 34 A4
Saginaw 76 C4
Saglouc = Salluit 70 C6
Sagua la Grande 86 B3
Sagunt 19 C5
Sagunto = Sagunt 19 C5
Sahagún 18 A3
Sahand, Kūh-e 46 C6
Sahara 52 D6
Saharan Atlas = Saharien,
  Atlas 52 B6
Saharanpur 42 E10
Saharien, Atlas 52 B6
Sahiwal 42 D8
Sahrawi = Western
  Sahara ■ 52 D3
Sa'id Bundâs 55 G3
Sa'īdābād = Sīrjān 44 D3
Sa'īdīyeh 46 C7
Saidpur 41 E7
Saidu Sharif 42 B8
Saigon = Thanh Pho Ho
  Chi Minh 38 B3
Saikhoa Ghat 41 D10
Saiki 33 G2
Sailolof 37 E4
Saimaa 8 C11
Saimaa = Saimaa 8 C11
Saimen = Saimaa 8 C11
St. Andrews 10 C5
St. Anthony 71 D8
St. Arnaud 62 C3
St-Augustin 71 D8
St. Augustine 83 E7
St. Austell 11 F4
St. Boniface 69 D10
St-Brieuc 12 B2
St. Catharines 77 C6
St. Christopher-Nevis = St.
  Kitts & Nevis ■ 87 C7
St. Cloud 75 C7
St. Croix 87 C7
St-Denis 12 B5
St-Dizier 13 B6
St. Elias, Mt. 68 B5
St-Étienne 13 D6
St-Flour 13 D5
St. Gallen = Sankt Gallen
  13 C8
St-Gaudens 12 E4
St-Georges 93 B7
St. George's 87 D7
St. George's Channel
  11 F3
St. Georges Hd. 63 C5
St. Gotthard P. = San
  Gottardo, P. del 13 C8
St. Helena 51 H3

St. Helena B. 58 E3
St. Helens 62 D4
St. Helier 11 G5
St-Hyacinthe 71 E6
St-Jean, L. 71 E6
St. John 71 E7
St. John's Antigua & B.
  87 C7
St. John's Canada 71 E8
St. Johns → 83 D7
St. Joseph 75 F7
St. Joseph, L. 71 D4
St. Kilda 10 C2
St. Kitts & Nevis ■ 87 C7
St-Laurent 92 A3
St. Lawrence → 71 E7
St. Lawrence, Gulf of
  71 E7
St. Lawrence I. 69 B2
St-Lô 12 B3
St. Louis Senegal 53 E2
St. Louis U.S.A. 75 F9
St. Lucia ■ 87 D7
St-Malo 12 B2
St-Marc 87 C5
St. Mary Pk. 62 B2
St. Marys 62 D4
St-Mathieu, Pte. 12 B1
St-Nazaire 12 C2
St-Omer 12 A5
St. Paul 75 C8
St. Peter Port 11 G5
St. Petersburg =
  Sankt-Peterburg 24 B3
St. Petersburg 83 F6
St-Pierre-et-Miquelon ☑
  71 E8
St-Quentin 13 B5
St-Tropez 13 E7
St. Vincent, G. 62 C2
St. Vincent & the
  Grenadines ■ 87 D7
Ste-Marie, Ile = Nosy
  Boraha 59 B9
Saintes 12 D3
Saintonge 12 D3
Saipan 64 H9
Sairang 41 F9
Sajama 91 G5
Sajószentpéter 16 D5
Sakākah 47 E5
Sakakawea, L. 74 B4
Sakartvelo = Georgia ■
  25 E5
Sakarya 25 E3
Sakata 32 D6
Sakhalin 31 D12
Sakon Nakhon 38 A2
Sala 9 D9
Sala Consilina 21 D5
Saladillo 94 D5
Salado → B. Aires,
  Argentina 94 D4
Salado → La Pampa,
  Argentina 94 D3
Salado → Santa Fe,
  Argentina 94 C4
Salaga 53 G5
Salālah 49 D5
Salamanca Chile 94 C2

Salamanca *Spain* 18 B3
Salamina 23 F4
Salar de Atacama 94 A3
Salar de Uyuni 91 H5
Salaverry 91 E3
Salawati 37 E4
Salayar 37 F2
Saldanha 58 E3
Sale *Australia* 63 C4
Salé *Morocco* 52 B4
Salekhard 28 C7
Salem *India* 43 P11
Salem *U.S.A.* 72 F1
Salerno 21 D5
Salgótarján 16 D4
Salihli 23 E7
Salihorsk 17 B8
Salima 59 A6
Salina *Italy* 21 E5
Salina *U.S.A.* 74 F6
Salina Cruz 85 D5
Salinas *Brazil* 93 F5
Salinas *Ecuador* 90 D2
Salinas *U.S.A.* 78 B2
Salinas Grandes 94 C3
Salinópolis 92 C4
Salisbury *Australia* 62 B2
Salisbury *U.K.* 11 F6
Salisbury *U.S.A.* 83 B7
Salisbury I. 70 C6
Salliq = Coral Harbour
   70 C5
Salluit 70 C6
Salmås 46 C6
Salmon → 72 D5
Salmon River Mts. 73 D6
Salon-de-Provence 13 E6
Salonica = Thessaloniki
   23 D4
Salonta 16 E5
Salsk 25 D5
Salso → 21 F4
Salt Creek 62 C2
Salt L. 62 B3
Salt Lake City 73 F8
Salta 94 A3
Saltillo 84 B4
Salto 94 C5
Salto → 20 C4
Salton Sea 78 D5
Salûm 54 B4
Salur 40 H4
Salvador 93 E6
Salvador, El ■ 85 E7
Salwa 44 E2
Salween → 41 J11
Salyan 25 F6
Salzach → 15 D7
Salzburg 15 E7
Salzgitter 14 B6
Salzwedel 15 B6
Sama 28 C7
Sama de Langreo =
   Langreo 18 A3
Samales Group 36 C2
Samangān □ 45 B7
Samani 45 B7
Samar 36 B3
Samara 24 C7
Samarinda 39 E5

Samarkand = Samarqand
   29 F7
Samarqand 29 F7
Sämarrä' 46 D5
Sambalpur 40 G5
Sambar, Tanjung 39 E4
Sambas 39 D3
Sambhal 42 E11
Sambhar 42 F9
Sambiase 21 E6
Sambir 17 D6
Samoa ■ 65 L13
Samokov 22 C4
Samos 23 F6
Samothráki = Mathraki
   21 E7
Samothráki 23 D5
Sampit 39 E4
Sampit, Teluk 39 E4
Samra 47 F5
Samsun 25 E4
Samui, Ko 38 C2
Samut Prakan 38 B2
Samut Songkhram 38 B2
San 53 F5
San Agustin, C. 36 C3
San Andrés, I. de 86 D3
San Andrés Tuxtla 85 D5
San Angelo 80 D3
San Antonio *Chile* 94 C2
San Antonio *U.S.A.* 80 E4
San Antonio, C. 86 B3
San Antonio Oeste 95 E4
San Benedetto del Tronto
   20 C4
San Bernardino 78 C4
San Bernardino Str. 36 B2
San Bernardo 94 C2
San Bernardo, I. de 90 B3
San Borja 91 F5
San Buenaventura =
   Ventura 78 C3
San Carlos *Argentina*
   94 C3
San Carlos *Chile* 94 D2
San Carlos *Phil.* 36 B2
San Carlos *Amazonas,
   Venezuela* 90 C5
San Carlos *Cojedes,
   Venezuela* 90 B5
San Carlos de Bariloche
   95 E2
San Carlos del Zulia 90 B4
San Cristóbal *Argentina*
   94 C4
San Cristóbal *Venezuela*
   90 B4
San Cristóbal de las Casas
   85 D6
San Diego 78 D4
San Diego, C. 95 G3
San Felipe *Chile* 94 C2
San Felipe *Venezuela*
   90 A5
San Fernando *Chile* 94 C2
San Fernando *La Union,
   Phil.* 36 A2
San Fernando *Pampanga,
   Phil.* 36 A2
San Fernando *Spain*
   18 D2

San Fernando *Trin. & Tob.*
   87 D7
San Fernando *U.S.A.*
   78 C3
San Fernando de Apure
   90 B5
San Fernando de Atabapo
   90 C5
San Francisco *Argentina*
   94 C4
San Francisco *U.S.A.*
   78 B1
San Francisco de Macorís
   87 C5
San Gottardo, P. del
   13 C8
San Ignacio *Bolivia* 91 G6
San Ignacio *Paraguay*
   94 B5
San Ildefonso, C. 36 A2
San Javier 91 G6
San Joaquín → 78 A2
San Jorge, G. 95 F3
San José *Costa Rica*
   86 E3
San Jose *Mind. Occ., Phil.*
   36 B2
San Jose *Nueva Ecija, Phil.*
   36 A2
San José *U.S.A.* 78 B2
San José de Chiquitos
   91 G6
San José de Jáchal 94 C3
San José de Mayo 94 C5
San José del Guaviare
   90 C4
San Juan *Argentina* 94 C3
San Juan *Phil.* 36 C3
San Juan *Puerto Rico*
   87 C6
San Juan → 86 D3
San Juan de los Morros
   90 B5
San Juan Mts. 79 B9
San Justo 94 C4
San Leandro 78 B1
San Lorenzo 90 C3
San Lorenzo, Mte. 95 F2
San Lucas 91 H5
San Lucas, C. 84 C2
San Luis 94 C3
San Luis Obispo 78 C2
San Luis Potosí 84 C4
San Marino 20 C4
San Marino ■ 20 C4
San Martín, L. 95 F2
San Matías 91 G7
San Matías, G. 95 E4
San Miguel 85 E7
San Miguel → 91 F6
San Miguel de Tucumán
   94 B3
San Narciso 36 A2
San Nicolás de los Arroyas
   94 C4
San Pedro 53 H4
San Pedro de las Colonias
   84 B4
San Pedro de Macorís
   87 C6

San Pedro del Paraná
   94 B5
San Pedro Sula 85 D7
San Pietro 21 E2
San Rafael *Argentina*
   94 C3
San Rafael *U.S.A.* 72 H2
San Remo 13 E7
San Roque *Argentina*
   94 B5
San Roque *Spain* 18 D3
San Rosendo 94 D2
San Salvador 85 E7
San Salvador de Jujuy
   94 A4
San Salvador I. 86 B5
San Sebastián = Donostia-
   San Sebastián 19 A5
San Sebastián 95 G3
San Severo 20 D6
San Valentin, Mte. 95 F2
San Vicente de la
   Barquera 18 A3
Sana' 49 D3
Sana → 20 B6
Sanaga → 56 D1
Sanana 37 E3
Sanandaj 46 D6
Sancti Spíritus 86 B4
Sancy, Puy de 13 D5
Sandakan 38 C5
Sandanski 22 D4
Sanday 10 B5
Sandgate 63 A5
Sandía 91 F5
Sandıklı 46 C2
Sandoa 56 F4
Sandomierz 16 C5
Sandoway = Thandwe
   41 H10
Sandusky 76 D4
Sandwip Chan. 41 F8
Sandy C. 62 D3
Sandy L. 69 C10
Sanford *Fla., U.S.A.* 83 E7
Sanford *N.C., U.S.A.*
   83 B8
Sanford, Mt. 69 B5
Sanga → 56 E3
Sangamner 43 K9
Sangar 31 C10
Sangeang 37 F1
Sangerhausen 15 C6
Sanggau 39 D4
Sangihe, Pulau 37 D3
Sangkapura 39 F4
Sangli 43 L9
Sangmélima 56 D2
Sangre de Cristo Mts.
   80 A1
Sanikiluaq 71 D6
Sanirajak 70 C5
Sanjo 33 E6
Sankt Gallen 13 C8
Sankt Moritz 13 C8
Sankt-Peterburg 24 B3
Sankt Pölten 15 D8
Sankuru → 56 E4
Sanliurfa 46 C4
Sanlúcar de Barrameda
   18 D2

Sanmenxia **35 C6**
Sannicandro Gargánico **20 D5**
Sant Antoni de Portmany **19 C6**
Sant Feliu de Guíxols **19 B7**
Sant Jordi, G. de **19 B6**
Santa Ana *Bolivia* **91 F5**
Santa Ana *El Salv.* **85 E7**
Santa Ana *U.S.A.* **78 D4**
Sant' Antíoco **21 E2**
Santa Barbara **78 C3**
Santa Catalina I. **78 D3**
Santa Catalina □ **94 B7**
Santa Clara **86 B4**
Santa Clotilde **90 D4**
Santa Coloma de Gramenet **19 B7**
Santa Cruz *Argentina* **95 G3**
Santa Cruz *Bolivia* **91 G6**
Santa Cruz *Phil.* **36 B2**
Santa Cruz *U.S.A.* **78 B1**
Santa Cruz ➝ **95 G3**
Santa Cruz de Tenerife **52 C2**
Santa Cruz do Sul **94 B6**
Santa Eugenia, Pta. de **84 B1**
Santa Fé *Argentina* **94 C4**
Santa Fe *U.S.A.* **79 C10**
Santa Filomena **93 D4**
Santa Inés, I. **95 G2**
Santa Isabel **94 D3**
Santa Isabel do Morro **93 E3**
Santa Lucia Range **78 C2**
Santa Maria *Brazil* **94 B6**
Santa Maria *U.S.A.* **78 C2**
Santa María ➝ **84 A3**
Santa Maria da Vitória **93 E5**
Santa Maria di Léuca, C. **21 E7**
Santa Marta **90 A4**
Santa Marta, Sierra Nevada de **90 A4**
Santa Maura = Lefkada **23 E3**
Santa Rosa *La Pampa, Argentina* **94 D4**
Santa Rosa *San Luis, Argentina* **94 D3**
Santa Rosa *Brazil* **94 B6**
Santa Rosa *Brazil* **93 G2**
Santa Vitória do Palmar **94 C6**
Santai **35 C5**
Santana, Coxilha de **94 C5**
Santana do Livramento **94 C5**
Santander **18 A4**
Santarém *Brazil* **92 C3**
Santarém *Portugal* **18 C1**
Santiago = Río Grande de Santiago ➝ **84 C3**
Santiago *Brazil* **94 B6**
Santiago *Chile* **94 C2**

Santiago ➝ **90 D3**
Santiago de Compostela **18 A1**
Santiago de Cuba **86 C4**
Santiago de los Caballeros **87 C5**
Santiago del Estero **94 B4**
Santo Amaro **93 E6**
Santo Ângelo **94 B6**
Santo Antônio do Leverger **93 F2**
Santo Domingo **87 C6**
Santo Tomás **91 F4**
Santo Tomé **94 B5**
Santo Tomé de Guayana = Ciudad Guayana **90 B6**
Santoña **18 A4**
Santorini **23 F5**
Santos **94 A7**
São Bernardo do Campo **93 G4**
São Borja **94 B5**
São Carlos **94 A7**
São Cristóvão **93 E6**
São Domingos **93 E4**
São Francisco **93 F5**
São Francisco ➝ **93 E6**
São Francisco do Sul **94 B7**
São Gabriel **94 C6**
São João da Madeira **18 B1**
São João del Rei **93 G5**
São João do Araguaia **92 D4**
São João do Piauí **92 D5**
São José do Rio Prêto **93 G4**
São Leopoldo **94 B6**
São Lourenço **93 G4**
São Lourenço ➝ **93 F2**
São Luís **92 C5**
São Marcos ➝ **93 F4**
São Marcos, B. de **92 C5**
São Mateus **93 F6**
São Paulo **94 A7**
São Paulo □ **94 A7**
São Roque, C. de **92 D6**
São Sebastião, I. de **94 A7**
São Tomé & Príncipe ■ **51 F4**
São Vicente, C. de **18 D1**
Saône ➝ **13 D6**
Saonek **37 E4**
Sapa rua **37 E3**
Sapele **53 G7**
Saposoa **91 E3**
Sapporo **32 B7**
Sapulpa **81 B5**
Saqqez **46 C6**
Sar-e Pol **45 B6**
Sar-e Pol □ **45 B6**
Sar Planina **22 C3**
Sarāb **46 C6**
Saragossa = Zaragoza **19 B5**
Saraguro **90 D3**
Saran, Gunung **39 E4**
Sarangani B. **36 C3**

Sarangani Is. **36 C3**
Sarangarh **40 G4**
Saransk **24 C6**
Sarapul **29 D6**
Sarasota **83 F6**
Saratov **24 C6**
Sarāvān **45 E5**
Saravane **38 A3**
Sarawak □ **39 D4**
Saray **22 D6**
Sarayköy **23 F7**
Sarbāz **45 E5**
Sarbīsheh **45 C4**
Sarda ➝ **40 D3**
Sardarshahr **42 E9**
Sardegna □ **21 D2**
Sardinia = Sardegna □ **21 D2**
Sardis **23 E7**
Sargodha **42 C8**
Sārī **44 B3**
Sangöl **23 E7**
Sarikamiş **46 B5**
Sarikei **39 D4**
Sark **11 G5**
Şarköy **23 D6**
Sarlat-la-Canéda **12 D4**
Sarmi **37 E5**
Sarmiento **95 F3**
Sarnia **71 D3**
Sarny **24 C2**
Sarolangun **39 E2**
Saronikos Kolpos **23 F4**
Sarre = Saar ➝ **13 B7**
Sarreguemines **13 B7**
Sarthe ➝ **12 C3**
Sartynya **28 C7**
Sarvestān **44 D3**
Sary-Tash **29 F8**
Saryshaghan **29 E8**
Sasaram **40 E3**
Sasebo **33 G1**
Saser **42 B10**
Saskatchewan □ **69 C9**
Saskatchewan ➝ **69 C9**
Saskatoon **69 C9**
Saskylakh **30 B9**
Sasovo **24 C5**
Sassandra **53 H4**
Sassandra ➝ **53 H4**
Sássari **21 D2**
Sassnitz **15 A7**
Sassuolo **20 B3**
Sasyk, Ozero **17 F9**
Sata-Misaki **33 H2**
Satadougou **53 F3**
Satara **43 L8**
Satmala Hills **43 J9**
Satna **40 E3**
Sátoraljaújhely **16 D5**
Satpura Ra. **43 J10**
Satu Mare **17 E6**
Satui **39 E5**
Saturnina ➝ **91 F7**
Sauðarkrókur **8 B2**
Saudi Arabia ■ **47 F6**
Sauerland **14 C4**
Sault Ste. Marie *Canada* **71 E5**

Sault Ste. Marie *U.S.A.* **76 A3**
Saumlaki **37 F4**
Saumur **12 C3**
Saunders, C. **65 F4**
Saurimo **56 F4**
Sava ➝ **22 B3**
Savage I. = Niue **65 L14**
Savalou **53 G6**
Savannah **83 C7**
Savannah ➝ **83 C7**
Savannakhet **38 A2**
Save ➝ **59 C6**
Säveh **46 D7**
Savelugu **53 G5**
Savoie □ **13 D7**
Savona **13 D8**
Savonlinna **8 C11**
Savoy = Savoie □ **13 D7**
Sawahlunto **39 E2**
Sawai **37 E3**
Sawai Madhopur **42 F10**
Sawatch Range **79 A9**
Sawu **37 F2**
Sawu Sea **37 F2**
Saxony = Sachsen □ **15 C7**
Saxony, Lower = Niedersachsen □ **14 B5**
Sayán **91 F3**
Sayan, Zapadnyy **30 D7**
Saydā **46 D3**
Sayghān **45 C6**
Sayhūt **49 D5**
Saylac = Zeila **49 E3**
Saynshand = Buyant-Uhaa **35 B6**
Sazanit **21 D2**
Sázava ➝ **16 D2**
Sazin **42 B8**
Scandicci **20 C3**
Scandinavia **8 C8**
Scarborough **11 D6**
Scebeli, Wabi ➝ **49 G3**
Schaffhausen **13 C8**
Schefferville = Kawawachikamach **71 D7**
Schelde ➝ **14 C3**
Schenectady **77 C9**
Schiermonnikoog **14 B4**
Schio **20 B3**
Schleswig **14 A5**
Schleswig-Holstein □ **14 A5**
Schouten I. **62 D4**
Schouten Is. = Supiori **37 E5**
Schwäbische Alb **14 D5**
Schwaner, Pegunungan **39 E4**
Schwarzwald **14 D5**
Schwedt **15 B8**
Schweinfurt **14 C6**
Schweiz = Switzerland ■ **13 C8**
Schwenningen = Villingen-Schwenningen **14 D5**
Schwerin **15 B6**
Schwyz **13 C8**

Sciacca 21 F4
Scilla 21 E5
Scilly, Isles of 11 G3
Scone 63 B5
Scotland □ 10 C4
Scott Glacier 96 A12
Scott Inlet 70 B6
Scottsbluff 74 E3
Scottsdale 62 D4
Scranton 77 D8
Scunthorpe 11 E6
Scutari = Shkodër 22 C2
Seaspray 63 C4
Seattle 72 C2
Sebastopol = Sevastopol
  25 E3
Sebha = Sabhā 54 C1
Şebinkarahisar 46 B4
Sebta = Ceuta 18 E3
Sebuku 39 E5
Sebuku, Teluk 39 D5
Secretary I. 65 F2
Secunderabad 43 L11
Sedalia 75 F8
Sedan 13 B6
Seddon 65 D6
Seddonville 65 D5
Sédhiou 53 F2
Sedova, Pik 28 B6
Seferihisar 23 E6
Segamat 39 D2
Segesta 21 F4
Seget 37 E4
Ségou 53 F4
Segovia = Coco → 86 D3
Segovia 18 B3
Segre → 19 B6
Séguéla 53 G4
Segura → 19 C5
Sehore 43 H10
Seinäjoki → 8 C10
Seine → 12 B4
Seistan = Sīstān 45 D5
Seistan, Daryācheh-ye =
  Sīstān, Daryācheh-ye
  45 D5
Sekayu 39 E2
Sekondi-Takoradi 53 H5
Selaru 37 F4
Selçuk 23 F6
Sele → 21 D5
Selebi-Pikwe 59 C5
Selenga = Selenge
  Mörön → 35 A5
Selenge Mörön → 35 A5
Seletan, Tanjung 39 E4
Sélibabi 53 E3
Selîma, El Wâhât el 54 D4
Selkirk 69 C10
Selkirk Mts. 69 C8
Selma 83 B8
Selpele 37 E4
Selu 37 F4
Selva 94 B4
Selvas 91 E5
Seman → 23 D2
Semarang 39 F4
Semey 29 D9
Semiozernoye 29 D7
Semipalatinsk = Semey
  29 D9

Semirara Is. 36 B2
Semitau 39 D4
Semiyarka 29 D8
Semiyarskoye = Semiyarka
  29 D8
Semmering P. 15 E8
Semnān 44 C3
Semnān □ 44 C3
Semporna 36 D1
Semuda 39 E4
Sena Madureira 91 E5
Senador Pompeu 92 D6
Senanga 58 B4
Sendai-Wan 32 D7
Senegal ■ 53 F3
Sénégal → 53 E2
Senge Khambab =
  Indus → 43 G5
Senhor-do-Bonfim 93 E5
Senigállia 20 C4
Senj 20 B5
Senja 8 B9
Senlis 13 B5
Senmonorom 38 B3
Sens 13 B5
Senta 22 B3
Sentani 37 E6
Seo de Urgel = La Seu
  d'Urgell 19 A6
Seoul 35 C7
Sept-Îles 71 D7
Sequoia △ 78 B3
Seram 37 E3
Seram Laut 37 E4
Seram Sea 37 E3
Serasan 39 D3
Serbia ■ 22 B3
Serdar 29 F6
Serdobsk 24 C5
Sergiyev Posad 24 B4
Serov 28 D7
Serowe 59 C5
Serpukhov 24 C4
Serres 22 D4
Serrinha 93 E6
Serua 37 F4
Serui 37 E5
Sesepe 37 E3
Setana 32 B6
Sète 13 E5
Sete Lagôas 93 F5
Sétif 52 A7
Setonaikai 33 F3
Settat 52 B4
Setúbal 18 C1
Setúbal, B. de 18 C1
Sevan, Ozero = Sevana
  Lich 25 E6

Sevana Lich 25 E6
Sevastopol 25 E3
Sevan → Canada 71 D5
Sevan → U.K. 11 F5
Severnaya Zemlya 30 B7
Severnye Uvaly 24 B6
Severo-Yeniseyskiy 30 C7
Severodvinsk 28 C4
Sevilla 18 D2
Seville = Sevilla 18 D2
Sevlievo 22 C5
Seward 69 B5
Seward Peninsula 69 B3
Sewer 37 F4
Seychelles ■ 26 J7
Seyðisfjörður 8 B3
Seymour 63 C4
Sfântu Gheorghe 17 F7
Sfax 54 B1
Shaanxi □ 35 C5
Shaba = Katanga □ 57 F4
Shaballe = Scebeli,
  Wabi → 49 G3
Shache 34 C2
Shackleton Ice Shelf
  96 A11
Shackleton Inlet 96 C15
Shadrinsk 29 D7
Shāhābād 44 B4
Shahdād 44 D4
Shahdād, Namakzār-e
  44 D4
Shahdadkot 42 F5
Shahgarh 42 F6
Shahjahanpur 42 F11
Shahr-e Kord 44 C2
Shahrig 42 D5
Shajapur 43 H10
Shakhty 25 D5
Shakhunya 24 B6
Shaki 53 G6
Shalqar 29 E6
Shām, Bādiyat ash 47 D4
Shām, J. ash 44 F4
Shamil 44 E4
Shammar, Jabal 47 F5
Shamo = Gobi 35 B6
Shamo, L. 55 G6
Shan □ 41 G12
Shandong □ 35 C6
Shangani → 59 B5
Shanghai 35 C7
Shangqiu 35 C6
Shangrao 35 D6
Shangshui 35 C6
Shannon 64 D6
Shannon → 11 E2
Shansi = Shanxi □ 35 C6
Shantou 35 D6
Shantung = Shandong □
  35 C6
Shanxi □ 35 C6
Shaoguan 35 D6
Shaoxing 35 C7
Shaoyang 35 D6
Shaqra' Si. Arabia 47 F6
Shaqrā' Yemen 49 E4
Shari 32 B9
Sharjah = Ash Shāriqah
  44 E3

Sharon 76 D5
Sharya 24 B6
Shashi 35 C6
Shasta, Mt. 72 F2
Shatt al Arab 47 E7
Shawan 34 B3
Shawinigan 71 E6
Shawnee 78 B5
Shchūchīnsk 29 D8
Shebele = Scebeli,
  Wabi → 49 G3
Sheboygan 76 C2
Sheffield 11 E6
Shekhupura 42 D8
Shelby 83 B7
Shelbyville 82 B4
Shellharbour 63 B5
Shenandoah → 77 E7
Shendam 53 G7
Shendī 55 E5
Shensi = Shaanxi □ 35 C5
Shenyang 35 B7
Sheopur Kalan 42 G10
Shepetivka 17 C8
Shepetovka = Shepetivka
  17 C8
Shepparton 63 C4
Sherbro I. 53 G3
Sherbrooke 71 E6
Sheridan 73 D10
Sherman 81 C5
Shetland Is. 10 A6
Shibām 49 D4
Shibata 33 E6
Shibecha 32 B9
Shibetsu 32 A8
Shīeli 29 E7
Shihchiachuangi =
  Shijiazhuang 35 C6
Shijiazhuang 35 C6
Shikarpur 42 F6
Shikoku □ 33 G3
Shikotsu-Ko 32 B7
Shilabo 49 F3
Shiliguri 40 D7
Shillong 41 E8
Shimla 42 D10
Shimoga 43 N9
Shimonoseki 33 G2
Shindand 42 C3
Shingū 33 G4
Shinyanga 57 E6
Shio-no-Misaki 33 G4
Shipchenski Prokhod
  22 C5
Shipki La 42 D11
Shiquan He = Indus →
  43 G5
Shīr Kūh 44 D3
Shiragami-Misaki 32 C7
Shīrāz 44 D3
Shire → 59 B7
Shiriya-Zaki 32 C7
Shīrvān 44 B4
Shirwa, L. = Chilwa, L.
  59 B7
Shivpuri 43 G10
Shizuoka 33 F6
Shklov = Shklow 17 A10
Shklow 17 A10

Shkodër **22 C2**
Shkumbini → **23 D2**
Shmidta, Ostrov **30 A7**
Sholapur = Solapur **43 L9**
Shoshone Mts. **72 G5**
Shqipëria = Albania ■ **23 D3**
Shreveport **81 C7**
Shrewsbury **11 E5**
Shrirampur **40 F7**
Shū **29 E8**
Shuangyashan **35 B8**
Shule **34 C2**
Shumagin Is. **69 C4**
Shumen **22 C6**
Shūr → **44 D3**
Shurugwi **59 B6**
Shūsf **45 D5**
Shūshtar **47 D7**
Shwebo **41 F10**
Shwegu **41 E11**
Shweli → **41 F11**
Shymkent **29 E7**
Shyok **42 B11**
Shyok → **42 B9**
Si Kiang = Xi Jiang → **35 D6**
Si-ngan = Xi'an **35 C5**
Siah **47 G6**
Siahan Range **42 F4**
Siaksriindrapura **39 D2**
Sialkot **42 C9**
Siam = Thailand ■ **38 A2**
Sian = Xi'an **35 C5**
Siantan **39 D3**
Siargao I. **36 C3**
Siasi **36 C2**
Siau **37 D3**
Šiauliai **24 B1**
Šibenik **20 C6**
Siberia **30 C8**
Siberut **39 E1**
Sibi **42 E5**
Sibil = Oksibil **37 E6**
Sibirtsevo **32 A3**
Sibiti **56 E2**
Sibiu **17 F7**
Sibolga **39 D1**
Sibsagar **41 D10**
Sibu **39 D4**
Sibuco **36 C2**
Sibuguey B. **36 C2**
Sibut **55 G2**
Sibutu **36 D1**
Sibuyan I. **36 B2**
Sibuyan Sea **36 B2**
Sichuan □ **34 C5**
Sicilia **21 F5**
Sicily = Sicilia **21 F5**
Sicuani **91 F4**
Siddipet **43 K11**
Sidi-bel-Abbès **52 A5**
Sidi Ifni **52 C3**
Sidley, Mt. **96 B18**
Sidon = Saydā **46 D3**
Sidra, G. of = Surt, Khalīj **54 B2**
Siedlce **17 B6**
Sieg → **14 C4**

Siegen **14 C5**
Siem Reap = Siemreab **38 B2**
Siemreab **38 B2**
Siena **20 C3**
Sieradz **16 C4**
Sierra Colorada **95 E3**
Sierra Gorda **94 A3**
Sierra Leone ■ **53 G3**
Sierra Madre Occidental **84 B3**
Sierra Nevada *Spain* **18 D4**
Sierra Nevada *U.S.A.* **72 G3**
Sifnos **23 F5**
Sighetu-Marmaţiei **17 E6**
Sigli **38 C1**
Siglufjörður **8 B2**
Sigsig **90 D3**
Sigüenza **19 B4**
Siguiri **53 F4**
Sikar **42 F9**
Sikasso **53 F4**
Sikhote Alin, Khrebet **32 A5**
Sikhote Alin Ra. = Sikhote Alin, Khrebet **32 A5**
Sikinos **23 F5**
Sikkim □ **40 D7**
Sil → **18 A2**
Silchar **41 E9**
Silesia = Śląsk **16 C3**
Silgarhi Doti **40 C3**
Silghat **41 D9**
Silifke **46 C3**
Siliguri = Shiliguri **40 D7**
Siling Co **34 C3**
Silistra **22 B6**
Silivri **22 D7**
Sillajhuay, Cordillera **91 G5**
Simanggang = Sri Aman **39 D4**
Simav **23 E7**
Simbirsk **24 C1**
Simeria **17 F6**
Simeulue **39 D1**
Simferopol **25 E3**
Simi **23 F6**
Simikot **40 C3**
Simla = Shimla **42 D10**
Simpson Desert **60 F6**
Simpson Pen. **70 C5**
Sinabang **39 D1**
Sinadogo **49 F4**
Sinai = Es Sînâ' **54 C5**
Sinai, Mt. = Mûsa, Gebel **47 E3**
Sinaloa de Leyva **84 B3**
Sincelejo **90 B3**
Sincorá, Serra do **93 E5**
Sind = Sindh □ **42 G3**
Sind Sagar Doab **42 D7**
Sindangan **36 C2**
Sindh □ **42 F6**
Sines **18 D1**
Sines, C. de **18 D1**
Singa **55 F5**
Singapore ■ **39 D2**

Singaraja **39 F5**
Singida **57 E6**
Singkaling Hkamti **41 E10**
Singkang **37 E2**
Singkawang **39 D3**
Singleton **63 B5**
Singora = Songkhla **38 C2**
Sinjai **37 F2**
Sinjär **46 C5**
Sinkat **55 E6**
Sinkiang = Xinjiang Uygur Zizhiqu □ **34 B3**
Sinni → **21 D6**
Sinop **25 E4**
Sintang **39 D4**
Sintra **18 C1**
Siocon **36 C2**
Siófok **16 E4**
Sioux City **75 D6**
Sioux Falls **74 D6**
Sioux Lookout **69 C10**
Siping **35 B7**
Sipura **39 E1**
Siquijor **36 C2**
Siracusa **21 F5**
Sirajganj **41 E7**
Siret → **17 F9**
Sirjän **44 D3**
Sirohi **43 G8**
Sironj **43 G10**
Siros = Syros **23 F5**
Sirsa **42 E9**
Sisak **20 B6**
Sisaket **38 A2**
Sisophon **38 B2**
Sïstän **45 D5**
Sïstän, Daryächeh-ye **45 D5**
Sïstän va Balüchestän □ **45 E5**
Sitapur **40 D3**
Sitges **19 B6**
Sitia **23 G6**
Sitka **69 C6**
Sittang Myit → **41 J11**
Sittoung = Sittang Myit → **41 J11**
Sittwe **41 G9**
Siuri **40 F6**
Sivas **25 F4**
Siverek **46 C4**
Sivrihisar **25 F3**
Sïwa **54 C4**
Siwalik Range **40 D4**
Siwan **40 D5**
Sjælland **9 D8**
Sjumen = Shumen **22 C6**
Skadarsko Jezero **22 C2**
Skagen **9 D8**
Skagerrak **9 D7**
Skagway **69 C6**
Skala-Podilska **17 D8**
Skala Podolskaya = Skala-Podilska **17 D8**
Skalat **17 D7**
Skardu **42 B9**
Skarżysko-Kamienna **16 C5**
Skeena → **68 C6**
Skegness **11 E7**

Skeldon = Corriverton **90 B7**
Skeleton Coast **58 C2**
Skellefteå **8 C10**
Skellefteälven → **8 C10**
Skiathos **23 E4**
Skien **9 D7**
Skierniewice **16 C5**
Skíkda **52 A7**
Skíros **23 E5**
Skole **17 D6**
Skopelos **23 E4**
Skopje **22 C3**
Skövyra **17 D9**
Skye **10 C3**
Skyros = Skíros **23 E5**
Śląsk **16 C3**
Slatina **22 B5**
Slave → **68 B8**
Slavgorod **29 D8**
Slavonski Brod **20 B7**
Slavuta **17 C8**
Slavyanka **32 B2**
Slavyansk = Slovyansk **25 D4**
Slawharad **17 B10**
Sleaford B. **62 B2**
Sleeper Is. **70 D5**
Sligeach = Sligo **11 D2**
Sligo **11 D2**
Sliven **22 C6**
Slobodskoy **24 B7**
Slobozia **22 B6**
Slonim **17 B7**
Slough **11 F6**
Slovak Rep. ■ **16 D4**
Slovakia = Slovak Rep. ■ **16 D4**
Slovakian Ore Mts. = Slovenské Rudohorie **16 D4**
Slovenia ■ **20 B5**
Slovenija = Slovenia ■ **20 B5**
Slovenska = Slovak Rep. ■ **16 D4**
Slovenské Rudohorie **16 D4**
Slovyansk **25 D4**
Sluch → **17 C8**
Słupsk **16 A3**
Slutsk **17 B8**
Smallwood Res. **71 D7**
Smara **52 C3**
Smarhon **17 A8**
Smederevo **22 B3**
Smithton **62 D4**
Smithtown **63 B5**
Smoky Bay **62 B1**
Smolensk **24 C3**
Smolikas, Oros **23 D3**
Smolyan **22 D5**
Smorgon = Smarhon **17 A8**
Smyrna = İzmir **23 E6**
Snake → **72 C4**
Snake I. **63 C4**
Snake River Plain **73 E7**
Sneek **14 B3**
Sněžka **16 C2**

Snøhetta 8 C7
Snowdon 11 E4
Snowdrift = Łutselk'e
 68 B8
Snowtown 62 B2
Snowy → 63 C4
Snowy Mts. 63 C4
Snyatyn 17 D7
Snyder 80 C3
Sobat, Nahr → 55 G5
Sobral 92 C5
Soc Trang 38 C3
Soch'e = Shache 34 C2
Sochi 25 E4
Société, Îs. de la 65 L15
Society Is. = Société, Îs.
 de la 65 L15
Socompa, Portezuelo de
 94 A3
Socotra 49 E5
Söderhamn 8 C9
Sodiri 55 F4
Sofia = Sofiya 22 C4
Sofia → 59 B9
Sofiya 22 C4
Sogamoso 90 B4
Sognefjorden 8 C7
Sohâg 54 C5
Soissons 13 B5
Sokal 17 C7
Söke 23 F6
Sokhumi 25 E5
Sokodé 53 G6
Sokol 24 B5
Sokółka 17 B6
Sokołów Podlaski 17 B6
Sokoto 53 F7
Solander I. 65 G2
Solano 36 A2
Solapur 43 L9
Soledad 90 B6
Soligalich 24 B5
Soligorsk = Salihorsk
 17 B8
Solikamsk 28 D6
Solimões = Amazonas →
 92 C3
Solingen 14 C4
Sologne 12 C4
Solok 39 E2
Solomon Is. ■ 64 K10
Solomon Sea 61 B9
Solon 35 B7
Solor 37 F2
Šolta 20 C6
Solțānābād 44 B4
Solunska Glava 22 D3
Solwezi 59 A5
Sõma Japan 32 D7
Soma Turkey 23 E6
Somali Rep. ■ 49 F4
Somalia = Somali Rep. ■
 49 F4
Somaliland □ 49 E4
Sombor 22 B3
Sombrerete 84 C4
Somerset I. 68 A10
Somes → 17 E6
Sommariva 63 A4

Somme → 12 A4
Somosierra, Puerto de
 18 B4
Somport, Puerto de 12 E3
Sóndrio 13 C8
Sonepur 40 G4
Song Cau 38 B3
Songea 57 G7
Songhua Jiang → 35 B8
Songkhla 38 C2
Songpan 34 C5
Sonipat 42 E10
Sonmiani 42 G5
Sono → 93 D4
Sonora → 84 B2
Sonsonate 85 E7
Soochow = Suzhou 35 C7
Soomaaliya = Somali
 Rep. ■ 49 F4
Sopi 37 D3
Sopot 16 A4
Sopron 16 E3
Sør-Rondane 96 B8
Sorel-Tracy 71 E6
Sórgono 21 D2
Soria 19 B4
Sorkh, Kuh-e 44 C4
Soroca 17 D9
Sorocaba 94 A7
Soroki = Soroca 17 D9
Sorong 37 E4
Soroti 57 D6
Sørøya 8 A10
Sorrento 63 C3
Sorsogon 36 B2
Sosnowiec 16 C4
Souanké 56 D2
Soudas, Ormos 23 G5
Sôul = Seoul 35 C7
Sources, Mt. aux 59 D5
Soure 92 D6
Souris → 69 D10
Sousa 92 D6
Sousse 54 A1
South Africa ■ 58 E4
South Australia □ 62 B2
South Bend 76 D2
South Carolina □ 83 C7
South China Sea 38 C4
South Dakota □ 74 C4
South East C. 62 D4
South Horr 57 D7
South I. 65 E3
South Invercargill 65 G3
South Korea ■ 35 C7
South Magnetic Pole
 96 A13
South Nahanni → 68 B7
South Natuna Is. = Natuna
 Selatan, Kepulauan
 39 D3
South Orkney Is. 96 A4
South Pagai, I. = Pagai
 Selatan, Pulau 39 E2
South Platte → 74 E4
South Pole 96 C
South Ronaldsay 10 B5
South Saskatchewan →
 69 C9

South Shetland Is. 96 A4
South Shields 11 D6
South Taranaki Bight
 64 C6
South Uist 10 C3
South West C. Australia
 62 D4
South West C. N.Z. 65 G2
Southampton 11 F6
Southampton I. 70 C5
Southbridge 65 E5
Southend-on-Sea 11 F7
Southern Alps 65 E4
Southern Indian L. 69 C10
Southern Ocean 96 A9
Southern Uplands 10 D5
Southland □ 65 F3
Southport 63 A5
Sovetsk Kaliningrad,
 Russia 24 B1
Sovetsk Kirov, Russia
 24 B6
Soweto 59 D5
Sozh → 17 C10
Spain ■ 18 C4
Spalding 62 B2
Spanish Town 86 C4
Sparta = Sparti 23 F4
Spartanburg 83 B7
Sparti 23 F4
Spartivento, C. Calabria,
 Italy 21 F6
Spartivento, C. Sard., Italy
 21 E2
Spassk Dalniy 32 A3
Spatha, Akra 23 G4
Spence Bay = Taloyoak
 68 B10
Spencer, C. 62 C2
Spencer G. 62 B2
Spenser Mts. 65 E5
Spey → 10 C5
Speyer 14 D5
Split 20 C6
Spokane 72 C5
Spoleto 20 C5
Sporyy Navolok, Mys
 28 B7
Spratly Is. 38 C4
Spree → 15 B7
Springfield N.Z. 65 E4
Springfield Ill., U.S.A.
 75 F10
Springfield Mass., U.S.A.
 77 C9
Springfield Mo., U.S.A.
 81 A7
Springfield Ohio, U.S.A.
 76 F4
Springfield Oreg., U.S.A.
 72 D2
Springhurst 63 C4
Springs 59 D5
Srbija = Serbia ■ 22 C4
Sre Ambel 38 B2
Sre Umbell = Sre Ambel
 38 B2
Srebrenica 20 B7
Sredinny Ra. = Sredinnyy
 Khrebet 31 D14

Sredinnyy Khrebet 31 D14
Srednevilyuysk 31 C10
Śrem 16 B3
Sremska Mitrovica 22 B2
Sri Aman 39 D4
Sri Lanka ■ 43 R12
Srikakulam 40 H4
Srinagar 42 B9
Stade 14 B5
Stafford 11 E5
Stakhanov 25 D4
Stalowa Wola 17 C6
Stamford 77 D9
Stanke Dimitrov 22 C4
Stanley Australia 62 D4
Stanley Falk. Is. 95 G5
Stanovoy Khrebet 31 D10
Stanovoy Ra. = Stanovoy
 Khrebet 31 D10
Stanthorpe 63 A5
Stara Planina 22 C4
Stara Zagora 22 C5
Starachowice 16 C5
Staraya Russa 24 B3
Starbuck I. 65 K15
Stargard Szczeciński
 16 B2
Staritsa 24 B3
Starogard Gdański 16 B4
Starokonstantinov =
 Starokonstyantyniv
 17 D8
Starokonstyantyniv 17 D8
Staryy Chartoriysk 17 C7
Staryy Oskol 24 C4
State College 77 D7
Staten, I. = Estados, I. de
 Los 95 G4
Statesville 83 B7
Stavanger 9 D7
Staveley 65 E4
Stavropol 25 D5
Stawell 62 C3
Stefanie L. = Chew Bahir
 55 H6
Stefansson Bay 96 A9
Steiermark □ 15 E8
Steinkjer 8 C8
Stendal 15 B6
Steornabhaigh =
 Stornoway 10 B3
Stepanakert = Xankändi
 25 F6
Stephens Creek 62 B3
Stephenville 71 E8
Stepnyak 29 D8
Sterlitamak 29 D6
Stettin = Szczecin 16 B2
Stettiner Haff 15 B8
Stettler 69 C8
Steubenville 76 D5
Stevenage 11 F6
Stevenson → 62 A2
Stewart → 68 B6
Stewart, I. 95 G2
Stewart I. 65 G2
Steyr 15 D8
Stillwater N.Z. 65 E4
Stillwater U.S.A. 80 A5
Štip 22 D4

Stirling **10 C5**
Stockerau **15 D9**
Stockholm **9 D9**
Stockport **11 E5**
Stockton **78 B2**
Stockton-on-Tees **11 D6**
Stoeng Treng **38 B3**
Stoke-on-Trent **11 E5**
Stokes Pt. **62 D3**
Stolac **20 C6**
Stolbovoy, Ostrov **30 B11**
Stolbtsy = Stowbtsy **17 B8**
Stolin **17 C8**
Stonehaven **10 C5**
Stony Tunguska = Tunguska, Podkamennaya → **30 C7**
Stora Lulevatten **8 B9**
Storavan **8 B9**
Store Bælt **9 D8**
Store Creek **63 B4**
Storm B. **62 D4**
Stormberge **59 E5**
Stornoway **10 B3**
Storozhinets = Storozhynets **17 D7**
Storozhynets **17 D7**
Storsjön **8 C8**
Storuman **8 B9**
Stowbtsy **17 B8**
Strahan **62 D4**
Stralsund **15 A7**
Stranraer **11 D4**
Strasbourg **13 B7**
Stratford *Canada* **76 C5**
Stratford *N.Z.* **64 C6**
Strathalbyn **62 C2**
Straubing **15 D7**
Streaky B. **62 B1**
Streaky Bay **62 B1**
Strelka **30 D7**
Strezhevoy **29 C8**
Strimonas → **23 D4**
Strómboli **21 E5**
Stronsay **10 B5**
Stroud Road **63 B5**
Strumica **22 D4**
Stryy **17 D6**
Strzelecki Cr. → **62 A2**
Stuart Ra. **62 A1**
Stung Treng = Stoeng Treng **38 B3**
Stuttgart **14 D5**
Styria = Steiermark □ **15 E8**
Suakin **55 E6**
Subansiri → **41 D9**
Subi **39 D3**
Subotica **16 E4**
Suceava **17 E8**
Suchou = Suzhou **35 C7**
Süchow = Xuzhou **35 C6**
Sucre **91 G5**
Sudair **47 F6**
Sudan ■ **55 E4**
Sudbury **71 E5**
Sûdd **55 G4**
Sudeten Mts. = Sudety **16 C3**

Sudety **16 C3**
Sudirman, Pegunungan **37 E5**
Sueca **19 C5**
Suez = El Suweis **54 C5**
Suez, G. of = Suweis, Khalîg el **54 C5**
Sugluk = Salluit **70 C6**
Şuḥār **44 E4**
Sühbaatar **35 A5**
Suihua **35 B7**
Sukadana **39 E3**
Sukagawa **33 E7**
Sukaraja **39 E4**
Sukhona → **28 C5**
Sukhothai **38 D2**
Sukhumi = Sokhumi **25 E5**
Sukkur **42 F6**
Sukkur Barrage **42 F6**
Sukumo **33 G3**
Sula, Kepulauan **37 E3**
Sulaiman Range **42 D6**
Sulawesi **37 E2**
Sulawesi Sea = Celebes Sea **37 D2**
Sulawesi Tengah □ **37 E2**
Sulawesi Tenggara □ **37 E2**
Sulima **53 G3**
Sulina **17 F9**
Sullana **90 D2**
Sultanpur **40 D4**
Sulu Arch. **36 C2**
Sulu Sea **36 C2**
Suluq **54 B3**
Sulzberger Ice Shelf **96 B17**
Sumalata **37 D2**
Sumatera **39 D2**
Sumatra = Sumatera **39 D2**
Sumba **37 F1**
Sumba, Selat **37 F1**
Sumbawa **39 F5**
Sumbawa Besar **39 F5**
Sumbe **56 G2**
Šumen = Shumen **22 C6**
Sumgait = Sumqayıt **25 E6**
Summerside **71 E7**
Šumperk **16 D3**
Sumqayıt **25 E6**
Sumter **83 C7**
Sumy **24 C3**
Sunbury **63 C3**
Sunda, Selat **39 F3**
Sunda Str. = Sunda, Selat **39 F3**
Sundarbans **41 G7**
Sundargarh **40 F5**
Sunderland **11 D6**
Sundsvall **8 C9**
Sungaigerong **39 E2**
Sungailiat **39 E3**
Sungaipakning **39 D2**
Sungaipenuh **39 E2**
Sungari = Songhua Jiang → **35 B8**

Sunghua Chiang = Songhua Jiang → **35 B8**
Sungurlu **46 B3**
Sunnyvale **78 B1**
Suntar **30 C9**
Supaul **40 D6**
Superior **75 B8**
Superior, L. **71 E5**
Suphan Dağı **46 C5**
Supiori **37 E5**
Suquṭra = Socotra **49 E5**
Sūr *Lebanon* **46 D3**
Şūr *Oman* **45 F4**
Sura → **24 B6**
Surabaja = Surabaya **39 F4**
Surabaya **39 F4**
Surakarta **39 F4**
Surat *Australia* **63 A4**
Surat *India* **43 J8**
Surat Thani **38 C1**
Suratgarh **42 E8**
Surgut **29 C8**
Suriapet **43 L11**
Surigao **36 C3**
Surinam = Suriname ■ **92 B2**
Suriname ■ **92 B2**
Suriname → **92 A2**
Surt **54 B2**
Surt, Khalīj **54 B2**
Surtsey **8 C1**
Suruga-Wan **33 F6**
Susanville **72 F3**
Susquehanna → **77 E7**
Susques **94 A3**
Susunu **37 E4**
Susurluk **23 E7**
Sutherland **58 E4**
Sutherland Falls **65 F2**
Sutlej → **42 E7**
Suttsu **32 B7**
Suva **64 L12**
Suva Planina **22 C4**
Suvorov Is. = Suwarrow Is. **65 L14**
Suwałki **17 A6**
Suwarrow Is. **65 L14**
Suweis, Khalîg el **54 C5**
Suzdal **24 B5**
Suzhou **35 C7**
Suzu **33 E5**
Suzu-Misaki **33 E5**
Svealand □ **9 D9**
Sverdrup Chan. **70 B4**
Sverdrup Is. **70 B4**
Sverige = Sweden ■ **9 D9**
Svetlogorsk = Svyetlahorsk **17 B9**
Svishtov **22 C5**
Svislach **17 B7**
Svizzera = Switzerland ■ **13 C8**
Svyetlahorsk **17 B9**
Swabian Alps = Schwäbische Alb **14 D5**
Swakopmund **58 C2**

Swan Hill **62 C3**
Swansea **11 F5**
Swatow = Shantou **35 D6**
Swaziland ■ **59 D6**
Sweden ■ **9 D9**
Sweetwater **80 C3**
Swellendam **58 E4**
Świdnica **16 C3**
Świdnik **17 C6**
Świebodzin **16 B2**
Świecie **16 B4**
Swift Current **69 C9**
Swindon **11 F6**
Swinemünde = Świnoujście **16 B2**
Świnoujście **16 B2**
Switzerland ■ **13 C8**
Sydney *Australia* **63 B5**
Sydney *Canada* **71 E7**
Sydra, G. of = Surt, Khalīj **54 B2**
Syktyvkar **28 C6**
Sylhet **41 E8**
Sylt **14 A5**
Sym **29 C9**
Syracuse **77 C7**
Syrdarya → **29 E7**
Syria ■ **46 D4**
Syrian Desert = Shām, Bādiyat ash **47 D4**
Syros **23 F5**
Syzran **24 C6**
Szczecin **16 B2**
Szczecinek **16 B3**
Szczeciński, Zalew = Stettiner Haff **15 B8**
Szczytno **16 B5**
Szechwan = Sichuan □ **34 C5**
Szeged **16 E5**
Székesfehérvár **16 E4**
Szekszárd **16 E4**
Szentes **16 E5**
Szolnok **16 E5**
Szombathely **16 E3**

T

Tabacal **94 A4**
Tabaco **36 B2**
Ṭābah **47 F5**
Ṭabas *Khorāsān, Iran* **45 C5**
Ṭabas *Yazd, Iran* **44 C4**
Tabatinga, Serra da **93 E5**
Tablas **36 B2**
Table B. **58 E3**
Table Mt. **58 E3**
Tábor **16 D2**
Tabora **57 F6**
Tabou **53 H4**
Tabrīz **46 C6**
Tabūk **47 E4**
Tacheng **34 B3**
Tacloban **36 B2**
Tacna **91 G4**
Tacoma **72 C2**
Tacuarembó **94 C5**
Tademaït, Plateau du **52 C6**

Tadjoura 49 E3
Tadmor 65 D5
Tadzhikistan = Tajikistan ■ 29 F8
Taegu = Daegu 35 C7
Taejŏn = Daejeon 35 C7
Tafalla 19 A5
Tafermear 37 F4
Taft 36 B3
Taftan 42 E2
Taftān, Küh-e 45 D5
Taga Dzong 41 D7
Taganrog 25 D4
Tagbilaran 36 C2
Tagliamento → 20 B4
Taguatinga 93 E5
Tagum 36 C3
Tagus = Tejo → 18 C1
Tahakopa 65 G3
Tahan, Gunung 38 D2
Tahat 52 D7
Tāherī 44 E3
Tahiti 65 L16
Tahoe, L. 72 G3
Tahoua 53 F7
Tahta 54 C5
Tahulandang 37 D3
Tahuna 37 D3
Taibei = T'aipei 35 D7
T'aichung 35 D7
Taidong 35 D7
Taieri → 65 G4
Taihape 64 C6
Tailem Bend 62 C2
Taimyr Peninsula = Taymyr, Poluostrov 30 B7
Tain 10 C4
T'ainan 35 D7
T'aipei 35 D7
Taiping 38 D2
Taitao, Pen. de 95 F1
Taiwan ■ 35 D7
Taiyuan 35 C6
Taizhong = T'aichung 35 D7
Ta'izz 49 E3
Tajikistan ■ 29 F8
Tajima 33 E6
Tajo = Tejo → 18 C1
Tak 38 A1
Takada 33 E6
Takaka 65 D5
Takamatsu 33 F4
Takaoka 33 E5
Takasaki 33 E6
Takayama 33 E5
Takefu 33 F5
Takengon 38 D1
Takeshima = Liancourt Rocks 33 F2
Tākestān 46 D7
Takev 38 B2
Takhār □ 45 B7
Takikawa 32 B7
Takla Makan 34 C3
Taklamakan Shamo = Takla Makan 34 C3

Talara 90 D2
Talas 29 E8
Talaud, Kepulauan 36 D3
Talaud Is. = Talaud, Kepulauan 36 D3
Talavera de la Reina 18 C3
Talayan 36 C2
Talbragar → 63 B4
Talca 94 D2
Talcahuano 94 D2
Talcher 40 G5
Taldy Kurgan = Taldyqorghan 29 E8
Taldyqorghan 29 E8
Tälesh, Kühhä-ye 46 C7
Tali Post 55 G5
Talibon 36 B2
Taliwang 39 F5
Tall 'Afar 46 C5
Talladega 82 C4
Tallahassee 83 D5
Tallangatta 63 C4
Tallinn 24 B1
Taloyoak 68 B10
Taltal 94 B2
Talwood 63 A4
Talyawalka Cr. → 62 B3
Tamale 53 G5
Tamanrasset 52 D7
Tamarang 63 B5
Tamatave = Toamasina 59 B9
Tambacounda 53 F3
Tambelan, Kepulauan 39 D3
Tambo de Mora 91 F3
Tambora 39 F5
Tambov 24 C5
Tâmega → 18 B1
Tamenglong 41 E9
Tamgak, Mts. 53 E7
Tamil Nadu □ 43 P10
Tammerfors = Tampere 8 C10
Tamo Abu, Banjaran 39 D5
Tampa 83 F6
Tampere 8 C10
Tampico 84 C5
Tamsagbulag 35 B6
Tamu 41 E10
Tamworth 63 B5
Tana → Kenya 57 E8
Tana → Norway 8 A11
Tana, L. 55 F6
Tanabe 33 G4
Tanahbala 39 E1
Tanahgrogot 39 E5
Tanahjampea 37 F2
Tanahmasa 39 E1
Tanahmerah 37 F10
Tanakura 33 F7
Tanami Desert 60 D5
Tanana → 69 B4
Tananarive = Antananarivo 59 B9
Tánaro → 13 D8
Tandag 36 C3
Tandil 94 D5

Tando Adam 42 G6
Tandou L. 62 B3
Taneatua 64 C7
Tanen Tong Dan = Dawna Ra. 41 J12
Tanezrouft 52 D6
Tanga 57 F7
Tanganyika, L. 57 F5
Tanger 52 A4
Tanggula Shan 34 C4
Tanghla Range = Tanggula Shan 34 C4
Tangier = Tanger 52 A4
Tangshan 35 C6
Tanimbar, Kepulauan 37 F4
Tanimbar Is. = Tanimbar, Kepulauan 37 F4
Taninthari = Tenasserim 38 B1
Tanjay 36 C2
Tanjore = Thanjavur 43 P11
Tanjung 39 E5
Tanjungbalai 39 D1
Tanjungbatu 39 D5
Tanjungkarang Telukbetung = Bandar Lampung 39 F3
Tanjungpandan 39 E3
Tanjungpinang 39 D2
Tanjungredeb 39 D5
Tanjungselor 39 D5
Tanout 53 F7
Tanta 54 B5
Tantung = Dandong 35 B7
Tanunda 62 B2
Tanzania ■ 57 F6
Taolanaro 59 D9
Taoudenni 52 D5
Tapa Shan = Daba Shan 35 C5
Tapajós → 92 C3
Tapaktuan 39 D1
Tapanui 65 F3
Tapauá → 91 E6
Tapeta 53 G4
Tapirapecó, Serra 90 C6
Tapti → 43 J8
Tapuae-o-Uenuku 65 D5
Tapul Group 36 C2
Taquari → 91 G7
Tara Australia 63 A5
Tara Russia 29 D8
Tara → Montenegro 22 C2
Tara → Russia 29 D8
Tarābulus Lebanon 46 D3
Tarābulus Libya 54 B1
Tarakan 39 D5
Taranaki □ 64 C6
Taranaki, Mt. 64 C6
Tarancón 19 B4
Taranga Hill 43 H8
Taranto 21 D6
Táranto, G. di 21 D6
Tarapacá 90 D5
Tararua Ra. 64 D6
Tarashcha 17 D10
Tarauacá 91 E4

Tarauacá → 91 E5
Tarawa 64 J12
Tarawera 64 C7
Tarawera, L. 64 C7
Taraz 29 E8
Tarazona 19 B5
Tarbagatay, Khrebet 29 E9
Tarbela Dam 42 B8
Tarbes 12 E4
Tarcoola 62 B1
Tarcoon 63 B4
Taree 63 B5
Tarfaya 52 C3
Târgovişte 22 B5
Târgu Jiu 17 F6
Târgu Mureş 17 E7
Tarifa 18 D3
Tarija 94 A4
Tariku → 37 E5
Tarim Basin = Tarim Pendi 34 C3
Tarim He → 34 C3
Tarim Pendi 34 C3
Taritatu → 37 E5
Tarkhankut, Mys 25 D3
Tarko Sale 28 C8
Tarkwa 53 G5
Tarlac 36 A2
Tarma 91 F3
Tarn → 12 D4
Tarnobrzeg 16 C5
Tarnów 16 C5
Tarnowskie Góry 16 C4
Taroom 63 A4
Taroudannt 52 B4
Tarragona 19 B6
Tarrasa = Terrassa 19 B7
Tarsus 46 C3
Tartagal 94 A4
Tartu 24 B2
Ţarţūs 46 D3
Tarutung 39 D1
Tash-Kömür 29 E8
Tash-Kumyr = Tash-Kömür 29 E8
Tashauz = Dashoguz 29 E6
Tashi Chho Dzong = Thimphu 41 D7
Tashkent = Toshkent 29 E7
Tashtagol 29 D9
Tasman B. 65 D5
Tasman Mts. 65 D5
Tasman Pen. 62 D4
Tasmania □ 62 D4
Tatabánya 16 E4
Tatar Republic = Tatarstan □ 29 D6
Tatarbunary 17 F9
Tatarsk 29 D8
Tatarstan □ 29 D6
Tateyama 33 F6
Tathra 63 C4
Tatnam, C. 71 D4
Tatra = Tatry 16 D4
Tatry 16 D4
Tatta 43 G5
Tat'ung = Datong 35 B6

Tatvan 46 C5
Taubaté 94 A7
Tauern 15 E7
Taumarunui 64 C6
Taumaturgo 91 E4
Taungdwingyi 41 G10
Taunggyi 41 G11
Taungup 41 H10
Taungup Taunggya 41 H9
Taunton 11 F5
Taunus 14 C5
Taupo 64 C7
Taupo, L. 64 C6
Tauranga 64 B7
Tauranga Harb. 64 B7
Taurianova 21 E6
Taurus Mts. = Toros
    Dağları 46 C3
Tavastehus = Hämeenlinna
    8 C10
Tavda 29 D7
Tavda → 29 D7
Tavira 18 D2
Tavoy 38 B1
Tawau 38 D5
Tawi-Tawi 36 C2
Tay → 10 C5
Tayabamba 91 E3
Taygetos Oros 23 F4
Taylakova 29 D8
Taylakovy = Taylakova
    29 D8
Taymä 47 F4
Taymyr, Oz. 30 B8
Taymyr, Poluostrov 30 B7
Taytay 36 B1
Taz → 28 C8
Taza 52 B5
Tazovskiy 28 C8
Tbilisi 25 E5
Tchad = Chad ■ 55 F2
Tchad, L. 55 F1
Tchibanga 56 E2
Tch'eng-tou = Chengdu
    35 C5
Tchibanga 56 E2
Tch'ong-k'ing =
    Chongqing 35 D5
Tczew 16 A4
Te Anau, L. 65 F2
Te Aroha 64 B6
Te Awamutu 64 C6
Te Ika a Maui = North I.
    64 B5
Te Kuiti 64 C6
Te Puke 64 B6
Te Waewae B. 65 G2
Te Wai Pounamu = South
    I. 65 E3
Tebakang 39 D4
Tébessa 52 A7
Tebicuary → 94 B5
Tebingtinggi 39 D1
Tecuci 22 B6
Tedzhen = Tejen 29 F7
Tefé 90 D6
Tegal 39 F3
Tegucigalpa 85 E7
Tehachapi 78 C3
Teheran = Tehrān 44 C2
Tehoru 37 E3

Tehrān 44 C2
Tehuantepec 85 D5
Tehuantepec, G. de 85 D5
Tehuantepec, Istmo de
    85 D6
Tejen 29 F7
Tejo → 18 C1
Tekapo, L. 65 E4
Tekeli 29 E8
Tekirdağ 22 D6
Tekkali 40 H5
Tel Aviv-Yafo 46 D3
Tela 85 D7
Telanaipura = Jambi
    39 E2
Telavi 25 E6
Telekhany = Tsyelyakhany
    17 B7
Teles Pires → 91 E7
Telford 11 E5
Tellicherry 43 P9
Telsen 95 E3
Teluk Anson = Teluk Intan
    39 D2
Teluk Betung = Bandar
    Lampung 39 F3
Teluk Intan 39 D2
Telukbutun 39 D3
Telukdalem 39 D1
Tema 53 G5
Temerloh 39 D2
Temir 29 E6
Temirtau Kazakhstan
    29 D8
Temirtau Russia 29 D9
Temma 62 D3
Tempe 79 D7
Temple 80 D5
Temuco 94 D2
Temuka 65 F4
Tenali 40 J3
Tenasserim 38 B1
Tenda, Colle di 13 D7
Tendaho 49 E3
Tenerife 52 C2
Tengah, Kepulauan 39 F5
Tengchong 34 D4
Tenggarong 39 E5
Tengiz Köli 29 D7
Tenkasi 43 Q10
Tennessee □ 82 B4
Tennessee → 76 F1
Tenom 38 C5
Tenterfield 63 A5
Teófilo Otoni 93 F5
Tepa 37 F3
Tepic 84 C4
Teplice 16 C1
Ter → 19 A7
Téramo 20 C4
Terang 62 C3
Terebovlya 17 D7
Terek → 25 E6
Terewah, L. 63 A4
Teridgerie Cr. → 63 B4
Termez = Termiz 29 F7
Términi Imerese 21 F4
Termiz 29 F7

Térmoli 20 C5
Ternate 37 D3
Terney 32 A5
Terni 20 C4
Ternopil 17 D7
Ternopol = Ternopil 17 D7
Terowie N.S.W., Australia
    63 B3
Terowie S. Austral.,
    Australia 62 B2
Terracina 20 D4
Terralba 21 E2
Terrassa 19 B7
Terre Haute 76 E2
Terschelling 14 B3
Teruel 19 B5
Teryaweynya L. 62 B3
Teshio 32 A7
Teshio-Gawa → 32 A7
Tesiyn Gol → 34 A4
Teslin 68 B6
Teslin → 68 B6
Tessalit 52 D6
Tetas, Pta. 94 A2
Tete 59 B6
Teterev → 17 C10
Teteven 22 C5
Tetiyev 17 D9
Tétouan 52 A4
Tetovo 22 C3
Teuco → 94 B4
Teun 37 F3
Teutoburger Wald 14 B5
Tewantin 63 A5
Texarkana 81 C6
Texas 63 A5
Texas □ 80 D4
Texas City 81 E6
Texel 14 B3
Teyvareh 45 C6
Tezpur 41 D9
Thabana Ntlenyana 59 D5
Thabazimbi 59 C5
Thailand ■ 38 A2
Thailand, G. of 38 B2
Thakhek 38 A2
Thal 42 C7
Thala La = Hkakabo Razi
    41 C11
Thallon 63 A4
Thames 64 B6
Thames → 11 F7
Thandwe 41 H10
Thane 43 K8
Thanh Pho Ho Chi Minh
    38 B3
Thanjavur 43 P11
Thar Desert 42 F7
Tharad 43 G7
Thargomindah 63 A3
Tharrawaddy 41 J10
Thasos 23 D5
Thaton 41 J11
Thaungdut 41 E10
Thayetmyo 41 H10
Thazi 41 G11
The Gulf = Persian Gulf
    44 E2
The Hague =
    's-Gravenhage 14 B3

The Pas 69 C9
The Wash 11 E7
Thebes = Thiva 23 E4
Theebine 63 A5
Thermopylae 23 E4
Thessaloniki 23 D4
Thessaloniki, Gulf of =
    Thessaloniki Kolpos
    23 D4
Thessaloniki Kolpos 23 D4
Thetford 11 E7
Thetford Mines 71 E6
Thevenard 62 B1
Thiel Mts. 96 C2
Thiers 13 D5
Thiès 53 F2
Thika 57 E7
Thimphu 41 D7
Thionville 13 B7
Thira = Santorini 23 F5
Thiruvananthapuram =
    Trivandrum 43 Q10
Thistle I. 62 C2
Thiva 23 E4
Þjórsá → 8 C1
Thohoyandou 59 C6
Thomas, L. 62 A2
Thomasville Ga., U.S.A.
    83 D6
Thomasville N.C., U.S.A.
    83 B7
Thompson 69 C10
Thrace 22 D6
Three Hummock I. 62 D3
Three Points, C. 53 H5
Thunder Bay 71 E5
Thung Song 38 C1
Thunkar 41 D8
Thüringer Wald 14 C6
Thurles 11 E3
Thurloo Downs 63 A3
Thurso 10 B5
Thurston I. 96 B2
Thylungra 63 A3
Tia 63 B5
Tian Shan 34 B3
Tianjin 35 C6
Tianshui 35 C5
Tiaret 52 A6
Tiber = Tevere → 20 D4
Tiberias, L. = Yam Kinneret
    46 D3
Tibesti 54 D2
Tibet = Xizang Zizhiqu □
    34 C3
Tibooburra 62 A3
Tiburón, I. 84 B2
Ticino → 13 D8
Tiddim 41 F9
Tidjikja 53 E3
Tidore 37 D3
Tien Shan = Tian Shan
    34 B3
Tien-tsin = Tianjin 35 C6
T'ienching = Tianjin 35 C6
Tientsin = Tianjin 35 C6
Tierra de Campos 18 A3
Tierra del Fuego, I. Gr. de
    95 G3
Tiétar → 18 C2

Tieyon 62 A1
Tifu 37 E3
Tighina 17 E9
Tigre → 90 D4
Tigris = Dijlah, Nahr →
47 E6
Tigyaing 41 F11
Tijuana 84 A1
Tikamgarh 43 G11
Tikhoretsk 25 D5
Tikiraqjuaq = Whale Cove
68 B10
Tikrīt 46 D5
Tiksi 30 B10
Tilamuta 37 D2
Tilburg 14 C3
Tilos 23 F6
Tilpa 63 B3
Timaru 65 F4
Timbuktu = Tombouctou
53 E5
Timimoun 52 C6
Timiris, Râs 53 E2
Timişoara 16 F5
Timmins 71 E5
Timok → 22 B4
Timor 37 F3
Timor Leste = East
Timor ■ 37 F3
Tinaca Pt. 36 C3
Tindouf 52 C4
Tingo Maria 91 E3
Tinian 64 H9
Tinjoub 52 C4
Tinnevelly = Tirunelveli
43 Q10
Tinogasta 94 B3
Tinos 23 F5
Tintinara 62 C3
Tioman, Pulau 39 D2
Tipongpani 41 D10
Tipperary 11 E2
Tīrān 44 C2
Tiranë 22 D2
Tiraspol 17 E9
Tire 23 E6
Tirebolu 25 E4
Tiree 10 C3
Tîrgovişte = Târgovişte
22 B5
Tîrgu Jiu = Târgu Jiu
17 F6
Tîrgu Mureş = Târgu Mureş
17 E7
Tirich Mir 42 A7
Tiritiri o te Moana =
Southern Alps 65 E4
Tīrnavos 23 E4
Tirodi 43 J11
Tirol □ 14 E6
Tirso → 21 E2
Tiruchchirappalli 43 P11
Tirunelveli 43 Q10
Tirupati 43 N11
Tiruppur 43 P10
Tiruvannamalai 43 N11
Tisa → 22 B3
Tisdale 69 C9
Tisza = Tisa → 22 B3
Tit-Ary 30 B10

Titicaca, L. 91 G5
Titule 57 D5
Tivaouane 53 F2
Tívoli 20 D4
Tiwï 45 F4
Tizi-Ouzou 52 A6
Tjirebon = Cirebon 39 F3
Tlaxiaco 84 D5
Tlemcen 52 B5
Toamasina 59 B9
Toay 94 D4
Toba Kakar 42 D6
Tobago 87 D7
Tobelo 37 D3
Tobermory 10 C3
Tobias Fornier 36 B2
Toboali 39 E3
Tobol → 29 D7
Toboli 37 E2
Tobolsk 29 D7
Tobruk = Tubruq 54 B3
Tobyl = Tobol → 29 D7
Tocantinópolis 92 D4
Tocantins □ 93 E4
Tocantins → 92 C4
Tocumwal 63 C4
Tocuyo → 90 A5
Todeli 37 E2
Todos os Santos, B. de
93 E6
Togian, Kepulauan 37 E2
Togliatti 24 C6
Togo ■ 53 G6
Toili 37 E2
Toinya 55 G4
Tojo 37 E2
Tokala 37 E2
Tōkamachi 33 E6
Tokanui 65 G3
Tokarahi 65 F4
Tokat 46 B4
Tokdo = Liancourt Rocks
33 E2
Tokelau Is. 65 K13
Tokmak 29 E8
Tokushima 33 F4
Tokuyama 33 F3
Tōkyō 33 F6
Tolaga Bay 64 C8
Tolbukhin = Dobrich
22 C6
Toledo *Spain* 18 C3
Toledo *U.S.A.* 76 D4
Toledo, Montes de 18 C3
Toliara 59 C8
Tolima 90 C3
Tolitoli 37 D2
Tolo, Teluk 37 E2
Toluca 84 D5
Tomakomai 32 B7
Tomar 18 C1
Tomaszów Mazowiecki
16 C4
Tombouctou 53 E5
Tombua 58 B2
Tomelloso 18 C4
Tomini 37 D2
Tomini, Teluk 37 E2

Tomorit 23 D3
Tomsk 29 D9
Tonantins 90 D5
Tondano 37 D2
Tonekābon 44 B2
Tonga ■ 65 L13
Tonga Trench 65 L13
Tongaren = Penrhyn
65 K15
Tongatapu 94 C2
Tongchuan 35 C5
Tonghua 35 B7
Tongjiang 35 B8
Tongking, G. of = Tonkin,
G. of 35 D5
Tongoy 94 C2
Tongsa Dzong 41 D8
Tongue → 74 B2
Tonk 42 F9
Tonkin, G. of 35 D5
Tonle Sap 38 B2
Tonnégrande 30 E
Toompine 63 A3
Toora 63 C4
Toowoomba 63 A5
Topeka 75 F7
Topki 29 D9
Topolobampo 84 B3
Torata 91 G4
Torbalı 23 E6
Torbat-e Heydārīyeh
44 C4
Torbat-e Jām 45 C5
Torbay □ 11 F5
Tordesillas 18 B3
Torgau 15 C7
Torino 13 D7
Torit 55 H5
Tormes → 18 B2
Torneå = Tornio 8 E12
Torneälven → 8 B10
Torneträsk 8 B9
Tornio 8 E12
Tornionjoki =
Torneälven → 8 B10
Tornquist 94 D3
Toro, Cerro del 94 B3
Toronto 71 E6
Toropets 24 B3
Tororo 57 D6
Toros Dağları 46 C3
Torre de Moncorvo 18 B2
Torre del Greco 21 D5
Torrejón de Ardoz 18 B4
Torrelavega 18 A3
Torremolinos 18 D3
Torrens, L. 62 B2
Torrent 19 C5
Torreón 84 B4
Torres Vedras 18 C1
Torrevieja 19 D5
Tortosa 19 B6
Tortosa, C. 19 B6
Ţorūd 44 C3
Toruń 16 B4
Tosa-Wan 33 G3
Toscana □ 20 C3
Toshkent 29 E7
Tostado 94 B4
Tosya 46 B3

Totma 24 A5
Totten Glacier 96 A12
Tottenham 63 B4
Tottori 33 F4
Toubkal, Djebel 52 B4
Tougan 53 F5
Touggourt 52 B7
Toul 13 B6
Toulon 13 E6
Toulouse 12 E4
Toummo 54 D1
Touraine 12 C4
Tourcoing 13 A5
Touriñán, C. 18 A1
Tournai 14 C3
Tournon-sur-Rhône 13 D6
Tours 12 C4
Towada 32 C7
Towada-Ko 32 C7
Towamba 63 C4
Towang 41 D8
Townsville 61 D8
Toya-Ko 32 B7
Toyama 33 E5
Toyama-Wan 33 E5
Toyohashi 33 F5
Toyooka 33 F4
Toyota 33 F5
Tozeur 52 B7
Tozkhurmato 46 D6
Trá Li = Tralee 11 E2
Trabzon 25 E4
Trafalgar, C. 18 D2
Trail 69 D8
Tralee 11 E2
Trancas 94 B3
Trang 38 C1
Trangan 37 F4
Trangie 63 B4
Trani 20 D7
Transantarctic Mts. 96 C
Transilvania 17 F7
Transilvanian Alps =
Carpaţii Meridionali
17 F7
Transylvania = Transilvania
17 F7
Trápani 21 E4
Traralgon 63 C4
Trasimeno, L. 20 C4
Traun 15 D8
Travemünde 15 B6
Travers, Mt. 65 E5
Travnik 20 B6
Trébbia → 13 D8
Trebič 16 D2
Trebinje 20 C7
Treinta y Tres 94 C5
Trelew 95 E3
Tremp 19 A6
Trenque Lauquen 94 D4
Trent → 11 E6
Trento 20 A3
Trenton 77 D8
Tres Arroyos 94 D4
Três Lagoas 93 G3
Tres Montes, C. 95 F1
Tres Puntas, C. 95 F3
Três Rios 93 G5

Treviso **20 B4**
Triabunna **62 D4**
Trichinopoly =
   Tiruchchirappalli **43 P11**
Trichur **43 P10**
Trida **63 B4**
Trier **14 D4**
Trieste **20 B4**
Triglav **20 A4**
Trikala **23 E3**
Trikora, Puncak **37 E5**
Trinidad *Bolivia* **91 F6**
Trinidad *Cuba* **86 B3**
Trinidad *Uruguay* **94 C5**
Trinidad *U.S.A.* **80 A1**
Trinidad & Tobago ■
   87 D7
Trinity → **81 E6**
Trinity B. **71 E8**
Trinity Range **72 F4**
Trinkitat **55 E6**
Tripoli = Tarābulus
   Lebanon **46 D3**
Tripoli = Tarābulus *Libya*
   54 B1
Tripoli **23 F4**
Tripura □ **41 F8**
Trivandrum **43 Q10**
Troglav **20 C6**
Trois-Rivières **71 E6**
Troitsko Pechorsk **28 C6**
Trollhättan **9 D8**
Tromsø **8 B9**
Tronador, Mte. **95 E2**
Trondheim **8 C8**
Trondheimsfjorden **8 C8**
Trout L. **68 B7**
Trouville-sur-Mer **12 B4**
Troy *Turkey* **23 E6**
Troy *Ala., U.S.A.* **82 D5**
Troy *N.Y., U.S.A.* **77 C9**
Troyes **13 B6**
Trucial States = United
   Arab Emirates ■ **44 F3**
Trudovoye **32 B8**
Trujillo *Honduras* **85 D7**
Trujillo *Peru* **91 E3**
Trujillo *Spain* **18 C3**
Trujillo *Venezuela* **90 B4**
Truk **64 J10**
Trundle **63 B4**
Truro *Canada* **71 E7**
Truro *U.K.* **11 F4**
Truskavets **17 D6**
Trutnov **16 C2**
Tsaratanana **59 B9**
Tsetserleg **34 B5**
Tshabong **58 D4**
Tshane **58 C4**
Tshela **56 E2**
Tshikapa **56 F4**
Tshwane = Pretoria **59 D5**
Tsiigehtchic **68 B6**
Tsimlyansk Res. =
   Tsimlyanskoye Vdkhr.
   25 D5
Tsimlyanskoye Vdkhr.
   25 D5
Tsinan = Jinan **35 C6**
Tsinghai = Qinghai □
   34 C4

Tsingtao = Qingdao **35 C7**
Tsirigo = Kythira **23 F4**
Tskhinvali **25 E5**
Tsna → **24 C5**
Tsuchiura **33 E7**
Tsugaru-Kaikyō **32 C7**
Tsumeb **58 B3**
Tsuruga **33 F5**
Tsuruoka **32 D6**
Tsushima **33 F1**
Tsuyama **33 F4**
Tsyelyakhany **17 B7**
Tual **37 F4**
Tuamotu, Îs. **65 L16**
Tuamotu Arch. = Tuamotu,
   Îs. **65 L16**
Tuamotu Ridge **65 M17**
Tuao **36 A2**
Tuapse **25 E4**
Tuatapere **65 G2**
Tubarão **94 B7**
Tübingen **14 D5**
Tubruq **54 B3**
Tubuaï, Îs. **65 M16**
Tucacas **90 A5**
Tucson **79 D7**
Tucumcari **80 B2**
Tucupita **90 B6**
Tucuruí **92 C4**
Tucuruí, Reprêsa de
   92 C4
Tudela **19 A5**
Tudmur **46 D4**
Tuen **63 A4**
Tuguegarao **36 A2**
Tui **18 A1**
Tukangbesi, Kepulauan
   37 F2
Tuktoyaktuk **68 B6**
Tukuyu **57 F6**
Tula **24 C4**
Tūlak **45 C5**
Tulare **78 B3**
Tulcán **90 C3**
Tulcea **17 F9**
Tulchyn **17 D9**
Tulita **68 B7**
Tulle **12 D4**
Tullibigeal **63 B4**
Tulsa **81 A6**
Tulua **90 C3**
Tum **37 E4**
Tumaco **90 C3**
Tumatumari **90 B7**
Tumba, L. **56 E3**
Tumbarumba **63 C4**
Tumbes **90 D2**
Tumby Bay **62 B2**
Tumeremo **90 B6**
Tumkur **43 N10**
Tump **42 F3**
Tumpat **38 C2**
Tumu **53 F5**
Tumucumaque, Serra
   92 B3
Tumut **63 C4**
Tuncurry **63 B5**
Tundzha → **22 D6**

Tungabhadra → **43 M11**
Tunguska, Nizhnyaya →
   30 C6
Tunguska,
   Podkamennaya →
   30 C7
Tunis **50 A1**
Tunisia ■ **50 B1**
Tunja **90 B4**
Tunnsjøen **8 D7**
Tunuyán → **94 C3**
Tupelo **82 B3**
Tupinambaranas **90 D7**
Tupiza **94 A3**
Tupungato, Cerro **94 C3**
Túquerres **90 C3**
Tura **30 C8**
Turabah **47 E5**
Tūrān **44 C4**
Țurayf **47 E4**
Turek **16 B4**
Turfan = Turpan **34 B3**
Turfan Basin = Turpan
   Pendi **34 B3**
Turfan Depression =
   Turpan Pendi **34 B3**
Tŭrgovishte **22 C6**
Turgutlu **23 E6**
Turhal **46 B4**
Turia → **19 C5**
Turiaçu **92 C4**
Turiaçu → **92 C4**
Turin = Torino **13 D7**
Turkana, L. **57 D7**
Turkestan = Türkistan
   29 E7
Turkey ■ **25 F4**
Türkistan **29 E7**
Türkmenabat **29 F7**
Türkmenbashi **29 E6**
Turkmenistan ■ **29 F6**
Turks & Caicos Is. ☑
   87 B5
Turku **9 C10**
Turnagain, C. **64 D7**
Turneffe Is. **85 D7**
Turnhout **14 C3**
Tŭrnovo = Veliko Tŭrnovo
   22 C5
Turnu Măgurele **22 C5**
Turnu Roşu, P. **17 F7**
Turpan **34 B3**
Turpan Pendi **34 B3**
Turukhansk **30 C6**
Tuscaloosa **82 C4**
Tuscany = Toscana □
   20 C3
Tuticorin **43 Q11**
Tutóia **92 C5**
Tutong **38 D4**
Tutrakan **22 B6**
Tuttlingen **14 E5**
Tutuala **37 F3**
Tutuila **65 L13**
Tutume **59 C5**
Tuvalu ■ **64 K12**
Tuxpan **84 C5**
Tuxtla Gutiérrez **85 D6**
Tuy = Tui **18 A1**
Tuz Gölü **25 F3**
Tūz Khurmātū =
   Tozkhurmato **46 D6**

Tuzla **20 B7**
Tver **24 B4**
Tweed Heads **63 A5**
Twin Falls **73 E6**
Twofold B. **63 C4**
Tyachiv **17 D6**
Tychy **16 C4**
Tyler **81 E6**
Tyre = Sūr **46 D3**
Tyrol = Tirol □ **14 E6**
Tyrrell → **62 C3**
Tyrrell, L. **62 C3**
Tyrrhenian Sea **21 E4**
Tyumen **29 D7**
Tzaneen **59 C6**
Tzukong = Zigong **35 D5**

U

U.S.A. = United States of
   America ■ **67 F10**
Uato-Udo **37 F3**
Uatumã → **90 D7**
Uaupés **90 D5**
Uaupés → **90 C5**
Ubá **93 G5**
Ubaitaba **93 E6**
Ubangi = Oubangi →
   56 E3
Ubauro **42 E6**
Ube **33 G2**
Úbeda **18 C4**
Uberaba **93 F4**
Uberlândia **93 F4**
Ubon Ratchathani **38 A2**
Ubort → **17 B9**
Ubundu **57 E5**
Ucayali → **90 D4**
Uchiura-Wan **32 B7**
Udagamandalam **43 P10**
Udaipur **43 G8**
Udaipur Garhi **40 D6**
Udgir **43 K10**
Udhampur **42 C9**
Údine **20 A4**
Udmurtia □ **28 D6**
Udon Thani **38 A2**
Udupi **43 N9**
Uele → **57 D4**
Uelzen **14 B6**
Ufa **29 D6**
Ugab → **58 C2**
Ugalla → **57 F6**
Uganda ■ **57 D6**
Ugljan **20 B5**
Ugolyak **30 C10**
Uibhist a Deas = South
   Uist **10 C3**
Uibhist a Tuath = North
   Uist **10 C3**
Uíge **56 F2**
Uinta Mts. **73 F8**
Uitenhage **59 E5**
Ujjain **43 H9**
Ujung Pandang **37 F1**
Ukhrul **41 E10**
Ukhta **28 C6**
Ukraine ■ **25 D3**
Ulaanbaatar **35 B5**
Ulaangom **34 A4**

Ulaanjirem 35 B5
Ulan Bator = Ulaanbaatar 35 B5
Ulan Ude 30 D8
Ulcinj 22 D2
Ule älv = Oulujoki → 8 B11
Ule träsk = Oulujärvi 8 C11
Uleåborg = Oulu 8 B11
Ulhasnagar 43 K8
Uliastay 34 B4
Ulladulla 63 C5
Ullapool 10 C4
Ulleungdo 33 E2
Ulm 14 D5
Ulmarra 63 A5
Ulster □ 11 D3
Ulubat Gölü 23 D7
Uludağ 23 D7
Ulungur He → 34 B3
Uluru 60 F5
Ulutau 29 E7
Ulverstone 62 D4
Ulyanovsk = Simbirsk 24 C6
Ulyasutay = Uliastay 34 B4
Umala 91 G5
'Umān = Oman ■ 48 C6
Uman 17 D10
Umaria 40 F3
Umarkot 43 G6
Umbrella Mts. 65 F13
Umeå 8 C10
Umeälven → 8 C10
Umera 37 E3
Umlazi 59 E6
Umm al Qaywayn 44 E3
Umm Durman = Omdurmân 55 E5
Umm Lajj 47 F4
Umm Ruwaba 55 F5
Umnak I. 69 C3
Umniati → 59 B5
Umtata = Mthatha 59 E5
Umuarama 93 G3
Umzimvubu 59 E5
Una → 20 B6
Unalaska 69 C3
Uncía 91 G5
Underbool 62 C3
Ungarie 63 B4
Ungarra 62 B2
Ungava, Pén. d' 70 C6
Ungava B. 70 D7
Ungeny = Ungheni 17 E8
Ungheni 17 E8
Ungwana B. 57 E8
União da Vitória 94 B6
Unimak I. 69 C3
United Arab Emirates ■ 44 F3
United Kingdom ■ 11 D5
United States of America ■ 67 F10
Unnao 40 D3
Unst 10 A6
Ünye 46 B4
Upata 90 B6
Upemba, L. 57 F5

Upington 58 D4
Upper Hutt 65 D6
Upper Volta = Burkina Faso ■ 53 F5
Uppsala 9 D9
Uqsuqtuuq = Gjoa Haven 68 B10
Ur 47 E6
Ural = Zhayyq → 29 E6
Ural 63 B4
Ural Mts. = Uralskie Gory 28 D6
Uralla 63 B5
Uralsk = Oral 24 C7
Uralskie Gory 28 D6
Uranquinty 63 C4
Uray 29 C7
Urbana 76 D1
Urbino 20 C4
Urbión, Picos de 19 A4
Urcos 91 F4
Urda 25 D6
Urewera △ 64 C7
Urfa = Sanliurfa 46 C4
Urganch 29 E7
Urgench = Urganch 29 E7
Uribia 90 A4
Urla 23 E6
Urmia = Orūmīyeh 46 C6
Uroševac 22 C3
Urubamba → 91 F4
Uruçara 90 D7
Uruçuí 92 D5
Uruguai → 94 B6
Uruguaiana 94 B5
Uruguay ■ 94 C5
Uruguay → 94 C5
Urumchi = Ürümqi 34 B4
Ürümqi 29 E9
Ürzhar 29 E9
Usakos 58 C3
Usedom 15 B8
Ushant = Ouessant, Î. d' 12 B1
Ushibuka 33 G2
Üshtöbe 29 E8
Ushuaia 95 G3
Usman 24 C4
Uspallata, P. de 94 C3
Uspenskiy 29 E8
Ussuriysk 32 B2
Ust-Ishim 29 D8
Ust-Kamenogorsk = Öskemen 29 E9
Ust-Karenga 31 D9
Ust-Kuyga 31 B11
Ust Muya 30 D9
Ust-Olenek 30 B10
Ust-Port 28 C9
Ust-Tsilma 28 C6
Ust-Urt = Ustyurt Plateau 29 E6
Ústí nad Labem 16 C2
Ústica 21 E4
Ustinov = Izhevsk 28 D6
Ustye 30 D7
Ustyurt Plateau 29 E6
Usu 34 B3
Usumacinta → 85 D6
Usumbura = Bujumbura 57 E5

Uta 37 E5
Utah □ 73 G8
Utiariti 91 F7
Utica 77 C8
Utrecht 14 B3
Utrera 18 D3
Utsunomiya 33 E6
Uttar Pradesh □ 42 F11
Uttaradit 38 A2
Uusikaupunki 9 C10
Uvat 29 D8
Uvinza 57 F6
Uvira 57 E5
Uvs Nuur 34 A4
'Uwairidh, Harrat al 47 F4
Uwajima 33 G3
Uyuni 91 H5
Uzbekistan ■ 29 E7
Uzerche 12 D4
Uzh → 17 C10
Uzhgorod = Uzhhorod 17 D6
Uzhhorod 17 D6
Uzice 22 C2
Uzunköprü 22 D6

V

Vaal → 58 D4
Vaasa 8 C10
Vác 16 E4
Vach = Vakh → 29 C8
Vadodara 43 H8
Vadsø 8 D13
Vaduz 13 C8
Vahsel B. 96 B5
Váhtjer = Gällivare 8 B10
Vaigach 28 B6
Vakh → 29 C8
Val-d'Or 71 E6
Valahia 22 B5
Valandovo 22 D4
Valcheta 95 E3
Valdai Hills = Valdayskaya Vozvyshennost 24 B3
Valdayskaya Vozvyshennost 24 B3
Valdepeñas 18 C4
Valdés, Pen. 95 E4
Valdez 69 B5
Valdivia 95 D2
Valdosta 83 D6
Valença 93 E6
Valença do Piauí 92 D5
Valence 13 D6
Valencia Spain 19 C5
Valencia Venezuela 90 A5
Valencia □ 19 C5
Valencia, de 19 C6
Valencia de Alcántara 18 C2
Valencia I. 11 F1
Valenciennes 13 A5
Valentim, Sa. do 92 D5
Valera 90 B4
Valjevo 22 B2
Vall de Uxó = La Vall d'Uixó 19 C5
Valladolid Mexico 85 C7
Valladolid Spain 18 B3
Valle de la Pascua 90 B5

Valledupar 90 A4
Vallejo 72 G2
Vallenar 94 B2
Valletta 21 G5
Valls 19 B6
Valognes 12 B3
Valona = Vlorë 23 D2
Valozhyn 17 A8
Valparaíso 94 C2
Vals, Tanjung 37 F5
Valsad 43 J8
Valverde del Camino 18 D2
Van 46 C5
Van, L. = Van Gölü 46 C5
Van Gölü 46 C5
Van Rees, Pegunungan 37 E5
Vanadzor 25 E5
Vancouver Canada 69 D7
Vancouver U.S.A. 72 D2
Vancouver I. 69 D7
Vänern 9 D8
Vangaindrano 59 C9
Vännäs 8 C9
Vannes 12 C2
Vanrhynsdorp 58 E3
Vantaa → 9 C11
Vanua Levu 64 L12
Vanuatu ■ 64 L11
Vapnyarka 17 D9
Varanasi 40 E4
Varangerfjorden 8 A11
Varaždin 20 A6
Varberg 9 D8
Vardak □ 45 C7
Vardar = Axios → 23 D4
Varese 13 D8
Varna 22 C6
Varzaneh 44 C3
Vasa = Vaasa 8 C10
Vasa Barris → 93 E6
Vascongadas = País Vasco □ 19 A4
Vasht = Khāsh 42 E2
Vasilevichi 17 B9
Vasilkov = Vasylkiv 17 C10
Västerås 9 D9
Västerdalälven → 8 C8
Västervik 9 D9
Vasto 20 C5
Vasylkiv 17 C10
Vatican City ■ 20 D4
Vatnajökull 8 C2
Vatra-Dornei 17 E7
Vättern 9 D8
Vaupés = Uaupés → 90 C5
Vawkavysk 17 B7
Vaygach, Ostrov 28 C6
Vedea → 22 C5
Vega 8 C15
Vegreville 69 C8
Vejer de la Frontera 18 D3
Velebit Planina 20 B5
Veles 22 D3
Vélez-Málaga 18 D3
Vélez Rubio 19 D4
Velhas → 93 F5
Velika Kapela 20 B5

Velikaya → 24 B2
Veliki Ustyug 24 A6
Velikiye Luki 24 B3
Veliko Tŭrnovo 22 C5
Velikonda Range 43 M11
Velletri 20 D4
Vellore 43 N11
Venado Tuerto 94 C4
Vendée □ 12 C3
Vendôme 12 C4
Venézia 20 B4
Venézia, G. di 20 B4
Venezuela ■ 90 B5
Venezuela, G. de 90 A4
Vengurla 43 M8
Venice = Venézia 20 B4
Venkatapuram 40 H3
Ventotène 21 D4
Ventoux, Mt. 13 D6
Ventspils 24 B1
Ventuarí → 90 C3
Ventura 78 C3
Venus B. 63 C4
Vera Argentina 94 B4
Vera Spain 19 D5
Veracruz 84 D4
Veraval 43 J7
Verbánia 13 D8
Vercelli 13 D8
Verde → 95 E3
Verden 14 B5
Verdun 13 B6
Vereeniging 59 D5
Verga, C. 53 F3
Veria 23 D4
Verín 18 B2
Verkhnevilyuysk 30 C10
Verkhniy Baskunchak
    25 D6
Verkhoyansk 31 C11
Verkhoyansk Ra. =
    Verkhoyanskiy Khrebet
    31 C10
Verkhoyanskiy Khrebet
    31 C10
Vermont □ 77 C9
Vernon Canada 69 C8
Vernon U.S.A. 80 B4
Véroia = Veria 23 D4
Verona 20 B3
Versailles 12 B5
Vert, C. 53 F2
Verviers 14 C3
Veselovskoye Vdkhr.
    25 D5
Vesoul 13 C7
Vesterålen 8 B9
Vestfjorden 8 B8
Vesúvio 21 D5
Vesuvius, Mt. = Vesúvio
    21 D5
Veszprém 16 E3
Vettore, Mte. 20 C4
Vezha 11 G5
Viacha 91 G5
Viamão 94 C6
Viana 92 C5
Viana do Alentejo 18 C2
Viana do Castelo 18 B1
Viangchan = Vientiane
    38 A2

Vianópolis 93 F4
Viaréggio 20 C3
Vibo Valéntia 21 E6
Vic 19 B7
Vicenza 20 B3
Vich = Vic 19 B7
Vichy 13 C5
Vicksburg 81 C8
Victor 43 J7
Victor Harbor 62 C2
Victoria Canada 69 D7
Victoria Chile 94 D2
Victoria □ 62 C3
Victoria, L. Africa 57 E6
Victoria, L. Australia 62 B3
Victoria, Mt. 41 G9
Victoria de Durango =
    Durango 84 C4
Victoria Falls 59 B5
Victoria I. 68 A8
Victoria Ld. 96 B14
Victorica 94 D3
Vicuña 94 C2
Vidin 22 C4
Vidisha 43 H10
Viedma 95 E4
Viedma, L. 95 F2
Vienna = Wien 15 D9
Vienne 13 D6
Vienne → 12 C4
Vientiane 38 A2
Vierzon 12 C5
Vietnam ■ 38 A3
Vieux-Fort, Pte. du 30 C
Vigan 35 A2
Vigévano 13 D8
Vigia 92 C4
Vigo 18 A1
Vijayawada 40 J3
Vijosë → 23 D2
Vikeke = Viqueque 37 F3
Vikna 8 C8
Vila do Bispo 18 D1
Vila Franca de Xira 18 C1
Vila Nova de Gaia 18 B1
Vila Real 18 B2
Vila-real de los Infantes
    19 C5
Vila Real de Santo António
    18 D2
Vila Velha 93 G5
Vilagarcía de Arousa
    18 A1
Vilanculos 59 C7
Vilanova i la Geltrú 19 B6
Vileyka 17 A8
Vilhelmina 8 C9
Vilhena 91 F6
Vilkitskogo, Proliv 30 B8
Vilkovo = Vylkove 17 F9
Villa Ángela 94 B4
Villa Bella 91 F5
Villa de María 94 B4
Villa Dolores 94 C3
Villa Hayes 94 B5
Villa María 94 C4
Villa Mazán 94 B3
Villa Montes 94 A4
Villa Ocampo 94 B5
Villacarrillo 18 C4

Villach 15 E7
Villaguay 94 C5
Villahermosa 85 D6
Villajoyosa 19 C5
Villalba 18 A2
Villanueva de la Serena
    18 C3
Villanueva y Geltrú =
    Vilanova i la Geltrú
    19 B6
Villarreal = Vila-real de los
    Infantes 19 C5
Villarrica Chile 95 D2
Villarrica Paraguay 94 B5
Villarrobledo 19 C4
Villaviciosa 18 A3
Villazón 94 A3
Villena 19 C5
Villeneuve-d'Ascq 13 A5
Villeneuve-sur-Lot 12 D4
Villingen-Schwenningen
    14 D5
Vilnius 24 C2
Vilyuy → 31 C10
Vilyuysk 31 C10
Viña del Mar 94 C2
Vinaròs 19 B6
Vindhya Ra. 43 H10
Vineland 77 E8
Vinkovci 20 B7
Vinnitsa = Vinnytsya 17 D9
Vinnytsya 17 D9
Viqueque 37 F3
Virac 36 B2
Viramgam 43 H8
Virden 69 D9
Vire 12 B3
Vírgenes, C. 95 G3
Virgin Is. (British) ☑ 87 C7
Virginia 59 D5
Virginia □ 77 F6
Virginia Beach 77 F8
Virovitica 20 B6
Virudunagar 43 Q10
Vis 20 C6
Visalia 78 B3
Visayan Sea 36 B2
Visby 9 D9
Viscount Melville Sd.
    70 B3
Višegrad 20 C7
Viseu Brazil 92 C4
Viseu Portugal 18 B2
Vishakhapatnam 40 J4
Viso, Mte. 13 D7
Vitebsk = Vitsyebsk 24 B3
Viterbo 20 C4
Viti Levu 64 L12
Vitigudino 18 B2
Vitória Brazil 93 G5
Vitória da Conquista 93 E5
Vitoria-Gasteiz 19 A4
Vitsyebsk 24 B3
Vittória 21 F5
Vittório Véneto 20 B4
Viveiro 18 A2
Vize 20 C6
Vizianagaram 40 H4
Vladikavkaz 25 E5

Vladimir 24 B5
Vladimir Volynskiy =
    Volodymyr-Volynskyy
    17 C7
Vladivostok 32 B2
Vlissingen 14 C2
Vlorë 23 D2
Vltava → 16 C2
Vogelkop = Doberai,
    Jazirah 37 E4
Vogelsberg 14 C5
Voghera 13 D8
Vohimarina = Iharana
    59 A10
Vohimena, Tanjon' i 59 D9
Voi 57 E7
Voiron 13 D6
Vojvodina □ 22 B2
Volga → 25 D6
Volga Hts. = Privolzhskaya
    Vozvyshennost 24 C6
Volgodonsk 25 D5
Volgograd 25 D5
Volgogradskoye Vdkhr.
    24 C5
Volkhov → 24 A3
Volkovysk = Vawkavysk
    17 B7
Volochanka 30 B7
Volodymyr-Volynskyy
    17 C7
Vologda 24 B4
Volos 23 E4
Volovets 17 D6
Volozhin = Valozhyn 17 A8
Volsk 24 C6
Volta, L. 53 G6
Volta Redonda 93 G5
Volterra 20 C3
Volturno → 20 D4
Volzhskiy 25 D5
Vorkuta 28 C7
Voronezh 24 C4
Vosges 13 B7
Vostok I. 65 L15
Vouga → 18 B1
Vouzela 18 D1
Voznesensk 25 D3
Vrangelya, Ostrov 31 B15
Vranje 22 C3
Vratsa 22 C4
Vrbas → 20 B6
Vršac 22 B3
Vryburg 58 D4
Vryheid 59 D6
Vukovar 20 B7
Vulcan 17 F6
Vulcanești 17 F9
Vulcano 21 E5
Vulkaneshty = Vulcanești
    17 F9
Vung Tau 38 B3
Vyatka = Kirov 28 D5
Vyatskiye Polyany 24 B7
Vyazma 24 B3
Vyborg 28 C3
Vychegda → 28 C5
Vychodné Beskydy 17 D5
Vylkove 17 F9
Vynohradiv 17 D6
Vyshniy Volochek 24 B3
Vyškov 16 D3

W

Waal → 14 C3
Wabash → 76 F1
Waco 80 D5
Wad Hamid 55 E5
Wad Medanî 55 F5
Waddington, Mt. 69 C7
Waddy Pt. 63 A5
Wadi Halfa 54 C4
Wafrah 47 E6
Wager B. 70 C5
Wager Bay 70 C4
Wagga Wagga 63 C4
Waghete 37 E5
Wah 42 C8
Wahai 37 E3
Waiau → 65 E5
Waibeem 37 E4
Waigeo 37 E4
Waihi 64 B6
Waihou → 64 B6
Waikabubak 37 F1
Waikaremoana, L. 64 C7
Waikari 65 E5
Waikato → 64 B6
Waikerie 62 B2
Waikokopu 64 C7
Waikouaiti 65 F3
Waimakariri → 65 E5
Waimate 65 F4
Wainganga → 43 K11
Waingapu 37 F2
Waiouru 64 C6
Waipara 65 E5
Waipawa 64 C7
Waipiro 64 C8
Waipoua Forest 64 A5
Waipu 64 A6
Waipukurau 64 D7
Wairakei 64 C7
Wairarapa, L. 65 D6
Wairoa 64 C7
Waitaki → 65 F4
Waitangi 64 A6
Waitara 64 C6
Waitomo Caves 64 C6
Waiuku 64 B6
Wajima 33 E6
Wajir 57 D8
Wakasa-Wan 33 F4
Wakatipu, L. 65 F3
Wakayama 33 F4
Wakefield 65 D5
Wakkanai 32 A7
Wakool 63 C3
Wakool → 62 C3
Wakre 37 E4
Wałbrzych 16 C3
Walcha 63 B5
Wałcz 16 B3
Wales □ 11 E4
Walgett 63 A4
Walgreen Coast 96 B1
Walla Walla 72 C4
Wallachia = Valahia 22 B5
Wallal 63 A4
Wallaroo 62 B2
Wallis & Futuna, Is. 64 L13
Wallowa Mts. 72 D5
Wallumbilla 63 A4

Walvis Bay 58 C2
Walvisbaai = Walvis Bay
58 C2
Wamba 57 D5
Wamena 37 E5
Wamulan 37 E3
Wana 42 C6
Wanaaring 63 A3
Wanaka 65 F3
Wanaka, L. 65 F3
Wandoan 63 A4
Wangal 37 F4
Wanganella 63 C3
Wanganui 64 C6
Wangaratta 63 C4
Wangary 62 B2
Wangerooge 14 B4
Wangiwangi 37 F2
Warangal 43 L11
Waratah 62 D4
Waratah B. 63 C4
Warburton 63 C4
Warburton → 62 A2
Ward 65 D6
Ward → 63 A4
Wardha 43 J11
Wardha → 43 K11
Warialda 63 A5
Wariap 37 E4
Warkopi 37 E4
Warner Mts. 72 F3
Warracknabeal 62 C3
Warragul 63 C4
Warrego → 63 B4
Warren Australia 63 B4
Warren U.S.A. 76 C4
Warrenville 63 A4
Warri 53 G7
Warrina 62 A2
Warrington U.K. 11 E5
Warrington U.S.A. 82 D4
Warrnambool 62 C3
Warsa 37 E5
Warsaw = Warszawa
16 B5
Warszawa 16 B5
Warta → 16 B2
Warthe = Warta → 16 B2
Waru 37 E4
Warwick 63 A5
Wasatch Ra. 73 F8
Wash, The 11 E7
Washim 43 J10
Washington 77 E7
Washington □ 72 C3
Washington, Mt. 77 B10
Wasian 37 E4
Wasior 37 E4
Waskaganish 71 D6
Wasserkuppe 14 C5
Watampone 37 E2
Waterbury 77 D9
Waterford 11 E3
Waterloo 75 D8
Watertown 77 C8
Waterville 77 B11
Watford 11 F6
Watrous 69 C9
Watsa 57 D5

Watson Lake 68 B7
Watsonville 78 B2
Wattiwarriganna Cr. →
62 A2
Watuata = Batuata 37 F2
Watubela, Kepulauan
37 E4
Watubela Is. = Watubela,
Kepulauan 37 E4
Wau = Wâw 55 G4
Wauchope 63 B5
Waukegan 76 C2
Waukesha 76 C1
Wausau 75 C10
Wauwatosa 76 C2
Waverley 64 C6
Wâw 55 G4
Wâw al Kabîr 54 C2
Waxahachie 81 C5
Wayabula 37 D3
Wayatinah 62 D4
Waycross 83 D6
Wazirabad 42 C9
We 38 C1
Weda 37 D3
Weda, Teluk 37 D3
Weddell I. 95 G4
Weddell Sea 96 A4
Wedderburn 62 C3
Wee Waa 63 B4
Weemelah 63 A4
Weiden 15 D7
Weifang 35 C6
Weimar 15 C6
Weipa 61 C7
Weir → 63 A4
Wejherowo 16 A4
Welbourn Hill 62 A1
Welkom 59 D5
Wellesley Is. 60 D6
Wellington Australia 63 B4
Wellington N.Z. 65 D6
Wellington, I. 95 F1
Wellington, L. 63 C4
Wellington Chan. 70 B4
Wels 15 D8
Welshpool 11 E5
Wemindji 71 D6
Wenatchee 72 C3
Wenchi 53 G5
Wenchow = Wenzhou
35 D7
Wendesi 37 E4
Wensu 34 B3
Wentworth 62 B3
Wenut 37 E4
Wenzhou 35 D7
Weri 37 E4
Werra → 14 C5
Werrimull 62 B3
Werris Creek 63 B5
Wersar 37 E4
Weser → 14 B5
Wesiri 37 F3
West Bank ■ 46 D3
West Bengal □ 40 F7
West Beskids = Západné
Beskydy 16 D4
West Falkland 95 G4
West Fjord = Vestfjorden
8 B8

West Ice Shelf 96 A11
West Palm Beach 83 F7
West Pt. 62 C2
West Virginia □ 76 E5
West Wyalong 63 B4
Westall, Pt. 62 B1
Westbury 62 D4
Westerland 14 A5
Western Australia □ 60 F3
Western Dvina =
Daugava → 24 B1
Western Ghats 43 N9
Western Sahara ■ 52 D3
Western Samoa =
Samoa ■ 65 L13
Western Sierra Madre =
Madre Occidental, Sierra
84 B3
Westerwald 14 C4
Westland △ 65 E4
Westland Bight 65 E4
Weston-super-Mare 11 F5
Westport Ireland 11 E2
Westport N.Z. 65 D4
Westray 11 B5
Wetar 37 F3
Wetaskiwin 69 C8
Wetzlar 14 C5
Wevok 69 B3
Wexford 11 E3
Weyburn 69 D9
Weymouth 11 F5
Wha Ti 68 B8
Whakaari = White I. 64 B7
Whakatane 64 B7
Whale → 70 D7
Whale Cove 68 B10
Whales, B. of 96 B16
Whangamata 64 B6
Whangamomona 64 C6
Whanganui △ 64 C6
Whangarei 64 A6
Whangarei Harb. 64 A6
Wheeling 76 E5
White → Ark., U.S.A.
81 C8
White → Ind., U.S.A.
76 E2
White Cliffs 62 B3
White I. 64 B7
White Nile = Nîl el
Abyad → 55 E5
White Russia = Belarus ■
24 C2
White Sea = Beloye More
8 B13
Whitecliffs 65 E4
Whitehaven 11 D5
Whitehorse 68 B6
Whitemark 62 D4
Whitianga 64 B6
Whitney, Mt. 78 B3
Whittlesea 63 C4
Wholdaia L. 68 B9
Whyalla 62 B2
Whyjonta 62 A3
Wichita 80 A5
Wichita Falls 80 C4
Wick 10 B5
Wickham, C. 62 C3
Wicklow Mts. 11 E3

Wieluń 16 C4
Wien 15 D9
Wiener Neustadt 15 E9
Wiesbaden 14 C5
Wight, I. of 11 F6
Wilcannia 62 B3
Wildspitze 14 E6
Wilhelm, Mt. 61 B8
Wilhelm II Coast 96 A11
Wilhelmshaven 14 B5
Wilkes-Barre 77 D8
Willandra Creek → 63 B4
Willemstad 87 D6
William Creek 62 A2
Williams Lake 69 C7
Williamsburg 77 F7
Williamsport 77 D7
Williamstown 63 C3
Williston 74 A3
Willunga 62 C2
Wilmington Australia
62 B2
Wilmington Del., U.S.A.
77 E8
Wilmington N.C., U.S.A.
83 B9
Wilpena Cr. → 62 B2
Wilson 83 B9
Wilson → 62 A3
Wilsons Promontory
63 C4
Wimmera → 62 C3
Winchester 11 F6
Wind River Range 73 E9
Windau = Ventspils 24 B1
Windhoek 58 C3
Windsor Australia 63 B5
Windsor Canada 71 E5
Wingen 63 B5
Wingham 63 B5
Winisk → 71 D5
Winnipeg 69 D10
Winnipeg, L. 69 C10
Winnipegosis L. 69 C9
Winona 75 C9
Winston-Salem 83 A7
Winterthur 13 C8
Winton Australia 61 E7
Winton N.Z. 65 G3
Wirrulla 62 B1
Wisconsin □ 75 C10
Wisła → 16 A4
Wismar 15 B6
Witbank = eMalahleni
59 D5
Wittenberge 15 B6
Wkra → 16 B5
Włocławek 16 B4
Włodawa 17 C6
Wokam 37 F4
Wolfsberg 15 E8
Wolfsburg 15 B6
Wolin 16 B2
Wollaston, Is. 95 H3
Wollaston Pen. 68 B8
Wollongong 63 B5
Wolverhampton 11 E5
Wondai 63 A5
Wongalarroo L. 63 B3
Wŏnsan 35 C7
Wonthaggi 63 C4

Woocalla 62 B2
Woodburn 63 A5
Woodenbong 63 A5
Woodend 63 C3
Woodland 72 G3
Woodroffe, Mt. 60 F5
Woods, L. of the 69 D10
Woodstock 71 E7
Woodville 64 D6
Woolamai, C. 63 C4
Woolgoolga 63 B5
Woombye 63 A5
Woomera 62 B2
Worcester S. Africa 58 E3
Worcester U.K. 11 E5
Worcester U.S.A. 77 C10
Workington 11 D5
Worms 14 D5
Worthing 11 F6
Wosi 37 E3
Wou-han = Wuhan 35 C6
Wousi = Wuxi 35 C7
Wowoni 37 E2
Wrangel I. = Vrangelya,
Ostrov 31 B15
Wrangell 69 C6
Wrangell Mts. 69 B5
Wrath, C. 10 B4
Wrexham 11 E5
Wright = Paranas 36 B3
Wrigley 68 B7
Wrocław 16 C3
Września 16 B3
Wu Jiang → 35 D5
Wuhan 35 C6
Wuhsi = Wuxi 35 C7
Wuhu 35 C6
Wukari 53 G7
Wuliaru 37 F4
Wulumuchi = Ürümqi
29 E9
Wuntho 41 F10
Wuppertal 14 C4
Würzburg 14 D5
Wutongqiao 34 D5
Wuwei 34 C5
Wuxi 35 C7
Wuyi Shan 35 D6
Wuzhong 35 C5
Wuzhou 35 D6
Wyandotte 76 C4
Wyandra 63 A4
Wyangala, L. 63 B4
Wyara, L. 63 A3
Wycheproof 62 C3
Wynbring 62 B1
Wyndham Australia 60 D4
Wyndham N.Z. 65 G3
Wynnum 63 A5
Wynyard 62 D4
Wyoming □ 73 E10
Wyong 63 B5

X

Xaafuun 49 E5
Xaafuun, Ras 49 E5
Xai-Xai 59 D6
Xainza 34 C3
Xalapa 84 D5
Xangongo 58 B3

Xankändi 25 F6
Xanthi 22 D5
Xapuri 91 F5
Xátiva 19 C5
Xi Jiang → 35 D6
Xiaguan 34 D5
Xiamen 35 D6
Xi'an 35 C5
Xiang Jiang → 35 D6
Xiangfan 35 C6
Xianggang = Hong Kong □
35 D6
Xiangquan He = Sutlej →
42 E7
Xiangtan 35 D6
Xiao Hinggan Ling 35 B7
Xichang 34 D5
Xigazê 34 D3
Xing'an 35 D6
Xingu → 92 C3
Xining 34 C5
Xinjiang Uygur Zizhiqu □
34 B3
Xinjin = Pulandian 35 C7
Xinxiang 35 C6
Xinyang 35 C6
Xinzhu 35 D7
Xique-Xique 93 E5
Xisha Qundao = Paracel Is.
38 A4
Xixabangma Feng 40 C5
Xixón = Gijón 18 A3
Xizang Zizhiqu □ 34 C3
Xuanhua 35 B6
Xúquer → 19 C5
Xuzhou 35 C6

Y

Ya'an 34 D5
Yaapeet 62 C3
Yablonovyy Khrebet
30 D9
Yablonovyy Ra. =
Yablonovyy Khrebet
30 D9
Yacuiba 94 A4
Yadgir 43 L10
Yahuma 56 D4
Yakima 72 C3
Yakovlevka 32 A3
Yakumo 32 B7
Yakutat 69 C6
Yakutsk 31 C10
Yala 38 C2
Yalinga 56 C4
Yalong Jiang → 34 D5
Yalova 22 D7
Yalta 25 E3
Yalutorovsk 29 D7
Yam Ha Melah = Dead Sea
47 E3
Yam Kinneret 46 D3
Yamagata 32 E7
Yamaguchi 33 F2
Yamal, Poluostrov 28 B8
Yamal Pen. = Yamal,
Poluostrov 28 B8
Yamantau, Gora 29 D6
Yamba N.S.W., Australia
63 A5

Yamba S. Austral.,
Australia 62 B3
Yãmbiõ 55 H4
Yambol 22 C6
Yamdena 37 F4
Yamethin 41 G11
Yamma Yamma, L. 62 A3
Yamoussoukro 53 G4
Yampil 17 D9
Yampol = Yampil 17 D9
Yamuna → 40 E3
Yamzho Yumco 34 D4
Yana → 31 B11
Yanac 62 C3
Yanbu 'al Baḥr 47 F4
Yancannia 62 B3
Yanco Cr. → 63 C4
Yandoon 41 J10
Yangambi 56 D4
Yangch'ü = Taiyuan 35 C6
Yangjiang 35 D6
Yangon = Rangoon
41 J11
Yangquan 35 C6
Yangtse = Chang Jiang →
35 C7
Yangtze Kiang = Chang
Jiang → 35 C7
Yanji 35 B7
Yanna 63 A4
Yanqi 34 B3
Yantabulla 63 A4
Yantai 35 C7
Yanykurgan =
Zhanaqorghan 29 E7
Yaoundé 56 D2
Yapen 37 E5
Yapen, Selat 37 E5
Yaqui → 84 B2
Yar-Sale 28 C8
Yaraka 61 E7
Yaransk 24 B6
Yardea P.O. 62 B2
Yaremcha 17 D7
Yarensk 28 C5
Yarí → 90 D4
Yarkand = Shache 34 C2
Yarkhun → 42 A8
Yarlung Ziangbo Jiang =
Brahmaputra → 41 F7
Yarmouth 71 E7
Yaroslavl 24 B4
Yarram 63 C4
Yarraman 63 A5
Yarranvale 63 A4
Yarras 63 B5
Yartsevo 30 C7
Yaselda 17 B8
Yasinya 17 D7
Yass 63 B4
Yatağan 23 F7
Yathkyed L. 68 B10
Yatsushiro 33 G2
Yavari → 90 D4
Yavatmal 43 J11
Yavoriv 17 D6
Yavorov = Yavoriv 17 D6
Yawatahama 33 G3
Yazd 44 D3
Yazd □ 44 C3

Yazdān 45 C1
Yazoo → 81 C8
Yebyu 41 K12
Yecla 19 C5
Yedintsy = Edineţ 17 D8
Yeelanna 62 B2
Yegros 94 B5
Yei 55 H5
Yekaterinburg 29 D7
Yelarbon 63 A5
Yelets 24 C4
Yelizavetgrad = Kirovohrad
25 D3
Yell 10 A6
Yellow = Huang He →
35 C6
Yellow Sea 35 C7
Yellowhead Pass 69 C8
Yellowknife 68 B8
Yellowstone → 74 B3
Yellowstone △ 73 D9
Yelsk 17 C9
Yemen ■ 49 D4
Yenangyaung 41 G10
Yenbo = Yanbu 'al Baḥr
47 F4
Yenda 63 B4
Yenice 23 E6
Yenisey → 28 B9
Yeniseysk 30 D7
Yeniseyskiy Zaliv 28 B9
Yenyuka 31 D10
Yeola 43 J9
Yeovil 11 F5
Yerbent 29 F6
Yerevan 25 F7
Yermak 29 D8
Yershov 24 D7
Yerushalayim = Jerusalem
47 E3
Yessey 30 C8
Yeu, Î. d' 12 C2
Yevpatoriya 25 D3
Yeysk 25 D4
Yezd = Yazd 44 D3
Yibin 35 D5
Yichang 35 C6
Yichun 35 B7
Yilan 35 B7
Yıldız Dağları 22 D6
Yinchuan 35 C5
Yingkou 35 B7
Yining 29 E9
Yinmabin 41 F10
Yishan 35 D5
Yiyang 35 D6
Yog Pt. 36 B2
Yogyakarta 39 F4
Yokadouma 56 D2
Yokkaichi 33 F5
Yokohama 33 F6
Yokosuka 33 F6
Yola 55 G1
Yonago 33 F3
Yonibana 53 G3
Yonkers 77 D9
Yonne → 13 C5
York U.K. 11 E6
York U.S.A. 77 E7

York, C. 61 C7
Yorke Pen. 62 B2
Yorkton 69 C9
Yos Sudarso, Pulau =
Dolak, Pulau 37 F5
Yosemite △ 78 B3
Yoshkar Ola 24 B6
Youghal 11 F3
Young 63 B4
Younghusband, L. 62 B2
Younghusband Pen.
62 C2
Youngstown 76 D5
Yozgat 25 F3
Ysyk-Köl 29 E8
Yu Jiang → 35 D6
Yü Shan 35 D7
Yuan Jiang → 35 D6
Yuba City 72 G3
Yübetsu 32 A8
Yucatán □ 85 C7
Yucatán, Canal de 85 C7
Yucatán, Península de
85 D7
Yucatan Channel =
Yucatán, Canal de
85 C7
Yuci 35 C6
Yugoslavia = Serbia ■
22 B3
Yukon → 69 B3
Yukon Territory □ 68 B6
Yukta 30 C8
Yuma 78 D5
Yumen 34 C4
Yungas 91 G5
Yunta 62 B2
Yurga 29 D9
Yuribei 28 B8
Yurimaguas 91 E3
Yuryung Kaya 30 B9
Yushu 34 C4
Yuzhno-Sakhalinsk
31 E12
Yvetot 12 B4

Z

Zāb al Kabīr → 46 C5
Zāb aş Şaghīr → 46 D5
Zābol □ 45 D6
Zāboli 45 E5
Zabrze 16 C4
Zacatecas 84 C4
Zadar 20 B5
Zadetkyi Kyun 38 C1
Zafra 18 C2
Żagań 16 C2
Zagazig 54 B5
Zagreb 20 B6
Zāgros, Kūhhā-ye 44 C2
Zagros Mts. = Zāgros,
Kūhhā-ye 44 C2
Zāhedān 45 D5
Zahlah 46 D3
Zaïre = Congo → 56 F2
Zaječar 22 C4
Zakhodnaya Dzvina =
Daugava → 24 B1

Zākhū 46 C5
Zakinthos = Zakynthos
23 F3
Zakynthos 23 F3
Zalaegerszeg 16 E3
Zalău 17 E6
Zaleshchiki = Zalishchyky
17 D7
Zalew Wiślany 16 A4
Zalingei 55 F3
Zalishchyky 17 D7
Zambeze → 59 B7
Zambezi = Zambeze →
59 B7
Zambezi 58 A4
Zambia ■ 59 B5
Zamboanga 36 C2
Zamora Mexico 84 D4
Zamora Spain 18 B3
Zamość 17 C6
Zanesville 76 E4
Zanjān 46 C7
Zanjān □ 46 C7
Zante = Zakynthos 23 F3
Zanzibar 57 F7
Zaouiet El-Kala = Bordj
Omar Driss 52 C7
Zaouiet Reggâne 52 C6
Zap Suyu = Zāb al
Kabīr → 46 C5
Zapadnaya Dvina =
Daugava → 24 B1
Západné Beskydy 16 D4
Zaporizhzhya 25 D4
Zaporozhye =
Zaporizhzhya 25 D4
Zara 46 C4
Zaragoza 19 B5
Zarand 44 D4
Zaranj 42 D2
Zaria 53 F7
Zaruma 90 D3
Zary 16 C2
Zarzis 54 B1
Zaskar Mts. 42 C10
Zāvareh 44 C3
Zawiercie 16 C4
Zāwiyat al Bayḍā = Al
Bayḍā 54 B3
Zāyandeh → 44 C3
Zaysan 29 E9
Zaysan Köli 29 E9
Zbarazh 17 D7
Zdolbuniv 17 C8
Zduńska Wola 16 C4
Zeebrugge 14 C2
Zeehan 62 D4
Zeila 49 E3
Zeitz 15 C7
Zelenograd 24 B4
Zemun 22 B3
Zenica 20 B6
Žepče 20 B7
Zêzere → 18 C1
Zgorzelec 16 C2
Zhabinka 17 B7
Zhailma 29 D7
Zhambyl = Taraz 29 E8
Zhangaqazaly 29 E7
Zhangaqûrghan 29 E7

Zhanghua 35 D7
Zhangjiakou 35 B6
Zhangye 34 C5
Zhangzhou 35 D6
Zhanjiang 35 D6
Zhanyi 34 D5
Zhaotong 34 D5
Zharkent 29 E8
Zhashkiv 17 D10
Zhayyq → 29 E6
Zhdanov = Mariupol
25 D4
Zhejiang □ 35 D7
Zhengzhou 35 C6
Zhezqazghan 29 E7
Zhigansk 30 C10
Zhilinda 30 B9
Zhitomir = Zhytomyr
17 C9
Zhlobin 17 B10
Zhmerinka = Zhmerynka
17 D9
Zhmerynka 17 D9
Zhob 42 D6
Zhodino = Zhodzina 17 A9
Zhodzina 17 A9
Zhongdian 34 D4
Zhongshan 35 D6
Zhumadian 35 C6
Zhytomyr 17 C9
Zibo 35 C6
Zielona Góra 16 C2
Zigey 55 F2
Zigong 35 C5
Ziguinchor 53 F2
Zile 46 B3
Zillah 54 C2
Zimbabwe ■ 59 B5
Zimnicea 22 C5
Zinder 53 F7
Zion △ 79 B6
Zirreh, Gowd-e 42 E3
Zlatograd 22 D5
Zlatoust 29 D6
Zlín 16 D3
Zmeinogorsk 29 D9
Znojmo 16 D3
Zolochev = Zolochiv
17 D7
Zolochiv 17 D7
Zomba 59 B7
Zongo 56 D4
Zonguldak 25 E3
Zorritos 90 D2
Zouar 54 D2
Zouérate = Zouïrât 52 D3
Zouïrât 52 D3
Zrenjanin 22 B3
Żufār 48 D5
Zug 13 C8
Zugspitze 14 E6
Zumbo 59 B6
Zunyi 35 D5
Zürich 13 C8
Zuwārah 54 B1
Zvishavane 59 C6
Zwelitsha 59 E5
Zwettl 15 D8
Zwickau 15 C7
Zwolle 14 B4
Żyrardów 16 B5

Projection:Hammer Equal Area